Theater of Memory: The Plays of Kālidāsa

TRANSLATIONS FROM THE ORIENTAL CLASSICS

Theater of Memory

The Plays of Kālidāsa

Edited by
BARBARA STOLER MILLER

Translated by
EDWIN GEROW
DAVID GITOMER
BARBARA STOLER MILLER

Columbia University Press
NEW YORK 1984

UNESCO COLLECTION OF REPRESENTATIVE WORKS
INDIAN SERIES

This book has been accepted in the Indian Series of the Translations Collection of the United Nations Educational, Scientific and Cultural Organization (UNESCO)

Library of Congress Cataloging in Publication Data

Kālidāsa.
Theater of memory.

(Translations from the Oriental classics)
I. Miller, Barbara Stoler. II. Title. III. Series.
PK3795.E5 1984 891.21 83-26362
ISBN 0-231-05838-1
ISBN 0-231-05839-X (pbk.)

Columbia University Press
New York Guildford, Surrey

Printed in the United States of America

Clothbound editions of Columbia University Press books are Smyth-sewn and printed on permanent and durable acid-free paper.

Book design by Ken Venezio.

CONTENTS

EDITOR'S PREFACE

If you want the bloom of youth and fruit of later years,
If you want what enchants, fulfills, and nourishes,
If you want heaven and earth contained in one name—
I say Śakuntalā and all is spoken.

J. W. von Goethe, "Willst du die Blüte..."

I have never read the Shakuntala of Kalidasa, and I never shall. I do not learn the language of the gods to amuse myself with love stories and literary trifles.

Vinoba Bhave, cited by V. S. Naipaul in
India: A Wounded Civilization

Śākuntalā, the heroine of Kālidāsa's play who inspired the German Romantic poet, was ignored by the traditional Indian ascetic. In India delight, even delight in the beauties of the natural world, is considered dangerous for an ascetic; it threatens to undermine his strict quest for perfection. Goethe was searching for forms and images that could express his ideal of man's integration with nature. The *Śākuntala,* first known to Goethe through the English translation of William Jones (published in 1789), appealed to him for the beauty of its imagery, the complexity of its structure (he modeled his prologue to *Faust* on Kālidāsa's to *Śākuntala*), and the unity of art and religion on which it was based.

The *Śākuntala* has had many enthusiastic admirers in the West as well as in India, where from the time of its composition in the early fifth century A.D., it has been considered a masterpiece of classical Indian literature. It has been translated often, into every European language, and has been the subject of commentaries and critical studies in Sanskrit and other Indian languages. But there has been little critical recognition of the two other known plays by Kālidāsa: the *Mālavikāgnimitra* and the *Vikramorvaśīya*.

This book began with the idea that the plays had to be studied, translated, and discussed in light of one another, for only in the context of the other plays could the conceptual depth and dramatic art of each one be appreciated. Edwin Gerow, David Gitomer, and I have known each other for more than ten years. We have all separately studied in Mysore at the Oriental Research Institute with Vidvan H.V. Nagaraja Rao. His vast knowledge of Sanskrit poetry, linguistic theory, and critical literature has influenced our ability to see the plays from various perspectives within the ancient Indian traditions of criticism. In the process of translating and interpreting the plays, we have all read the commentaries attached to them, as well as the relevant theoretical writings on poetics and dramaturgy that are cited in the bibliography. Although each of us has translated only one play, we have frequently criticized each other's work.

The different styles of translation evident in each of the works reflect the literary tastes of the translators, but the differences are consonant with stylistic differences in the plays. Though they may all be broadly classed as "dramatic romances," significant variations in character, story, and emphasis mark the particular genre and achievement of each play. The *Śākuntala* with its rich mythological layers and vast cosmic landscape is the model of the most "serious" Indian dramatic form, which we may call "heroic romance." The *Vikramorvaśīya*, whose protagonists are a celestial nymph and a mortal king, is more lyrical and fantastic in places, but it is also a romance that concludes in a ceremonious royal ritual. The *Mālavikāgnimitra* is a version of Indian "secular romance," set in the king's palace and pleasure garden. The buffoon's constant presence contributes greatly to its tone of quasi-pompous irony. While love comes into conflict with duty and anger in the other plays, here the conflict is minor and the main foil for love is parodied ritual and humor. Edwin Gerow's frequent use of rhyme and fixed metrical structure in translating the verses, as well as the "pompous" diction he chooses for the prose of certain characters, seem appropriate to the poetic constraints of this play. David Gitomer and I have intentionally employed freer rhythmic forms and more varied levels of diction.

Although the texts of the plays have been individually edited many times in their various recensions, there is no single critical edition of all of them. The *Kālidāsa Lexicon* of A. Scharpé represents a textual summary of the best printed editions. Since the texts of the plays have not been transmitted as a unit (only one commentator, Kāṭayavema, comments on all three), we have each chosen to follow the text we felt to be most faithful to the style of Kālidāsa. Details of these choices are given in the translators' notes to the plays. The varied length of these notes depends on the relative complexity of the textual problems. The problems of the *Mālavikāgnimitra* text are minimal, while those of the other two plays still defy solution. Notes are not intended to be comprehensive. Some merely indicate variant readings, while others contain supplementary information that may illuminate a passage, or an idea. Notes are not marked in the body of the translation; they are keyed to act and verse, with a plus sign (+) used to indicate prose following a particular verse. The reader is advised to consult them after first reading the introductory essays and the translations.

We have also written three essays in which we offer different perspectives on the nature and interpretation of Kālidāsa's dramatic art, and which are intended to help the modern reader enter the universe of classical Sanskrit drama. My essay first attempts to set the poet and his plays within the cultural and religious context of the Gupta period. I then turn to an analysis of the performance, language, structure, and meaning of the plays in terms of material provided within the plays themselves and in contemporary literary and epigraphical sources. My appreciation of ancient theater has grown during discussions with my friend and colleague Helen Bacon, who has taught me to read both Greek and Sanskrit plays more carefully. Edwin Gerow's essay analyzes the plays in terms of the Sanskrit theories of drama and poetics, especially those of Bharata and Dhanaṁjaya. David Gitomer's study of classical Indian stagecraft focuses on how Kālidāsa's plays were performed, so that the reader may visualize some of the specifics of such a performance: the playhouse and its stage, costumes, makeup, acting style, stage directions, and dance. David thanks the dancer Nadine Berardi for her help in interpreting some points of performance technique. We all thank Karen Mitchell for helping us to clarify our presentation.

Kālidāsa's theater is expressed through elaborately stylized verses, dialogues, dance gestures, sounds, and signs of emotion. We feel that these plays can be appreciated today, even in translated versions, as paradigms for understanding the frustration and fulfillment of human desire and duty in a complex world. Their performance can take place within the imagination of a sensitive reader, whom the Sanskrit critics call a *sahṛdaya,* one whose heart shares aesthetic joy, or a *rasika,* one who enjoys the subtleties of art.

BARBARA STOLER MILLER

A NOTE ON SANSKRIT PRONUNCIATION

Indic words are rendered in Roman script, using international conventions for transliteration. In reading Sanskrit words, the accent may be placed on a syllable when this is heavy. A syllable is heavy if it contains a long simple vowel (*ā, ī, ū, ṝ*), a dipthong (*e, o, ai, au*), or a short vowel followed by more than one consonant. It should be noted that the aspirated consonants *kh, gh, ch, jh, ṭh, ḍh, th, dh, ph,* and *bh,* are considered single consonants in the Sanskrit alphabet.

Vowels, except *a,* are given their full value as in Italian or German:

a	as *u* in c*u*t
ā	as *a* in f*a*ther
i	as *i* in p*i*t
ī	as *i* in mach*i*ne
u	as *u* in p*u*t
ū	as *u* in r*u*le
ṛ	a short vowel; as *ir* in b*ir*d, but often rendered *ri* in Anglicized words
e	as *ay* in s*ay*
ai	as *ai* in *ai*sle
o	as *o* in g*o*
au	as *ow* in c*ow*
ṁ	nasalizes the preceding vowel and makes the syllable heavy
ḥ	a rough breathing vowel, replacing an original *s* or *r*; occurs only at the end of a syllable or word and makes the syllable heavy

Most consonants are analogous to the English, if the distinction between aspirated and nonaspirated consonants is observed; for example, the aspirated consonants *th* and *ph* must never be pronounced as in English *th*in and *ph*ial, but as in ho*th*ouse and she*ph*erd (similarly, *kh, gh, ch, jh, dh, bh*). The differences between the Sanskrit "cerebral" *ṭ, ṭh, ḍ, ḍh, ṇ, ṣ* and "dental" *t, th, d, dh, n, s* are another distinctive feature of the language. The dentals are formed with the tongue against the teeth, the cerebrals with the tongue flexed back along the palate. Note also:

g	as *g* in *g*oat
ṅ	as *n* in i*n*k, or si*n*g
c	as *ch* in *ch*urch
ñ	as *ñ* in Spanish se*ñ*or
ś	as *s* in *s*ugar

Introduction: Kālidāsa's Dramatic Universe

KĀLIDĀSA'S WORLD AND HIS PLAYS

BARBARA STOLER MILLER

Kālidāsa: Servant of the Goddess and Devotee of Śiva

Although Kālidāsa is the acknowledged master-poet of Sanskrit, we lack any historical evidence of his life. Throughout the centuries the quality of his poetry attracted many legends to his name. These are known from sources in Sanskrit and other languages. When the Tibetan Lama Tāranātha wrote his *History of Buddhism in India* in the seventeenth century, the legendary Kālidāsa was included among the spiritual adepts of India. Tāranātha recounts the tale of Kālidāsa's transformation from fool to poet through a series of events that bring him the grace of the goddess Kālī.[1] It is a parable filled with magic, paradox, and allusions to the power of speech.

When the brahman Vararuci was living in the royal temple of King Bhīmaśukla of Banaras, the king wanted to offer the princess Vāsantī in marriage to the brahman. Vāsantī arrogantly said, "I am a greater scholar than Vararuci and therefore I cannot serve him." So Vararuci thought, "I must trick her!" He said, "Let me ask my learned teacher, who is a hundred times more intelligent than I am. The king might well offer Vāsantī to him."

Now, in Magadha there lived a handsome cowherd. Vararuci saw him sitting on the branch of a tree while he cut it with an ax and he knew that he was a great fool. Vararuci led him away and had him bathed and annointed. He had him dressed in the garb of a brahman pandit and made him memorize the Sanskrit words "*oṁ svasti.*" He told him, "When you come to where the king is holding court, offer flowers to him and say only *oṁ svasti.* If anyone asks any question, do not try to answer."

Though he tried to carry out these instructions, the cowherd only uttered the nonsense syllables *u-śa-ta-ra* after offering flowers to the king. But Vararuci cleverly construed a benedictory verse to Śiva out of them:

> Umā with Rudra is he,
> Śaṅkara with Viṣṇu—
> Taking his twanging trident,
> Rampant, may Śiva protect you!

Then Vāsantī asked the fool questions on the import of words and the like, but he did not reply. Vararuci said, "Why should a profound scholar like my teacher answer the questions of a woman?" Tricking her in this way, Vararuci fled to the south.

When the cowherd was taken to the temple, he said nothing. But he was visibly delighted to see the picture of a cow among the animals painted on the outer wall of the temple. He thus revealed himself to be a cowherd.

"Alas, this is a mere cowherd!" Vāsantī cried when she realized that she had been cheated. But she thought, "If he has intelligence, I am going to teach him grammar." By examining him, however, she found him to be an utter fool. Vāsantī became angry and ordered him to gather flowers for her every day.

There was in Magadha an image of the goddess Kālī made by a celestial sculptor. The cowherd worshiped her daily with bunches of flowers and great reverence. Once, in the early morning, he went to gather flowers for Vāsantī to use in worship. One of her maids wanted to tease him. She concealed herself behind the image, chewing a ball of betel nut. When the cowherd finished his usual prayers, the maid put the remnants of her chewing into his hand. He thought the goddess herself had presented it to him, so he swallowed it. Instantly, unlimited knowledge of logic and grammar dawned in him and he became a great poet.

He took a red lotus in his right hand, a blue lotus in his left hand. "Though the red lotus is beautiful, its stem is rough. Though the blue lotus is small, its stem is soft. Which of the two does she prefer?" Thinking thus, he said to Vāsantī:

> My right hand holds a red lotus,
> a blue lotus rests in my left;

rough is one stem, the other is soft—
lotus-eyed lady, which will you take?

When she heard this, she realized that he had become learned and showed him great respect. From his great reverence for the goddess Kālī, he came to be known as Kālidāsa, the servant of Kālī. From then on he became the crowning jewel of all poets.

Kālidāsa's literary reputation is based on six surviving works that are generally attributed to him by modern critics and commentators.[2] The coherent language, poetic technique, style, and sentiment that these works express seem to be the product of a single mind. The poems include a lyric monologue of nature, *Meghadūta* (The Cloud Messenger), and two long lyric narratives, *Raghuvaṁśa* (The Lineage of Raghu) and *Kumārasaṁbhava* (The Birth of Śiva's Son). There are three dramas, all of which begin with prologues that refer to Kālidāsa as the author. The title of each play is a composite word that includes the name of the play's heroine combined with the name of the hero or a central idea in her story: *Mālavikāgnimitra* (Mālavikā and Agnimitra), *Vikramorvaśīya* (Urvaśī Won by Valor), and *Abhijñānaśākuntala* (Śakuntalā and the Ring of Recollection). The last is often referred to in critical literature by the abbreviated title *Śākuntala* and popularly as *Śakuntalā*, after the heroine's name. A seventh work, a collection of lyric verses called *Ṛtusaṁhāra* (Cycle of the Seasons) is also attributed to Kālidāsa, but some authorities doubt his authorship on grounds of style.[3]

There are passages in all of Kālidāsa's work that show how intimately he knew the cities and countryside of the North Indian landscape. The exquisite detail with which he describes the city of Ujjayinī and the hills and rivers of Malwa in the *Meghadūta* points to his attachment to the region.[4] In this poem the lovelorn demigod gives his messenger the cloud directions to break its journey in order to visit Ujjayinī.

Though it diverts you
on your way northward,
do not fail to see the roofs
of Ujjayinī's stuccoed palaces—

if you are not enchanted there
by the way the city women's eyes
tremble in alarm at your bolts
of lightning, you are cheated.

Reaching the region of Avantī
where old village men tell Udayana's tale,
proceed to Ujjayinī,
the city of splendor I told you about—
it is like a shining fragment
torn from the sky by fallen demigods
who brought a token of virtue to earth
when the fruit of purity withered.

He tells the cloud to approach the great Śiva temple of Mahākāla in Ujjayinī as a worshiper.[5]

You should journey to the holy shrine
of Caṇḍeśvara, lord of the fierce goddess,
preceptor of the triple world,
where Śiva's gnomes will greet you with awe,
seeing in you the blue of their master's throat—
its grove is fanned by fragrant river winds,
laden with lotus pollen and scented
by the ablutions of girls playing in the water.

If you arrive at Mahākāla temple
at another time, cloud,
stay there until the sun descends
over the horizon
and perform the drumming patterns
for twilight rites to celebrate Śiva—
the sound of your deep thunder
will win you eternal reward.

Girdles ringing to rhythmic steps,
hands weary from waving yak-tail whisks
whose handles are inlaid with jewels,
the dancing girls there,

feeling your first raindrops
like balm on the nailmarks of love,
will throw you glances
as long as a line of swarming bees.

Then, suspended in a magic circle
over a forest of trees with raised arms,
glowing with the deep red of sunset,
like a freshly opened crimson flower,
be Śiva's bloody elephant hide
as he begins his wild dance—
his wife will watch your devotion
with the still eye of subdued fear.

That Kālidāsa was a devotee of Śiva and the Goddess is evident from his work as well as from his legends. The powerful images of nature that dominate his poetry and drama are ultimately determined by his conception of Śiva's creative mystery. This is implicit in the doctrine of Śiva's eight manifest forms (*aṣṭamūrti*), which he states in the benediction of the *Śākuntala*.[6]

The water that was first created,
the sacrifice-bearing fire, the priest,
the time-setting sun and moon,
audible space that fills the universe,
what men call nature, the source of all seeds,
the air that living creatures breathe—
through his eight embodied forms,
may Lord Śiva come to bless you!

The natural world of Kālidāsa's poetry is never a static landscape; it reverberates with Śiva's presence. Nature functions not as a setting or allegorical landscape but as a dynamic surface on which the unmanifest cosmic unity plays. This unity is Śiva; his creative nature is expressed through the eight essential principles of empirical existence: the elements, (water, fire, ether, earth, air) the sun and the moon, and the ritual sacrificer, who is integrated into this cosmic system. In the sustained interplay of these basic constituents of nature, the creation and destruction of life occur. Śiva is present in each aspect of life and fulfills all the functions that the eight forms collectively perform.

The conception of Śiva's eight manifest forms has inherent in it the identification of Śiva himself with Nature (*prakṛti*), the female half of his cosmic totality. Śiva is called "The God Who Is Half Female" (*ardhanārīśvara*).[7] The male and female aspects of existence, *puruṣa* and *prakṛti,* separately personified as Śiva and the goddess Umā, are bound into a single androgynous figure. These concepts are fundamental to the meaning of Kālidāsa'a poetry; in his dramas they set the romantic relationship between the hero and heroine in a definite religious context.

The King as Hero and Patron

The hero in each play is a king whose character is shaped by the poet's view of kingship and its relation to cosmic order. Kālidāsa shared with the ancient priesthood of Vedic brahmans a belief that nature's structure is constantly recreated by ritual sacrifice.[8] In the Vedic rites of royal consecration (*rājasūya*), the symbols of the ritual link all the elements of the world to the king, so that he stands at the center of the universe. It is through the king that the natural, social, and divine worlds have unity and order.[9] The king's supernatural nature is indicated by his intimate associations with the Vedic gods. According to Manu, an ancient authority on Hindu law, a king is composed of eternal particles of eight divine powers, and because of them he surpasses all other created beings.[10] He is the human counterpart of Indra, king of the gods, and is his equal in many ways.[11]

The high qualities of kingship that Kālidāsa's heroes possess qualify them to be called royal sages. The epithet "royal sage" (*rājarṣi*) signifies that the king's spiritual power is equal to his martial strength and moral superiority. He is a sage (*ṛṣi*) by virtue of his discipline (*yoga*), austerity (*tapas*), and knowledge of sacred law (*dharma*). It is his religious duty to keep order in the cosmos by guarding his kingdom; in this he is like a sage guarding the realm of holy sacrifice. His responsibility to guide and protect those beneath him involves him in acts of penance that place him in the highest position of the temporal and spiritual hierarchy.

The ideal royal sage is a figure of enormous physical strength and energy who also has the power to control his senses.[12] The conflict between desire (*kāma*) and duty (*dharma*) that is enacted in each of Kālidāsa's dramas involves a tension between the energy of physical passion and the constraints of self-control. In two of the plays, the *Vikramorvaśīya* and the *Śākuntala,* the tension is resolved in the king's recognition of his son and heir. Each boy is portrayed as a natural warrior despite his birth in a hermitage and his education in religious practice. Royal power combined with religious discipline makes the prince destined to be "a king who turns the wheel of empire" (*cakravartin*), a universal emperor whose great spiritual and temporal conquests mark him with divinity.[13]

That Kālidāsa enjoyed royal patronage is strongly suggested by the central role that the figure of the king plays in his dramas and in his epic *Raghuvaṁśa*. The sense of the world that one gets from Kālidāsa's work is consonant with historical, geographical, and linguistic factors supporting the Indian tradition that associates the poet with the Gupta monarch Candragupta II, who ruled most of northern India from about A.D. 375 to A.D. 415.[14] His capital was Pāṭaliputra, an ancient capital of the Gangetic valley.

While we have no way of establishing Kālidāsa's exact dates, an upper limit is provided by an inscription on the shrine of Aihole, dated A.D. 634, in which he is praised as a great poet.[15] Another seventh-century tribute is found in the epic *Harṣacarita*. Its author Bāṇabhaṭṭa, the court poet of Harṣa of Kanauj, pays tribute to Kālidāsa by saying "No one fails to feel delight when Kālidāsa's verses are recited; they are sweet and dense, like clusters of buds."[16]

The history of northern India during the first three centuries A.D. is dominated by the Scythian dynasty of Kushan rulers. The origin of the Gupta dynasty dates to the period of Kushan decline, but details are few and the exact succession of rulers is uncertain. Inscriptions and coins give evidence that Candragupta II was the third major ruler in the dynasty, which was founded by his grandfather, Candragupta I, in the beginning of the fourth century A.D. The first Candragupta seems to have been a minor ruler in the area of Bihar; he extended his domain by marrying Kumāradevī, a princess of the powerful Licchavi tribe that controlled Pāṭaliputra. In honor of this alliance, he proclaimed a new era, and early Gupta gold coins bear figures of himself and his bride. He was succeeded by his son Samudragupta, whose military accomplishments are the subject of a lengthy panegyric inscribed on a stone pillar found at the site of Kauśāmbī, near Allahabad. Samudragupta used various devices of war and diplomacy to extend his territory to the east, west, and south. This inscription, publicizing the king's prowess and his conquest of the earth (*pṛthivīvijaya*), is written in elegant Sanskrit poetic style.[17] It is notable that the description of the legendary Raghu's world conquest (*digvijaya*) in the fourth canto of the *Raghuvaṁśa* parallels this account of Samudragupta's victories.[18] To please Candragupta II, Kālidāsa may well have woven events in the life of Samudragupta into his epic narrative.

Candragupta II ascended to the throne in about A.D. 375. Early in his reign he suppressed rebellions in Bengal and pushed the Kushans to the banks of the Indus river. Some time after A.D. 390 he launched a successful war against the Śaka satraps of Malwa, annexed the territory, and established a provincial capital in Ujjayinī. By his conquest of the Śaka ruler of western India during the first decade of the fifth century A.D., Candragupta II ended several hundred years of foreign domination of lands on the coast of the Arabian Sea.

Following the practice of his father Samudragupta, who used the word *parākrama,* which means "courage," as his personal signature in epithets on royal coins and inscriptions, Candragupta II used *vikrama,* which means "valor." His titles Vikramāditya, Śrīvikrama, Ajitavikrama, Siṁhavikrama, and Vikramāṅka appear on varieties of gold coins minted during his reign.[19] It is by the title Vikramāditya, meaning "one who is like the sun in valor," that Candragupta II is generally known in literary accounts. Vikramāditya became a legendary royal name in western India. One popular tradition placed him during the first century B.C., when he was supposed to have routed an early wave of Śaka invaders and founded the Vikrama era.[20] But of all the Vikramādityas known to history, Candragupta II was the earliest, and it seems clear that his exploits are the basis of the legend.

Inscriptions document that Candragupta's daughter Prabhāvatīgupta married the crown prince of the neighboring Vākāṭaka state. The prince died shortly after becoming king, leaving his wife as regent for their young son.[21] Literary accounts relate various stories about Kālidāsa as ambassador and poet at the Vākāṭaka court.[22] In ancient India it was usual for poets to serve as ambassadors, and it is possible that Kālidāsa was the Gupta emperor's envoy to his daughter's court on more than one occasion. The poet's knowledge of administration and court life, as well as of geography, suggests that he could have held such an official post.

The case in favor of Kālidāsa's connection with Candragupta II is strengthened by allusions in Kālidāsa's works. For example, the word *vikrama* in the title *Vikramorvaśīya* may refer to Candragupta II, whose royal epithets all contained the word. Clues come from another play, of which Candragupta II is more obviously the subject—*Devīcandragupta* (The Queen and Candragupta).[23] It is known only from fragments preserved in other works, but the basic plot is clear. It revolves around Prince Candragupta's heroic rescue, in female disguise, of his impotent elder brother's wife, Queen Dhruvadevī, who has been abducted by a Śaka king. After killing the Śaka, Candragupta has his brother murdered, ascends the throne, and marries Dhruvadevī. We know from inscriptions that Dhruvadevī was the wife of Candragupta II, but there is no historical evidence of her prior marriage to the short-lived Rāmagupta. The abduction and rescue scene with which the *Vikramorvaśīya* begins may well have its source in the same events on which the *Devīcandragupta* was based.

The name Kumāra in the *Kumārasaṁbhava* and in Acts Four and Five of the *Vikramorvaśīya* may refer to the king's son and successor, Kumāragupta. Act Five ends in a rite consecrating Vikrama's son as the crown prince; and the association of him with Kumāra, the son of Śiva, is made explicit by the divine sage Nārada. In this case there would be an implied identification between Śiva and the king. The early Gupta kings were worshipers of Viṣṇu, but Śaivism was well established throughout the region of their empire and the rulers were ecumenical in their patronage.[24] Candragupta II styles himself "paramabhāgavata."[25] The Bhāgavata cult of this time was a syncretic warrior religion whose adherents worshiped Śiva and the Goddess as aspects of Lord Viṣṇu, whom they call Bhagavān.[26] Candragupta II is praised by one of his court poets for coming in person to dedicate the Śiva cave at Udayagiri.[27]

Kumāragupta, while preserving his family's Vaiṣṇava allegiance in the majority of his official records, seems to have also favored the Śaivite cult of Kumāra Skanda. On his coins, the peacock, vehicle of the war god aspect of Śiva's son, is often substituted for the eagle Garuḍa, the vehicle of Viṣṇu that regularly appears as the royal emblem on Gupta coins.[28]

Classical Culture and Kālidāsa's Dramas

In studying the historical documents, the literature, and the visual arts of Gupta India, one is repeatedly struck by the heterogeneity of cultural values expressed in these works.[29] Even at the height of Gupta classicism (c. A.D. 350–470), the harmonious ideal of Sanskrit culture seems to only partially represent the artistic attitudes and practices of the society. Most literary compositions traditionally placed in the Gupta period are complex, multilayered works that display and play with conflicting philosophies of life and art.

The sources of classical Indian drama probably antedate the Gupta period. The earliest extant works are fragments of plays attributed to the Buddhist poet Aśvaghoṣa, who is associated with the court of the Kushan ruler Kaniṣka. Kālidāsa certainly had other predecessors; plays attributed to the dramatic poets Bhāsa, Saumilla, and Kaviputra are mentioned in the prologue of the *Mālavikāgnimitra*. There is also evidence of early monologue plays (*bhāṇa*) and popular theater.[30]

But it was during the Gupta period that drama seems to have emerged as a sophisticated form of public literature. Plays like Śūdraka's satiric romance the *Mṛcchakaṭika* (The Little Clay Cart), Viśākhadatta's political dramas the *Mudrārākṣasa* (The Minister's Signet Ring) and the *Devīcandragupta*,[31] as well as Kālidāsa's dramatic romances, were performed before discerning audiences. The formal and thematic complexity of the plays accords well with principles codified in the earliest Indian work on dramatic theory, the *Nāṭyaśāstra* attributed to Bharata, which was probably compiled during the Gupta period on the basis of older sources.[32]

Bharata's dramatic theory recognizes the emotional and ethical instruction afforded by the spectacle of theater. Like Aristotle, Bharata stresses the emotional satisfaction that spectators may enjoy through the action of drama. Although their modes of ordering experience are significantly different, Greek tragedy and Indian heroic romance (*nāṭaka*) were conceived and performed as sources of pleasure and insight for the audience.

In a Greek tragedy, the struggle is between the actors and a superior force, whether society or cosmic order. Its outcome affects the fate of every person in the story, and by extension that of the human audience.[33] When Aristotle discusses the emotional effect of a tragedy on an audience, he speaks of the pleasure of witnessing fearful and pitiful events, and of catharsis, or purification, a concept that Aristotle himself never precisely explains. Its meaning remains controversial among scholars, but it seems to imply the transformation of painful and destructive emotions of fear and pity into the pleasure associated with insight.

Indian heroic romances represent human emotions in a theatrical universe of symbolically charged characters and events in order to lead the audience into a state of extraordinary pleasure and insight. The goal of a Sanskrit drama is to re-establish emotional harmony in the microcosm of the audience by exploring the deeper relations that bind apparent conflicts of existence. The manifestation of these relations produces the intense aesthetic experience called *rasa*. All Kālidāsa's plays focus on the critical tension between desire and duty that is aesthetically manifest in the relation of the erotic sentiment (*śṛṅgārarasa*) to the heroic (*vīrarasa*).

The production of *rasa* is basic to classical Indian theater. The concept is difficult to translate in a single word. Though "sentiment" and "mood," the conventional translations, approximate its meaning, *rasa* more literally means the "flavor" or "taste" of something. The *rasa* is essentially the flavor that the poet distills from a given emotional situation in order to present it for aesthetic appreciation. In Indian aesthetic theory human emotion (*bhāva*) is thought to exist in the heart as latent impressions left by past experiences. Early theorists divide emotion into eight categories, each of which has the potential to become a *rasa,* a state of emotional integration. The eight *rasa*s are the erotic, the heroic, the comic, the pathetic, the furious, the horrible, the marvelous, and the disgusting.[34] Every drama or dramatic episode has a dominant *rasa;* of these the erotic and the heroic are of central importance throughout Sanskrit drama.

In Bharata's mythic account, drama is a holy presentation that the gods originated to offer ethical instruction through diversion when people were no longer listening to Vedic scriptures. According to legend the first production of a play took place at the popular rainy-season festival of Indra known as the "Banner Festival."[35] Kālidāsa states that the first production took place in celebration of the marriage of Śiva and the goddess Pārvatī. For centuries, Indian dramas have been presented on the occasion of a seasonal festival, the birth of a son, a marriage, a royal consecration, a political victory, or any auspicious event.

The ideal of education through dramatic spectacle is codified in Bharata's definition of drama (*nāṭya*). The god Brahmā speaks to the gathered demons who threaten the performance.[36]

In drama there is no exclusive representation of you demons or of the gods. Drama is a representation of the emotional states of the threefold universe. It includes concerns of duty (*dharma*), play (*krīḍa*), material gain (*artha*), peace (*śama*), mirth (*hāsya*) war (*yuddha*), desire (*kāma*), and death (*vadha*). It teaches duty to those who violate duty, desire to those addicted to love; it reprimands those who behave rudely, promotes restraint in those who are disciplined; it gives courage to cowards, energy to heroes; it enlightens fools and gives learning to learned men.

In the *Mālavikāgnimitra,* Kālidāsa invokes the view of the ancient sages that drama, though men have many tastes, can delight everyone: it is a balanced visual rite of the gods; its wild and gentle modes appear in Śiva's androgynous body; and human action, arising from the three strands of Nature, produces its various forms of *rasa*.[37]

The *Nāṭyaśāstra* contains references to the medley of spectators who assemble to enjoy a dramatic performance. Though the audience is limited in size by the necessity that the most subtle gestures of hand and eye be visible, the diversity of the audience in an Indian theater is alluded to in Bharata's theory of theatrical success.[38] Bharata stresses the reward a king will gain if he presents dramatic performances as a gift to his subjects and an offering to the gods.[39]

Visual Poetry in Performance

In the *Kumārasaṁbhava,* Kālidāsa uses the technical vocabulary of Bharata to describe the first dramatic production, as it was presented to Śiva and Pārvatī in celebration of their marriage.[40]

The divine pair watched the first play performed
by celestial nymphs acting with graceful gestures;
subtleties of style were developed in plot episodes
and the musical drama emerged in modulating moods.

Kālidāsa says nothing about the subject of the play that Śiva and Pārvatī watched, but the techniques referred to in the verse leave little doubt that he knew the abstract theatrical conventions codified in the *Nāṭyaśāstra* and composed his dramas for performance in this style.

In the *Mālavikāgnimitra,* the king's wives and members of the court study dance and drama. Mālavikā, the heroine of the play, is a student of the palace dancing master, Gaṇadāsa. The beginning of the second act of the play is devoted to a dramatic competition in which she interprets a love song in dance. The performance is much appreciated by the king and the entire audience. In discussing it, Kālidāsa's characters apply concepts of dramatic theory. The learned nun gives her judgment of its technical perfection:[41]

The meaning was set forth
with gestures and interwoven words,
dance steps followed time,
truth was in every mood,
the portrayal was gentle
and seemed natural to her limbs;
emotion wrought emotion from the matter—
it was a very work of passion.

In the *Vikramorvaśīya* the plot turns on Urvaśī's role as the goddess Lakṣmī in a play called "Lakṣmī's Bridegroom Choice" that is presented before Indra, the king of the gods. Urvaśī is the prize pupil of Bharata, the legendary theoretician of drama who is an offstage character in this play; she performs in the plays he directs for the pleasure of the gods. In the introduction to Act Three, we learn about the play's performance from a dialogue between two students of Bharata. The lyrics were composed by the goddess Sarasvatī herself and the various sentiments were portrayed. During the performance Urvaśī was so preoccupied by her love for Purūravas that she uttered his name in answer to a question about her choice of a husband, when she should have answered Puruṣottama, an epithet of Viṣṇu. Her mistake destroyed the dramatic mood for the celestial audience. Because she allowed personal emotion to interfere with her role as an actress, Urvaśī is cursed by Bharata to lose her place in heaven.[42]

These examples suggest that the drama was patronized by royalty and that kings and queens supported the training of actors and dancers. Permanent troupes of actors were probably associated with major courts. Royal palaces contained a theater with a stage backed by a greenroom, in which the actors and actresses put on their makeup and costumes and waited to enter the stage. Stage directions in the texts indicate entrances and exits, as well instructions for specific movements and actions onstage. In the prologues and within the plays a director is portrayed as a high-caste brahman who demands strict attention to detail, like a priest supervising a sacred ritual.

In Bharata's terminology, the bare text of a drama is called "poetry" (*kāvya*), while the text arranged for performance is called "drama" (*nāṭya*). In later critical literature, drama is called "visual poetry" (*dṛśyakāvya*) as opposed to "aural poetry" (*śravyakāvya*) because it presents us with a world to see.[43]

It is through stylized enactment, including gesture, verbal delivery, costume, makeup, and conventional signs of emotion, that the special atmosphere of traditional Indian theater is created. The word for acting in Sanskrit is *abhinaya*.[44] It comes from the root *nī,* which means "to lead," the same root from which are derived the words for the protagonists, the dramatic hero (*nāyaka*) and heroine (*nāyikā*). *Abhinaya* effectively leads the play toward the audience. The term refers to every means by which this object is achieved and to the synthesis resulting from the combination of its aspects. Bharata analyzes acting into four components.

1. Acting through the body (*āṅgika*), relating to gestures and movements of the body, hands, and eyes.

2. Acting through speech (*vācika*), relating to voice intonation, recitation, and singing.

3. Acting through accessories (*āhārya*), which include makeup, costume, and jewelry—scenery and props are little used, since suggestive gestures and descriptive verses function to evoke scenes and objects for the audience.

4. Acting through signs of emotion (*sāttvika*), relating to the physical manifestations of emotional states, such as tears, change of color, voice trembling, and fainting.

A language of gesture developed as a distinctive feature of the Indian stage from the earliest times. Particular importance was given to the use of hands and eyes for translating ideas, objects, and emotions into aesthetic statements. The expressive eyes and supple wrists and fingers of the figures painted in the Ajanta caves give ancient evidence of this preoccupation.[45]

Kālidāsa's plays, so rich in verbal images, depend on gesture for the full expression of their texts. In the first meeting of Śakuntalā and Duṣyanta, the heroine barely speaks. The king recites verse after verse, set against the rhythms of the Prakrit dialogue of her two friends. While this verbal poetry is being presented, the heroine represents her responses through gesture and dance, visually expressing the text through her movements. At one point, the stage direction specifies that she is to show the bee's "attack" while the king addresses the bee:[46]

Bee, you touch the quivering
corners of her frightened eyes;
you hover softly near
to whisper secrets in her ear;
a hand brushes you away,
but you drink her lips' treasure—

while the truth we seek defeats us,
you are truly blessed.

Like the verse, which portrays the bee by means of a few essential traits, quivering and fluttering gestures of fingers and eyes would be used to represent the erratic movements of the bee.

Gestures are made up of both natural and conventional movements. The natural motions of birds and animals in love or in flight are the basis for many stylized forms. The movements of an elephant or a wild goose to represent a voluptuous woman's gait are conventions of both literature and dance. In the various schools of classical Indian dance, great emphasis is placed on the artist's ability to enter the spirit of birds, animals, and flowers. A teacher might ask his pupil to live the life of a lotus by watching the lotus pond from dawn until sunset to carefully absorb the nature of the flower.[47]

Gestures thus learned are not intended to imitate nature realistically, but rather to recreate the experience of it. Gestures function not only to make vivid pictures, but also to communicate abstract ideas and to suggest nuances of emotion. An actor would have to control a whole range of gestures to communicate the motions and emotions that are fundamental to the production of *rasa* in each of Kālidāsa's plays.

In the Indian theater acting is considered a discipline (*yoga*) whereby the actor and acted become one. Arduous training is essential to the perfect acting (*abhinaya*) that can produce *rasa*. The gestures, however carefully learned and conventionalized, must not be mechanical; they must appear ceremonious, graceful, and spontaneous. An actor or actress, like a yogi, must cultivate a spontaneity that transcends learned conventions and the limitations of the stage. Intense concentration allows the performer to become absorbed in creating scenes that put the audience in intimate touch with vital aspects of nature and human psychology.

The text of a classical Indian drama begins with an invocation (*nāndī*) and a prologue (*prastāvana*). The prologue to each of Kālidāsa's plays introduces elements that are basic to the dramatic structure: prose (*gadya*), verse (*padya*), and song (*gītā*); bilingual dialogue, with the director speaking Sanskrit and his assistant or the actress speaking a lower-status Prakrit language. There is also the contrast between normative codes, cited by the director, and the practical aspects of art, expressed by the assistant or the actress.[48]

We know from the *Nāṭyaśāstra* that the prologue was preceded by elaborate preliminary ceremonies that established the ritual context of a play. The invocation was the concluding verse of these ceremonies.[49] The ceremonies and the prologue effectively draw the audience into the realm of the theater, focusing perception on the cosmic creator Śiva and then shifting it to the director, the actor, and the audience for whose sake the play is produced.

In each play, the end of the prologue marks a transition to the action of the drama itself. The first entrance of the characters occurs in swift movements that capture the mind of the audience and expose the underlying tensions of the plot. In the *Mālavikāgnimitra,* two maids burst on the scene, one rushing to the theater hall, the other bringing a ring from the royal jeweler to the chief queen. Their lively dialogue defines the palace intrigue based on the king's attraction to Mālavikā's beauty and artistic skill. The *Vikramorvaśīya* begins with the sudden entry of celestial nymphs in distress, followed by the king mounted on his aerial chariot. They enlist his help to rescue Urvaśī, who has been abducted by demons, thus creating the opportunity for the hero and heroine to fall in love.

In the *Śākuntala* we witness the king hunting a fleeing antelope in the sacred forest where Śakuntalā dwells. The movement of the chase creates a sense of uncertainty and excitement for the mind's eye as it is drawn deeper into a mythical world. The poet's intention to pierce the boundaries of ordinary time and space is suggested by the king's description of the way in which his perspective is altered as he enters the forest (1.9):

What is small suddenly looms large,
split forms seem to reunite,
bent shapes straighten before my eyes—
from the chariot's speed
nothing ever stays distant or near.

The swift rhythms of the entry in each play give way to dialogue, poetry, and action that slow down the sense of time. Details of nature and physical signs of emotion are represented in order to arrest the attention of the audience and intensify aesthetic participation in the dramatic process. The movements of the actors in the opening scene also serve to fix the symbolic geography of the stage, where specific zones represent different realms of the dramatic universe. The zones in a single play may represent heaven and earth, as well as forest, mountain, city, and palace.[50] The actor moves from one zone to another by walking around the stage in a stylized gait (*parikrama*), thereby indicating that the scene has shifted. He can thus transport the audience vast distances. There are no fixed limits on the time of a play, and the imaginative space in which its action occurs can be fantastic.

The pattern of alternating tempos and movements that begins each play is characteristic of its structure. Acts are introduced by interludes and preludes that sharpen these shifts.[51] The dialogues in these scenes often reveal crucial events of the plot that have taken place offstage, such as the curse of Urvaśī by Bharata. The play ends with the hero's recitation of a benediction, called "Bharata's speech" (*bharatavākya*). It marks the resolution of dramatic conflicts and rehearses the nature of dramatic success:[52]

May the king serve nature's good!
May priests honor the goddess of speech!
And may Śiva's dazzling power
destroy my cycle of rebirths!

Classical Language and the Languages of Drama

The techniques of performance used in the classical Indian theater were appropriate to the complicated verbal texts of Kālidāsa's dramas. These multilingual poetic dramas reflect an ancient Indian preoccupation with the nature of language. From the time of the earliest attempts to collect and codify the hymns of the *Ṛg Veda,* Indian culture placed high value on recording subtle linguistic distinctions. In order to assure the precise pronunciation, transmission, and preservation of the hymns, the brahmanic scholars carefully analyzed the language of oral poetry in these sacred texts and began to speculate on the structure and function of speech. Linguistic science developed in India in the middle of the first millennium B.C. and received systematic expression in the work of Pāṇini, a grammarian of the fifth century B.C.

By basing his analyses not only on the sacred language of the *Ṛg Veda* but on the spoken language of his time and region, Pāṇini was able to liberate the older linguistic techniques from their narrow purpose and to apply them to a codification of the language of his day. The language he codified is called Sanskrit (*saṁskṛta,* from the root *kṛ* "to make" with the prefix *sam* "together"), which means "put together," "codified," "classified." It is the classical language of India, and this language itself became the criterion of what is classical in Indian culture.

Sanskrit was the hieratic language of the brahman priests from ancient times. Under various rulers, it was also the status language of royal administration and poetry. The conservative values which it came to represent made the language increasingly regularized and artificial. During the Gupta period, it was promoted as the courtly language of literature and official communications, such as inscriptions on monuments, land-grant plates, seals, and coins. The widespread use of Sanskrit is at least partially responsible for the term "Classical Age" that is given to the Gupta period.

Although the tradition that was expressed in and through

Sanskrit was dominant in the classical tradition, this should not blind us to the dynamism that always characterized Indian culture beneath the surface of seeming linguistic and cultural uniformity. Sanskrit never really supplanted other languages. Various other post-Vedic dialects continued to develop independently of Sanskrit; the grammarians referred to them by the collective term Prakrit (*prākṛta,* a derivative of the noun *prakṛti,* from the root *kṛ* "to make," with the prefix *pra* "before"), which means "original" or "natural." The orthodox traditions expressed in brahmanical language and culture faced continual challenges in ancient times. The most significant of these was Buddhism, which remained strong throughout the Gupta period. To borrow the sociologist W. F Werthheim's musical analogy, one could say of Gupta India that "beneath the dominant theme there always exist different sets of values, which are to a certain degree, adhered to among certain social groups and which function as a kind of counterpoint to the leading melody."[53]

Kālidāsa is the only early Sanskrit author besides Aśvaghoṣa known to have composed both poems and plays. Kālidāsa's poems, like the Gupta inscriptions, are in courtly Sanskrit. The high tone of the poetry prevails and excursions into humor or lower registers of language and thought are rare. In their digressive elegance, the poems were for a select audience of men who could concentrate on the sustained subtleties of a refined literary language.[54]

The demands of the theater generated conventions of composition that were distinct from those of classical poetry. The art of Kālidāsa's plays is deliberately more eclectic than that of his poems. Languages, characters, and plots from the idealized epic universe are juxtaposed with elements from popular literature and everyday life. A fundamental clue to this is the language of his dramas.

An acute sensitivity to spoken language enabled Kālidāsa to effectively use the linguistic conventions that defined dramatic character. In most classical drama the Sanskrit language was deliberately mixed with several stylized forms of "natural" language, the dramatic Prakrits. Linguistic diversity was conventionalized in the plays and formalized in the *Nāṭyaśāstra*.[55] Sanskrit was the language spoken by twice-born men: the king, his advisers, and others of high status in religious or political spheres. It was occasionally spoken by a woman of learning, such as the nun in the *Mālavikāgnimitra*. The brahman buffoon (*vidūṣaka*), the women of the court, city, and hermitage, as well as various minor characters, spoke different Prakrits. This mixture represents the multilingual nature of Indian society, where contrasting languages have served to define layers of the social hierarchy. The languages and the value systems encoded in them were woven into the intricate patterns of the classical drama.

The contrast between Sanskrit and the Prakrits overlaps with the distinction between verse (*padya*) and prose (*gadya*). The majority of verses in the plays are in Sanskrit; Prakrits are used mainly for prose dialogues and descriptions, with Prakrit verse reserved for songs. The Sanskrit verses, rich in imagery and metaphor, share the quantitative metrical forms and aesthetic norms of classical poetry. The Prakrit verses are more lyrical, emphasizing figures of sound, such as alliteration and rhyme. The verses express imaginative landscapes and nuances of emotion that are crucial to the *rasa* of a drama. The prose, whether in Sanskrit or Prakrit, is relatively free of embellishments and usually communicates ideas and events rather directly. An exception is the Prakrit prose of the buffoon, which regularly contains puns and humorous similes.

There are cases where the Prakrit prose seems to "translate" the Sanskrit verse it accompanies, or where it summarizes the plot. In these situations the Prakrit is primarily a special pronunciation of Sanskrit,[56] grammatically similar despite differences in form and diction. One suspects that a member of the audience who spoke a Prakrit, but knew barely any Sanskrit, could enjoy the play on some level by listening to the Prakrit and watching the actors' gestures. But a full appreciation of Kālidāsa's plays demands an understanding of both Sanskrit and Prakrit.

Once codified, the dramatic Prakrits became increasingly removed from the colloquial languages on which they had been based and required special practice for one to understand them. As aids for educated readers, the pandits composed Sanskrit transliterations (*chāyās*). These occur in old commentaries and appear in the earliest manuscripts of the plays. The *chāyās* may help Sanskrit readers to understand the Prakrit dialogues and songs without effort, but they do not preserve the aesthetically significant verbal polyphony and musical contours of the original texts. These are equally impossible to reproduce in English translation, since no distinctions of dialect adequately capture the Prakrits. However, contrastive sound patterns and levels of diction in English may hint at the effect. Compare the director's verse describing summer with the actress' song in the prologue of the *Śākuntala*:[57]

DIRECTOR:
To plunge in fresh waters
swept by scented forest winds
and dream in soft shadows
of the day's ripened charms.

ACTRESS (*singing*):
Sensuous women
in summer love
weave
flower earrings
from fragile petals
of mimosa
while wild bees
kiss them gently.

In the remainder of the prologue, the poet portrays how the Prakrit song enchants the audience and transports it into the magical world of the theater.

The Prakrits are more fluid than textbook definitions would have one believe. This may be the result of mixture in textual transmission, but it is not unlikely that Kālidāsa blended three dramatic Prakrits: Śaurasenī, used for prose and spoken mainly by women, Māhārāṣṭrī, the medium of songs, and Māgadhī, spoken by untutored characters like the fisherman, the two policemen, and young boys. We find definite features of Māhārāṣṭrī in the Śaurasenī speeches. There is considerable variation within Kālidāsa's plays, strongly suggesting that he was exploiting the dramatic effect of the Prakrits, perhaps drawing variants from local or regional dialects of his day and stylizing them to emphasize tendencies in those dialects. He used various Prakrits in conventional ways as verbal signs of gender and social rank, but he also used them to complicate and enrich the verbal expressions of complex psychological states.[58] This can be better understood if we examine how contrasts of language contribute to the delineation of characters in the plays.

The Heroine and the King

The hero and heroine, as well as the clusters of characters that surround them, appear as symbolic personalities, defined by language and gender. Males are kings, princes, sages, buffoons, ministers, priests, generals, chamberlains, dancing masters, students, policemen, and fishermen. Females are nymphs, queens, princesses, nuns, ascetics, doorkeepers, bow-bearers, and serving maids. With the exception of the buffoon and other comic characters, like the policemen, the male characters in Kālidāsa's plays generally speak Sanskrit. With the exception of the nun in *Mālavikāgnimitra,* the female characters speak Prakrit.

In the microcosm of the Indian theater, the resolution of psychological, social, and religious disharmonies is enacted by characters who represent generic types. They are not unique individuals with personal destinies, like Shakespeare's Hamlet or Lear.[59] Indian characters live within stylized social contexts that reflect the hierarchical nature of traditional Indian society. The hierarchies are equally strict in the hermitages of Kaṇva and Mārīca or at the courts of Duṣyanta and his divine counterpart Indra.

Kālidāsa's dramas achieve their aesthetic and moral impact not through the conflicts of individuals but through the perennial human conflict between duty (*dharma*) and desire (*kāma*). His dramatic expositions are rooted in an ancient Indian scheme for reconciling life's multiple possibilities. The scheme is called the "four human pursuits" (*puruṣārtha*) and is divided into a wordly triad of duty (*dharma*), material gain (*artha*), and pleasure (*kāma*), plus a supermundane concern for liberation from worldly existence (*mokṣa*).[60]

The conflict is transformed into aesthetic experience by the poet's skillful presentation of his characters' emotional reactions to various situations.[61] When a poet explores the emotional reactions of a king or other exalted person through the medium of a traditional story, the drama is known as a *nāṭaka*. Insofar as this type of drama combines two major *rasas,* the heroic and the erotic, it is reasonably termed "heroic romance." Dramatic romance in Western literature, represented by examples such as Aeschylus' *Oresteia,* Euripides' *Alcestis,* or Shakespeare's *The Tempest* is comparable in many ways, though the mode of these plays may not be heroic.[62] The *Śākuntala* is the model of this genre, and the *Vikramorvaśīya* is also generally classified as such. Although later critics consider the *Mālavikāgnimitra* to be a *prakaraṇa,* or "secular romance," on the basis of its invented story and the levity of its plot, the play is called a *nāṭaka* in its prologue. Kālidāsa doubtless used the designation to indicate a broader category of plays than later critics allowed.[63]

In each of Kālidāsa's plays the hero and heroine are the focal dramatic vehicles for exposing the states of mind of the poet and his audience. The heroes of the plays are royal sages whose character is expressed according to the norms of classical society and dramatic theory. The nature of Kālidāsa's heroines is more enigmatic. They are goddess-like, but sexually and emotionally vulnerable. Śakuntalā is the daughter of a nymph and a royal sage, inappropriately living in an ascetics' grove. When the play begins, her adoptive father has gone on a pilgrimage to avert some threat to her. In his absence, she meets Duṣyanta and agrees to a secret love-wedding. Mālavikā is a princess living in disguise as a serving maid in a foreign kingdom, where she falls uncontrollably in love with the king. Urvaśī is a powerful celestial nymph, kidnaped by demons in heaven and cursed by her teacher for loving a mortal.

In some measure each of the heroines embodies both the goddess of beauty and fortune, Lakṣmī, and goddess of speech, Vāk. Kālidāsa, like the ancient singers of the *Ṛg Veda,* identifies himself with the sacred power of language. In their hymns the Vedic poets stress that their language does not serve the function of separating elements of the cosmos. Instead it is a unifying force, personified as Vāk. She is seen by the poets as a manifestation of their own power to communicate with the divine, to unify men with nature and the cosmos.[64]

The first beginning of Speech was when wise men appeared, engaged in giving names. From their love for the world they revealed their best, most perfectly guarded secret.

With the sacrifice, they followed the path of Speech. They found her within the sages. They brought her out and divided her into diverse parts. Seven singers join in praising her.

One man looks, but does not see Speech. One listens, but does not hear Speech. To another she discloses herself like a richly arrayed, passionate woman to her lord.

In another hymn,[65] where Vāk speaks of herself, she introduces herself as moving with the host of gods in mighty strides while she carries the great gods. She enters the stage of the world and reveals herself to him whom she loves. She identifies her own origin in the waters. Born in the waters of creation, Speech is the voice of the waters, the creative sound flowing from nature.

Thus Vāk, basically an abstraction, emerges in the *Ṛg Veda* as a beautiful celestial water nymph, an *apsaras,* who assumes many shapes. Later tradition has her manifesting herself in the tumultuous sounds of the river goddesses Gaṅgā and Yamunā, or as Sarasvatī, the daughter of lightning and voice of the thunder who later became the tutelary goddess of poets. As she continues to manifest herself in the imaginations of Indian poets, Vāk is not a fixed idea or image. Rather, her attributes are found in various forms, and her powerful cosmic energy (*śakti*) works in diverse ways to arouse men and to bear the fruit of their inspiration. This goddess can readily transfer her energy to the male who consorts with her.

In Indian dramatic theory each performance is conceived as a conflict between opposing forces of existence.[66] The dramatic union of the hero with the heroine is a substitute for the Vedic sacrificial union of Indra, king of the gods, with Vāk. The heroine appears as a beautiful nymph whose spontaneous love embraces the hero and leads him beyond the world of everyday experience into the imaginative universe where dichotomies of sensual desire (*kāma*) and sacred duty (*dharma*) are reintegrated. The heroine's presence, through her various forms and transformations, reassures the audience that the energy of nature is always available to reintegrate conflicting aspects of life. The plays, like the elaborately carved railings of early Buddhist stūpas and the cave paintings of Ajanta, as well as Hindu temples, teem with forms of religiously auspicious natural beauty, personified in the images of voluptuous nymphs.

The heroine is characteristically interchangeable with elements of nature, whose procreative energies she personifies. The parts of her body are conventionally equated with natural objects. One could make lists of equations for her every part, from hair to toenail tips, including brows, nose, earlobes, neck creases, navel, hips, buttocks, thighs, etc. The exiled nature spirit (*yakṣa*) of the *Meghadūta* describes his nymph-wife to the cloud as he begs it to carry his message:[67]

In twining creepers I see your body,
in eyes of startled does your glance,
in the moon the glow and shadow of your cheek,
in the peacocks' crested plumes your hair,

in the flowing waters' quick ripples
the capricious frown on your brow,
but no single object ever holds
an image of your likeness.

The strength of this conception among Indian poets is underscored by Bhartṛhari's more cynical view.[68]

Her breasts, those fleshy protuberances,
are compared to golden bowls;
her face, a vile receptacle of phlegm,
is likened to the moon;
her thighs, dank with urine,
are said to rival the elephant's trunk—
this despicable form is made venerable
by the ornaments of poets.

The heroine's body is an object of worship; poetic ornaments are like the auspicious ornaments placed on an image in religious ritual or on a bride for her marriage ritual.[69] These put the wearer in a sacred state in which she is transformed from a nubile creature whose sexual power invites violence and threatens to produce chaos into a fecund vessel for the production of offspring. As the heroine of drama or poetry she is the vehicle for transforming erotic passion (*rati*) into the aesthetic experience of love (*śṛṅgārarasa*), which incorporates the erotic and transcends the limitations of its particularity.[70]

The patterns of the Indian dramatic universe move toward a closure in which the magic of the heroine's fertility produces an environment of auspicious relations expressive of cosmic renewal. It is a universe in which all forms of life are organically related, where voluptuous young women share their fertility with trees in elaborate vegetation rites, where a woman's feet are ornamented with ritual anklets and red lac before she kicks the tree with her left foot to make it bloom.[71]

In the *Mālavikāgnimitra,* when the lost princess is found by the chief queen's low-caste half-brother and sent to his sister as an offering, her arrival magically coincides with the coming of spring. The king sees her in a painting of court ladies as the goddess of spring incarnate. Mālavikā is sent by the queen to the grove of Lakṣmī, goddess of fortune, to perform the annual aśoka blossom ritual called "Bringing the Pregnant Aśoka Tree Through the Labor of Birth."[72]

The king encounters her there and through a series of metaphors, he evokes her as a goddess composed of every spring flower.[73] The king's evocation establishes an identification of Mālavikā with both the goddess of the grove, Lakṣmī, and her seasonal transformation, the goddess of spring, Mādhavī. When the flower-maid Bakulāvalikā adorns Mālavikā for the aśoka blossom ritual, she says: "Your foot shines like a hundred-petaled red lotus; may you be constantly at the king's side!" The ritual of spring simultaneously brings her into contact with the tree and the king. This ritual in the grove is the crucial scene of the drama. Its fulfillment assures the king's political victory and the revelation of Mālavikā's true identity.

Urvaśī, heroine of the *Vikramorvaśīya* is known from the *Ṛg Veda* and the *Śatapatha Brāhmaṇa* as a stern nymph who enacts a marriage rite of fertility culminating in the sacrificial death of her consort.[74] In Kālidāsa's story, which bears striking resemblance to several popular versions,[75] she is a celestial courtesan, the delicate yet powerful weapon of Indra, born from the thigh of the ascetic Nārāyaṇa when he was seduced by a group of nymphs. It was this ascetic who gave her to Indra. She is kidnaped by some demons, rescued by the mortal king Purūravas and twice cursed for loving him—once to descend to earth, another time to be transformed into a creeper for entering a sacred grove of Śiva's son Kumāra, where women are forbidden.[76]

Her disappearance in the grove makes Purūravas lose his normal sense of reality. In his madness, he magically learns to understand the language of the animals, birds, plants, clouds, and the river to whom he speaks verses in Sanskrit, as well as in Apabhraṁśa Prakrit.[77]

The Apabhraṁśa stanzas[78] function as more concrete, naturally descriptive intensifiers of the king's Sanskrit verses. Each is accompanied, as we learn from the stage directions, by a series of dance movements. There are also Māhārāṣṭrī songs intended to delineate the condition and sentiment of the king by means of a metaphor in which the king shares his emotion with some creature of nature. The verses are introduced whenever the king goes from one object of nature to another for inquiry, providing another level of verbal description and musical counterpoint to the king's conventional expressions of grief in Sanskrit. In the original text the singer of these verses is ambiguous; the translation designates the voice as "A Singer Offstage."[79]

Having entered the grove and searched in vain for Urvaśī, he begins his lamentations in Sanskrit:[80]

> Rain clouds rising to shield the world
> from the sun relieve summer's fierce heat—
> now in this pain of my love's desertion
> beautiful days seem to mock my grief.

A dance called *carcarī* follows, accompanied by a song in Apabraṁśa:

> Cloud, withdraw! Why have you started
> this endless downpour that covers the skies?
> Yet if I see my love while roaming the earth
> I'll endure whatever you do.

After another Prakrit song and a Sanskrit verse, a voice offstage sings in Māhārāṣṭrī, referring to the king:

> Bereft of his mate, flooded with grief
> he stumbles, sluggish in love's desertion—
> in a mountain grove aflame with blossoms
> the elephant lord slackens his stride.

The verses evoke Urvaśī's presence in various objects of nature. The king is able to recognize her only when he picks up the charmed jewel composed of red lac fallen from Pārvatī's feet. He embraces the creeper and finds himself in the arms of Urvaśī. This jewel is later stolen by a vulture and found when the bird is shot by an arrow bearing a legend that reveals the archer to be the son of Urvaśī and the king, born in secret and hidden by her among forest ascetics to protect herself from her obligation to return to heaven after the king has seen his son. Indra intervenes, negates the curse, and allows her to stay with Purūravas, thus averting the potential catastrophe.

Śakuntalā is known from Vedic literature as a nymph who conceived her superhuman son Bharata at a sacred place called Nāḍapit.[81] In the *Mahābhārata* episode on which Kālidāsa based his drama, Śakuntalā is identified as the daughter born of a union between the nymph Menakā and the royal sage Viśvāmitra. Menakā, meaning "woman," is a paradigmatic figure of feminine beauty. It is noteworthy that the wife of the mountain-king Himālaya, and the mother of Pārvatī, has a variant of this name, Menā. Menakā is sent to seduce Viśvāmitra when his ascetic powers threaten the gods. She succeeds and becomes pregnant with a daughter whom she bears and abandons to birds of prey near a river. The birds worship and protect her until another great sage, the ascetic Kaṇva, finds her and brings her to live in his forest hermitage as his daughter. Having found her among the śakunta birds, he names her Śakuntalā.

Kālidāsa shapes the epic story to focus attention on details of Śakuntalā's semidivine origin and her role within the universe of Śiva. The epic story begins with the scene of a tumultuous hunt in which Duṣyanta kills numerous forest animals. The play begins with the benediction to Śiva and the prologue, followed by a scene in which the king enters with his charioteer, armed with a bow and arrow, like "the wild bowman Śiva, hunting the dark antelope." The intensity of the hunt is interrupted by two ascetics, who identify the antelope as a creature of sage Kaṇva's hermitage.[82]

The entire scene is set with great economy and magical speed by the black buck as he penetrates the forest and charges the atmosphere with danger. Kālidāsa portrays the elegant animal altered by the violence of the hunt (1.7):

> The graceful turn of his neck
> as he glances back at our speeding car,
> his haunches folded into his chest
> in fear of my speeding arrow;
> the open mouth dropping
> half-chewed grass on our path—
> watch how he leaps, bounding on air,
> barely touching the earth!

The antelope is Śakuntalā's "son," adopted by her when it was orphaned as a fawn. This scene shows the king captivated by the graceful creature of nature he is bent on killing. His passion threatens the calm of the forest and the animal it is his duty to protect. This is the prelude to Duṣyanta's discovery of Śakuntalā. As the buffoon aptly jests to the king "you've turned that ascetics' grove into a pleasure garden."

It is summertime as the drama begins. Śakuntalā is in the dangerous state of being a nubile virgin. The king's physical presence arouses the whole world of nature. When he enters the hermitage, he hides behind a tree to watch Śakuntalā and her friends watering the trees of the ascetics' grove. While they are watering the trees and plants, the friends notice that the spring Mādhavī vine she loves like a sister is blossoming unseasonably, clinging to the male mango tree. A bee in the grove lustily attacks Śakuntalā, giving the king a chance to reveal himself as her protector. As her apparent inaccessibility to him vanishes with the revelation that she is not the child of a brahman hermit, but of a warrior sage, he pursues her insistently, controlled only by her weak resistance. Finally passion overwhelms them both and they consummate their love in a secret *gāndharva* marriage of mutual consent. Śakuntalā transfers her creative energy from the forest animals and plants she nurtured by her touch to her human lover, she herself becoming pregnant in the process. Soon after their union, the king is recalled to his capital and leaves Śakuntalā behind. He gives her his signet ring as a sign of their marriage and promises to send for her.

Act Four, which critics consider to be the core, or womb (*garbha*) of the drama, begins with Śakuntalā distracted by her lover's parting and negligent of her religious duties in the hermitage. She ignores the approach of the irascible sage Durvāsas, arouses his wrath, and incurs his curse.[83] The wrath has its fulfillment in Śakuntalā herself, who rises to anger when she is later rejected by the king. The curse makes the king forget her, until he sees the ring again. Kaṇva learns from the voice of the forest, Vāk herself, that Śakuntalā is pregnant. He presides over the ceremonies that sanctify her marriage and poignantly arranges for her departure from the hermitage. The ascetic women come to worship her, and two hermit boys who had been sent to gather flowers from the trees in the woods enter with offerings of jewels and garments produced by the forest trees. The scene of her last moments in the hermitage is an emotional ritual of breaking her bonds with it. On the way to the king's capital, Śakuntalā and her escorts stop to worship at the river shrine of Indra's consort, Śacī. There she loses the ring and brings Durvāsas' curse into effect, so that the king does not remember her. When she is rejected by the king and abandoned by the ascetics, Śakuntalā, in her anger, invokes the earth to open and receive her. Before the eyes of the king's astonished priest, a light in the shape of a woman appears and carries her off. Eventually the ring is retrieved by a fisherman and when the king sees it, the curse is broken.

But Duṣyanta transgressed his duty in the hermitage, and he too has to undergo a trial of separation before he is ready to be reunited with Śakuntalā. The fire of parted love that the king experiences as he worships her in his memory consecrates him for the sacred work of destroying cosmic demons that threaten the gods. After he has done this, he is transported by Indra's charioteer to the hermitage of the divine ascetic Mārīca on the celestial mountain called Golden Peak. The scene of their descent in Indra's aerial chariot recalls and parallels the earlier entry of Duṣyanta and his earthly charioteer into the forest near Kaṇva's hermitage, where he first encountered Śakuntalā.

In this enchanted grove of coral trees, the king observes a child. As he analyzes his attraction to the boy, the king's Sanskrit is set in contrast with the Prakrit speeches of two female ascetics and the hermit boy whom Duṣyanta begins to suspect is his own son. The scene recalls and parallels the scene in the first act, when Duṣyanta discovers Śakuntalā in the company of her two friends in the hermitage of Kaṇva. One notes the formality of his language and the directness of the women's speech, as well as the legalism of his conceptions in contrast with the spontaneity of the women's thought and judgment. The scene culminates in a Prakrit pun on Śakuntalā's name, followed by her appearance before the contrite king. The fugue-like interplay of Sanskrit prose and verse with Prakrit prose emphasizes the tension between emotional responses and socially ordained behavior, which is Kālidāsa's major theme. He is not advocating unrestrained passion, but passion tempered by duty and duty brought alive by passion. Once the balance of these vital forces is restored, the king can recognize Śakuntalā as his wife and the great mother of a son who will turn the wheel of empire. Duṣyanta's victory over the demons, unlike his wanton pursuit of the antelope, is an act of heroism that entitles him to love.

Although the more austere aspects of suffering are focused on in Greek tragedy, the end of Oedipus in *Oedipus at Colonus* is not so different. The world view of Greek tragedy seems to presume the irreconcilability of forces such as passion and duty; their clash is violent, but neither passion nor duty is inevitably crushed. Within Greek tragedies, the conservative community often appears as the chorus, articulating traditional morality in a grieving, ominous voice. The chorus' relationship to the other actors may be one of fugue-like tension, or it may sound a single key that is stubbornly sustained, defeating attempts to modulate it. Victory may mean the triumph of the social order, but heroic efforts can transform it, as in the *Oresteia*. In spite of necessity (*anankē*), there is in some tragedies a transcendence that parallels the kind of integration inherent in the creative forces that dominate Indian romance.

In terms of Kālidāsa's aesthetics, creativity is regenerated by the magic power of the goddess, whom he embodies as Mālavikā, Urvaśī, and Śakuntalā. These heroines are endowed with physical forms, language, dance movements, and magical relations to nature that make beauty come to life in the dramatic process. Duṣyanta is bound to Śakuntalā by shared emotions and by a child who is the fulfillment of love and heroism. This is also true of Vikrama and Urvaśī.

Among Kālidāsa's heroes, only Agnimitra is not based on a mythological character. Agnimitra is a historical king known from inscriptions as a Śuṅga prince who served as his father's viceroy in Vidiśā, the ancient capital of eastern Malwa, which is described in the *Meghadūta*.[84] In the drama, King Agnimitra, vexed by the upstart king of Vidarbha, orders his army to crush him, and then, in an act of royal generosity, divides the conquered territory between two princes of Vidarbha, one of whom is Mālavikā's brother. Although both bear reference to Candragupta II, Purūravas[85] and Duṣyanta[86] are known in epic genealogies as brilliant kings of the lunar race, descended from the creator Brahmā. As mythic kings, each enters a union with a nymph who bears him a remarkable son.

In all the plays, circumstances draw the hero away from strict adherence to his orthodox role as the embodiment of duty and deep into the realm of emotions, where passionate desire is the dominant force. In this realm his Prakrit-speaking companion, the privileged brahman buffoon (*vidūṣaka*),[87] replaces the Sanskrit-speaking generals, ministers, and chamberlains as his main adviser. His proverbial gluttony, carelessness, and cowardice give a broad caricature of the normally sacred brahman. Although his words and actions often remind one of Shakespearean clowns like Touchstone and Feste, he is ultimately less complex.

As the king's "minister of amorous affairs," the buffoon indulges the king and frequently commits the critical errors that propel the plot to its conclusion. He speaks a comic Prakrit in contrast with the king's heroic Sanskrit and is as obsessed with satisfying his hunger for sweets as the king is with satisfying his erotic desires. His literal interpretation of *rasa* as a feast of flavors makes the underlying metaphor of love absurdly concrete. His humor provides the comic sentiment (*hāsyarasa*) that gives Kālidāsa's plays a particular liveliness.

Kālidāsa's heroes are not just kings and lovers, but connoisseurs of natural beauty and art. Agnimitra is a lover of dance and theater, as is Purūravas. Duṣyanta appreciates music and practices painting. Their responses to art within the plays reflect the poet's own conception of aesthetic experience. In addition to the prologue, each play contains distinct statements on art; notable are Act Two of the *Mālavikāgnimitra,* the interlude to Act Three of the *Vikramorvaśīya,* and the garden scene in Act Six of the *Śākuntala.* According to Kālidāsa, aesthetic pleasure, like deep love, depends on attention to detail and continual discovery of new associations.

Kālidāsa's Aesthetic of Memory

In the prologue of the *Śākuntala,* the director and the audience are so enchanted by the actress's song of summer that they are transported beyond mundane concerns. On awakening, the director recognizes its effect:

> The mood of your song's melody
> carried me off by force,
> just as the swift dark antelope
> enchanted King Duṣyanta.

The actress' singing, like the beautiful movements of the magical antelope, or the art of poetry, makes the audience "forget" the everyday world (*laukika*) and enter the fantastic (*alaukika*) realm of imagination that is latent within them.

The entire play is a reenactment of this idea. The mind of the poet, the hero, and the audience is symbolized here by the director, who holds together the various strands of the theater so that the *rasa* of the play can be realized and savored.[88]

In religious and literary texts there is a recurrent association between memory and love; one of the Sanskrit words for memory (*smara*) is a common epithet of the god of love.[89] Memory is crucial to the production of romantic sentiment throughout Sanskrit literature. Forgetfulness and memory function prominently in several works: the epic *Rāmāyaṇa,* the play *Avimāraka* attributed to Bhāsa; Bhavabhūti's drama the *Uttararāmacarita;* the collection of love-thief poems called the *Caurapañcāśikā,* attributed to Bilhaṇa; and Jayadeva's dramatic lyrical poem, the *Gītagovinda.*[90]

In this Sanskrit literature, an act of remembering is a conventional technique for relating the antithetical modes of love-in-separation (*vipralambha-śṛṅgāra*) and love-in-union (*saṁbhoga-śṛṅgāra*). In the *Caurapañcāśika,* for example, each of the verses is a miniature painting of the princess with whom the poet enjoyed an illicit love. For his recklessness in this love he is condemned to death. The love-thief's final thoughts are details of his mistress' beauty:

> Even now,
> I remember her eyes
> restlessly closed after love,
> her slender body limp,
> fine cloths and heavy hair loose—
> a wild goose in a thicket of lotuses of passion.
> I shall recall her in my next life
> and even at the end of time.

By remembering the exquisite details of her physical beauty and her behavior in love, he brings her into his presence and the lovers are reunited in his mind. Even as a literary convention of intense love, memory has the power to break through the logic of everyday experience—it makes visible what is invisible, obliterates distances, reverses chronologies, and fuses what is ordinarily separate.

We find both this vivid form of remembering and memory of a deeper metaphysical kind working throughout Kālidāsa's plays, most explicitly in the fifth, sixth, and seventh acts of the *Śākuntala*. When he emphasizes the role of memory in aesthetic experience, Kālidāsa seems to be basing his conception on established philosophical notions. Later theorists of *rasa* take this analysis further. Indian epistemologists hold that whatever we perceive by means of the sense organs leaves an impression on the mind. Memory occurs when a latent impression is awakened.[91] Indian literary theorists define memory as a recollection of a condition of happiness or misery, whether it was conceived in the mind or actually occurred.[92] In what is considered one of the key passages of Sanskrit aesthetics, the tenth-century Kashmiri philosopher Abhinavagupta explains what Kālidāsa means by "memory." It is not discursive recollection of past events, but rather an intuitive insight into the past that transcends personal experience, into the imaginative universe that beauty evokes.[93]

To illustrate this Abhinavagupta cites the final verse from the opening scene of Act Five of the *Śākuntala*.[94] The king and the buffoon are listening to a song being sung by Lady Haṁsapadikā, whom the king once loved and forgot. The king muses to himself: "Why did hearing the song's words fill me with such strong desire? I'm not parted from anyone I love . . ."

Seeing rare beauty,
hearing lovely sounds,
even a happy man
becomes strangely uneasy . . .
perhaps he remembers,
without knowing why,
loves of another life
buried deep in his being.

When the king looks at Śakuntalā at the end of Act Five, his clouded memory struggles to clarify what he feels intuitively, increasing the intensity of their "separation" for the audience. When his vivid memory is restored by seeing the ring, the image of the bee in Haṁsapadikā's song becomes visible in the picture he paints of Śakuntalā and her friends as he first saw them in the hermitage. He uses the painting to represent his experience, but love makes him create a picture of such perfection that he rises in anger to chastise the painted bee who attacks Śakuntalā. When the buffoon "reminds" him that he is raving at a picture, he awakens from tasting the joy of love and returns to the painful reality of separation (6.21):

My heart's affection made me feel
the joy of seeing her—
but you reminded me again
that my love is only a picture.

This episode evokes for the audience the first meeting of the king and Śakuntalā, that unique moment of sensory and emotional awareness in which their mutual passion sowed the seed of separation, various levels of memory experience, and then reconciliation. The richly developed counterpoint of the final act is built from latent impressions of images and events that accumulate throughout the play.[95] By sharing these with Duṣyanta as he moves through the enchanted celestial grove to find his son and Śakuntalā, the audience participates in the celebration of their reunion.

SANSKRIT DRAMATIC THEORY AND KĀLIDĀSA'S PLAYS

EDWIN GEROW

Historical Considerations

Any discussion of Kālidāsa's historical relation to the theory of Sanskrit drama is caught in a conundrum: is the theory a codification based on Kālidāsa's works, or do the works reflect an already conventional theory, on which the plays were modeled?[1] Both are in some sense true, making it likely that classical Indian drama and early dramaturgy grew in parallel and mutual development.

Kālidāsa's only certain predecessor, Aśvaghoṣa,[2] writes with obvious knowledge of the dramatic conventions that are fully developed in Kālidāsa's works. Evidence also exists for a pre-Aśvaghoṣa drama, and for some kind of teaching associated with its styles.[3] Much has been written in speculation on the Vedic and even extra-Indian relations of this early art form,[4] but the problem is one of literary archaeology, rather than literary study, for all the relevant information is gleaned from texts that are neither dramatic nor literary-critical.[5] The first evidence that is solidly within the dramatic mode, beside the fragments of Aśvaghoṣa's dramas, is the *Nāṭyaśāstra* of Bharata, generally considered to be a compilation of settled traditions rather than an authored work and roughly contemporaneous with Kālidāsa.[6]

The "Model" of the Sanskrit Drama

All three of Kālidāsa's dramas illustrate the essentials of the theory presented in the *Nāṭyaśāstra*. This text and its tenth-century abridgment, the *Daśarūpaka* of Dhanaṁjaya, provide an explicit model that attempts to account both for the form of the drama and its achievement.[7] By "form" is meant the peculiar adaptation necessary to turn a story (*itihāsa*), into a vehicle of drama, a plot (*itivṛtta*). According to Indian dramatic theory, form is manifest in the elements of character, language, and setting,[8] as well as in plot.[9] The elements interact to produce the play's emotional integration or *rasa*,[10] which, as formulated by the theoretical tradition, is a resolution of sentiments sufficiently general to abolish the mundane distinctions between audience, actor, and author. Thus, the formal and the purposive aspects of the dramatic theory are inextricably linked. Emotional reintegration is seen both as a "goal" and as the ultimate criterion of selection for the elements, determining what and in what order language, character, and theatrical effects are employed.

Both the means and ends of a drama are variable. Just as theorists recognize at least eight states of *rasa* as being sufficiently universal to animate a play,[11] they recognize ten modes, or genres, of representation (*daśa-rūpaka*).[12] The variety here is somewhat misleading. Although ten genres are differentiated, the theory clearly reflects the view that underlying the variety is a single model for drama itself, and that the model itself is realized in only one genre, the *nāṭaka*, or "heroic romance."[13]

For this reason, the discussion of the *nāṭaka* as one among ten genres is somewhat deficient in the treatises. In fact, the entire theory of representation, especially the theory of character and plot, may be taken to imply the *nāṭaka*. The *nāṭaka* is characterized chiefly by its subject matter: a "well-known" story, invariably epic, involving a suitable hero and apposite action.[14] It must be treated "fully," that is, in at least five acts, but not prolixly, not exceeding ten.[15] Its dominant *rasa* can only be the erotic (*śṛṅgāra*) or the heroic (*vīra*).[16]

Of the ten genres presented in the standard treatises only three are well represented in the dramatic literature: the *nāṭaka* (heroic romance), the *prakaraṇa* (secular romance), and the *prahasana* (farce). Since our task is to define the *nāṭaka,* I will resort to the same artificial distinctions used by the theoreticians to differentiate it from the other genres. The *prakaraṇa* is different from the *nāṭaka* in two chief points: its subject is invented rather than traditional, and its hero is a worldly character rather than a mythical epic persona.[17] Śūdraka's *Mṛcchakaṭika* (*The Little Clay Cart*), with an impoverished brahman merchant as the hero and a courtesan as the heroine, serves as the standard exemplification of the genre. In terms of structure, plot, and even sentiment, the *prakaraṇa* is indistinguishable from the *nāṭaka*.

The *prahasana* differs more markedly. Its *rasa* is the comic, and its hero is a jokester.[18] The remaining genres are known from only a few examples and may, like the *prahasana,* have developed from popular origins.[19] Many may represent types that were only imperfectly "Sanskritized" and did not survive the collapse of classical culture—except perhaps as folk art.

Kālidāsa's three dramas illustrate only two of the types. The *Śākuntala* and the *Vikramorvaśīya* are both *nāṭakas,* complete manifestations of its formal possibilities.[20] The *Mālavikāgnimitra* is a *prakaraṇa,* with scenes and characters drawn from the poet's experience or other mundane sources rather than the epic past.

The *Śākuntala* is the *nāṭaka* par excellence. The *Mālavikāgnimitra,* a *prakaraṇa,* is in its own prologue termed a *nāṭaka,* probably used loosely by Kālidāsa in the general sense of "drama."[21] The problem would appear to be that the hero of a *nāṭaka* is supposed to be a king, whereas that of a *prakaraṇa* is not. Agnimitra, though a king, is certainly more worldly than mythic. Also, although the plot has historical overtones, it is invented, not "epic."

Some later critics also deem the *Vikramorvaśīya* an imperfect *nāṭaka,* probably because it is designated *t(r)oṭaka* rather than *nāṭaka* in one version of the prologue.[22] The meaning of *t(r)oṭaka* is obscure, but it probably refers to the "musical" quality of a play, apparent here in the songs and dances of the fourth act and in the emphasis on poetry of language as against poetry of plot.[23]

Character

It has been said that the characters of a Sanskrit drama are not so much stylizations of familiar individuals as they are personifications of role types embedded in Indian culture.[24] Drama is a celebration of hierarchy, not in the sense that the powerful always triumph but rather that in a well-ordered universe identities are in some sense given and not acquired, and that relations are reasonable and not arbitrary. That implies that the character which is one's identity is a constituent of an ordered whole.

The drama is indeed an ordered whole, but the first instance of that order would appear to be founded on the paradox that character in the drama is adventitiously assumed by the player rather than given—as the Indian world view expects. Shakespeare's comment that "all the world's a stage" applies in a different sense in classical India. Western man increasingly sees his character as arbitrarily assumed like that of a dramatic persona, defined by circumstances and environment and prey to extrinsic authorities. A character in an Indian drama is precisely unlike one in the world, for in the world he is destroyed should he perversely attempt to choose his role. Being a player is itself part of the grand hierarchy, even for countersocial types: burglars, dacoits, sannyasis, or prostitutes. The Sanskrit play begins with a short ceremony in which the director and his assistant, or an actress, celebrate their magical function of turning pretense into reality.

The *nāṭaka* celebrates a reality of the highest type, the ideal hierarchy that is *dharma;* its characters are drawn from a rather restricted circle of epic heroes and heroines. Their myths are in one way or another responsible for the other world, the everyday world outside the theater. Duṣyanta and Śakuntalā are the father and mother of the ancestor of the Indian nation, Bharata. Purūravas is the Indian Orpheus, but one who wins back his Eurydice from the other world. In later dramas by other writers, such as Bhavabhūti, the god-king Rāma figures prominently, but his character is still that of the dharmic hero responsible for the maintenance and succor of his dependents. He is by definition "courteous, kindly, generous, competent, gentle-spoken, popular, pure, eloquent, well-descended, stable, young, intelligent, energetic, with a fine memory, insightful, artistic, self-respecting, courageous, consistent, vigorous, learned in the sciences, and observant of *dharma* . . . under all circumstances, steadfast."[25]

Such a character is the hero or protagonist (*nāyaka*) of the *nāṭaka*. The hero of the *prakaraṇa* is fundamentally the same character, minus the epic attributes. The notion of such a stylized protagonist is related to the nature of the drama itself, for in the absence of such a hero, we no longer have a *nāṭaka*.[26]

The idea that a certain kind of hero is essential to the play reflects the Indian view that character and action are not adventitiously related. In an important sense, nothing "happens" to the hero, for he is suited to the action that constitutes the play. In the case of the *nāṭaka,* the "best" hero is by nature possessed of an action that entirely suits him. It would be jarring for the Indian audience to find that it did not, or that something "happened" to him to deny him the fruits of that action, or that he was prey to forces beyond his ken, as in many kinds of modern antihero drama and in Greek tragedy. Sanskrit drama is rooted in a belief that such forces are within our ken.

It is the careful management of the adventitious that above all marks the Sanskrit drama. Great care is taken to assure the audience that unexpected events do not fundamentally alter a character, or the proprieties of the character's actions. Two strategies are employed, one of which we see in both the *Śākuntala* and the *Vikramorvaśīya*. Circumstances that do threaten to separate the lovers, such as the curse of Durvāsas or the grove of Kumāra, are reduced to temporary illusions, thus incidentally excusing the characters of whatever faults may derive from their deluded actions. In the *prakaraṇa,* the delusion has a more human face, such as the nun's reluctance to divulge the secret of Mālavikā's birth in the *Mālavikāgnimitra*.[27]

The idea that character is constant is reinforced by many facets of Indian social and religious custom, especially the notion of *karma,* with its attendant corollaries that every action bears inescapable fruit and that this life is not the only theater in which the drama of *karma* is played out. But it is insufficient to view drama simply as a reflection of life. To do so deprives us of key insights into the source of drama's power, its aesthetic appeal—it is no more for the Indian than for the Westerner merely a mirror of reality. Indeed, the presumptions of the Indian drama make drama itself a problem, for if character is a constant, and action largely predictable, just how can interest in that action by that character be excited and sustained? Part of the answer would appear to derive from the notion of the imbroglio. There must intervene a confusion, a curse, or a mistake that serves as the test of character. Much of the audience's enjoyment of such scenes derives from its superior knowledge, for it recognizes the mistake, as the characters do not: the audience is the locus of the fundamental truth that character is not permanently altered.

This says as much about the ways we in the West *achieve* constancy of character as it does about the Indian drama. For a Western audience, alteration of character, involving reevaluation and self-illumination, is, in theory, the prime source of interest; drama that fails in this dynamic respect is often considered to be of a lower order.[28] We have to take another set of cultural spectacles into the Sanskrit theater if we hope to participate in what is going on.

Since the true protagonist is inseparable from the nature and quality of his action, and must therefore be successful, the exploration of failure is, in the Indian view, a self-defeating task. In other words, the "tragic" perspective is an inappropriate way of viewing Sanskrit drama.[29] Though there is no single view of "tragedy," Western tragedians and theorists, beginning with Aeschylus, Sophocles, Euripides, and Aristotle, all seem to focus on the individual's distance from the world in which he finds himself. The tragedy is not, as Aristotle often points out, the equivalent of downfall or death, though the word is popularly much used in that sense; for we are all mortal, and our tragedy as such would be a commonplace. Rather tragedy resides in a conflict, the seemingly ineluctable opposition of the man's good and the good of those who constitute his universe. Oedipus wanted to find out who he was, and the citizens needed to eliminate from their midst the cause of their misery. Oedipus was that cause. Therefore his quest implied his own destruction. The classical tragedy is always in some form self-induced in terms of a "tragic flaw" (*hamartia*), but rarely with the logical purity and necessity played out by Oedipus. Tragedy seems to presume the possibility that in some ultimate sense, all is not well with the world, that man, because of what he truly is, may perish in the interest of others.

The tragic view thus presumes a notion of the individual whose existence and moral status are separable from, and possibly irreconcilable with, the community in which he finds himself. In certain modern writers, such as Heidegger and Kierkegaard, this tragic sense may appear simply as alienation, not requiring any action at all. In this sense, tragedy seems antithetical to the basic Indian notion that the ultimate good of an individual is integrally bound to the good of all. In drama this means that any separation of the protagonist is a temporary and resolvable condition.

The other characters in a Sanskrit drama are also reflections of model roles, chosen in part for the manner in which they help to articulate the character and action of the protagonist.

The character of the heroine (*nāyikā*) reflects that of her partner; she is a virtuous female (*satī*), the propriety of whose actions is founded ultimately on their redemption of the hero's actions. The importance of the heroine generally reflects the prevalence of the erotic sentiment in the dramas, either as the main theme, as in all Kālidāsa's plays, or as a minor and subdominant theme, as in the second half of the *Mṛcchakaṭika*.

In the Indian notion of a virtuous woman, submissiveness and energy coexist in an uneasy tension. Like the epic heroines Sāvitrī and Damayantī, Urvaśī wins her lover back, and indeed controls his every action, from her position as a semidivine nymph.[30] Still the critics have had some difficulty with the *Vikramorvaśīya,* finding in it much of the same thematic material also found in the *Śākuntala,* but presented with such incongruities as to vitiate its effect. One major problem lies in the character of Urvaśī, who does not seem suitable to the hero. In terms of the ancient myth on which the play is based, their separation is natural, but their union is against nature. Kālidāsa leaves this unresolved, for although the hero and heroine are reunited according to the dramatic canons, with Urvaśī becoming a wife and queen, she remains so only for the duration of Purūravas' life—ultimately Urvaśī is an immortal.

Among subordinate characters, the chief is the *vidūṣaka,* a privileged buffoon, but also the king's "minister of amorous affairs," a companion and foil for the king's sentimental and private life.[31] The *vidūṣaka* is often the arranger who conspires to bring the heroine and hero together, as in the *Mālavikāgnimitra* or Act Two of the *Śākuntala.* His efforts usually succeed despite himself, and are always threatened by his own inveterate gourmandise and self-indulgence, or by the hostility of other female characters. In what must be the major example of *lèse majesté* in the Sanskrit drama, the buffoon in the *Śākuntala* is sent to represent the king in ceremonies undertaken by the queen-mother!

The significance of the term is obscure, seemingly made

from the root *duṣ,* meaning "spoil." It hardly implies a moral judgment of his actions, but may evoke a reminiscence of his origins; he is always a "fallen" brahman, who fails even to speak Sanskrit, much less behave like a brahman. Thus, in our map of characters, the *vidūṣaka* is the only character who ought to be doing something else. He has the "wrong" character, by convention if not by nature. Thus even confusion and misguidedness are brought within the purview of the dramatist and his audience. The *vidūṣaka* of the *Śākuntala* is one of the best developed, if least typical, of these characters. He is possessed of a genuine sympathy for the king, but his go-between role is overshadowed by the lofty aims of the play itself.

Other stock characters of dramatic literature, such as the king's cruel brother-in-law (*śyāla*) or the sophisticated man-about-town (*viṭa*), are rarely or never used by Kālidāsa. In their place, Kālidāsa offers a variety of well-defined but atypical ones, such as the ascetic Śārṅgarava, whose anger at the king when he accompanies Śakuntalā to the palace seems to surpass the stylized conventions governing the expression of emotion in Sanskrit drama. The *Mālavikāgnimitra* has several notable female roles, for example: Irāvatī, the jealous rival to Mālavikā, witty, a bit violent, and probably drunk; and the noble nun, companion to the queen, intercessor and eventual key to the dénouement.

Plot

The notion of character, as we have seen, coincides with what action is thought proper to the stage. The hero is such because he superintends the play's main action, which is always suitable to his character, and enjoys its fruit. Underlying the notion of plot is a theory of action that, in its structure, purposiveness, and fructibility, has been taken to resemble a theory of ritual action.[32]

The action of a complete play is analyzed into five components (*avasthā*), which define the origin, direction, and success of any motivated action: (1) the motive (*ārambha*), subjectively expressed as desire, in which all action begins; (2) the effort (*prayatna*), the first objectification of the motive; (3) the hope of attainment (*prāptyāśā*), which presumes a response in the objective world sustaining and furthering the effort; (4) the eventuation (*niyatāpti*), wherein the subjective and objective phases of the action are brought together, promising a certain outcome; (5) the attainment of the fruit (*phalaprāpti*), which is both the termination of the hope and the realization of the original motive.

The commentatorial tradition and the theoretical literature further divide a play into five junctures (*saṁdhis*) each of which formulates one of these moments of the main action. To emphasize that they are moments of the play, and not of "real" action, a set of five distinctive names is given to them: (1) *mukha,* face; (2) *pratimukha,* reflection of the *mukha;* (3) *garbha,* womb; (4) *vimarśa,* reconsideration; (5) *nirvahaṇa,* dénouement.[33]

The components of action and the dramatic moments are evident in the *Śākuntala*. We may take the king as the hero and his action as that of winning Śakuntalā as his rightful wife.[34] The play is both a love story, especially in the first three acts, and a story of dharmic duty. Kālidāsa's innovation was to introduce the theme of *dharma* into the story as the complication, the means of separating and then reuniting the lovers. The plot is divided by the commentator Rāghavabhaṭṭa into five dramatic moments which dovetail with the five components of action.

1. The king happens on Śakuntalā and conceives a passion for her, which is from the beginning rightful. Act One is thus the "face" of the drama, in which the "motive" of action occurs.

2. The king engages the buffoon to work some contrivance whereby he can remain in the hermitage and pursue (*prayatna*) his beloved. The lovers are united, but immediately

parted by *dharma,* the king's royal business, and by Gautamī, the guardian of Śakuntalā's virtue. Acts Two and Three thus "reflect" what was begun in Act One.

3. The "womb" of the drama is always a period of separation, wherein hope of reunion is affirmed despite absence. The hope here is that of a lawful state of wedlock, completing the secret tryst of Act Three. This is manifest on Śakuntalā's part as she responds to the king's suit by leaving the hermitage for the royal capital. The king's rejection of her, which seems, in the *Mahābhārata* version, the act of a Don Juan turned indifferent, is made suitable to our drama by the device of the sage's curse, which relieves Duṣyanta of both his memory and his responsibility. By it the king's hope for the "physical" Śakuntalā, though seemingly canceled, is really born anew, in a form he is not yet able to recognize. This central section includes Act Four and the portion of Act Five up to the removal of Śakuntalā's veil in the presence of the king.

4. The "reconsideration" begins with that violent confrontation, which results in Śakuntalā's withdrawal to heaven, continues with the king's lamentations after recovering his memory, and ends with his recall to *dharma* by an appeal from Indra (*niyatāpti*). During Acts Four, Five, and Six, the lovers are separated, in mind if not in fact. The certainty of the lovers' relation now resides in the realization that they behave "out of character" in each other's absence, and can be what they are only in each other's presence. Thus, *dharma,* the fulfilling of one's proper role, which first separated them, now in effect reunites them. This section continues from Śakuntalā's rejection in Act Five through the end of Act Six.

5. The "dénouement" bears fruit on two levels: physically, the young son born of their affair; dharmically, their reunion in conformity with family and brahmanical tradition. This is Act Seven.

In the *Mālavikāgnimitra,* though the tone is lighter, the same contest of love and propriety is at issue. Like Śakuntalā's, Mālavikā's destiny is to rise from concubinage to wifehood, once her "nature" is transformed into "status." The major differences are the setting—the harem, in contrast to the hermitages of Kaṇva and Mārīca, and the contesting queens, one jealous of her rank, the other of her rival. The plot proceeds from the king's seeing Mālavikā's picture to the meeting contrived through the contest of the dancing masters. The separation arranged by the jealous queens involves Mālavikā's going to prison, instead of to heaven. During this, the king falls into a stylized crisis of despair, which is relieved only by the intervention, not of Indra's charioteer, but of the king's own buffoon, who simulates a snake bite with uncharacteristic initiative. Mālavikā's legitimation is only partially a result of her having pleased the queen by making the aśoka tree blossom. The dénouement is also a function of the two background plots involving the king's military expedition.

The same basic outline is evident in the *Vikramorvaśīya,* whose plot resemblance to the *Śākuntala* even includes an ornament as the device of reunion. The effect of the play is, however, very different, partly because of the problematical plot. Kālidāsa has romanticized this ancient story even more than he did the *Mahābhārata* story of Śakuntalā.[35] In the Vedic version, Urvaśī implacably spurns Purūravas' pleas to return to him. In Kālidāsa's play this dénouement is weakened and the plot multiplies adventitious improbabilities to the limit. The hero and heroine are united no less than four times, with Urvaśī and her two curses playing the decisive role in each case. Recovering his love so often reduces the force of Purūravas' laments, but then it is the sequence of disunions that increases the intensity of each succeeding one, until in the end Urvaśī is lost as the king gains his son.

The plot is clearly not of major importance. It seems almost a pretext for the lamentations of Purūravas. The play is thus more a dramatic lyric whose beautiful verses and songs[36] sometimes celebrate union but chiefly separation. It culminates in the fourth act, virtually a soliloquy of more than seventy verses, wherein Purūravas, in a state of madness over his love's disappearance, imagines her in a variety of animals and plants. This unique act, though imitated by later authors, points again to the difficulty of assigning the *Vikramorvaśīya* to a genre. The play is better viewed as a radical variant of the *nāṭaka* form exemplified by the *Śākuntala*. The main interest is not on the drama of character and plot (*nāṭya*), but on the visual and auditory arts of dance, music, pantomime, and song (*nṛtya*). The story is more a vehicle than an integral part of the art, much like the melodramas that underlie many of the most popular Western operas.[37]

An important role in all the dramas is played by the notion of subplot (*patākā*), the subsidiary story line that intersects the main plot whenever it is necessary either to complicate it or to resolve it. In the *Śākuntala,* the subplots are provided by the curse of Durvāsas, which separates the lovers under the image of inexorable *dharma* and thus points the way to proper resolution, and the incidents surrounding the ring, which restores the king's memory. The war of the gods and demons is another subsidiary plot that contributes to the resolution.

In the *Mālavikāgnimitra,* the chief subplots are the royal expedition, whose disentanglement legitimizes Mālavikā, and the aśoka blossom ritual, which reconciles her with the queen. The scenes involving Irāvatī, no less than Dhāriṇi, are not secondary, for the main action here is in the harem and concerns not only Mālavikā's introduction into it but the resolution of its quarrels.

In the *Vikramorvaśīya,* the subplots are few: the pair of curses that bring Urvaśī to earth and then abstract her again. But, as we have seen, the play's entire plot is less well developed.

Aesthetic Response

Ideally the *nāṭaka,* or its secular counterpart, the *prakaraṇa,* has inherent in its dramatic structure a measure of completion, a fulfillment of the seeds of action in characters suited to it. We may well ask what the proper aesthetic response to such a drama is. In other words, what is the Indian counterpart to Aristotle's notion of catharsis?

The concept of *rasa* was developed by the Indian aestheticians in an effort to account for the peculiar pleasure of the Sanskrit drama. Although the concept accumulated many philosophical and even religious connotations,[38] it was in origin primarily an evocation of the drama's "completeness" or "perfection." It was a response to the manifestation of potentialities presented in a drama—like a meal in which all the tastes and ingredients of the various dishes are perfected and harmonized. The drama was the complete art form, uniting poetry, dialogue, acting, song, dance, and thus music and sculpture.

For the aestheticians, the first "whole" is that of the action itself, its triumph in a character suited to it. By this manifestation of action, stylized almost to the point of ritual,[39] the audience is then brought into contact with a character whose nature, actions, and social persona are wholly appropriate to him. The action of the drama is "complete" in a third sense when the audience (*sahṛdaya,* those who share their hearts) is reintegrated with, and in, its own nature. This brief communion, which transcends the ordinary reality of the audience-actor-author trichotomy, is called *rasa*. Though only an emotion, or "affect," it is a token of a more profound reality that exists in all of us. The writers speak of *rasa* in terms of joy (*ānanda*), amazement (*camatkāra*), and similar words that suggest the religious-philosophical borderland in which drama works. But the drama of any culture can only be a rehearsal of its most deeply rooted fears and values. Just as Western tragedy expresses a fear of disintegration, classical Indian drama celebrates the ideal of union.

In practical terms, an audience cannot experience *rasa* as such, for its commonality is always colored by one or another of the basic emotions that constitute the human psyche and determine its potential for experience—here Freud and the aestheticians seem to share common ground. The texts enumerate at least eight such fundamental emotional propensities,[40] but chief among them is *śṛṅgāra,* the erotic sentiment. As we have seen, most of the major dramas are centered in the erotic, but the heroic *rasa* is also frequent; the rest as principals are rare or limited to certain genres. Some of the eight are not found animating any known drama; they perhaps derive from popular art forms that have not survived or were hypothesized from epic and story literature—the horrible, for example, abounds in the Purāṇas. As secondary or complementary emotions, all eight *rasas* are known in dramatic literature, along with various "transitory" emotions that were not considered capable of ever sustaining a whole dramatic work.

Indian theories of literature fall into two main categories, which in some ways resemble expressionist and aesthetic theories of the West. The former and perhaps older, with clear connections to Vedic theories of the "self-established text," grew chiefly in the context of the classical lyric poetry. It has for all intents and purposes been absorbed into the aesthetic theory from the time of the brilliant and eclectic tenth century text *Dhvanyāloka*.[41]

The aesthetic view is well illustrated in the *Nāṭyaśāstra,* where the term *rasa* is first used in a properly theoretical sense, and is clearly understood as a metaphor for its literal sense "flavor."[42] Not surprisingly, the aesthetic mode of understanding poetry was first developed in terms of drama rather than of strophic poetry. Drama, among all the arts that use language, is notable for the totality and immediacy of its effect on a real audience, an effect conveyed through language but derived from more fundamental kinesthetic and empathetic modes of response to events witnessed.

The aesthetic strain of Indian thinking on poetics has clear antecedents in Indian epic literature, particularly the *Rāmāyaṇa,* which is said to have been the "first poem" (*ādikāvya*), composed by the "first poet" (*ādikavi*), Vālmīki: it is said to have been born of a moment of emotional intensity, wherein the poet transformed his grief (*śoka*) at witnessing the cruel bereavement of a lovebird into poetry (*śloka,* the original verse form of Sanskrit poetry).[43] The manifest form of language is here grounded in an inspiration that is emotional yet already reflective, to which it uniquely gives voice. It is no accident that in later *rasa* theory, *śoka* is counted as the emotional ground of one of the eight *rasas,* the pathetic (*karuṇa*),[44] now understood as the message of Vālmīki's grief.

We cannot pursue here the many problems, both historical and psychological, that arise from the idea that the dramatic process is informed by an emotional awareness shared by audience, actors, and poet.[45] However, it is necessary to stress the dual paradox that exists for the poet and the audience: (1) the constructional paradox, a "stasis" that results in a "development"; (2) the appreciational paradox, a varied and diverted perception that ultimately is one and the same. How the multiplicity and the unity are related is the key problem of Indian aesthetics, and many theories have been proposed. The most influential of the solutions is that of the tenth-century Kashmiri thinker Abhinavagupta,[46] who notes the formal isomorphism of the aesthetic problem to that of the philosopher, especially the nondualist (*advaita*) philosopher. Abhinavagupta proceeds to treat dramatic aesthetics as a prolegomenon to the true conquest of the nature of things (*saṁsāra*). The drama is a metaphor of creation in general, and, on its appreciational side, a formula for acquiring the sense of unity that survives through all diversity. It is different from the philosophical problem in that its form of universality is still emotional—it is grounded in the diversity of the human realm rather than in the unity of the cosmic. According to this analysis, it is the capacity to feel that distinguishes us from the universe and gives us hope of salvation.

If one looks at the *Rāmāyaṇa,* one can get a better sense of the aesthetic problem, and of the solution provided by Kālidāsa's dramas. The epic poem concerns, among other themes, the separation of the lovers Rāma and Sītā, and thus bears out its symbolic opening, the separation of the lovebird from its mate. But in what sense does the poem itself manifest the emotion of grief at separation?

There has been much discussion over the authenticity of the poem's final section, the Uttarakāṇḍa, which is generally regarded as a later addition.[47] But this addition gives the poem a certain aesthetic unity and fulfills the promise of the symbolic beginning—itself perhaps an interpolation. Were the story to end after Rāma's restoration as king and his reconciliation with Sītā, the poem would be the usual Indian tale of success against odds and a validation of royal character. "Woe" would be reduced to a mere complication of the story. The final section is problematic precisely in that it turns the tale around. Events force Rāma to banish Sītā, much as he was once banished, but this time without hope of reconciliation. The political and opportunistic nature of his motives have long been the subject of scholarly and religious debate, for these would be inconsistent with his character. Not only is Sītā pregnant with Rāma's twin sons, but Rāma tricks her into accompanying Lakṣmaṇa into the forest, where the ever-faithful Lakṣmaṇa has been given orders to abandon her. She finds her way to Vālmīki's hermitage and we are spared a "tragic" finale—but the lovers have been finally and willfully separated.

We are left with the dilemma that the poem can be integrated emotionally only at the expense of Rāma's character, and vice versa, if the last section is rejected. It is possible to see Rāma's rejection of Sītā as an act of self-discipline, akin to the penance (*tapas*) of an ascetic, and thus heroic; but even so, the mode of heroism changes from warrior heroism to compassionate heroism. Here, as generally in Indian literary works, a change of character is regarded as a defect or blemish on the plot, and the plot that involves such a sudden change (Aristotle's *peripeteia*) is thought weak and incomplete. These assertions are merely corollaries of the *rasa* theory itself, but the relative "failure" of the *Rāmāyaṇa* is instructive when compared to Kālidāsa's treatment of these problems.

As a solution to the constructional paradox, Kālidāsa has devised a plot that is essentially circular, returning to itself through a set of concentric circles that are defined in terms of emotional contrasts. As a solution to the appreciational paradox, Kālidāsa has clearly reestablished the homogeneity of plot and character by the device of recasting all the events of the play into a world of pretense and illusion, whereby the characters are merely tested, not altered. Thus the emotional impact of the play remains integral even in its development. Both solutions are evident in the *Śākuntala*—note the parallelism of Acts One and Seven, the inversion of Acts Two and Six, the reversal of Acts Three and Five, and the crucial significance of Act Four, which formalizes the marriage of Śakuntalā, a process that takes her from the natural world of the forest and confers on her a new, social status. The propriety of the reunion of the king and Śakuntalā is expressed in the certitude of their respective characters, as sketched out in the chance meeting in the first act (where the king shows his subservience to *dharma* and is thereupon rewarded with the prophecy of a son) and reaffirmed, through every complication, until the final culmination.

The emotions themselves do not change, but their mode of relation changes as the conditions of love and duty (*kāma* and *dharma*) develop from external and contingent opposites into necessary complementarities.[48] Love, or heroic duty, is thus turned into *rasa* by the play itself, which means that emotional value is translated from its natural, or contingent, mode into one of integral necessity. In this resides the peculiar pleasure of Sanskrit drama, and the source of its power. It is a revelation of certainty that reawakens in us a sense of our common humanity, a sentiment usually overlaid by the cares and limitations of our individual selves.

The Indian play, exemplified by the *Śākuntala,* is indeed a "play," in the metaphysical sense that its workings reveal the nature of things. It is not a "drama" in the Aristotelian sense of an "imitation," having an existence apart from the things it imitates and a form proper to itself.[49] The Aristotelian poetic may be said to differ fundamentally from the classical Indian on another point as well and to constitute an "anti-aesthetic."

Given his notion that pleasure is properly an adjunct of "right activity," never a goal as such, Aristotle has some difficulty in dealing with the peculiar pleasure of the arts.[50] It appears that pleasure is only an adjunct to learning—the emphasis is on what we learn by imitation, and pleasure lies in the learning. Enjoyment is displaced in favor of more intellective goals. In tragedy, pity and fear are not the issues but rather their cleansing. This too is achieved by an intellective mechanism, a recognition (*anagnōrisis*) which is the goal of the plot-maker and the sign of the best plots.[51]

In India, the aesthetic emphasis of the Hindu dramatic theory may be contrasted with the Buddhist attitude toward enjoyment, which is based on a theory that denigrates the value of pleasure itself. "All life is suffering," according to the Buddha's insight into the nature of things. The role of art is rendered problematic here insofar as there is no "proper" pleasure to be aimed at. Pure art is, as for Plato, a waste of time. Art is redeemable only as a didactic exercise, which is evident in the work of Aśvaghoṣa.[52]

In canonical Hinduism, where ultimate reality is interpreted as a mode of universal enjoyment, the noncognitive and emotional aspects of art are emphasized. Upaniṣadic texts speak of the ultimate (*brahma*) as joy (*ānanda*). Abhinavagupta asserts that *rasa* is to be enjoyed and that in this enjoyment arises the connection of *rasa* with the ultimate, which is also to be enjoyed (*āsvādya*).[53]

The Achievement of the Plays

If the *Śākuntala* is the *nāṭaka* par excellence, it is also unique in Sanskrit literature for its moral intensity. In it the poet has had the inspiration to construct a romantic plot that goes beyond the obvious circumstantial obstacles to true love, such as rivals, potions, and villains. He has worked out a subtle dialectic of its essential oppositions in terms of the other major *rasa,* the heroic. The reconciliation offered is one that transcends even the ideal integration of the play's dominant *rasa*. The view that seems to have informed this play is that the various modes of aesthetic experience, the eight *rasas*, involve a fundamental harmony that must be evident for any one of them to be truly manifest.[54] The *Śākuntala* is thus for art what the *Bhagavad Gītā* has become for moral speculation. It addresses basic social issues that perhaps allow only an aesthetic resolution.

The *Vikramorvaśīya*, as suggested above, excels on another plane altogether. If it is judged only as a *nāṭaka*, it impresses with its imperfections. Rather it seems to have other aesthetic goals. Though its *rasa* is erotic, the counterbalance is not the high seriousness of *dharma*, but the seemingly external or "natural" opposition between human and divine. Purūravas is either ecstatically happy, when Urvaśī is present, or despondent, when she is absent, and nothing he does brings her close or takes her away. The intensity of his passion for her is seemingly the only theme, and one which is best communicated by song and poetry, as in the fourth act. The novelty of this play might be said to consist in its use of the dramatic format to present an essentially lyrical message.

The *Mālavikāgnimitra* is an example of a more popular and common type of drama.[55] It is distinguished neither by its erotic sentiment nor by its plot of the lovers' reconciliation, but by its contrasts and intrigues, which are more unabashedly comic and seem to parody those of the heroic romance. Here *vīra*, the heroic, is present only in the subplot that serves as a pretext for Mālavikā's eventual admission into the status of queen. *Dharma* itself is not an issue; it is a given—it is the social convention of the court, manipulated by the drunken Irāvatī, the ever-ingenious buffoon, and the lovesick king himself, who is embarassed when caught so frequently. The chief queen, Dhāriṇī, whose anger gives rise to the major complications of the plot, is moved less by jealousy than by the threat to her rank. Kālidāsa's remarkable skills here have not produced a new genre; rather they have been employed to set off the poet's infatuation with the female character. Nowhere else in the ancient dramatic literature is there such a variety of able and resourceful heroines. We might allege here that character constitutes the excellence of this play, in contrast with clearer examples of the secular comedy, and that Kālidāsa was in fact attempting to bring under the format of the *nāṭaka* the independent females of story literature.[56]

Kālidāsa's poems and plays reveal an astonishing command of diverse subjects and styles, and yet show an equally remarkable coherence of tone and quality. Across the evident variety, it is the *rasa* that most markedly unites the work of Kālidāsa. To the extent that his works excel according to the canons of the *rasa* aesthetic, they become standards for an Indian literature that seeks in *rasa* to express its ideal.[57]

THE THEATER IN KĀLIDĀSA'S ART

DAVID GITOMER

The Playhouse and Its Stage

When demons tried to break up the performance of the first drama because it shamed them, Brahmā ordered that a playhouse be built to protect the performance.[1] Indeed, the only structures remaining from antiquity that can be identified with any certainty as theaters are caves cut in rock in central and eastern India. Also in eastern India may be found open pavilions used for dance and drama attached to temples of much later date than the caves.[2] The temple-theaters of Kerala (*kūtaṁbalam*), home of the regional Sanskrit dramatic form known as Kūṭiyāṭṭam, certainly provide a valuable source of comparison with the buildings described by Bharata in the second chapter of the *Nāṭyaśāstra,* but they fit Bharata's prescriptions only in a few dimensions.[3] Unfortunately, the lovely oblong, intimate "playhouse for mortals," its whitewashed walls decorated with paintings of "creeping vines, men, women, and their sensual pleasures," was made of wood and brick; all specimens have perished. Exact interpretation of the *Nāṭyaśāstra*'s account is therefore difficult.[4]

Although playhouses of small, medium, and large scale, and triangular, rectangular, and square shapes are described, most attention is given to the medium rectangular variety; it may be taken as a norm. Ninety-six feet in length, forty-eight in width, but divided so that equal halves were given over to audience and performers, these halls could have accommodated no more than 200 spectators sitting on a mat-covered floor (perhaps on rising levels, though this is only specified for the square type of playhouse), with benches for the distinguished and elderly on the sides.[5] Wooden pillars supported the roof, which was possibly thatched.

At least four of these pillars stood away from the walls within the audience area. Each was associated with one of the four classes (*varṇas*). Whether they were to designate seating areas for these classes or whether they symbolically represented the dismembered unity of the primal man embodied in the building's site plan is difficult to say. They certainly indicate that the sanctuary of the fifth Veda, divinely created out of the other four that knowledge might be extended even to the lowly śūdras, was in its ideal at least a place for all people.[6]

The part of the house which was the domain of the performers was again subdivided, but in exactly what way is the subject of controversy.[7] It is agreed that there was a backstage area, the *nepathya* or *nepathyagṛha,* a kind of greenroom where the actors and actresses put on costumes and makeup, waited to make their entrances, and spoke when the script called for offstage voices. It seems that there was a wall between the backstage area and the stage, with two doorways cut near the center for entrances and exits.[8] Although the chapter of the *Nāṭyaśāstra* which describes the playhouse does not mention them, there are references elsewhere in the text to sliding curtains over these doors which could be thrown aside quickly for agitated entrances, such as that of Purūravas at the end of the prologue to the *Vikramorvaśīya.* The manner of these entrances is reflected in one of the names for this curtain, *javanikā* (from *java,* a primary derivative of *jū,* to be quick, to impel). A more doubtful derivation of the term associates it with *javana* ("Ionian," probably to mean Greco Bactrian); such a borrowing would parallel the designation of the female bow-bearers in Sanskrit dramas as *yavanyaḥ.*[9]

Between the doors were two large drums; clustered around them were the other musicians of the ensemble, which seems to have provided an almost continuous accompaniment to any dance-drama. The area occupied by the musical personnel would have reduced the acting area still further. Some interpret the text to mean that this section was elevated above the downstage and called by a separate name, *raṅgaśīrṣa*. The downstage (*raṅgapīṭha*) was flanked on either side by mysteriously named areas called *mattavāraṇī,* "intoxicated elephant."[10] These may have been used as an additional playing area, or perhaps as boxes for important persons such as the king and his party. Pillars defining the *mattavāraṇī* area further reduced the stage, so that the actual playing area may have been as small as twelve feet square; another scheme works out to a rectangular 24′ × 12′.

Consecration, Preliminaries, and the Gateway to the Drama

Every aspect of the construction of the playhouse, from the laying of the string to measure the foundation to the drawing of a *maṇḍala* for the installation and worship of gods in the building, was part of a great ritual, undertaken at the proper astrological moment, which drew on traditional modes of Vedic sacrifice and recapitulated Indra's defeat of the demons who threatened to destroy the primal drama.[11] Indra was the prototype of the hero (*nāyaka*) in the heroic mood (*vīrarasa*), that is, the prototype of the king. The final consecration of the playhouse involved the smashing of a pot (to ensure that the king would smash his enemies and that the dramatic preceptor would smash all obstacles to his performance), the illumination of a torch with which the preceptor then ran throughout the playhouse to the cacophonous accompaniment of the percussion ensemble, and a ritual combat that was only considered auspicious when blood was drawn.[12]

The weapon Indra used to smash the demons to pieces (*jarjarīkṛtasarvāṅgā*) is known as a *jarjara;* it is the flagstaff of his own auspicious banner, which was donated as a gift to the performers.[13] The violent ceremony described above was not repeated after the theater was consecrated, but was evoked before every performance in the preliminary ritual called the *pūrvaraṅga*, which included song and dance.[14] During these preliminaries the director had to carry the *jarjara* while singing dramatic songs and executing a complex series of movements and gestures borrowed from the vocabulary of the dance-drama in order to propitiate the gods and ward off evil from the playhouse. The final refrain was sung in praise of the *jarjara*.[15]

The first part of the preliminaries gave the musicians an opportunity to get themselves settled and warm up. The second part was divided into nine sections. In addition to its ritual function, it gave some of the performers a chance to move around on the stage, to stretch their limbs and vocal chords before what was undoubtedly the ordeal of a performance. Meanwhile the audience filtered in and was drawn into the mood of the play to be performed by the songs, dances, and verbal dialogue of the preliminary entertainment.[16] The length of these proceedings was not strictly fixed; that they could become overlong and tiresome is shown by the director's first line after the benedictory stanzas in both Bhaṭṭa Nārāyaṇa's epic drama *Veṇīsaṁhāra* and Harṣadeva's court romance *Ratnāvalī:* "Enough of these drawn-out preliminaries!" Jagaddhara, the commentator on *Veṇīsaṁhāra,* says that destruction of the aesthetic mood (*rasabhaṅga*) can result from overly long preliminaries, doubtless from the wearing away of the audience's expectations.

A benedictory stanza (*nāndī*) opens the "gateway to the drama" (*raṅgadvāra*), and it is here that our printed texts of the plays begin.[17] The division of the play into acts and a further separation of prologues, interludes, etc. from the acts themselves need only have been reflected on stage by a break in the action for the normal exits and entrances, since successive scenes in a Sanskrit play invariably begin with different characters from the preceding one. This does not mean that there were not also extended intermissions between certain acts during which musical interludes might be played to set or change a mood.

How long were the performances, and at what time of day were they given? In Kūṭiyāṭṭam, each act of a play is given a name and subjected to such intense elaboration that several nights may be required for the completion of an act. Each night the performance begins well into the evening and goes on for hours. It is not the regular practice to stage an entire play in any given "season." In many manuscripts and commentaries of Sanskrit plays, such names are attached to individual acts, giving rise to the impression that this may have been the practice in later times for the Sanskrit drama as well. But from the *Kāma Sūtra,* which contains much valuable information on the theater, as well as from prologues to various plays, we see that plays might be performed at any time, especially if a king's whim commanded it.[18] Urvaśī must hastily return to heaven when Indra desires to see her in the play "Lakṣmī's Bridegroom Choice." The *Nāṭyaśāstra* prescribes the time of day for the performance of plays of particular styles and themes, but the chief determining factor for performance time is *rasa.*[19] (A similar situation prevails today with regard to North Indian classical music composed in various rāgas.) Plays such as Kālidāsa's, in which the erotic mood (*śṛṅgārarasa*) is predominant, are to be staged in the evening. Other types of plays, such as those which develop the sentiments of the heroic or the pathetic, are to be performed in the daytime.

From this we may conclude that only the romances needed lighting, which was accomplished by means of torches or oil lamps. Such lighting could produce tremendous dramatic effect, but was incapable of illuminating the entire playing area. Even in the case of daylight performances, the subtlety of facial expressions, gestures, and modes of vocalization required proximity between audience and performers. For this reason the *Nāṭyaśāstra* recommends that the playhouse not be excessively large.[20]

The Company and Its Stagecraft: Costumes and Makeup

Roles were usually assigned to the appropriate gender, but transvestite roles were known, as were all-male and all-female troupes.[21] Bharata cautions the director to distribute roles according to physical type, and to a certain extent according to personality. In general, some fleshiness was considered an attractive sign of health. Chapter 35 of the *Nāṭyaśāstra,* which deals with distribution of roles, confuses its descriptions of a person ideally suited to play a particular role, the appearance of an actor in the role, and the personality of the character. These descriptions may not seem very enlightening:

A woman with the following qualities should be given the role of a heroine (*nāyikā*): She should be endowed with a good physical form, good qualities, character, and youth. She should be pure, affectionate, and sweet, and speak charming words with a lovely voice. She should be consistent in the exercise [of dramatic art] and conversant with tempos, rhythms, and the aesthetic moods. She should possess all the kinds of ornaments, and [be] adorned with garlands and scents.[22]

But the description of a woman disqualified from portraying a *nāyikā* helps to clarify what is desired:

But a woman should not be made a heroine in any theatrical show if she smiles on the wrong occasions, is rough in appearance, has an uneven gait and movement, persistent anger, a miserable look, and is always haughty and fickle. These are the characteristics that the producers of plays should know about.[23]

Actors who are to portray kings and princes are described as handsome, tall, of dignified gait, and wise. By contrast, the buffoon is described as dwarfish, hunchbacked, baldheaded, red-eyed, and having big teeth.[24]

Actually the *vidūṣaka*'s appearance is an exaggeration of stereotyped brahman features—obesity from gorging on food served as part of the rituals and baldness due to regular tonsure. Both the buffoon in *Mālavikāgnimitra* (4.17+) and the one in *Vikramorvaśīya* (2.0, 5.11+) are described as looking like monkeys. The buffoon also carried a crooked stick called a *kuṭilaka*, perhaps a comic counterpart to the *jarjara*.

Among the members of a typical theatrical company the *Nāṭyaśātra* lists a crown maker, an ornament maker, a garland maker, a dyer, and a dresser.[25] Obviously costumes were important and elaborate; from Bharata's description, items of costume seem to constitute a code of identity comprising rank, occupation, and geographical origin.[26] A striking element to the Western spectator would have been the heavy use of ornaments, largely of gold. Like the Bharata Nāṭyam dancers of today, royal persons of both sexes might be expected to wear crowns, necklaces, rings, bracelets, arm bands, earrings, and garlands. In addition, women would wear jeweled girdles and three types of ankle ornaments—ankle bracelets, a string of tiny bells, and hollow leg bangles containing stone chips which would rattle.[27] Bharata was aware of the hazards of excessive ornamentation and advised:

> In the production of plays too many ornaments should not be used, for these will cause fatigue to the actors and actresses while executing prolonged movements. Moreover, weighed down with heavy ornaments one cannot move much, and one so weighed down is likely to be exhausted and to faint. Hence [in a dramatic production] ornaments made of pure gold should not be used, but those made of lac and slightly inlaid with jewels will not bring exhaustion [to the wearers in a play].[28]

To this day Indian dancers wear stage ornaments made of lac covered with gold leaf.

The clothing of the costumes, in keeping with the non-theatrical dress of ancient times, would consist mostly of draped, rather than fitted and stitched apparel. The *Nāṭyaśāstra* seems to assume that the director knows in most cases how to dress his characters, for the notes concerning costume are generally to remind him that the particular characters must be dressed in particular ways, rather than specifying what the costume is. There is a helpful threefold division of costume into white, multicolored, and dirty.[29] The first is prescribed for those "observing some auspicious rite or a vow at the conjunction of some special phase of the moon and stars"; this would apply to Queen Auśīnarī in Act Three of *Vikramorvaśīya,* and possibly to both Purūravas and Urvaśī in Act Five. All ministers and brahmans wear white. Multicolored costumes are worn by, among others, kings and gandharvas, which would include Citraratha in Act One of the *Vikramorvaśīya*. Chamberlains, sages, and Buddhist monks (presumably nuns as well, such as Kauśikī in *Mālavikāgnimitra*) wear robes of a color called *kāṣāya,* a kind of brownish red. Ascetics wear garments fashioned from tree bark, tattered strips of cloth, and animal skins; this should be kept in mind when visualizing Śakuntalā in the early acts of the play, the other residents of the *āśrama,* and the female ascetic Satyavatī who appears in the fifth act of the *Vikramorvaśīya*. Lastly, lunatics and intoxicated persons were to appear in soiled costume; this would apply to the tipsy Irāvatī in the *Mālavikāgnimitra* and the raving Purūravas. The text also specifies various kinds of crowns, hairstyles, and beards.

The section of the *śāstra* that deals with makeup is largely concerned with the mixing of pigments to produce the shade appropriate to various castes, regions, and stations in life.[30] If the contemporary practice of regional drama and dance forms is any clue, makeup would have also served to make the extensive vocabulary of eye gestures, the *dṛṣṭis,* more visible to the audience.

A review of the vocabulary of *dṛṣṭis,* as well as those of gestures, postures, leg movements, arm movements, and coordinated motions, might create the impression that this theater was purely a theater of technique. Yet a number of remarks in chapters 23 and 25 of the *Nāṭyaśāstra* specifically relating to makeup would seem to indicate a very different kind of involvement of the actor with his art:

One should not enter the stage in his own natural appearance. His own body should be covered with paints and decorations.[31]

After covering the body and its [natural] color with paints and cosmetics, an actor should assume the nature of the person whose character he is to represent.[32]

Just as the soul [of a person] after renouncing the nature proper to [his own] body assumes another character relating to the body of an animal (a yogic practice), so a person having [a different color] and makeup adopts the behavior connected with the clothes he wears.[33]

Just as a man who renounces his own nature [and] body and assumes another's nature by entering into his body (a yogic power), so the wise actor, thinking within himself "I am he," should represent the states of another person by speech, gait, gesture, and other movements.[34]

Taken together these statements imply that the actor would undergo a kind of transformation in the long process of putting on makeup and costume. The result of this process is the external manifestation of the elements of character *within* the conventional vocabulary of technique of the Sanskrit stage.

Movement and Symbolic Space

Thus prepared, the actor enters the stage in a gait consonant with his character, the aesthetic mood being developed, the place, and the situation. These gaits are prescribed in chapter 13 of the *Nāṭyaśāstra*. Using technical terms, the text enjoins an erect but graceful and relaxed entrance posture for characters of high and middle degree. The position of the feet, the height to which they are raised in walking, even the tempo of the gait are detailed: characters of higher degree move more slowly and deliberately.[35]

A few examples will show the exacting specificity of the prescriptions. The position for women standing in conversation when in the erotic mood (either playful or determined) is called *avahittha sthāna*.[36] This is a contraposto pose (*abhaṅga*) in which the weight is shifted to one side (in this case the right), and one knee is slightly flexed. The left foot is *sama* ("even," i.e., facing front and normally parallel to the other) and the right is *tryaśra* ("triangular," or oblique). When a passionate woman walks, she starts from this posture, with her right hand in *kaṭakāmukha* (thumb holding bent forefinger, ring finger and little finger raised and bent)[37] placed against her navel, and the left hand pointing downwards. She raises her right foot gracefully to a height of one *tāla* (about a tenth of body length), throwing her weight on the left. As she swings her left hand out (the *latā* gesture) and brings it back to the navel, the right hand moves to the hip, the right side is bent and the right foot comes down. The fingers of the left hand, beginning with the forefinger, are moved outward (*udveṣṭita*),[38] the left foot put forward, and the right hand swings away from the body. Then the woman walks forward five steps with the body slightly bent, the head gracefully held and the chest raised (*udvāhita*).[39]

The description of the gaits in the *Nāṭyaśāstra* not only includes dancelike movements which reflect a psychological state, as above, they may also be instructions for miming particular actions in the absence of props. In both the *Śākuntala* and the *Vikramorvaśīya* the king must represent riding in a chariot.[40] Beginning in *samapāda sthāna* (feet in *sama,* one *tāla* apart; general equilibrium of the body called *sauṣṭhava* observed),[41] he begins to move forward with short quick steps. To show that he is riding in a chariot he mimes holding a bow with one hand and the chariot pole with the other. The charioteer follows along with parallel steps, with his hands in *kaṭakāmukha* to represent the use of whip and reins. Bharata seems to suggest here that the horses may be represented by dancers with masks. In the chapter on costume there are instructions for making masks.[42] Moreover, descriptions are given of the gaits of different animals.[43] This would mean that in Duṣyanta's deer hunt and Purūravas' encounter with the creatures of the grove, the absence of animal characters from the text of the play would not necessarily imply their absence from the stage.

Flying is another type of movement that could be represented by a special gait. The character must first make a special movement to indicate jumping into the sky. When the commentator Rāghavabhaṭṭa explains the stage direction at *Śākuntala* 6.25, *ityudbhrāntakena niṣkrāntā,* "flying into the air [the nymph Sānumatī] exits," he glosses *udbhrāntakena* with *utplutikaraṇena,* meaning that the recommended motion is one of the special *karaṇas* [movements involving the body as a whole] used for jumping (*utpluti*).[44] This is not a category of *karaṇa* recognized in the *Nāṭyaśāstra* (nor does *udbhrāntaka* occur as a technical term anywhere in the literature); perhaps that is why Raghavan has described a similar piece of stage business, the nymphs' taking off for heaven at the end of Act One of *Vikramorvaśīya* (*ākāśotpatanaṁ rūpayanti,* "they mime jumping into the sky"), as being accomplished with the *vṛścika karaṇa.*[45] Raghavan interprets this pose as having the left leg planted stationary on the ground and the right leg thrown back and bent so as to resemble the uplifted tail of a scorpion (*vṛścika*). Actual movement in the air would be represented by any one of sixteen foot movements (*cārīs*) designated for use in the air (*ākāśikya*).[46] This would apply to the flying done by the nymphs in Acts One, Two and Three of the *Vikramorvaśīya,* the nymph Sānumatī in Act Six of the *Śākuntala,* as well as to the aerial chariot scenes in Act One of the *Vikramorvaśīya* and Act Seven of the *Śākuntala.*

There is another stage direction which bears on the representation of sky travel. Urvaśī and Citralekhā enter in Acts Two and Three *ākāśayānena,* as does Sānumatī near the beginning of Act Six in the *Śākuntala.* The same expression is used to describe the entrance of King Duṣyanta and Mātali in Act Seven. Since in the last instance the two are further described as *rathādhirūḍha,* "mounted on a chariot," and since nymphs would have no need of a vehicle for aerial travel, this stage direction should be interpreted as "traveling in the sky," which is Kāṭayavema's gloss in the *Vikramorvaśīya,* or perhaps "by the skyway," meaning a certain zone of the stage designated for flying entrances. "By aerial chariot" (found in some translations) would be either redundant or inappropriate. The most similar reference in the *Nāṭyaśāstra* is *ākāśagamana,* which only means "going in the sky";[47] aerial foot movements and looking downward are prescribed to suggest flight.

Movement on the stage served not only to display psychological traits and to represent by mime conventions modes of travel impossible on a stage—riding in a chariot, flying, traveling by boat—it also served to change the scene of the action. The absence of sets both permitted and necessitated that the space of the stage represent a number of locales. When a character moves from one to another locale he announces his intention, executes a *parikrama* or "walking around" (but this should not be taken in the sense of random walking), "walking about," or "making a round of the stage," and announces his arrival at the destination.[48] Sometimes he will observe something as he moves, or he may see his destination before he reaches the spot; for this the stage direction would be *parikramyāvalokya ca,* "walking around and looking."

By this convention the stage becomes a totally fluid space in which divisions are established by dialogue and movement. As easily as these divisions are brought into being they may be dissolved, only to have new ones established. The author of the *Nāṭyaśāstra* understands that setting is entirely a thing of the imagination and urges the widest use of the convention of *kakṣyāvibhāga,* the partition of theatrical space:

> When zonal divisions are established [the spectator] can understand houses and cities, pleasure gardens and rivers, hermitages as well as forests, the earth and the oceans, the three worlds and the moving and immovable things in them, the realms of the earth and the seven continents, the various mountains, the invisible world, the earth's surface and the nether world. . . . And within a city or forest or mountain [further] zones can be represented.[49]

In all three plays *Kālidāsa* uses the technique to transport the audience through both earthly and cosmic spaces. The opening of the *Śākuntala* follows Duṣyanta from the forest into Kaṇva's hermitage, which he explores until he comes across Śakuntalā and her friends. In Act One of the *Vikramorvaśīya* and Act Seven of the *Śākuntala* there is movement from the sky to a mountain top. The fourth act of the *Vikramorvaśīya* is virtually a journey through the mountain grove where Urvaśī has been transformed into a creeper. Purūravas passes from lake to mountain to cave to river and beyond in his search; some form of the stage direction *parikrama* occurs fifteen times.

Characters entering when others are already onstage are assumed to be in a different symbolic locale. These characters who enter later show their awareness of the ones already onstage by turning to the right.[50] Kālidāsa's exploitation of this aspect of the convention allows him to reveal the interplay of passions and conflicting loyalties in his characters. There are eavesdropping scenes in every play, but a good example might be the third act of the *Mālavikāgnimitra*.[51] The interlude dialogue between the nun's maid and the guardian of the grove informs us that both the king and Mālavikā are pining for each other. After the two servants exit, the king enters telling the buffoon of his miserable condition. Soon Mālavikā enters to have her foot decorated for the ceremony of kicking the aśoka tree. Since she enters later she cannot see the king and the buffoon. The buffoon, however, sees her, which the audience knows not only from his remark but because he executes a stylized gesture of "seeing her" at 3.5+. Mālavikā then reveals her lovesickness to the maid Bakulāvalikā while the king and buffoon listen and comment. Next the intoxicated jealous junior queen Irāvatī enters with her maid Nipuṇikā. They do not see the king and buffoon at first, nor do the men see them. But when the king enters to speak to Mālavikā, Irāvatī watches the king's gallantry for a few moments before she rushes in and surprises all four of them.

There is another group of conventions which permit private feelings to be excluded from others on stage but shared with the audience. These are the three types of asides.[52]

1. *Ātmagatam,* "to oneself." This is a kind of thinking out loud; the character exposes deliberations and feelings not intended for the ears of anyone on stage. It was doubtless indicated by some gesture or posture, but none of the texts specify the movement.

2. *Janāntikam,* "in a stage whisper." This is a private remark of one character to another. Later texts agree that this is

to be represented by the *tripatāka* hand gesture,[53] in which the ring finger is bent down, the thumb slightly curved inward, and the other fingers are outstretched. The *Nāṭyaśāstra* describes this gesture, mentioning its use in *vāraṇa,* "warding off" (presumably others from a conversation), but does not specifically prescribe it for *janāntikam.* The *Sāhityadarpaṇa,*[54] however, explicitly states that the *tripatāka* is to be held up in such a way as to shut out others from the conversation.

3. *Apavārya,* "secretly." Various writers have made an attempt to distinguish between *janāntikam* and *apavārya,* but their explanations do not accord with the examples in extant dramas.[55]

Other stage directions relating to speaking and listening are:

Ākāśe, "in the air." This can indicate the use of an offstage voice, often that of a celestial (e.g., *Śākuntala* 4.10+, but see 5.0). When used to describe an onstage character's speech (e.g., *Śākuntala* 3.1+, *Vikramorvaśīya* 4.25), it means that the person being addressed is not on stage. *Ākāśabhāṣitam* may be in the form of half of an imaginary dialogue.[56]

Ākarṇya, "listening" and *karṇaṁ dattvā,* literally "giving ear." Both of these are used when the sound has originated in the backstage area (*nepathya*).

Nepathye, "backstage," "in the wings." Among the principal uses are the announcement of calamitous and marvelous events (the stealing of the gem at the beginning of the *Vikramorvaśīya,* Act Five; the flowering of the aśoka at *Mālavikāgnimitra* at 4.17+) and eulogies from panegyrist-bards (*Śākuntala* 5.6+; *Vikramorvaśīya* 5.20; *Mālavikāgnimitra* 2.11+, 5.0).

Karṇe, literally "in the ear." The audience does not hear the speech at all. Kālidāsa only uses this in *Mālavikāgnimitra* (1.8+, 4.2+, 4.17+).

Gesture Language and Stage Directions

Almost every action performed on the stage was performed in mime. Even those which are straightforward and appear to offer little scope for development ("Urvaśī mimes writing and tossing the letter," at *Vikramorvaśīya* 2.11+) could be performed in a naturalistic sort of mime (*lokadharmī*) or by the specified technical conventions (*nāṭyadharmī*).[57] The choice was the director's and the artist's. There was also room for interpretation in the degree of elaboration given to a particular representation. In the *Śākuntala* 1.15+, the watering of the trees could be mimed according to the gestures prescribed by the *Nāṭyaśāstra,* or all these gestures and movements could be incorporated into a prolonged dance.[58] The same is true of Mālavikā's kicking the aśoka tree at *Mālavikāgnimitra* 3.15+.

The classical vocabulary of gestures was employed to convey images, ideas, and narrative sequences from verses—information external to the character himself. In this way the gesture language could function as a kind of sign language. The treatment of Sanskrit verses in the Kūṭiyāṭṭam theater of Kerala is instructive in this regard. The actor first recites the verse in a kind of slow chant. Then he repeats the verse in gestures, explicating every verbal element with visual precision—to the great delight of connoisseurs.

One could imagine the chamberlain at *Śākuntala* 6.4 representing the effects in the natural world of the king's banning of the spring festival. Another example is *Vikramorvaśīya* 3.6, where the king compares the face of the brightening evening sky to a woman tying up her disheveled black hair when her lover (here, the moon, the real cause of the sky's brightness) returns after a long absence. When Purūravas reads Urvaśī's love letter (at 2.12) he might act out the lines "Why do fair breezes / of paradise grove burn / as I toss on my bed / of crushed coral blossoms?" In fact, the stage direction at 4.12+ is "the king dances, acting out the verse," supporting the theory that the fourth act in its Northern Recension represents a staged version of the original text. The notion of gesture as sign language also allows for the possibility that many of the creatures the king meets in the fourth act are mimed by the king himself in a tour de force of solo acting.

In attempting to make concrete the stage directions concerning emotions and other mental states (such as thinking, remembering), we are confronted with a variety of partly overlapping classification schemes from which to draw information. First there is the description of the manifestations of the *sthāyibhāvas,* the eight permanent emotions which underlie the aesthetic moods;[59] among them fear (*bhaya*) and astonishment (*vismaya*) frequently figure in stage directions. Then there are the 33 transitory emotional states (*vyabhicāribhāvas*)[60] which flow in and out of the permanent emotions; some of them are used in stage directions, e.g., joy (*harṣa*), remembrance (*smṛti*), shame (*vrīḍa*), and despair (*viṣāda*). Also to be taken into account is the lengthy catalogue of gestures for every part of the body, many of which are accompanied by suggestions for use in depicting particular emotions and situations. From another perspective, chapters 24 and 25 of the *Nāṭyaśāstra* cover a variety of acting problems, some of which have to do with portraying emotions.

Lastly there are the eight *sāttvika* states, the involuntary responses of paralysis, perspiration, horripilation, change of voice, trembling, change of color, weeping, and fainting.[61] There is controversy about whether these were intended to be "acted" in imitation of the character's response to an emotion, or whether they were actually to be manifested by the actor in his identification with the role.[62] The actor's transformation when he puts on his makeup, and the *Nāṭyaśāstra*'s own explanation of *sattva* ("true essence"), would seem to indicate the latter. The actor's identification, however, is an aesthetic identification; if successful, he achieves the "involuntary" response through an act of artistic concentration or meditation (*samādhi*).[63] Ideally the rehearsed gestural representation would subside and the simpler *sāttvika* state would prevail.[64] If unsuccessful, the actor could rely on the prescribed depiction through gestures, etc. In its derivation from a detached, though intense, state of concentration, rather than from an undiscriminated emotional response, the actor's art parallels the spectator's experience of *rasa*.

With this dynamic in view, here are suggestions for portrayal of some of the emotional states which occur in all three plays, culled from various sections of the *Nāṭyaśāstra:*

Harṣa (joy, excitement, delight)
Śākuntala 2.15+, 4.3+, 6.6+, 7.20+.
Vikramorvaśīya 1.10+, 2.9+, 2.11+, 2.13+, 5.0.
Mālavikāgnimitra 3.5+, 3.6+, 3.14+, 4.2+, 4.5+, 4.6+, 5.3+.
Brightness of the face and eyes, using sweet words, embracing, horripilation, tears, perspiration, etc.[65] The *sāttvika* state of horripilation should be represented on the stage by repeated shivers, hairs standing on the hand, and by touching the body.[66] The *sāttvika* state of perspiration should be represented on the stage by taking up a fan, wiping off sweat and looking for a breeze.[67]

Vrīḍa (shame, embarrassment, modesty, bashfulness, shyness)
Śākuntala 4.5+, 4.6+.
Vikramorvaśīya 1.11+, 2.15+.
Mālavikāgnimitra 4.10+, 5.7+, 5.17+.
Covered face, thinking with downcast face, drawing lines on the ground, touching clothes and rings, biting the nails, etc.[68]

Bhaya (fear)
Śākuntala 5.26+, 6.0, 6.3+.
Vikramorvaśīya 1.4+.
Mālavikāgnimitra 3.17+, 5.10+.
Trembling hands and feet, palpitation of the heart, paralysis, dryness of the mouth, licking the lips, perspiration, tremor, hurried movements, wide open eyes.[69] The *sāttvika* state of paralysis should be represented on the stage by being inactive, inert, senseless, and stiff.[70]

Vismaya (amazement, surprise, astonishment)
Śākuntala 1.7+, 4.4+, 4.10+, 5.29+, 5.30+, 7.9+, 7.13+, 7.20+.
Vikramorvaśīya 5.6+.
Mālavikāgnimitra 3.1+, 5.9+.
Opening the eyes wide, looking without blinking the eyes, much eyebrow movement, horripilation, moving the head to and fro, crying "wonderful!" etc.[71] Joy, tears, fainting.[72]

Viṣāda (despair, dejection, despondence, dismay)
Śākuntala 2.0, 3.5+, 5.17+, 5.21+.
Vikramorvaśīya 2.2+, 2.17+, 2.18+, 3.9+, 3.11+, 5.15+.
Mālavikāgnimitra 4.1+, 4.3+, 4.6+, 5.14+.
Characters of high and middle degree: looking about for allies,

thinking about means [to achieve the lost goal], loss of energy, absentmindedness, deep breathing, etc. Characters of low degree: running about aimlessly, looking down, drying up of the mouth, licking the corner of the mouth, sleep, deep breathing, trance.[73]

Smṛti (remembrance)
Śākuntala 4.12+
Vikramorvaśīya 2.18+, 5.14+.
Mālavikāgnimitra 3.5+.
Raising and nodding of the head, looking down, raising the eyebrows.[74]

Saṁbhrama (confusion, agitation, flurry, bewilderment; *sasaṁbhramam*—"flustered")
Occurrences are too numerous to list exhaustively. Examples are:
Śākuntala 1.9+, 1.19+, 1.21+, 1.29+, 6.25+.
Vikramorvaśīya 2.19+.
Mālavikāgnimitra 3.17+, 3.19+, 4.3+, 4.4+.
This is one of the most commonly used stage directions in the whole of Sanskrit drama. The term itself does not appear in the *Nāṭyaśāstra,* but seems to have replaced the older term *vidrava*[75] since *saṁbhrama* appears in its place in the later lists of subdivisions of the *garbha* ("gestation"), the third of the five *saṁdhis,* or junctures, described above by Gerow. *Vidrava,* which Ghosh translates "panicky commotion," is defined as flurry caused by fear from a king or a fire. *Daśarūpaka* defines *saṁbhrama* as *śaṅkātrāsau,* both of which are *vyabhicāribhāvas,* or transitory states.[76] *Śaṅkā* (apprehension) is to be represented on stage by glancing repeatedly, dryness of the mouth, licking the lips, change of facial color, dry lips, loss of voice.[77] The *sāttvika* state of change of color is to be achieved by putting pressure on the artery.[78] *Trāsa* (fearful trembling) is represented by shaking of limbs, tremors of the body, paralysis, horripilation, speaking with a choked voice, and talking about irrelevant matters.[79]

Spectator and Performance Success

In classical Sanskrit aesthetic theory, the role of the connoisseur is equally or more important in the production of *rasa* than that of the poet or artist. In terms of actual theatrical production, it is the spectator's response to the performance that in the end determines its success; Bharata's concentration on the characteristics of the ideal spectator makes this clear.[80] He or she (Bharata makes specific reference to women spectators)[81] must possess, in addition to virtuous character and detailed knowledge of the drama, the special capability of empathy called *sahṛdayatva* ("with-heartedness," tantamount to "connoisseurship") which allows the spectator to become one with the performer:

> One who experiences delight when he sees the delightful, experiences grief when the sorrowful is presented, experiences anger in the presentation of anger, and fear when confronting the frightening—such a person is regarded as the superior spectator. Therefore it is the person who is able to enter into the particular imitation [*anukaraṇa,* that is, the dramatic representation] of an emotional state, and is graced with these qualities who is known as a [true] spectator of that performance.[82]

Bharata specifies particular audience responses to a successful evocation of each of the eight sentiments. More generally he states that these spontaneous reactions will range from smiles and expressions of empathy through shouts of approval to continuous and swelling applause accompanied by shivers of joy as the audience rises from its seats throwing gifts of cloth and rings onto the stage. All these responses are expressions of success in human (*mānuṣī*) terms.[83] The attainment of the highest degree of excellence in performance, however, is regarded from the perspective of the gods. When the response is not a tumultuous commotion, when there is in fact not the slightest sound or disturbance among the audience, even in a packed house—that success is regarded as divine (*daivī*).[84]

The Plays

Śakuntalā and the Ring of Recollection

TRANSLATED BY BARBARA STOLER MILLER

CHARACTERS

Players in the prologue:
DIRECTOR: Director of the players and manager of the theater (*sūtradhāra*).
ACTRESS: The lead actress (*naṭī*).

Principal roles:
KING: Duṣyanta, the hero (*nāyaka*); ruler of Hastināpura; a royal sage of the lunar dynasty of Puru.
ŚAKUNTALĀ: The heroine (*nāyikā*); daughter of the royal sage Viśvāmitra and the celestial nymph Menakā; adoptive daughter of the ascetic Kaṇva.
BUFFOON: Māḍhavya, the king's comical brahman companion (*vidūṣaka*).

Members of Kaṇva's hermitage:
ANASŪYĀ and PRIYAṀVADĀ: Two young female ascetics; friends of Śakuntalā.
KAṆVA: Foster father of Śakuntalā and master of the hermitage; a sage belonging to the lineage of the divine creator Marīci, and thus related to Mārīca.
GAUTAMĪ: The senior female ascetic.
ŚĀRṄGARAVA and ŚĀRADVATA: Kaṇva's disciples.

Various inhabitants of the hermitage: a monk with his two

pupils, two boy ascetics (named Gautama and Nārada), a young disciple of Kaṇva, a trio of female ascetics.

Members of the king's forest retinue:
CHARIOTEER: Driver of the king's chariot (*sūta*).
GUARD: Raivataka, guardian of the entrance to the king's quarters (*dauvārika*).
GENERAL: Commander of the king's army (*senāpati*).
KARABHAKA: Royal messenger.

Various attendants, including Greco-Bactrian bow-bearers (*yavanyaḥ*).

Members of the king's palace retinue:
CHAMBERLAIN: Vātāyana, chief officer of the king's household (*kañcukī*).
PRIEST: Somarāta, the king's religious preceptor and household priest (*purohita*).
DOORKEEPER: Vetravatī, the female attendant who ushers in visitors and presents messages (*pratīhārī*).
PARABHṚTIKĀ and MADHUKARIKĀ: Two maids assigned to the king's garden.
CATURIKĀ: A maidservant.

City dwellers:
MAGISTRATE: The king's low-caste brother-in-law (*śyāla*); chief of the city's policemen.
POLICEMEN: Sūcaka and Jānuka.
FISHERMAN: An outcaste.

Celestials:
MĀRĪCA: A divine sage; master of the celestial hermitage in which Śakuntalā gives birth to her son; father of Indra, king of the gods, whose armies Duṣyanta leads.
ADITI: Wife of Mārīca.
MĀTALI: Indra's charioteer.
SĀNUMATĪ: A nymph; friend of Śakuntalā's mother Menakā.

Various members of Mārīca's hermitage: two female ascetics, Mārīca's disciple Gālava.

BOY: Sarvadamana, son of Śakuntalā and Duṣyanta; later known as Bharata.

Offstage voices:

VOICE OFFSTAGE: From the backstage area or dressing room (*nepathye*); behind the curtain, out of view of the audience. The voice belongs to various players before they enter the stage, such as the monk, Śakuntalā's friends, the buffoon, Mātali; also to figures who never enter the stage, such as the angry sage Durvāsas, the two bards who chant royal panegyrics (*vaitālikau*).

VOICE IN THE AIR: A voice chanting in the air (*ākāśe*) from somewhere offstage: the bodiless voice of Speech quoted in Sanskrit by Priyaṁvadā (4.4); the voice of a cuckoo who represents the trees of the forest blessing Śakuntalā in Sanskrit (4.11); the voice of Haṁsapadikā singing a Prakrit love song (5.1).

Aside from Duṣyanta, Śakuntalā, and the buffoon, most of the characters represent types that reappear in different contexts within the play itself, an aspect of the circular structure of the play in which complementary relations are repeated. In terms of their appearance, the following roles might be played by the same actor or actress:

Kaṇva—Mārīca
Gautamī—Aditi
Anasūyā and Priyaṁvadā—
  Sānumatī and Caturikā—
  Two Ascetic Women in the hermitage of Mārīca
Charioteer—Mātali
Monk—Sārṅgarava
General—Chamberlain
Karabhaka—Priest

The setting of the play shifts from the forest hermitage (Acts 1–4) to the palace (Acts 5–6) to the celestial hermitage (Act 7). The season is early summer when the play begins and spring during the sixth act; the passage of time is otherwise indicated by the birth and boyhood of Śakuntalā's son.

ACT ONE

The water that was first created,
the sacrifice-bearing fire, the priest,
the time-setting sun and moon,
audible space that fills the universe,
what men call nature, the source of all seeds,
the air that living creatures breathe—
through his eight embodied forms,
may Lord Śiva come to bless you! (1)

PROLOGUE

DIRECTOR (*looking backstage*): If you are in costume now, madam, please come on stage!
ACTRESS: I'm here, sir.
DIRECTOR: Our audience is learned. We shall play Kālidāsa's new drama called *Śakuntalā and the Ring of Recollection*. Let the players take their parts to heart!
ACTRESS: With you directing, sir, nothing will be lost.
DIRECTOR: Madam, the truth is:

I find no performance perfect
until the critics are pleased;
the better trained we are
the more we doubt ourselves. (2)

ACTRESS: So true . . . now tell me what to do first!
DIRECTOR: What captures an audience better than a song?

Sing about the new summer season and its pleasures:

To plunge in fresh waters
swept by scented forest winds
and dream in soft shadows
of the day's ripened charms. (3)

ACTRESS (*singing*):

Sensuous women
in summer love
weave
flower earrings
from fragile petals
of mimosa
while wild bees
kiss them gently. (4)

DIRECTOR: Well sung, madam! Your melody enchants the audience. The silent theater is like a painting. What drama should we play to please it?

ACTRESS: But didn't you just direct us to perform a new play called *Śakuntalā and the Ring of Recollection?*

DIRECTOR: Madam, I'm conscious again! For a moment I forgot.

The mood of your song's melody
carried me off by force,
just as the swift dark antelope
enchanted King Duṣyanta. (5)

(*They both exit; the prologue ends. Then the king enters with his charioteer, in a chariot, a bow and arrow in his hand, hunting an antelope.*)

CHARIOTEER (*watching the king and the antelope*):

I see this black buck move
as you draw your bow
and I see the wild bowman Śiva,
hunting the dark antelope. (6)

KING: Driver, this antelope has drawn us far into the forest. There he is again:

The graceful turn of his neck
as he glances back at our speeding car,
the haunches folded into his chest
in fear of my speeding arrow,
the open mouth dropping
half-chewed grass on our path—
watch how he leaps, bounding on air,
barely touching the earth. (7)

(*He shows surprise.*)
Why is it so hard to keep him in sight?
CHARIOTEER: Sir, the ground was rough. I tightened the reins to slow the chariot and the buck raced ahead. Now that the path is smooth, he won't be hard to catch.
KING: Slacken the reins!
CHARIOTEER: As you command, sir.
(*He mimes the speeding chariot.*)
Look!

Their legs extend as I slacken the reins,
plumes and manes set in the wind, ears angle back;
our horses outrun their own clouds of dust,
straining to match the antelope's speed. (8)

KING: These horses would outrace the steeds of the sun.

What is small suddenly looms large,
split forms seem to reunite,
bent shapes straighten before my eyes—
from the chariot's speed
nothing ever stays distant or near. (9)

CHARIOTEER: The antelope is an easy target now.
(*He mimes the fixing of an arrow.*)
VOICE OFFSTAGE: Stop! Stop, king! This antelope belongs to our hermitage! Don't kill him!
CHARIOTEER (*listening and watching*): Sir, two ascetics are protecting the black buck from your arrow's deadly aim.

KING (*showing confusion*): Rein in the horses!
CHARIOTEER: It is done!
(*He mimes the chariot's halt. Then a monk enters with two pupils, his hand raised.*)
MONK: King, this antelope belongs to our hermitage.

Withdraw your well-aimed arrow! Your weapon
should rescue victims, not destroy the innocent! (10)

KING: I withdraw it.
(*He does as he says.*)
MONK: An act worthy of the Puru dynasty's shining light!

Your birth honors
the dynasty of the moon!
May you beget a son
to turn the wheel of your empire! (11)

THE TWO PUPILS (*raising their arms*): May you beget a son to turn the wheel of your empire!
KING (*bowing*): I welcome your blessing.
MONK: King, we were going to gather firewood. From here you can see the hermitage of our master Kaṇva on the bank of the Mālinī river. If your work permits, enter and accept our hospitality.

When you see the peaceful rites of devoted ascetics,
you will know how well your scarred arm protects us. (12)

KING: Is the master of the community there now?
MONK: He went to Somatīrtha, the holy shrine of the moon, and put his daughter Śakuntalā in charge of receiving guests. Some evil threatens her, it seems.
KING: Then I shall see her. She will know my devotion and commend me to the great sage.
MONK: We shall leave you now.
(*He exits with his pupils.*)
KING: Driver, urge the horses on! The sight of this holy hermitage will purify us.

CHARIOTEER: As you command, sir.
(*He mimes the chariot's speed.*)
KING (*looking around*): Without being told one can see that this is a grove where ascetics live.
CHARIOTEER: How?
KING: Don't you see—

Wild rice grains under trees
where parrots nest in hollow trunks,
stones stained by the dark oil
of crushed iṅgudī nuts,
trusting deer who hear human voices
yet don't break their gait,
and paths from ponds streaked
by water from wet bark cloth. (13)

CHARIOTEER: It is perfect.
KING (*having gone a little inside*): We should not disturb the grove! Stop the chariot and let me get down!
CHARIOTEER: I'm holding the reins. You can dismount now, sir.
KING (*dismounting*): One should not enter an ascetics' grove in hunting gear. Take these!
(*He gives up his ornaments and his bow.*)
Driver, rub down the horses while I pay my respects to the residents of the hermitage!
CHARIOTEER: Yes, sir!
(*He exits.*)
KING: This gateway marks the sacred ground. I will enter.
(*He enters, indicating he feels an omen.*)

The hermitage is a tranquil place,
yet my arm is quivering . . .
do I feel a false omen of love
or does fate have doors everywhere? (14)

VOICE OFFSTAGE: This way, friends!
KING (*straining to listen*): I think I hear voices to the right of the grove. I'll find out.

(*Walking around and looking.*)
Young female ascetics with watering pots cradled on their hips are coming to water the saplings.
(*He mimes it in precise detail.*)
This view of them is sweet.

These forest women have beauty
rarely seen inside royal palaces—
the wild forest vines far surpass
creepers in my pleasure garden. (15)

I'll hide in the shadows and wait.
(*Śakuntalā and her two friends enter, acting as described.*)
ŚAKUNTALĀ: This way, friends!
ANASŪYĀ: I think Father Kaṇva cares more about the trees in the hermitage than he cares about you. You're as delicate as a jasmine, yet he orders you to water the trees.
ŚAKUNTALĀ: Anasūyā, it's more than Father Kaṇva's order. I feel a sister's love for them.
(*She mimes the watering of trees.*)
KING (*to himself*): Is this Kaṇva's daughter? The sage does show poor judgment in imposing the rules of the hermitage on her.

The sage who hopes to subdue
her sensuous body by penances
is trying to cut firewood
with a blade of blue-lotus leaf. (16)

Let it be! I can watch her closely from here in the trees.
(*He does so.*)
ŚAKUNTALĀ: Anasūyā, I can't breathe! Our friend Priyaṁvadā tied my bark dress too tightly! Loosen it a bit!
ANASŪYĀ: As you say.
(*She loosens it.*)
PRIYAṀVADĀ: (*laughing*): Blame your youth for swelling your breasts. Why blame me?
KING: This bark dress fits her body badly, but it ornaments her beauty . . .

A tangle of duckweed adorns a lotus,
a dark spot heightens the moon's glow,
the bark dress increases her charm—
beauty finds its ornaments anywhere. (17)

ŚAKUNTALĀ (*looking in front of her*): The new branches on this mimosa tree are like fingers moving in the wind, calling to me. I must go to it!
(*Saying this, she walks around.*)
PRIYAṀVADĀ: Wait, Śakuntalā! Stay there a minute! When you stand by this mimosa tree, it seems to be guarding a creeper.
ŚAKUNTALĀ: That's why your name means "Sweet-talk."
KING: "Sweet-talk" yes, but Priyaṁvadā speaks the truth about Śakuntalā:

Her lips are fresh red buds,
her arms are tendrils,
impatient youth is poised
to blossom in her limbs. (18)

ANASŪYĀ: Śakuntalā, this is the jasmine creeper who chose the mango tree in marriage, the one you named "Forestlight." Have you forgotten her?
ŚAKUNTALĀ: I would be forgetting myself!
(*She approaches the creeper and examines it.*)
The creeper and the tree are twined together in perfect harmony. Forestlight has just flowered and the new mango shoots are made for her pleasure.
PRIYAṀVADĀ (*smiling*): Anasūyā, don't you know why Śakuntalā looks so lovingly at Forestlight?
ANASŪYĀ: I can't guess.
PRIYAṀVADĀ: The marriage of Forestlight to her tree makes her long to have a husband too.
ŚAKUNTALĀ: You're just speaking your own secret wish.
(*Saying this, she pours water from the jar.*)
KING: Could her social class be different from her father's? There's no doubt!

She was born to be a warrior's bride,
for my noble heart desires her—
when good men face doubt,
inner feelings are truth's only measure. (19)

Still, I must learn everything about her.
ŚAKUNTALĀ (*flustered*): The splashing water has alarmed a bee. He is flying from the jasmine to my face.
(*She dances to show the bee's attack.*)
KING (*looking longingly*):

Bee, you touch the quivering
corners of her frightened eyes,
you hover softly near
to whisper secrets in her ear;
a hand brushes you away,
but you drink her lips' treasure—
while the truth we seek defeats us,
you are truly blessed. (20)

ŚAKUNTALĀ: This dreadful bee won't stop. I must escape.
(*She steps to one side, glancing about.*)
Oh! He's pursuing me . . . Save me! Please save me! This mad bee is chasing me!
BOTH FRIENDS (*laughing*): How can we save you? Call King Duṣyanta. The grove is under his protection.
KING: Here's my chance. Have no fear . . .
(*With this half-spoken, he stops and speaks to himself.*)
Then she will know that I am the king . . . Still, I shall speak.
ŚAKUNTALĀ (*stopping after a few steps*): Why is he still following me?
KING (*approaching quickly*):

While a Puru king rules the earth
to punish evildoers,
who dares to molest
these innocent young ascetics? (21)

(*Seeing the king, all act flustered.*)

ANASŪYĀ: Sir, there's no real danger. Our friend was frightened when a bee attacked her.
(*She points to Śakuntalā.*)
KING (*approaching Śakuntalā*): Does your ascetic practice go well?
(*Śakuntalā stands speechless.*)
ANASŪYĀ: It does now that we have a special guest. Śakuntalā, go to our hut and bring the ripe fruits. We'll use this water to bathe his feet.
KING: Your kind speech is hospitality enough.
PRIYAṀVADĀ: Please sit in the cool shadows of this shade tree and rest, sir.
KING: You must also be tired from your work.
ANASŪYĀ: Śakuntalā, we should respect our guest. Let's sit down.
(*All sit.*)
ŚAKUNTALĀ (*to herself*): When I see him, why do I feel an emotion that the forest seems to forbid?
KING (*looking at each of the girls*): Youth and beauty complement your friendship.
PRIYAṀVADĀ (*in a stage whisper*): Anasūyā, who is he? He's so polite, fine looking, and pleasing to hear. He has the marks of royalty.
ANAYSŪYĀ: I'm curious too, friend. I'll just ask him.
(*Aloud.*)
Sir, your kind speech inspires trust. What family of royal sages do you adorn? What country mourns your absence? Why does a man of refinement subject himself to the discomfort of visiting an ascetics' grove?
ŚAKUNTALĀ: (*to herself*): Heart, don't faint! Anasūyā speaks your thoughts.
KING (*to himself*): Should I reveal myself now or conceal who I am? I'll say it this way:
(*Aloud.*)
Lady, I have been appointed by the Puru king as the officer in charge of religious matters. I have come to this sacred forest to assure that your holy rites proceed unhindered.

ANASŪYĀ: Our religious life has a guardian now.
(*Śakuntalā mimes the embarrassment of erotic emotion.*)
BOTH FRIENDS (*observing the behavior of Śakuntalā and the king; in a stage whisper*): Śakuntalā, if only your father were here now!
ŚAKUNTALĀ (*angrily*): What if he were?
BOTH FRIENDS: He would honor this distinguished guest with what he values most in life.
ŚAKUNTALĀ: Quiet! Such words hint at your hearts' conspiracy. I won't listen.
KING: Ladies, I want to ask about your friend.
BOTH FRIENDS: Your request honors us, sir.
KING: Sage Kaṇva has always been celibate, but you call your friend his daughter. How can this be?
ANASŪYĀ: Please listen, sir. There was a powerful royal sage of the Kauśika clan . . .
KING: I am listening.
ANASŪYĀ: He begot our friend, but Kaṇva is her father because he cared for her when she was abandoned.
KING: "Abandoned"? The word makes me curious. I want to hear her story from the beginning.
ANASŪYĀ: Please listen, sir. Once when this great sage was practicing terrible austerities on the bank of the Gautamī river, he became so powerful that the jealous gods sent a nymph named Menakā to break his self-control.
KING: The gods dread men who meditate.
ANASŪYĀ: When springtime came to the forest with all its charm, the sage saw her intoxicating beauty . . .
KING: I understand what happened then. She is the nymph's daughter.
ANASŪYĀ: Yes.
KING: It had to be!

> No mortal woman could give birth to such beauty—
> lightning does not flash out of the earth. (22)

(*Śakuntalā stands with her face bowed. The king continues speaking to himself.*)

My desire is not hopeless. Yet, when I hear her friends teasing her about a bridegroom, a new fear divides my heart.

PRIYAṀVADĀ (*smiling, looking at Śakuntalā, then turning to the king*): Sir, you seem to want to say more.

(*Śakuntalā makes a threatening gesture with her finger.*)

KING: You judge correctly. In my eagerness to learn more about your pious lives, I have another question.

PRIYAṀVADĀ: Don't hesitate! Ascetics can be questioned frankly.

KING: I want to know this about your friend:

Will she keep the vow of hermit life
only until she marries . . .
or will she always exchange
loving looks with deer in the forest? (23)

PRIYAṀVADĀ: Sir, even in her religious life, she is subject to her father, but he does intend to give her to a suitable husband.

KING (*to himself*): His wish is not hard to fulfill.

Heart, indulge your desire—
now that doubt is dispelled,
the fire you feared to touch
is a jewel in your hands. (24)

ŚAKUNTALĀ (*showing anger*): Anasūyā, I'm leaving!

ANASŪYĀ: Why?

ŚAKUNTALĀ: I'm going to tell Mother Gautamī that Priyaṁvadā is talking nonsense.

ANASŪYĀ: Friend, it's wrong to neglect a distinguished guest and leave as you like.

(*Śakuntalā starts to go without answering.*)

KING (*wanting to seize her, but holding back, he speaks to himself*): A lover dare not act on his impulsive thoughts!

I wanted to follow the sage's daughter,
but decorum abruptly pulled me back;
I set out and returned again
without moving my feet from this spot. (25)

PRIYAṀVADĀ (*stopping Śakuntalā*): It's wrong of you to go!
ŚAKUNTALĀ (*bending her brow into a frown*): Give me a reason why!
PRIYAṀVADĀ: You promised to water two trees for me. Come here and pay your debt before you go!
(*She stops her by force.*)
KING: But she seems exhausted from watering the trees:

Her shoulders droop, her palms
are red from the watering pot—
even now, breathless sighs
make her breasts shake;
beads of sweat on her face
wilt the flower at her ear;
her hand holds back
disheveled locks of hair. (26)

Here, I'll pay her debt!
(*He offers his ring. Both friends recite the syllables of the name on the seal and stare at each other.*)
Don't mistake me for what I am not! This is a gift from the king to identify me as his royal official.
PRIYAṀVADĀ: Then the ring should never leave your finger. Your word has already paid her debt.
(*She laughs a little.*)
Śakuntalā, you are freed by this kind man . . . or perhaps by the king. Go now!
ŚAKUNTALĀ (*to herself*): If I am able to . . .
(*Aloud.*)
Who are you to keep me or release me?
KING (*watching Śakuntalā*): Can she feel toward me what I feel toward her? Or is my desire fulfilled?

She won't respond directly to my words,
but she listens when I speak;
she won't turn to look at me,
but her eyes can't rest anywhere else. (27)

VOICE OFFSTAGE: Ascetics, be prepared to protect the creatures of our forest grove! King Duṣyanta is hunting nearby!

Dust raised by his horses' hooves
falls like a cloud of locusts swarming
at sunset over branches of trees
where wet bark garments hang. (28)

In terror of the chariots, an elephant
charged into the hermitage
and scattered the herd of black antelope,
like a demon foe of our penances—
his tusks garlanded with branches
from a tree crushed by his weight,
his feet tangled in vines
that tether him like chains. (29)

(*Hearing this, all the girls are agitated.*)

KING (*to himself*): Oh! My palace men are searching for me and wrecking the grove. I'll have to go back.

BOTH FRIENDS: Sir, we're all upset by this news. Please let us go to our hut.

KING (*showing confusion*): Go, please. We will try to protect the hermitage.

(*They all stand to go.*)

BOTH FRIENDS: Sir, we're ashamed that our bad hospitality is our only excuse to invite you back.

KING: Not at all. I am honored to have seen you.

(*Śakuntalā exits with her two friends, looking back at the king, lingering artfully.*)

I have little desire to return to the city. I'll join my men and have them camp near the grove. I can't control my feelings for Śakuntalā.

My body turns to go,
my heart pulls me back,
like a silk banner
buffeted by the wind. (30)

(*All exit.*)

END OF ACT ONE

ACT TWO

(*The buffoon enters, despondent.*)

BUFFOON (*sighing*): My bad luck! I'm tired of playing sidekick to a king who's hooked on hunting. "There's a deer!" "There's a boar!" "There's a tiger!" Even in the summer midday heat we chase from jungle to jungle on paths where trees give barely any shade. We drink stinking water from mountain streams foul with rusty leaves. At odd hours we eat nasty meals of spit-roasted meat. Even at night I can't sleep. My joints ache from galloping on that horse. Then at the crack of dawn, I'm woken rudely by a noise piercing the forest. Those sons of bitches hunt their birds then. The torture doesn't end—now I have sores on top of my bruises. Yesterday, we lagged behind. The king chased a buck into the hermitage. As luck would have it, an ascetic's daughter called Śakuntalā caught his eye. Now he isn't even thinking of going back to the city. This very dawn I found him wide-eyed, mooning about her. What a fate! I must see him after his bath.
(*He walks around, looking.*)
Here comes my friend now, wearing garlands of wild flowers. Greek women carry his bow in their hands. Good! I'll stand here pretending my arms and legs are broken. Maybe then I'll get some rest.
(*He stands leaning on his staff. The king enters with his retinue, as described.*)
KING (*to himself*):

> My beloved will not be easy to win,
> but signs of emotion revealed her heart—
> even when love seems hopeless,
> mutual longing keeps passion alive. (1)

(*He smiles.*)
A suitor who measures his beloved's state of mind by his own desire is a fool.

She threw tender glances
though her eyes were cast down,
her heavy hips swayed
in slow seductive movements,
she answered in anger
when her friend said, "Don't go!"
and I felt it was all for my sake . . .
but a lover sees in his own way. (2)

BUFFOON (*still in the same position*): Dear friend, since my hands can't move to greet you, I have to salute you with my voice.
KING: How did you cripple your limbs?
BUFFOON: Why do you ask why I cry after throwing dust in my eyes yourself?
KING: I don't understand.
BUFFOON: Dear friend, when a straight reed is twisted into a crooked reed, is it by its own power, or is it the river current?
KING: The river current is the cause.
BUFFOON: And so it is with me.
KING: How so?
BUFFOON: You neglect the business of being a king and live like a woodsman in this awful camp. Chasing after wild beasts every day jolts my joints and muscles till I can't control my own limbs anymore. I beg you to let me rest for just one day!
KING: (*to himself*): He says what I also feel. When I remember Kaṇva's daughter, the thought of hunting disgusts me.

I can't draw my bowstring
to shoot arrows at deer
who live with my love
and teach her tender glances. (3)

BUFFOON: Sir, you have something on your mind. I'm crying in a wilderness.

KING (*smiling*): Yes, it is wrong to ignore my friend's plea.
BUFFOON: Live long!
(*He starts to go.*)
KING: Dear friend, stay! Hear what I have to say!
BUFFOON: At your command, sir!
KING: When you have rested, I need your help in some work that you will enjoy.
BUFFOON: Is it eating sweets? I'm game!
KING: I shall tell you. Who stands guard?
GUARD (*entering*): At your command, sir!
KING: Raivataka! Summon the general!
(*The guard exits and reenters with the general.*)
GUARD: The king is looking this way, waiting to give you his orders. Approach him, sir!
GENERAL (*looking at the king*): Hunting is said to be a vice, but our king prospers:

> Drawing the bow only hardens his chest,
> he suffers the sun's scorching rays unburned,
> hard muscles mask his body's lean state—
> like a wild elephant, his energy sustains him. (4)

(*He approaches the king.*)
Victory, my lord! We've already tracked some wild beasts. Why the delay?
KING: Māḍhavya's censure of hunting has dampened my spirit.
GENERAL (*in a stage whisper, to the buffoon*): Friend, you stick to your opposition! I'll try to restore our king's good sense. (*Aloud.*)
This fool is talking nonsense. Here is the king as proof:

> A hunter's belly is taut and lean,
> his slender body craves exertion;
> he penetrates the spirit of creatures
> overcome by fear and rage;
> his bowmanship is proved
> by arrows striking a moving target—
> hunting is falsely called a vice.
> What sport can rival it? (5)

BUFFOON (*angrily*): The king has come to his senses. If you keep chasing from forest to forest, you'll fall into the jaws of an old bear hungry for a human nose . . .
KING: My noble general, we are near a hermitage; your words cannot please me now.

Let horned buffaloes plunge into muddy pools!
Let herds of deer huddle in the shade to eat grass!
Let fearless wild boars crush fragrant swamp grass!
Let my bowstring lie slack and my bow at rest! (6)

GENERAL: Whatever gives the king pleasure.
KING: Withdraw the men who are in the forest now and forbid my soldiers to disturb the grove!

Ascetics devoted to peace
possess a fiery hidden power,
like smooth crystal sunstones
that reflect the sun's scorching rays. (7)

GENERAL: Whatever you command, sir!
BUFFOON: Your arguments for keeping up the hunt fall on deaf ears!
(*The general exits.*)
KING (*looking at his retinue*): You women, take away my hunting gear! Raivataka, don't neglect your duty!
RETINUE: As the king commands!
(*They exit.*)

BUFFOON: Sir, now that the flies are cleared out, sit on a stone bench under this shady canopy. Then I'll find a comfortable seat too.
KING: Go ahead!
BUFFOON: You first, sir!
(*Both walk about, then sit down.*)
KING: Māḍhavya, you haven't really used your eyes because you haven't seen true beauty.
BUFFOON: But you're right in front of me, sir!
KING: Everyone is partial to what he knows well, but I'm speaking about Śakuntalā, the jewel of the hermitage.

BUFFOON (*to himself*): I won't give him a chance!
(*Aloud.*)
Dear friend, it seems that you're pursuing an ascetic's daughter.
KING: Friend, the heart of a Puru king wouldn't crave a forbidden fruit . . .

The sage's child is a nymph's daughter,
rescued by him after she was abandoned,
like a fragile jasmine blossom
broken and caught on a sunflower pod. (8)

BUFFOON (*laughing*): You're like the man who loses his taste for dates and prefers sour tamarind! How can you abandon the gorgeous gems of your palace?
KING: You speak this way because you haven't seen her.
BUFFOON: She must be delectable if you're so enticed!
KING: Friend, what is the use of all this talk?

The divine creator imagined perfection
and shaped her ideal form in his mind—
when I recall the beauty his power wrought,
she shines like a gemstone among my jewels. (9)

BUFFOON: So she's the reason you reject the other beauties!
KING: She stays in my mind:

A flower no one has smelled,
a bud no fingers have plucked,
an uncut jewel, honey untasted,
unbroken fruit of holy deeds—
I don't know who is destined
to enjoy her flawless beauty. (10)

BUFFOON: Then you should rescue her quickly! Don't let her fall into the arms of some ascetic who greases his head with iṅgudī oil!
KING: She is someone else's ward and her guardian is away.
BUFFOON: What kind of passion did her eyes betray?

KING: Ascetics are timid by nature:

Her eyes were cast down in my presence,
but she found an excuse to smile—
modesty barely contained the love
she could neither reveal nor conceal. (11)

BUFFOON: Did you expect her to climb into your lap when she'd barely seen you?
KING: When we parted her feelings for me showed despite her modesty.

"A blade of kuśa grass
pricked my foot,"
the girl said for no reason
after walking a few steps away;
then she pretended to free
her bark dress from branches
where it was not caught
and shyly glanced at me. (12)

BUFFOON: Stock up on food for a long trip! I can see you've turned that ascetics' grove into a pleasure garden.
KING: Friend, some of the ascetics recognize me. What excuse can we find to return to the hermitage?
BUFFOON: What excuse? Aren't you the king? Collect a sixth of their wild rice as tax!
KING: Fool! These ascetics pay tribute that pleases me more than mounds of jewels.

Tribute that kings collect
from members of society decays,
but the share of austerity
that ascetics give lasts forever. (13)

VOICE OFFSTAGE: Good, we have succeeded!
KING (*listening*): These are the steady, calm voices of ascetics.
GUARD (*entering*): Victory, sir! Two boy ascetics are waiting near the gate.
KING: Let them enter without delay!

GUARD: I'll show them in.
(*He exits; reenters with the boys.*)
Here you are!
FIRST BOY: His majestic body inspires trust. It is natural when a king is virtually a sage.

His palace is a hermitage
with its infinite pleasures,
the discipline of protecting men
imposes austerities every day—
pairs of celestial bards praise
his perfect self-control,
adding the royal word "king"
to "sage," his sacred title. (14)

SECOND BOY: Gautama, is this Duṣyanta, the friend of Indra?
FIRST BOY: Of course!
SECOND BOY:

It is no surprise that this arm of iron
rules the whole earth bounded by dark seas—
when demons harass the gods, victory's hope
rests on his bow and Indra's thunderbolt. (15)

BOTH BOYS (*coming near*): Victory to you, king!
KING (*rising from his seat*): I salute you both!
BOTH BOYS: To your success, sir!
(*They offer fruits.*)
KING (*accepting their offering*): I am ready to listen.
BOTH BOYS: The ascetics know that you are camped nearby and send a petition to you.
KING: What do they request?
BOTH BOYS: Demons are taking advantage of Sage Kaṇva's absence to harass us. You must come with your charioteer to protect the hermitage for a few days!
KING: I am honored to oblige.
BUFFOON (*in a stage whisper*): Your wish is fulfilled!
KING (*smiling*): Raivataka, call my charioteer! Tell him to bring the chariot and my bow!
GUARD: As the king commands!

(*He exits.*)
BOTH BOYS (*showing delight*):

> Following your ancestral duties
> suits your noble form—
> the Puru kings are ordained
> to dispel their subjects' fear. (16)

KING (*bowing*): You two return! I shall follow.
BOTH BOYS: Be victorious!
(*They exit.*)
KING: Māḍhavya, are you curious to see Śakuntalā?
BUFFOON: At first there was a flood, but now with this news of demons, not a drop is left.
KING: Don't be afraid! Won't you be with me?
BUFFOON: Then I'll be safe from any demon . . .
GUARD (*entering*): The chariot is ready to take you to victory . . . but Karabhaka has just come from the city with a message from the queen.
KING: Did my mother send him?
GUARD: She did.
KING: Have him enter then.
GUARD: Yes.
(*He exits; reenters with Karabhaka.*)
Here is the king. Approach!
KARABHAKA: Victory, sir! Victory! The queen has ordered a ceremony four days from now to mark the end of her fast. Your Majesty will surely give us the honor of his presence.
KING: The ascetics' business keeps me here and my mother's command calls me there. I must find a way to avoid neglecting either!
BUFFOON: Hang yourself between them the way Triśaṅku hung between heaven and earth.
KING: I'm really confused . . .

> My mind is split in two
> by these conflicting duties,
> like a river current split
> by boulders in its course. (17)

(*Thinking.*)
Friend, my mother has treated you like a son. You must go back and report that I've set my heart on fulfilling my duty to the ascetics. You fulfill my filial duty to the queen.
BUFFOON: You don't really think I'm afraid of demons?
KING (*smiling*): My brave brahman, how could you be?
BUFFOON: Then I can travel like the king's younger brother.
KING: We really should not disturb the grove! Take my whole entourage with you!
BUFFOON: Now I've turned into the crown prince!
KING (*to himself*): This fellow is absent-minded. At any time he may tell the palace women about my passion. I'll tell him this:
(*Taking the buffoon by the hand, he speaks aloud.*)
Dear friend, I'm going to the hermitage out of reverence for the sages. I really feel no desire for the young ascetic Śakuntalā.

What do I share with a rustic girl
reared among fawns, unskilled in love?
Don't mistake what I muttered
in jest for the real truth, friend! (18)

(*All exit.*)

END OF ACT TWO

ACT THREE

(*A disciple of Kaṇva enters, carrying kuśa grass for a sacrificial rite.*)

DISCIPLE: King Duṣyanta is certainly powerful. Since he entered the hermitage, our rites have not been hindered.

Why talk of fixing arrows?
The mere twang of his bowstring
clears away menacing demons
as if his bow roared with death. (1)

I'll gather some more grass for the priests to spread on the sacrificial altar.
(*Walking around and looking, he calls aloud.*)
Priyaṁvadā, for whom are you bringing the ointment of fragrant lotus root fibers and leaves?
(*Listening.*)
What are you saying? Śakuntalā is suffering from heat exhaustion? They're for rubbing on her body? Priyaṁvadā, take care of her! She is the breath of Father Kaṇva's life. I'll give Gautamī this water from the sacrifice to use for soothing her.
(*He exits; the interlude ends. Then the king enters, suffering from love, deep in thought, sighing.*)
KING:

I know the power ascetics have
and the rules that bind her,
but I cannot abandon my heart
now that she has taken it. (2)

(*Showing the pain of love.*)

Love, why do you and the moon both contrive to deceive lovers by first gaining our trust?

> Arrows of flowers and cool moon rays
> are both deadly for men like me—
> the moon shoots fire through icy rays
> and you hurl thunderbolts of flowers. (3)

(*Walking around.*)
Now that the rites are concluded and the priests have dismissed me, where can I rest from the weariness of this work?
(*Sighing.*)
There is no refuge but the sight of my love. I must find her.
(*Looking up at the sun.*)
Śakuntalā usually spends the heat of the day with her friends in a bower of vines on the Mālinī riverbank. I shall go there.
(*Walking around, miming the touch of breeze.*)
This place is enchanted by the wind.

> A breeze fragrant with lotus pollen
> and moist from the Mālinī waves
> can be held in soothing embrace
> by my love-scorched arms. (4)

(*Walking around and looking.*)

> I see fresh footprints
> on white sand in the clearing,
> deeply pressed at the heel
> by the sway of full hips. (5)

I'll just look through the branches.
(*Walking around, looking, he becomes joyous.*)
My eyes have found bliss! The girl I desire is lying on a stone couch strewn with flowers, attended by her two friends. I'll eavesdrop as they confide in one another.
(*He stands watching. Śakuntalā appears as described, with her two friends.*)

BOTH FRIENDS (*fanning her affectionately*): Śakuntalā, does the breeze from this lotus leaf please you?

ŚAKUNTALĀ: Are you fanning me?
(*The friends trade looks, miming dismay.*)
KING (*deliberating*): Śakuntalā seems to be in great physical pain. Is it the heat or is it what is in my own heart?
(*Miming ardent desire.*)
My doubts are unfounded!

Her breasts are smeared with lotus balm,
her lotus-fiber bracelet hangs limp,
her beautiful body glows in pain—
love burns young women like summer heat,
but its guilt makes them more charming. (6)

PRIYAṀVADĀ (*in a stage whisper*): Anasūyā, Śakuntalā has been pining since she first saw the king. Could he be the cause of her sickness?
ANASŪYĀ: She must be suffering from lovesickness. I'll ask her . . .
(*Aloud.*)
Friend, I have something to ask you. Your pain seems so deep . . .
ŚAKUNTALĀ (*raising herself halfway*): What do you want to say?
ANASŪYĀ: Śakuntalā, though we don't know what it is to be in love, your condition reminds us of lovers we have heard about in stories. Can you tell us the cause of your pain? Unless we understand your illness, we can't begin to find a cure.
KING: Anasūyā expresses my own thoughts.
ŚAKUNTALĀ: Even though I want to, suddenly I can't make myself tell you.
PRIYAṀVADĀ: Śakuntalā, my friend Anasūyā means well. Don't you see how sick you are? Your limbs are wasting away. Only the shadow of your beauty remains . . .
KING: What Priyaṁvadā says is true:

Her cheeks are deeply sunken,
her breasts' full shape is gone,
her waist is thin, her shoulders bent,
and the color has left her skin—

tormented by love,
she is sad but beautiful to see,
like a jasmine creeper
when hot wind shrivels its leaves. (7)

ŚAKUNTALĀ: Friends, who else can I tell? May I burden you?
BOTH FRIENDS: We insist! Sharing sorrow with loving friends makes it bearable.
KING:

Friends who share her joy and sorrow
discover the love concealed in her heart—
though she looked back longingly at me,
now I am afraid to hear her response. (8)

ŚAKUNTALĀ: Friend, since my eyes first saw the guardian of the hermits' retreat, I've felt such strong desire for him!
KING: I have heard what I want to hear.

My tormentor, the god of love,
has soothed my fever himself,
like the heat of late summer
allayed by early rain clouds. (9)

ŚAKUNTALĀ: If you two think it's right, then help me to win the king's pity. Otherwise, you'll soon pour sesame oil and water on my corpse . . .
KING: Her words destroy my doubt.
PRIYAMVADĀ (*in a stage whisper*): She's so dangerously in love that there's no time to lose. Since her heart is set on the ornament of the Puru dynasty, we should rejoice that she desires him.
ANASŪYĀ: What you say is true.
PRIYAMVADĀ (*aloud*): Friend, by good fortune your desire is in harmony with nature. A great river can only descend to the ocean. A jasmine creeper can only twine around a mango tree.
KING: Why is this surprising when the twin stars of spring serve the crescent moon?

ANASŪYĀ: What means do we have to fulfill our friend's desire secretly and quickly?
PRIYAṀVADĀ: "Secretly" demands some effort. "Quickly" is easy.
ANASŪYĀ: How so?
PRIYAṀVADĀ: The king was charmed by her loving look; he seems thin these days from sleepless nights.
KING: It's true . . .

This golden armlet
slips to my wrist
without touching the scars
my bowstring has made;
its gemstones are faded
by tears of secret pain
that every night wets my arm
where I bury my face. (10)

PRIYAṀVADĀ (*thinking*): Compose a love letter and I'll hide it in a flower. I'll deliver it to his hand on the pretext of bringing an offering to the deity.
ANASŪYĀ: This subtle plan pleases me. What does Śakuntalā say?
ŚAKUNTALĀ: I'll try my friend's plan.
PRIYAṀVADĀ: Then compose a poem to declare your love!
ŚAKUNTALĀ: I'm thinking, but my heart trembles with fear that he'll reject me.
KING (*delighted*):

The man you fear will reject you
waits longing to love you, timid girl—
a suitor may lose or be lucky,
but the goddess always wins. (11)

BOTH FRIENDS: Why do you belittle your own virtues? Who would cover his body with a piece of cloth to keep off cool autumn moonlight?
ŚAKUNTALĀ (*smiling*): I'm trying to follow your advice.
(*She sits thinking.*)

KING: As I gaze at her, my eyes forget to blink.

She arches an eyebrow,
struggling to compose the verse—
the down rises on her cheek,
showing the passion she feels. (12)

ŚAKUNTALĀ: I've thought of a verse, but I have nothing to write it on.
PRIYAMVADĀ: Engrave the letters with your nail on this lotus leaf! It's as delicate as a parrot's breast.
ŚAKUNTALĀ (*miming what Priyaṁvadā described*): Listen and tell me if this makes sense!
BOTH FRIENDS: We're both paying attention.
ŚAKUNTALĀ (*singing*):

I don't know
your heart,
but day and night
for wanting you,
love violently
tortures
my limbs,
cruel man. (13)

KING (*suddenly revealing himself*):

Love torments you, slender girl,
but he completely consumes me—
daylight spares the lotus pond
while it destroys the moon. (14)

BOTH FRIENDS (*looking, rising with delight*): Welcome to the swift success of love's desire!
(*Śakuntalā tries to rise.*)
KING: Don't exert yourself!

Limbs lying among crushed petals
like fragile lotus stalks
are too weakened by pain
to perform ceremonious acts. (15)

ANASŪYĀ: Then let the king sit on this stone bench!
(*The king sits; Śakuntalā rises in embarrassment.*)
PRIYAṀVADĀ: The passion of two young lovers is clear. My affection for our friend makes me speak out again now.
KING: Noble lady, don't hesitate! It is painful to keep silent when one must speak.
PRIYAṀVADĀ: We're told that it is the king's duty to ease the pain of his suffering subjects.
KING: My duty, exactly!
PRIYAṀVADĀ: Since she first saw you, our dear friend has been reduced to this sad condition. You must protect her and save her life.
KING: Noble lady, our affection is shared and I am honored by all you say.
ŚAKUNTALĀ (*looking at Priyaṁvadā*): Why are you keeping the king here? He must be anxious to return to his palace.
KING:

If you think that my lost heart
could love anyone but you,
a fatal blow strikes a man
already wounded by love's arrows! (16)

ANASŪYĀ: We've heard that kings have many loves. Will our dear friend become a sorrow to her family after you've spent time with her?
KING: Noble lady, enough of this!

Despite my many wives,
on two the royal line rests—
sea-bound earth
and your friend. (17)

BOTH FRIENDS: You reassure us.
PRIYAṀVADĀ (*casting a glance*): Anasūyā, this fawn is looking for its mother. Let's take it to her!
(*They both begin to leave.*)
ŚAKUNTALĀ: Come back! Don't leave me unprotected!
BOTH FRIENDS: The protector of the earth is at your side.

ŚAKUNTALĀ: Why have they gone?
KING: Don't be alarmed! I am your servant.

Shall I set moist winds in motion
with lotus-leaf fans to cool your pain,
or rest your soft red lotus feet
on my lap to stroke them, my love? (18)

ŚAKUNTALĀ: I cannot sin against those I respect! (*Standing as if she wants to leave.*)
KING: Beautiful Śakuntalā, the day is still hot.

Why should your frail limbs
leave this couch of flowers
shielded by lotus leaves
to wander in the heat? (19)

(*Saying this, he forces her to turn around.*)
ŚAKUNTALĀ: Puru king, control yourself! Though I'm burning with love, how can I give myself to you?
KING: Don't fear your elders! The father of your family knows the law. When he finds out, he will not blame you.

The daughters of royal sages often marry
in secret and then their fathers bless them. (20)

ŚAKUNTALĀ: Release me! I must ask my friends' advice!
KING: Yes, I shall release you.
ŚAKUNTALĀ: When?
KING:

Only let my thirsting mouth
gently drink from your lips,
the way a bee sips nectar
from a fragile virgin blossom. (21)

(*Saying this, he tries to raise her face. Śakuntalā evades him with a dance.*)
VOICE OFFSTAGE: Red goose, bid farewell to your gander! Night has arrived!

ŚAKUNTALĀ (*flustered*): Puru king, Mother Gautamī is surely coming to ask about my health. Hide behind this tree!
KING: Yes.
(*He conceals himself and waits. Then Gautamī enters with a vessel in her hand, accompanied by Śakuntalā's two friends.*)
BOTH FRIENDS: This way, Mother Gautamī!
GAUTAMĪ (*approaching Śakuntalā*): Child, does the fever in your limbs burn less?
ŚAKUNTALĀ: Madam, I do feel better.
GAUTAMĪ: Kuśa grass and water will soothe your body.
(*She sprinkles Śakuntalā's head.*)
Child, the day is ended. Come, let's go back to our hut!
(*She starts to go.*)
ŚAKUNTALĀ (*to herself*): My heart, even when your desire was within reach, you were bound by fear. Now you'll suffer the torment of separation and regret.
(*Stopping after a few steps, she speaks aloud.*)
Bower of creepers, refuge from my torment, I say goodbye until our joy can be renewed . . .
(*Sorrowfully, Śakuntalā exits with the other women.*)
KING (*coming out of hiding*): Fulfillment of desire is fraught with obstacles.

Why didn't I kiss her face
as it bent near my shoulder,
her fingers shielding lips
that stammered lovely warning? (22)

Should I go now? Or shall I stay here in this bower of creepers that my love enjoyed and then left?

I see the flowers her body pressed
on this bench of stone,
the letter her nails inscribed
on the faded lotus leaf,
the lotus-fiber bracelet
that slipped from her wrist—
my eyes are prisoners
in this empty house of reeds. (23)

VOICE IN THE AIR: King!

When the evening rituals begin,
shadows of flesh-eating demons swarm
like amber clouds of twilight,
raising terror at the altar of fire. (24)

KING: I am coming.
(*He exits.*)

END OF ACT THREE

ACT FOUR

(*The two friends enter, miming the gathering of flowers.*)

ANASŪYĀ: Priyaṁvadā, I'm delighted that Śakuntalā chose a suitable husband for herself, but I still feel anxious.
PRIYAṀVADĀ: Why?
ANASŪYĀ: When the king finished the sacrifice, the sages thanked him and he left. Now that he has returned to his palace women in the city, will he remember us here?
PRIYAṀVADĀ: Have faith! He's so handsome, he can't be evil. But I don't know what Father Kaṇva will think when he hears about what happened.
ANASŪYĀ: I predict that he'll give his approval.
PRIYAṀVADĀ: Why?
ANASŪYĀ: He's always planned to give his daughter to a worthy husband. If fate accomplished it so quickly, Father Kaṇva won't object.
PRIYAṀVADĀ (*looking at the basket of flowers*): We've gathered enough flowers for the offering ceremony.
ANASŪYĀ: Shouldn't we worship the goddess who guards Śakuntalā?
PRIYAṀVADĀ: I have just begun.
(*She begins the rite.*)
VOICE OFFSTAGE: I am here!
ANASŪYĀ (*listening*): Friend, a guest is announcing himself.
PRIYAṀVADĀ: Śakuntalā is in her hut nearby, but her heart is far away.
ANASŪYĀ: You're right! Enough of these flowers!
(*They begin to leave.*)

VOICE OFFSTAGE: So . . . you slight a guest . . .

Since you blindly ignore
a great sage like me,
the lover you worship
with mindless devotion
will not remember you,
even when awakened—
like a drunkard who forgets
a story he just composed! (1)

PRIYAṀVADĀ: Oh! What a terrible turn of events! Śakuntalā's distraction has offended someone she should have greeted.
(*Looking ahead.*)
Not just an ordinary person, but the angry sage Durvāsas himself cursed her and went away in a frenzy of quivering, mad gestures. What else but fire has such power to burn?
ANASŪYĀ: Go! Bow at his feet and make him return while I prepare the water for washing his feet!
PRIYAṀVADĀ: As you say.
(*She exits.*)
ANASŪYĀ (*after a few steps, she mimes stumbling*): Oh! The basket of flowers fell from my hand when I stumbled in my haste to go.
(*She mimes the gathering of flowers.*)
PRIYAṀVADĀ (*entering*): He's so terribly cruel! No one could pacify him! But I was able to soften him a little.
ANASŪYĀ: Even that is a great feat with him! Tell me more!
PRIYAṀVADĀ: When he refused to return, I begged him to forgive a daughter's first offense, since she didn't understand the power of his austerity.
ANASŪYĀ: Then? Then?
PRIYAṀVADĀ: He refused to change his word, but he promised that when the king sees the ring of recollection, the curse will end. Then he vanished.
ANASŪYĀ: Now we can breathe again. When he left, the king himself gave her the ring engraved with his name. Śakuntalā will have her own means of ending the curse.

PRIYAṀVADĀ: Come friend! We should finish the holy rite we're performing for her.

(*The two walk around, looking.*)

Anasūyā, look! With her face resting on her hand, our dear friend looks like a picture. She is thinking about her husband's leaving, with no thought for herself, much less for a guest.

ANASŪYĀ: Priyaṁvadā, we two must keep all this a secret between us. Our friend is fragile by nature; she needs our protection.

PRIYAṀVADĀ: Who would sprinkle a jasmine with scalding water?

(*They both exit; the interlude ends. Then a disciple of Kaṇva enters, just awakened from sleep.*)

DISCIPLE: Father Kaṇva has just returned from his pilgrimage and wants to know the exact time. I'll go into a clearing to see what remains of the night.

(*Walking around and looking.*)

It is dawn.

> The moon sets over the western mountain
> as the sun rises in dawn's red trail—
> rising and setting, these two bright powers
> portend the rise and fall of men. (2)
>
> When the moon disappears, night lotuses
> are but dull souvenirs of its beauty—
> when her lover disappears, the sorrow
> is too painful for a frail girl to bear. (3)

ANASŪYĀ (*throwing aside the curtain and entering*): Even a person withdrawn from worldly life knows that the king has treated Śakuntalā badly.

DISCIPLE: I'll inform Father Kaṇva that it's time for the fire oblation.

(*He exits.*)

ANASŪYĀ: Even when I'm awake, I'm useless. My hands and feet don't do their work. Love must be pleased to have made

our innocent friend put her trust in a liar . . . but perhaps it was the curse of Durvāsas that changed him . . . otherwise, how could the king have made such promises and not sent even a message by now? Maybe we should send the ring to remind him. Which of these ascetics who practice austerities can we ask? Father Kaṇva has just returned from his pilgrimage. Since we feel that our friend was also at fault, we haven't told him that Śakuntalā is married to Duṣyanta and is pregnant. The problem is serious. What should we do?
PRIYAṀVADĀ (*entering, with delight*): Friend, hurry! We're to celebrate the festival of Śakuntalā's departure for her husband's house.
ANASŪYĀ: What's happened, friend?
PRIYAṀVADĀ: Listen! I went to ask Śakuntalā how she had slept. Father Kaṇva embraced her and though her face was bowed in shame, he blessed her: "Though his eyes were filled with smoke, the priest's oblation luckily fell on the fire. My child, I shall not mourn for you . . . like knowledge given to a good student I shall send you to your husband today with an escort of sages."
ANASŪYĀ: Who told Father Kaṇva what happened?
PRIYAṀVADĀ: A bodiless voice was chanting when he entered the fire sanctuary.
(*Quoting in Sanskrit.*)

Priest, know that your daughter
carries Duṣyanta's potent seed
for the good of the earth—
like fire in mimosa wood. (4)

ANASŪYĀ: I'm joyful, friend. But I know that Śakuntalā must leave us today and sorrow shadows my happiness.
PRIYAṀVADĀ: Friend, we must chase away sorrow and make this hermit girl happy!
ANASŪYĀ: Friend, I've made a garland of mimosa flowers. It's in the coconut-shell box hanging on a branch of the mango tree. Get it for me! Meanwhile I'll prepare the special ointments of deer musk, sacred earth, and blades of dūrvā grass.

PRIYAṀVADĀ: Here it is!
(*Anasūyā exits; Priyaṁvadā gracefully mimes taking down the box.*)
VOICE OFFSTAGE: Gautamī! Śārṅgarava and some others have been appointed to escort Śakuntalā.
PRIYAṀVADĀ (*listening*): Hurry! Hurry! The sages are being called to go to Hastināpura.
ANASŪYĀ (*reentering with pots of ointments in her hands*): Come, friend! Let's go!
PRIYAṀVADĀ (*looking around*): Śakuntalā stands at sunrise with freshly washed hair while the female ascetics bless her with handfuls of wild rice and auspicious words of farewell. Let's go to her together.
(*The two approach as Śakuntalā enters with Gautamī and other female ascetics, and strikes a posture as described. One after another, the female ascetics address her.*)
FIRST FEMALE ASCETIC: Child, win the title "Chief Queen" as a sign of your husband's high esteem!
SECOND FEMALE ASCETIC: Child, be a mother to heroes!
THIRD FEMALE ASCETIC: Child, be honored by your husband!
BOTH FRIENDS: This happy moment is no time for tears, friend.
(*Wiping away her tears, they calm her with dance gestures.*)
PRIYAṀVADĀ: Your beauty deserves jewels, not these humble things we've gathered in the hermitage.
(*Two boy ascetics enter with offerings in their hands.*)
BOTH BOYS: Here is an ornament for you!
(*Everyone looks amazed.*)
GAUTAMĪ: Nārada, my child, where did this come from?
FIRST BOY: From Father Kaṇva's power.
GAUTAMĪ: Was it his mind's magic?
SECOND BOY: Not at all! Listen! You ordered us to bring flowers from the forest trees for Śakuntalā.

One tree produced this white silk cloth,
another poured resinous lac to redden her feet—
the tree nymphs produced jewels in hands
that stretched from branches like young shoots. (5)

PRIYAMVADĀ (*watching Śakuntalā*): This is a sign that royal fortune will come to you in your husband's house.
(*Śakuntalā mimes modesty.*)
FIRST BOY: Gautama, come quickly! Father Kaṇva is back from bathing. We'll tell him how the trees honor her.
SECOND BOY: As you say.
(*The two exit.*)
BOTH FRIENDS: We've never worn them ourselves, but we'll put these jewels on your limbs the way they look in pictures.
ŚAKUNTALĀ: I trust your skill.
(*Both friends mime ornamenting her. Then Kaṇva enters, fresh from his bath.*)
KAṆVA:

My heart is touched with sadness
since Śakuntalā must go today,
my throat is choked with sobs,
my eyes are dulled by worry—
if a disciplined ascetic
suffers so deeply from love,
how do fathers bear the pain
of each daughter's parting? (6)

(*He walks around.*)
BOTH FRIENDS: Śakuntalā, your jewels are in place; now put on the pair of silken cloths.
(*Standing, Śakuntalā wraps them.*)
GAUTAMĪ: Child, your father has come. His eyes filled with tears of joy embrace you. Greet him reverently!
ŚAKUNTALĀ (*modestly*): Father, I welcome you.
KAṆVA: Child,

May your husband honor you
the way Yayāti honored Śarmiṣṭhā.
As she bore her son Puru,
may you bear an imperial prince. (7)

GAUTAMĪ: Sir, this is a blessing, not just a prayer.
KAṆVA: Child, walk around the sacrifical fires!

(*All walk around; Kaṇva intoning a prayer in Vedic meter.*)

Perfectly placed around the main altar,
fed with fuel, strewn with holy grass,
destroying sin by incense from oblations,
may these sacred fires purify you! (8)

You must leave now!
(*Looking around.*)
Where are Śārṅgarava and the others?
DISCIPLE (*entering*): Here we are, sir!
KAṆVA: You show your sister the way!
ŚĀRṄGARAVA: Come this way!
(*They walk around.*)
KAṆVA: Listen, you trees that grow in our grove!

Until you were well watered
she could not bear to drink;
she loved you too much
to pluck your flowers for her hair;
the first time your buds bloomed,
she blossomed with joy—
may you all bless Śakuntalā
as she leaves for her husband's house. (9)

(*Miming that he hears a cuckoo's cry.*)

The trees of her forest family
have blessed Śakuntalā—
the cuckoo's melodious song
announces their response. (10)

VOICE IN THE AIR:

May lakes colored by lotuses mark her path!
May trees shade her from the sun's burning rays!
May the dust be as soft as lotus pollen!
May fragrant breezes cool her way! (11)

(*All listen astonished.*)

GAUTAMĪ: Child, the divinities of our grove love you like your family and bless you. We bow to you all!
ŚAKUNTALĀ (*bowing and walking around; speaking in a stage whisper*): Priyaṁvadā, though I long to see my husband, my feet move with sorrow as I start to leave the hermitage.
PRIYAṀVADĀ: You are not the only one who grieves. The whole hermitage feels this way as your departure from our grove draws near.

Grazing deer
drop grass,
peacocks
stop dancing,
vines loose
pale leaves
falling
like tears. (12)

ŚAKUNTALĀ (*remembering*): Father, before I leave, I must see my sister, the vine Forestlight.
KAṆVA: I know that you feel a sister's love for her. She is right here.
ŚAKUNTALĀ: Forestlight, though you love your mango tree, turn to embrace me with your tendril arms! After today, I'll be so far away . . .
KAṆVA:

Your merits won you the husband
I always hoped you would have
and your jasmine has her mango tree—
my worries for you both are over. (13)

Start your journey here!
ŚAKUNTALĀ (*facing her two friends*): I entrust her care to you.
BOTH FRIENDS: But who will care for us?
(*They wipe away their tears.*)
KAṆVA: Anasūyā, enough crying! You should be giving Śakuntalā courage!
(*All walk around.*)

ŚAKUNTALĀ: Father, when the pregnant doe who grazes near my hut gives birth, please send someone to give me the good news.
KAṆVA: I shall not forget.
ŚAKUNTALĀ (*miming the interrupting of her gait*): Who is clinging to my skirt?
(*She turns around.*)
KAṆVA: Child,

> The buck whose mouth you healed with oil
> when it was pierced by a blade of kuśa grass
> and whom you fed with grains of rice—
> your adopted son will not leave the path. (14)

ŚAKUNTALĀ: Child, don't follow when I'm abandoning those I love! I raised you when you were orphaned soon after your birth, but now I'm deserting you too. Father will look after you. Go back!
(*Weeping, she starts to go.*)
KAṆVA: Be strong!

> Hold back the tears that blind
> your long-lashed eyes—
> you will stumble if you cannot see
> the uneven ground on the path. (15)

ŚĀRṄGARAVA: Sir, the scriptures prescribe that loved ones be escorted only to the water's edge. We are at the shore of the lake. Give us your message and return!
ŚAKUNTALĀ: We shall rest in the shade of this fig tree.
(*All walk around and stop; Kaṇva speaks to himself.*)
What would be the right message to send to King Duṣyanta?
(*He ponders.*)
ŚAKUNTALĀ (*in a stage whisper*): Look! The wild goose cries in anguish when her mate is hidden by lotus leaves. What I'm suffering is much worse.
ANASŪYĀ: Friend, don't speak this way!

This goose spends
every long night
in sorrow
without her mate,
but hope lets her
survive
the deep pain
of loneliness. (16)

KAṆVA: Śārṅgarava, speak my words to the king after you present Śakuntalā!

ŚĀRṄGARAVA: As you command, sir!

KAṆVA:

Considering our discipline,
the nobility of your birth
and that she fell in love with you
before her kinsmen could act,
acknowledge her with equal rank
among your wives—
what more is destined for her,
the bride's family will not ask. (17)

ŚĀRṄGARAVA: I grasp your message.

KAṆVA: Child, now I must instruct you. We forest hermits know something about worldly matters.

ŚĀRṄGARAVA: Nothing is beyond the scope of wise men.

KAṆVA: When you enter your husband's family:

Obey your elders, be a friend to the other wives!
If your husband seems harsh, don't be impatient!
Be fair to your servants, humble in your happiness!
Women who act this way become noble wives;
sullen girls only bring their families disgrace. (18)

But what does Gautamī think?

GAUTAMĪ: This is good advice for wives, child. Take it all to heart!

KAṆVA: Child, embrace me and your friends!

ŚAKUNTALĀ: Father, why must Priyaṁvadā and my other friends turn back here?
KAṆVA: They will also be given in marriage. It is not proper for them to go there now. Gautamī will go with you.
ŚAKUNTALĀ (*embracing her father*): How can I go on living in a strange place, torn from my father's side, like a vine torn from the side of a sandalwood tree growing on a mountain slope?
KAṆVA: Child, why are you so frightened?

> When you are your husband's honored wife,
> absorbed in royal duties and in your son,
> born like the sun to the eastern dawn,
> the sorrow of separation will fade. (19)

(*Śakuntalā falls at her father's feet.*)
Let my hopes for you be fulfilled!
ŚAKUNTALĀ (*approaching her two friends*): You two must embrace me together!
BOTH FRIENDS (*embracing her*): Friend, if the king seems slow to recognize you, show him the ring engraved with his name!
ŚAKUNTALĀ: Your suspicions make me tremble!
BOTH FRIENDS: Don't be afraid! It's our love that fears evil.
ŚĀRṄGARAVA: The sun is high in the afternoon sky. Hurry, please!
ŚAKUNTALĀ (*facing the sanctuary*): Father, will I ever see the grove again?
KAṆVA:

> When you have lived for many years
> as a queen equal to the earth
> and raised Duṣyanta's son
> to be a matchless warrior,
> your husband will entrust him
> with the burdens of the kingdom
> and will return with you
> to the calm of this hermitage. (20)

GAUTAMĪ: Child, the time for our departure has passed. Let

your father turn back! It would be better, sir, if you turn back yourself. She'll keep talking this way forever.
KAṆVA: Child, my ascetic practice has been interrupted.
ŚAKUNTALĀ: My father's body is already tortured by ascetic practices. He must not grieve too much for me!
KAṆVA (*sighing*):

When I see the grains of rice
sprout from offerings you made
at the door of your hut,
how shall I calm my sorrow! (21)

(*Śakuntalā exits with her escort.*)
BOTH FRIENDS (*watching Śakuntalā*): Śakuntalā is hidden by forest trees now.
KAṆVA: Anasūyā, your companion is following her duty. Restrain yourself and return with me!
BOTH FRIENDS: Father, the ascetics' grove seems empty without Śakuntalā. How can we enter?
KAṆVA: The strength of your love makes it seem so.
(*Walking around in meditation.*)
Good! Now that Śakuntalā is on her way to her husband's family, I feel calm.

A daughter belongs to another man—
by sending her to her husband today,
I feel the satisfaction
one has on repaying a loan. (22)

(*All exit.*)

END OF ACT FOUR

ACT FIVE

(*The king and the buffoon enter; both sit down.*)

BUFFOON: Pay attention to the music room, friend, and you'll hear the notes of a song strung into a delicious melody . . . the lady Haṁsapadikā is practicing her singing.
KING: Be quiet so I can hear her!
VOICE IN THE AIR (*singing*):

Craving sweet
new nectar,
you kissed
a mango bud once—
how could you
forget her, bee,
to bury your joy
in a lotus? (1)

KING: The melody of the song is passionate.
BUFFOON: But did you get the meaning of the words?
KING: I once made love to her. Now she reproaches me for loving Queen Vasumatī. Friend Māḍhavya, tell Haṁsapadikā that her words rebuke me soundly.
BUFFOON: As you command!
(*He rises.*)
But if that woman grabs my hair tuft, it will be like a heavenly nymph grabbing some ascetic . . . there go my hopes of liberation!
KING: Go! Use your courtly charm to console her.
BUFFOON: What a fate!
(*He exits.*)

KING (*to himself*): Why did hearing the song's words fill me with such strong desire? I'm not parted from anyone I love . . .

Seeing rare beauty,
hearing lovely sounds,
even a happy man
becomes strangely uneasy . . .
perhaps he remembers,
without knowing why,
loves of another life
buried deep in his being. (2)

(*He stands bewildered. Then the king's chamberlain enters.*)
CHAMBERLAIN: At my age, look at me!

Since I took this ceremonial bamboo staff
as my badge of office in the king's chambers
many years have passed; now I use it
as a crutch to support my faltering steps. (3)

A king cannot neglect his duty. He has just risen from his seat of justice and though I am loath to keep him longer, Sage Kaṇva's pupils have just arrived. Authority to rule the world leaves no time for rest.

The sun's steeds were yoked before time began,
the fragrant wind blows night and day,
the cosmic serpent always bears earth's weight,
and a king who levies taxes has his duty. (4)

Therefore, I must perform my office.
(*Walking around and looking.*)

Weary from ruling them like children,
he seeks solitude far from his subjects,
like an elephant bull who seeks cool shade
after gathering his herd at midday. (5)

(*Approaching.*)
Victory to you, king! Some ascetics who dwell in the forest at

the foothills of the Himālayas have come. They have women with them and bring a message from Sage Kaṇva. Listen, king, and judge!

KING (*respectfully*): Are they Sage Kaṇva's messengers?

CHAMBERLAIN: They are.

KING: Inform the teacher Somarāta that he should welcome the ascetics with the prescribed rites and then bring them to me himself. I'll wait in a place suitable for greeting them.

CHAMBERLAIN: As the king commands.

(*He exits.*)

KING (*rising*): Vetravatī, lead the way to the fire sanctuary.

DOORKEEPER: Come this way, king!

KING (*walking around, showing fatigue*): Every other creature is happy when the object of his desire is won, but for kings success contains a core of suffering.

High office only leads to greater greed;
just perfecting its rewards is wearisome—
a kingdom is more trouble than it's worth,
like a royal umbrella one holds alone. (6)

TWO BARDS OFFSTAGE: Victory to you, king!

FIRST BARD:

You sacrifice your pleasures every day
to labor for your subjects—
as a tree endures burning heat
to give shade from the summer sun. (7)

SECOND BARD:

You punish villains with your rod of justice,
you reconcile disputes, you grant protection—
most relatives are loyal only in hope of gain,
but you treat all your subjects like kinsmen. (8)

KING: My weary mind is revived.

(*He walks around.*)

DOORKEEPER: The terrace of the fire sanctuary is freshly washed and the cow is waiting to give milk for the oblation.

Let the king ascend!
KING: Vetravatī, why has Father Kaṇva sent these sages to me?

Does something hinder their ascetic life?
Or threaten creatures in the sacred forest?
Or do my sins stunt the flowering vines?
My mind is filled with conflicting doubts. (9)

DOORKEEPER: I would guess that these sages rejoice in your virtuous conduct and come to honor you.
(*The ascetics enter; Śakuntalā is in front with Gautamī; the chamberlain and the king's priest are in front of her.*)
CHAMBERLAIN: Come this way, sirs!
ŚĀRṄGARAVA: Śāradvata, my friend:

I know that this renowned king is righteous
and none of the social classes follows evil ways,
but my mind is so accustomed to seclusion
that the palace feels like a house in flames. (10)

ŚĀRADVATA: I've felt the same way ever since we entered the city.

As if I were freshly bathed, seeing a filthy man,
pure while he's defiled, awake while he's asleep,
as if I were a free man watching a prisoner,
I watch this city mired in pleasures. (11)

ŚAKUNTALĀ (*indicating she feels an omen*): Why is my right eye twitching?
GAUTAMĪ: Child, your husband's family gods turn bad fortune into blessings!
(*They walk around.*)
PRIEST (*indicating the king*): Ascetics, the guardian of sacred order has left the seat of justice and awaits you now. Behold him!
ŚĀRṄGARAVA: Great priest, he seems praiseworthy, but we expect no less.

Boughs bend, heavy with ripened fruit,
clouds descend with fresh rain,
noble men are gracious with wealth—
this is the nature of bountiful things. (12)

DOORKEEPER: King, their faces look calm. I'm sure that the sages have confidence in what they're doing.
KING (*seeing Śakuntalā*):

Who is she? Carefully veiled
to barely reveal her body's beauty,
surrounded by the ascetics
like a bud among withered leaves. (13)

DOORKEEPER: King, I feel curious and puzzled too. Surely her form deserves closer inspection.
KING: Let her be! One should not stare at another man's wife!
ŚAKUNTALĀ (*placing her hand on her chest, she speaks to herself*): My heart, why are you quivering? Be quiet while I learn my noble husband's feelings.
PRIEST (*going forward*): These ascetics have been honored with due ceremony. They have a message from their teacher. The king should hear them!
KING: I am paying attention.
SAGES (*raising their hands in a gesture of greeting*): May you be victorious, king!
KING: I salute you all!
SAGES: May your desires be fulfilled!
KING: Do the sages perform austerities unhampered?
SAGES:

Who would dare obstruct the rites
of holy men whom you protect—
how can darkness descend
when the sun's rays shine? (14)

KING: My title "king" is more meaningful now. Is the world blessed by Father Kaṇva's health?

SAGES: Saints control their own health. He asks about your welfare and sends this message . . .
KING: What does he command?
ŚĀRṄGARAVA: At the time you secretly met and married my daughter, affection made me pardon you both.

We remember you to be a prince of honor;
Śakuntalā is virtue incarnate—
the creator cannot be condemned
for mating the perfect bride and groom. (15)

And now that she is pregnant, receive her and perform your sacred duty together.
GAUTAMĪ: Sir, I have something to say, though I wasn't appointed to speak:

She ignored her elders
and you failed to ask her kinsmen—
since you acted on your own,
what can I say to you now? (16)

ŚAKUNTALĀ: What does my noble husband say?
KING: What has been proposed?
ŚAKUNTALĀ (*to herself*): The proposal is as clear as fire.
ŚĀRṄGARAVA: What's this? Your Majesty certainly knows the ways of the world!

People suspect a married woman who stays
with her kinsmen, even if she is chaste—
a young wife should live with her husband,
no matter how he despises her. (17)

KING: Did I ever marry you?
ŚAKUNTALĀ (*visibly dejected, speaking to herself*): Now your fears are real, my heart!
ŚĀRṄGARAVA:

Does one turn away from duty in contempt
because his own actions repulse him? (18a)

KING: Why ask this insulting question?

ŚĀRṄGARAVA:

Such transformations take shape
when men are drunk with power. (18b)

KING: This censure is clearly directed at me.
GAUTAMĪ: Child, this is no time to be modest. I'll remove your veil. Then your husband will recognize you.
(*She does so.*)
KING (*staring at Śakuntalā*):

Must I judge whether I ever married
the flawless beauty they offer me now?
I cannot love her or leave her, like a bee
near a jasmine filled with frost at dawn. (19)

(*He shows hesitation.*)
DOORKEEPER: Our king has a strong sense of justice. Who else would hesitate when beauty like this is handed to him?
ŚĀRṄGARAVA: King, why do you remain silent?
KING: Ascetics, even though I'm searching my mind, I don't remember marrying this lady. How can I accept a woman who is visibly pregnant when I doubt that I am the cause?
ŚAKUNTALĀ (*in a stage whisper*): My lord casts doubt on our marriage. Why were my hopes so high?
ŚĀRṄGARAVA: It can't be!

Are you going to insult the sage
who pardons the girl you seduced
and bids you keep his stolen wealth,
treating a thief like you with honor? (20)

ŚĀRADVATA: Śārṅgarava, stop now! Śakuntalā, we have delivered our message and the king has responded. He must be shown some proof.
ŚAKUNTALĀ (*in a stage whisper*): When passion can turn to this, what's the use of reminding him? But, it's up to me to prove my honor now.
(*Aloud.*)
My noble husband . . .

(*She breaks off when this is half-spoken.*)
Since our marriage is in doubt, this is no way to address him. Puru king, you do wrong to reject a simple-hearted person with such words after you deceived her in the hermitage.
KING (*covering his ears*): Stop this shameful talk!

Are you trying to stain my name
and drag me to ruin—
like a river eroding her own banks,
soiling water and uprooting trees? (21)

ŚAKUNTALĀ: Very well! If it's really true that fear of taking another man's wife turns you away, then this ring will revive your memory and remove your doubt.
KING: An excellent idea!
ŚAKUNTALĀ (*touching the place where the ring had been*): I'm lost! The ring is gone from my finger.
(*She looks despairingly at Gautamī.*)
GAUTAMĪ: The ring must have fallen off while you were bathing in the holy waters at the shrine of the goddess near Indra's grove.
KING (*smiling*): And so they say the female sex is cunning.
ŚAKUNTALĀ: Fate has shown its power. Yet, I will tell you something else.
KING: I am still obliged to listen.
ŚAKUNTALĀ: One day, in a jasmine bower, you held a lotus-leaf cup full of water in your hand.
KING: We hear you.
ŚAKUNTALĀ: At that moment the buck I treated as my son approached. You coaxed it with the water, saying that it should drink first. But he didn't trust you and wouldn't drink from your hand. When I took the water, his trust returned. Then you jested, "Every creature trusts what its senses know. You both belong to the forest."
KING: Thus do women further their own ends by attracting eager men with the honey of false words.

GAUTAMĪ: Great king, you are wrong to speak this way. This child raised in an ascetics' grove doesn't know deceit.
KING: Old woman,

When naive female beasts show cunning,
what can we expect of women who reason?
Don't cuckoos let other birds nurture
their eggs and teach the chicks to fly? (22)

ŚAKUNTALĀ (*angrily*): Evil man! you see everything distorted by your own ignoble heart. Who would want to imitate you now, hiding behind your show of justice, like a well overgrown with weeds?
KING (*to himself*): Her anger does not seem feigned; it makes me doubt myself.

When the absence of love's memory
made me deny a secret affair with her,
this fire-eyed beauty bent her angry brows
and seemed to break the bow of love. (23)

(*Aloud.*)
Lady, Duṣyanta's conduct is renowned, so what you say is groundless.
ŚAKUNTALĀ: All right! I may be a self-willed wanton woman! But it was faith in the Puru dynasty that brought me into the power of a man with honey in his words and poison in his heart.
(*She covers her face at the end of the speech and weeps.*)
ŚĀRṄGARAVA: A willful act unchecked always causes pain.

One should be cautious
in forming a secret union—
unless a lover's heart is clear,
affection turns to poison. (24)

KING: But sir, why do you demean me with such warnings? Do you trust the lady?

ŚĀRṄGARAVA (*scornfully*): You have learned everything backwards.

If you suspect the word of one
whose nature knows no guile,
then you can only trust
people who practice deception. (25)

KING: I presume you speak the truth. Let us assume so. But what could I gain by deceiving this woman?
ŚĀRṄGARAVA: Ruin.
KING: Ruin? A Puru king has no reason to want his own ruin!
ŚĀRADVATA: Śārṅgarava, this talk is pointless. We have delivered our master's message and should return.

Since you married her, abandon her or take her—
absolute is the power a husband has over his wife. (26)

GAUTAMĪ: You go ahead.
(*They start to go.*)
ŚAKUNTALĀ: What? Am I deceived by this cruel man and then abandoned by you?
(*She tries to follow them.*)
GAUTAMĪ (*stopping*): Śārṅgarava my son, Śakuntalā is following us, crying pitifully. What will my child do now that her husband has refused her?
ŚĀRṄGARAVA (*turning back angrily*): Bold woman, do you still insist on having your way?
(*Śakuntalā trembles in fear.*)

If you are what the king says you are,
you don't belong in Father Kaṇva's family—
if you know that your marriage vow is pure,
you can bear slavery in your husband's house. (27)

Stay! We must go on!
KING: Ascetic, why do you disappoint the lady too?

The moon only makes lotuses open,
the sun's light awakens lilies—
a king's discipline forbids him
to touch another man's wife. (28)

ŚĀRṄGARAVA: If you forget a past affair because of some present attachment, why do you fear injustice now?
KING (*to the priest*): Sir, I ask you to weigh the alternatives:

Since it's unclear whether I'm deluded
or she is speaking falsely—
should I risk abandoning a wife
or being tainted by another man's? (29)

PRIEST (*deliberating*): I recommend this . . .
KING: Instruct me! I'll do as you say.
PRIEST: Then let the lady stay in our house until her child is born. If you ask why: the wise men predict that your first son will be born with the marks of a king who turns the wheel of empire. If the child of the sage's daughter bears the marks, congratulate her and welcome her into your palace chambers. Otherwise, send her back to her father.
KING: Whatever the elders desire.
PRIEST: Child, follow me!
ŚAKUNTALĀ: Mother earth, open to receive me!
(*Weeping, Śakuntalā exits with the priest and the hermits. The king, his memory lost through the curse, thinks about her.*)
VOICE OFFSTAGE: Amazing! Amazing!
KING (*listening*): What could this be?
PRIEST (*reentering, amazed*): King, something marvelous has occurred!
KING: What?
PRIEST: When Kaṇva's pupils had departed,

The girl threw up her arms and wept,
lamenting her misfortune . . . then . . . (30a)

KING: Then what?
PRIEST:

Near the nymph's shrine a ray of light
in the shape of a woman carried her away. (30b)

(*All mime amazement.*)
KING: We've already settled the matter. Why discuss it further?

PRIEST (*observing the king*): May you be victorious!
(*He exits.*)
KING: Vetravatī, I am bewildered. Lead the way to my chamber!
DOORKEEPER: Come this way, my lord!
(*She walks forward.*)
KING:

> I cannot remember marrying
> the sage's abandoned daughter,
> but the pain my heart feels
> makes me suspect that I did. (31)

(*All exit.*)

END OF ACT FIVE

ACT SIX

(The king's wife's brother, who is city magistrate, enters with two policemen leading a man whose hands are tied behind his back.)

BOTH POLICEMEN (*beating the man*): Speak, thief! Where'd you steal this handsome ring with the king's name engraved in the jewel?

MAN (*showing fear*): Peace, sirs! I wouldn't do a thing like that.

FIRST POLICEMAN: Don't tell us the king thought you were some famous priest and gave it to you as a gift!

MAN: Listen, I'm a humble fisherman who lives near Indra's grove.

SECOND POLICEMAN: Thief, did we ask you about your caste?

MAGISTRATE: Sūcaka, let him tell it all in order! Don't interrupt him!

BOTH POLICEMEN: Whatever you command, chief!

MAN: I feed my family by catching fish with nets and hooks.

MAGISTRATE (*mocking*): What a pure profession!

MAN:

> The work I do
> may be vile
> but I won't deny
> my birthright—
> a priest
> doing his holy rites
> pities the animals
> he kills. (1)

MAGISTRATE: Go on!

MAN: One day as I was cutting up a red carp, I saw the shining stone of this ring in its belly. When I tried to sell it, you grabbed me. Kill me or let me go! That's how I got it!

MAGISTRATE: Jānuka, I'm sure this ugly butcher's a fisherman by his stinking smell. We must investigate how he got the ring. We'll go straight to the palace.

BOTH POLICEMEN: Okay. Go in front, you pickpocket!

(*All walk around.*)

MAGISTRATE: Sūcaka, guard this villain at the palace gate! I'll report to the king how we found the ring, get his orders, and come back.

BOTH POLICEMEN: Chief, good luck with the king!

(*The magistrate exits.*)

FIRST POLICEMAN: Jānuka, the chief's been gone a long time.

SECOND POLICEMAN: Well, there are fixed times for seeing kings.

FIRST POLICEMAN: Jānuka, my hands are itching to tie on his execution garland.

(*He points to the man.*)

MAN: You shouldn't think about killing a man for no reason.

SECOND POLICEMAN (*looking*): I see our chief coming with a letter in his hand. It's probably an order from the king. You'll be thrown to the vultures or you'll see the face of death's dog again . . .

MAGISTRATE (*entering*): Sūcaka, release this fisherman! I'll tell you how he got the ring.

FIRST POLICEMAN: Whatever you say, chief!

SECOND POLICEMAN: The villain entered the house of death and came out again.

(*He unties the prisoner.*)

MAN (*bowing to the magistrate*): Master, how will I make my living now?

MAGISTRATE: The king sends you a sum equal to the ring.

(*He gives the money to the man.*)

MAN (*bowing as he grabs it*): The king honors me.

FIRST POLICEMAN: This fellow's certainly honored. He was lowered from the execution stake and raised up on a royal elephant's back.

SECOND POLICEMAN: Chief, the reward tells me this ring was special to the king.

MAGISTRATE: I don't think the king valued the stone, but when he caught sight of the ring, he suddenly seemed to remember someone he loved, and he became deeply disturbed.

FIRST POLICEMAN: You served him well, chief!

SECOND POLICEMAN: I think you better served this king of fish.

(*Looking at the fisherman with jealousy.*)

MAN: My lords, half of this is yours for your good will.

FIRST POLICEMAN: It's only fair!

MAGISTRATE: Fisherman, now that you are my greatest and dearest friend, we should pledge our love over kadamba-blossom wine. Let's go to the wine shop!

(*They all exit together; the interlude ends. Then a nymph named Sānumatī enters by the skyway.*)

SĀNUMATĪ: Now that I've performed my assigned duties at the nymph's shrine, I'll slip away to spy on King Duṣyanta while the worshipers are bathing. My friendship with Menakā makes me feel a bond with Śakuntalā. Besides, Menakā asked me to help her daughter.

(*Looking around.*)

Why don't I see preparations for the spring festival in the king's palace? I can learn everything by using my mental powers, but I must respect my friend's request. So be it! I'll make myself invisible and spy on these two girls who are guarding the pleasure garden.

(*Sānumatī mimes descending and stands waiting. Then a maid servant named Parabhṛtikā, "Little Cuckoo," enters, looking at a mango bud. A second maid, named Madhukarikā, "Little Bee," is following her.*)

FIRST MAID:

Your pale green stem
tinged with pink
is a true sign
that spring has come—
I see you,
mango-blossom bud,
and I pray
for a season of joy. (2)

SECOND MAID: What are you muttering to yourself?

FIRST MAID: A cuckoo goes mad when she sees a mango bud.

SECOND MAID (*joyfully rushing over*): Has the sweet month of spring come?

FIRST MAID: Now's the time to sing your songs of love.

SECOND MAID: Hold me while I pluck a mango bud and worship the god of love.

FIRST MAID: Only if you'll give me half the fruit of your worship.

SECOND MAID: That goes without saying . . . our bodies may be separate, but our lives are one . . .

(*Leaning on her friend, she stands and plucks a mango bud.*)

The mango flower is still closed, but this broken stem is fragrant.

(*She makes the dove gesture with her hands.*)

Mango-blossom bud,
I offer you to Love
as he lifts
his bow of passion.
Be the first
of his flower arrows
aimed at lonely girls
with lovers far away! (3)

(*She throws the mango bud.*)

CHAMBERLAIN (*angrily throwing aside the curtain and entering*): Not now, stupid girl! When the king has banned the festival of spring, how dare you pluck a mango bud!

BOTH MAIDS (*frightened*): Please forgive us, sir. We don't know what you mean.
CHAMBERLAIN: Did you not hear that even the spring trees and the nesting birds obey the king's order?

The mango flowers bloom without spreading pollen,
the red amaranth buds, but will not bloom,
cries of cuckoo cocks freeze though frost is past,
and out of fear, Love holds his arrow half-drawn. (4)

BOTH MAIDS: There is no doubt about the king's great power!
FIRST MAID: Sir, several days ago we were sent to wait on the queen by Mitrāvasu, the king's brother-in-law. We were assigned to guard the pleasure garden. Since we're newcomers, we've heard no news.
CHAMBERLAIN: Let it be! But don't do it again!
BOTH MAIDS: Sir, we're curious. May we ask why the spring festival was banned?
SĀNUMATĪ: Mortals are fond of festivals. The reason must be serious.
CHAMBERLAIN: It is public knowledge. Why should I not tell them? Has the scandal of Śakuntalā's rejection not reached your ears?
BOTH MAIDS: We only heard from the king's brother-in-law that the ring was found.
CHAMBERLAIN (*to himself*): There is little more to tell.
(*Aloud.*)
When he saw the ring, the king remembered that he had married Śakuntalā in secret and had rejected her in his delusion. Since then the king has been tortured by remorse.

Despising what he once enjoyed,
he shuns his ministers every day
and spends long sleepless nights
tossing at the edge of his bed—
when courtesy demands that
he converse with palace women,
he stumbles over their names,
and then retreats in shame. (5)

SĀNUMATĪ: This news delights me.
CHAMBERLAIN: The festival is banned because of the king's melancholy.
BOTH MAIDS: It's only right.
VOICE OFFSTAGE: This way, sir!
CHAMBERLAIN (*listening*): The king is coming. Go about your business!
BOTH MAIDS: As you say.
(*Both maids exit. Then the king enters, costumed to show his grief, accompanied by the buffoon and the doorkeeper.*)
CHAMBERLAIN (*observing the king*): Extraordinary beauty is appealing under all conditions. Even in his lovesick state, the king is wonderful to see.

> Rejecting his regal jewels,
> he wears one golden bangle
> above his left wrist;
> his lips are pale with sighs,
> his eyes wan from brooding at night—
> like a gemstone ground in polishing,
> the fiery beauty of his body
> makes his wasted form seem strong. (6)

SĀNUMATĪ (*seeing the king*): I see why Śakuntalā pines for him though he rejected and disgraced her.
KING (*walking around slowly, deep in thought*):

> This cursed heart slept
> when my love came to wake it,
> and now it stays awake
> to suffer the pain of remorse. (7)

SĀNUMATĪ: The girl shares his fate.
BUFFOON (*in a stage whisper*): He's having another attack of his Śakuntalā disease. I doubt if there's any cure for that.
CHAMBERLAIN (*approaching*): Victory to the king! I have inspected the grounds of the pleasure garden. Let the king visit his favorite spots and divert himself.
KING: Vetravatī, deliver a message to my noble minister

Piśuna: "After being awake all night, we cannot sit on the seat of justice today. Set in writing what your judgment tells you the citizens require and send it to us!"
DOORKEEPER: Whatever you command!
(*She exits.*)
KING: Vātāyana, attend to the rest of your business!
CHAMBERLAIN: As the king commands!
(*He exits.*)
BUFFOON: You've cleared out the flies. Now you can rest in some pretty spot. The garden is pleasant now in this break between morning cold and noonday heat.
KING: Dear friend, the saying "Misfortunes rush through any crack" is absolutely right:

> Barely freed by the dark force
> that made me forget Kaṇva's daughter,
> my mind is threatened by an arrow
> of mango buds fixed on Love's bow. (8)

BUFFOON: Wait, I'll destroy the love god's arrow with my wooden stick.
(*Raising his staff, he tries to strike a mango bud.*)
KING (*smiling*): Let it be! I see the majesty of brahman bravery. Friend, where may I sit to divert my eyes with vines that remind me of my love?
BUFFOON: Didn't you tell your maid Caturikā, "I'll pass the time in the jasmine bower. Bring me the drawing board on which I painted a picture of Śakuntalā with my own hand!"
KING: Such a place may soothe my heart. Show me the way!
BUFFOON: Come this way!
(*Both walk around; the nymph Sānumatī follows.*)
The marble seat and flower offerings in this jasmine bower are certainly trying to make us feel welcome. Come in and sit down!
(*Both enter the bower and sit.*)
SĀNUMATĪ: I'll hide behind these creepers to see the picture he's drawn of my friend. Then I'll report how great her husband's passion is.

(*She does as she says and stands waiting.*)

KING: Friend, now I remember everything. I told you about my first meeting with Śakuntalā. You weren't with me when I rejected her, but why didn't you say anything about her before? Did you suffer a loss of memory too?

BUFFOON: I didn't forget. You did tell me all about it once, but then you said, "It's all a joke without any truth." My wit is like a lump of clay, so I took you at your word . . . or it could be that fate is powerful . . .

SĀNUMATĪ: It is!

KING: Friend, help me!

BUFFOON: What's this? It doesn't become you! Noblemen never take grief to heart. Even in storms, mountains don't tremble.

KING: Dear friend, I'm defenseless when I remember the pain of my love's bewilderment when I rejected her.

> When I cast her away, she followed her kinsmen,
> but Kaṇva's disciple harshly shouted, "Stay!"
> The tearful look my cruelty provoked
> burns me like an arrow tipped with poison. (9)

SĀNUMATĪ: The way he rehearses his actions makes me delight in his pain.

BUFFOON: Sir, I guess that the lady was carried off by some celestial creature or other.

KING: Who else would dare to touch a woman who worshiped her husband? I was told that Menakā is her mother. My heart suspects that her mother's companions carried her off.

SĀNUMATĪ: His delusion puzzled me, but not his reawakening.

BUFFOON: If that's the case, you'll meet her again in good time.

KING: How?

BUFFOON: No mother or father can bear to see a daughter parted from her husband.

KING:

Was it dream or illusion or mental confusion,
or the last meager fruit of my former good deeds?
It is gone now, and my heart's desires are
like riverbanks crumbling of their own weight. (10)

BUFFOON: Stop this! Isn't the ring evidence that an unexpected meeting is destined to take place?

KING (*looking at the ring*): I only pity it for falling from such a place.

Ring, your punishment is proof
that your fate is as flawed as mine—
you were placed in her lovely fingers,
glowing with crimson nails, and you fell. (11)

SĀNUMATĪ: The real pity would have been if it had fallen into some other hand.

BUFFOON: What prompted you to put the signet ring on her hand?

SĀNUMATĪ: I'm curious too.

KING: I did it when I left for the city. My love broke into tears and asked, "How long will it be before my noble husband sends news to me?"

BUFFOON: Then? What then?

KING: Then I placed the ring on her finger with this promise:

One by one, day after day,
count each syllable of my name!
At the end, a messenger will come
to bring you to my palace. (12)

But in my cruel delusion, I never kept my word.

SĀNUMATĪ: Fate broke their charming agreement!

BUFFOON: How did it get into the belly of the carp the fisherman was cutting up?

KING: While she was worshiping at the shrine of Indra's wife, it fell from her hand into the Gaṅgā.

BUFFOON: It's obvious now!

SĀNUMATĪ: And the king, doubtful of his marriage to Śakuntalā, a female ascetic, was afraid to commit an act of injustice. But why should such passionate love need a ring to be remembered?

KING: I must reproach the ring for what it's done.

BUFFOON (*to himself*): He's gone the way of all madmen . . .

KING:

> Why did you leave her delicate finger
> and sink into the deep river? (13a)

Of course . . .

> A mindless ring can't recognize virtue,
> but why did I reject my love? (13b)

BUFFOON (*to himself again*): Why am I consumed by a craving for food?

KING: Oh ring! Have pity on a man whose heart is tormented because he abandoned his love without cause! Let him see her again!

(*Throwing the curtain aside, the maid Caturikā enters, with the drawing board in her hand.*)

CATURIKĀ: Here's the picture you painted of the lady.

(*She shows the drawing board.*)

BUFFOON: Dear friend, how well you've painted your feelings in this sweet scene! My eyes almost stumble over the hollows and hills.

SĀNUMATĪ: What skill the king has! I feel as if my friend were before me.

KING:

> The picture's imperfections are not hers,
> but this drawing does hint at her beauty. (14)

SĀNUMATĪ: Such words reveal that suffering has increased his modesty as much as his love.

BUFFOON: Sir, I see three ladies now and they're all lovely to look at. Which is your Śakuntalā?

SĀNUMATĪ: Only a dim-witted fool like this wouldn't know such beauty!
KING: You guess which one!
BUFFOON: I guess Śakuntalā is the one you've drawn with flowers falling from her loosened locks of hair, with drops of sweat on her face, with her arms hanging limp and tired as she stands at the side of a mango tree whose tender shoots are gleaming with the fresh water she poured. The other two are her friends.
KING: You are clever! Look at these signs of my passion!

> Smudges from my sweating fingers
> stain the edges of the picture
> and a tear fallen from my cheek
> has raised a wrinkle in the paint. (15)

Caturikā, the scenery is only half-drawn. Go and bring my paints!
CATURIKĀ: Noble Māḍhavya, hold the drawing board until I come back!
KING: I'll hold it myself.
(*He takes it, the maid exits.*)

> I rejected my love when she came to me,
> and now I worship her in a painted image—
> having passed by a river full of water,
> I'm longing now for an empty mirage. (16)

BUFFOON (*to himself*): He's too far gone for a river now! He's looking for a mirage!
(*Aloud.*)
Sir, what else do you plan to draw here?
SĀNUMATĪ: He'll want to draw every place my friend loved.
KING:

> I'll draw the river Mālinī
> flowing through Himālaya's foothills
> where pairs of wild geese nest in the sand
> and deer recline on both riverbanks,

where a doe is rubbing her left eye
on the horn of a black buck antelope
under a tree whose branches
have bark dresses hanging to dry. (17)

BUFFOON (*to himself*): Next he'll fill the drawing board with mobs of ascetics wearing long grassy beards.
KING: Dear friend, I've forgotten to draw an ornament that Śakuntalā wore.
BUFFOON: What is it?
SĀNUMATĪ: It will suit her forest life and her tender beauty.
KING:

I haven't drawn the mimosa flower on her ear,
its filaments resting on her cheek,
or the necklace of tender lotus stalks,
lying on her breasts like autumn moonbeams. (18)

BUFFOON: But why does the lady cover her face with her red lotus-bud fingertips and stand trembling in fear?
(*Looking closely.*)
That son-of-a-bee who steals nectar from flowers is attacking her face.
KING: Drive the impudent rogue away!
BUFFOON: You have the power to punish criminals. You drive him off!
KING: All right! Bee, favored guest of the flowering vines, why do you frustrate yourself by flying here?

A female bee waits on a flower,
thirsting for your love—
she refuses to drink
the sweet nectar without you. (19)

SĀNUMATĪ: How gallantly he's driving him away!
BUFFOON: When you try to drive it away, this creature becomes vicious.
KING: Why don't you stop when I command you?

Bee, if you touch the lips of my love
that lure you like a young tree's virgin buds,
lips I gently kissed in festivals of love,
I'll hold you captive in a lotus flower cage. (20)

BUFFOON: Why isn't he afraid of your harsh punishment?
(*Laughing, he speaks to himself.*)
He's gone crazy and I'll be the same if I go on talking like this.
(*Aloud.*)
But sir, it's just a picture!
KING: A picture? How can that be?
SĀNUMATĪ: When I couldn't tell whether it was painted, how could he realize he was looking at a picture?
KING: Dear friend, are you envious of me?

My heart's affection made me feel
the joy of seeing her—
but you reminded me again
that my love is only a picture. (21)

(*He wipes away a tear.*)
SĀNUMATĪ: The effects of her absence make him quarrelsome.
KING: Dear friend, why do I suffer this endless pain?

Sleepless nights prevent our meeting in dreams;
her image in a picture is ruined by my tears. (22)

SĀNUMATĪ: You have clearly atoned for the suffering your rejection caused Śakuntalā.
CATURIKĀ (*entering*): Victory my lord! I found the paint box and started back right away . . . but I met Queen Vasumatī with her maid Taralikā on the path and she grabbed the box from my hand, saying, "I'll bring it to the noble lord myself!"
BUFFOON: You were lucky to get away!
CATURIKĀ: The queen's shawl got caught on a tree. While Taralikā was freeing it, I made my escape.
KING: Dear friend, the queen's pride can quickly turn to anger. Save this picture!

BUFFOON: You should say, "Save yourself!"
(*Taking the picture, he stands up.*)
If you escape the woman's deadly poison, then send word to me in the Palace of the Clouds.
(*He exits hastily.*)
SĀNUMATĪ: Even though another woman has taken his heart and he feels indifferent to the queen, he treats her with respect.
DOORKEEPER (*entering with a letter in her hand*): Victory, king!
KING: Vetravatī, did you meet the queen on the way?
DOORKEEPER: I did, but when she saw the letter in my hand, she turned back.
KING: She knows that this is official and would not interrupt my work.
DOORKEEPER: King, the minister requests that you examine the contents of this letter. He said that the enormous job of reckoning the revenue in this one citizen's case had taken all his time.
KING: Show me the letter!
(*The girl hands it to him and he reads barely aloud.*)
What is this? "A wealthy merchant sea captain named Dhanamitra has been lost in a shipwreck and the laws say that since the brave man was childless, his accumulated wealth all goes to the king." It's terrible to be childless! A man of such wealth probably had several wives. We must find out if any one of his wives is pregnant!
DOORKEEPER: King, it's said that one of his wives, the daughter of a merchant of Ayodhyā, has performed the rite to ensure the birth of a son.
KING: The child in her womb surely deserves his paternal wealth. Go! Report this to my minister!
DOORKEEPER: As the king commands!
(*She starts to go.*)
KING: Come here a moment!
DOORKEEPER: I am here.
KING: Is it his offspring or not?

When his subjects lose a kinsman,
Duṣyanta will preserve the estates—
unless there is some crime.
Let this be proclaimed. (23)

DOORKEEPER: It shall be proclaimed loudly.
(*She exits; reenters.*)
The king's order will be as welcome as rain in the right season.
KING (*sighing long and deeply*): Families without offspring whose lines of succession are cut off lose their wealth to strangers when the last male heir dies. When I die, this will happen to the wealth of the Puru dynasty.
DOORKEEPER: Heaven forbid such a fate!
KING: I curse myself for despising the treasure I was offered.
SĀNUMATĪ: He surely has my friend in mind when he blames himself.
KING:

I abandoned my lawful wife, the holy ground
where I myself planted my family's glory,
like earth sown with seed at the right time,
ready to bear rich fruit in season. (24)

SĀNUMATĪ: But your family's line will not be broken.
CATURIKĀ (*in a stage whisper*): The king is upset by the story of the merchant. Go and bring noble Māḍhavya from the Palace of the Clouds to console him!
DOORKEEPER: A good idea!
(*She exits.*)
KING: Duṣyanta's ancestors are imperiled.

Our fathers drink the yearly libation
mixed with my childless tears,
knowing that there is no other son
to offer the sacred funeral waters. (25)

(*He falls into a faint.*)
CATURIKĀ (*looking at the bewildered king*): Calm yourself, my lord!

SĀNUMATĪ: Though a light shines, his separation from Śakuntalā keeps him in a state of dark depression. I could make him happy now, but I've heard Indra's consort consoling Śakuntalā with the news that the gods are hungry for their share of the ancestral oblations and will soon conspire to have her husband welcome his lawful wife. I'll have to wait for the auspicious time, but meanwhile I'll cheer my friend by reporting his condition.
(*She exits, flying into the air.*)
VOICE OFFSTAGE: Help! Brahman-murder!
KING (*regaining consciousness, listening*): Is it Māḍhavya's cry of pain? Who's there?
DOORKEEPER: King, your friend is in danger. Help him!
KING: Who dares to threaten him?
DOORKEEPER: Some invisible spirit seized him and dragged him to the roof of the Palace of the Clouds.
KING (*getting up*): Not this! Even my house is haunted by spirits.

When I don't even recognize
the blunders I commit every day,
how can I keep track
of where my subjects stray? (26)

VOICE OFFSTAGE: Dear friend! Help! Help!
KING (*breaking into a run*): Friend, don't be afraid! I'm coming!
VOICE OFFSTAGE (*repeating the call for help*): Why shouldn't I be afraid? Someone is trying to split my neck in three, like a stalk of sugar cane.
KING (*casting a glance*): Quickly, my bow!
BOW-BEARER (*entering with a bow in hand*): Here are your bow and quiver.
(*The king takes his bow and arrows.*)
VOICE OFFSTAGE:

I'll kill you as a tiger kills struggling prey!
I'll drink fresh blood from your tender neck!
Take refuge now in the bow Duṣyanta lifts
to calm the fears of the oppressed! (27)

KING (*angrily*): How dare you abuse my name? Stop, carrion-eater! Or you will not live!
(*He strings his bow.*)
Vetravatī, lead the way to the stairs!
DOORKEEPER: This way, king.
(*All move forward in haste.*)
KING (*searching around*): There is no one here!
VOICE OFFSTAGE: Help! Help! I see you. Don't you see me? I'm like a mouse caught by a cat! My life is hopeless!
KING: Don't count on your powers of invisibility! My magical arrows will find you. I aim this arrow:

It will strike its doomed target
and spare the brahman it must save—
a wild goose can extract the milk
and leave the water untouched. (28)

(*He aims the arrow. Then Indra's charioteer Mātali enters, having released the buffoon.*)
MĀTALI: King!

Indra sets demons as your targets;
draw your bow against them!
Send friends gracious glances
rather than deadly arrows! (29)

KING (*withdrawing his arrow*): Mātali, welcome to great Indra's charioteer!
BUFFOON (*entering*): He tried to slaughter me like a sacrifical beast and this king is greeting him with honors!
MĀTALI (*smiling*): Your Majesty, hear why Indra has sent me to you!
KING: I am all attention.
MĀTALI: There is an army of demons descended from one-hundred-headed Kālanemi, known to be invincible . . .
KING: I have already heard it from Nārada, the gods' messenger.

MĀTALI:

He is invulnerable to your friend Indra,
so you are appointed to lead the charge—
the moon dispels the darkness of night
since the sun cannot drive it out. (30)

Take your weapon, mount Indra's chariot, and prepare for victory!
KING: Indra favors me with this honor. But why did you attack Māḍhavya?
MĀTALI: I'll tell you! From the signs of anguish Your Majesty showed, I knew that you were despondent. I attacked him to arouse your anger.

A fire blazes when fuel is added;
a cobra provoked raises its hood—
men can regain lost courage
if their emotions are roused. (31)

KING (*in a stage whisper*): Dear friend, I cannot disobey a command from the lord of heaven. Inform my minister Piśuna of this and tell him this for me:

Concentrate your mind on guarding my subjects!
My bow is strung to accomplish other work. (32)

BUFFOON: Whatever you command!
(*He exits.*)
MĀTALI: Mount the chariot, Your Majesty!
(*The king mimes mounting the chariot; all exit.*)

END OF ACT SIX

ACT SEVEN

(*The king enters with Mātali by the skyway, mounted on a chariot.*)

KING: Mātali, though I carried out his command, I feel unworthy of the honors Indra gave me.

MĀTALI (*smiling*): Your Majesty, neither of you seems satisfied.

You belittle the aid you gave Indra
in face of the honors he conferred,
and he, amazed by your heroic acts,
deems his hospitality too slight. (1)

KING: No, not so! When I was taking leave, he honored me beyond my heart's desire and shared his throne with me in the presence of the gods:

Indra gave me a garland of coral flowers
tinged with sandalpowder from his chest,
while he smiled at his son Jayanta,
who stood there barely hiding his envy. (2)

MĀTALI: Don't you deserve whatever you want from Indra?

Indra's heaven of pleasures has twice
been saved by rooting out thorny demons—
your smooth-jointed arrows have now done
what Viṣṇu once did with his lion claws. (3)

KING: Here too Indra's might deserves the praise.

When servants succeed in great tasks,
they act in hope of their master's praise—
would dawn scatter the darkness
if he were not the sun's own charioteer? (4)

MĀTALI: This attitude suits you well!
(*He moves a little distance.*)
Look over there, Your Majesty! See how your own glorious fame has reached the vault of heaven!

Celestial artists are drawing your exploits
on leaves of the wish-granting creeper
with colors of the nymphs' cosmetic paints,
and bards are moved to sing of you in ballads. (5)

KING: Mātali, in my desire to do battle with the demons, I did not notice the path we took to heaven as we climbed through the sky yesterday. Which course of the winds are we traveling?
MĀTALI:

They call this path of the wind Parivaha—
freed from darkness by Viṣṇu's second stride,
it bears the Gaṅgā's three celestial streams
and turns stars in orbit, dividing their rays. (6)

KING: Mātali, this is why my soul, my senses, and my heart feel calm.
(*He looks at the chariot wheels.*)
We've descended to the level of the clouds.
MĀTALI: How do you know?
KING:

Crested cuckoos fly between the spokes,
lightning flashes glint off the horses' coats,
and a fine mist wets your chariot's wheels—
all signs that we go over rain-filled clouds. (7)

MĀTALI: In a moment you'll be back in your own domain, Your Majesty.
KING (*looking down*): Our speeding chariot makes the mortal world appear fantastic. Look!

Mountain peaks emerge as the earth descends,
branches spread up from a sea of leaves,
fine lines become great rivers to behold—
the world seems to hurtle toward me. (8)

MĀTALI: You observe well! (*He looks with great reverence.*) The beauty of earth is sublime.
KING: Mātali, what mountain do I see stretching into the eastern and western seas, rippled with streams of liquid gold, like a gateway of twilight clouds?
MĀTALI: Your Majesty, it is called the "Golden Peak," the mountain of the demigods, a place where austerities are practiced to perfection.

Mārīca, the descendant of Brahmā,
a father of both demons and gods,
lives the life of an ascetic here
in the company of Aditi, his wife. (9)

KING: One must not ignore good fortune! I shall perform the rite of circumambulating the sage.
MĀTALI: An excellent idea!
(*The two mime descending.*)
KING (*smiling*):

The chariot wheels make no sound,
they raise no clouds of dust,
they touch the ground unhindered—
nothing marks the chariot's descent. (10)

MĀTALI: It is because of the extraordinary power that you and Indra both possess.
KING: Mātali, where is Mārīca's hermitage?
MĀTALI (*pointing with his hand*):

Where the sage stands staring at the sun,
as immobile as the trunk of a tree,
his body half-buried in an ant hill,
with a snake skin on his chest,
his throat pricked by a necklace
of withered thorny vines,
wearing a coil of long matted hair
filled with nests of śakunta birds. (11)

KING: I do homage to the sage for his severe austerity.

MĀTALI (*pulling hard on the chariot reins*): Great king, let us enter Mārīca's hermitage, where Aditi nurtures the celestial coral trees.
KING: This tranquil place surpasses heaven. I feel as if I'm bathing in a lake of nectar.
MĀTALI (*stopping the chariot*): Dismount, Your Majesty!
KING (*dismounting*): Mātali, what about you?
MĀTALI: I have stopped the chariot. I'll dismount too.
(*He does so.*)
This way, Your Majesty!
(*He walks around.*)
You can see the grounds of the ascetics' grove ahead.
KING: I am amazed!

> In this forest of wish-fulfilling trees
> ascetics live on only the air they breathe
> and perform their ritual ablutions
> in water colored by golden lotus pollen.
> They sit in trance on jeweled marble slabs
> and stay chaste among celestial nymphs,
> practicing austerities in the place
> that others seek to win by penances. (12)

MĀTALI: Great men always aspire to rare heights!
(*He walks around, calling aloud.*)
O venerable Śākalya, what is the sage Mārīca doing now? What do you say? In response to Aditi's question about the duties of a devoted wife, he is talking in a gathering of great sages' wives.
KING (*listening*): We must wait our turn.
MĀTALI (*looking at the king*): Your Majesty, rest at the foot of this aśoka tree. Meanwhile, I'll look for a chance to announce you to Indra's father.
KING: As you advise . . .
(*He stops.*)
MĀTALI: Your Majesty, I'll attend to this.
(*He exits.*)

KING (*indicating he feels an omen*):

I have no hope for my desire.
Why does my arm throb in vain?
Once good fortune is lost,
it becomes constant pain. (13)

VOICE OFFSTAGE: Don't be so wild! Why is his nature so stubborn?
KING (*listening*): Unruly conduct is out of place here. Whom are they reprimanding?
(*Looking toward the sound, surprised.*)
Who is this child, guarded by two female ascetics? A boy who acts more like a man.

He has dragged this lion cub
from its mother's half-full teat
to play with it, and with his hand
he violently tugs its mane. (14)

(*The boy enters as described, with two female ascetics.*)
BOY: Open your mouth, lion! I want to count your teeth!
FIRST ASCETIC: Nasty boy, why do you torture creatures we love like our children? You're getting too headstrong! The sages gave you the right name when they called you "Sarvadamana, Tamer-of-everything."
KING: Why is my heart drawn to this child, as if he were my own flesh? I don't have a son. That is why I feel tender toward him . . .
SECOND ASCETIC: The lioness will maul you if you don't let go of her cub!
BOY (*smiling*): Oh, I'm scared to death!
(*Pouting.*)
KING:

This child appears to be
the seed of hidden glory,
like a spark of fire
awaiting fuel to burn. (15)

FIRST ASCETIC: Child, let go of the lion cub and I'll give you another toy!
BOY: Where is it? Give it to me!
(*He reaches out his hand.*)
KING: Why does he bear the mark of a king who turns the wheel of empire?

> A hand with fine webs connecting the fingers
> opens as he reaches for the object greedily,
> like a single lotus with faint inner petals
> spread open in the red glow of early dawn. (16)

SECOND ASCETIC: Suvratā, you can't stop him with words! The sage Mārkaṇḍeya's son left a brightly painted clay bird in my hut. Get it for him!
FIRST ASCETIC: I will!
(*She exits.*)
BOY: But until it comes I'll play with this cub.
KING: I am attracted to this pampered boy . . .

> Lucky are fathers whose laps give refuge
> to the muddy limbs of adoring little sons
> when childish smiles show budding teeth
> and jumbled sounds make charming words. (17)

SECOND ASCETIC: Well, he ignores me.
(*She looks back.*)
Is one of the sage's sons here?
(*Looking at the king.*)
Sir, please come here! Make him loosen his grip and let go of the lion cub! He's tormenting it in his cruel child's play.
KING (*approaching the boy, smiling*): Stop! You're a great sage's son!

> When self-control is your duty by birth,
> why do you violate the sanctuary laws
> and ruin the animals' peaceful life,
> like a young black snake in a sandal tree? (18)

SECOND ASCETIC: Sir, he's not a sage's son.

KING: His actions and his looks confirm it. I based my false assumption on his presence in this place.
(*He does what she asked; responding to the boy's touch, he speaks to himself.*)

Even my limbs feel delighted
from the touch of a stranger's son—
the father at whose side he grew
must feel pure joy in his heart. (19)

SECOND ASCETIC (*examining them both*): It's amazing! Amazing!
KING: What is it, madam?
SECOND ASCETIC: This boy looks surprisingly like you. He doesn't even know you, and he's acting naturally.
KING (*fondling the child*): If he's not the son of an ascetic, what lineage does he belong to?
SECOND ASCETIC: The family of Puru.
KING (*to himself*): What? His ancestry is the same as mine . . . so this lady thinks he resembles me. The family vow of Puru's descendants is to spend their last days in the forest.

As world protectors they first choose
palaces filled with sensuous pleasures,
but later, their homes are under trees
and one wife shares the ascetic vows. (20)

(*Aloud.*)
But mortals cannot enter this realm on their own.
SECOND ASCETIC: You're right, sir. His mother is a nymph's child. She gave birth to him here in the hermitage of Mārīca.
KING (*in a stage whisper*): Here is a second ground for hope!
(*Aloud.*)
What famed royal sage claims her as his wife?
SECOND ASCETIC: Who would even think of speaking the name of a man who rejected his lawful wife?
KING (*to himself*): Perhaps this story points to me. What if I ask the name of the boy's mother? No, it is wrong to ask about another man's wife.

FIRST ASCETIC (*returning with a clay bird in her hand*): Look, Sarvadamana, a śakunta! Look! Isn't it lovely?

BOY: Where's my mother?

BOTH ASCETICS: He's tricked by the similarity of names. He wants his mother.

SECOND ASCETIC: Child, she told you to look at the lovely clay śakunta bird.

KING (*to himself*): What? Is his mother's name Śakuntalā? But names can be the same. Even a name is a mirage . . . a false hope to herald despair.

BOY: I like this bird!

(*He picks up the toy.*)

FIRST ASCETIC (*looking frantically*): Oh, I don't see the amulet-box on his wrist!

KING: Don't be alarmed! It broke off while he was tussling with the lion cub.

(*He goes to pick it up.*)

BOTH ASCETICS: Don't touch it! Oh, he's already picked it up!

(*With their hands on their chests, they stare at each other in amazement.*)

KING: Why did you warn me against it?

FIRST ASCETIC: It contains the magical herb called Aparājitā, honored sir. Mārīca gave it to him at his birth ceremony. He said that if it fell to the ground no one but his parents or himself could pick it up.

KING: And if someone else does pick it up?

FIRST ASCETIC: Then it turns into a snake and strikes.

KING: Have you two seen it so transformed?

BOTH ASCETICS: Many times.

KING (*to himself, joyfully*): Why not rejoice in the fulfillment of my heart's desire?

(*He embraces the child.*)

SECOND ASCETIC: Suvratā, come, let's tell Śakuntalā that her penances are over.

(*Both ascetics exit*).

BOY: Let me go! I want my mother!
KING: Son, you will greet your mother with me.
BOY: My father is Duṣyanta, not you!
KING: This contradiction confirms the truth.
(*Śakuntalā enters, wearing the single braid of a woman in mourning.*)
ŚAKUNTALĀ: Even though Sarvadamana's amulet kept its natural form instead of changing into a snake, I can't hope that my destiny will be fulfilled. But maybe what my friend Sānumatī reports is right.
KING (*looking at Śakuntalā*): It is Śakuntalā!

Wearing dusty gray garments,
her face gaunt from penances,
her bare braid hanging down—
she bears with perfect virtue
the trial of long separation
my cruelty forced on her. (21)

ŚAKUNTALĀ (*seeing the king pale with suffering*): He doesn't resemble my noble husband. Whose touch defiles my son when the amulet is protecting him?
BOY (*going to his mother*): Mother, who is this stranger who calls me "son"?
KING: My dear, I see that you recognize me now. Even my cruelty to you is transformed by your grace.
ŚAKUNTALĀ (*to herself*): Heart, be consoled! My cruel fate has finally taken pity on me. It is my noble husband!
KING:

Memory chanced to break my dark delusion
and you stand before me in beauty,
like the moon's wife Rohiṇī
as she rejoins her lord after an eclipse. (22)

ŚAKUNTALĀ: Victory to my noble husband! Vic . . .
(*She stops when the word is half-spoken, her throat choked with tears.*)

KING: Beautiful Śakuntalā,

Even choked by your tears,
the word "victory" is my triumph
on your bare pouting lips,
pale-red flowers of your face. (23)

BOY: Mother, who is he?
ŚAKUNTALĀ: Child, ask the powers of fate!
KING (*falling at Śakuntalā's feet*):

May the pain of my rejection
vanish from your heart;
delusion clouded my weak mind
and darkness obscured good fortune—
a blind man tears off a garland,
fearing the bite of a snake. (24)

ŚAKUNTALĀ: Noble husband, rise! Some crime I had committed in a former life surely came to fruit and made my kind husband indifferent to me.
(*The king rises.*)
But how did my noble husband come to remember this woman who was doomed to pain?
KING: I shall tell you after I have removed the last barb of sorrow.

In my delusion I once ignored
a teardrop burning your lip—
let me dry the tear on your lash
to end the pain of remorse! (25)

(*He does so.*)
ŚAKUNTALĀ (*seeing the signet ring*): My noble husband, this is the ring!
KING: I regained my memory when the ring was recovered.
ŚAKUNTALĀ: When it was lost, I tried in vain to convince my noble husband who I was.

KING: Let the vine take back this flower as a sign of her union with spring.
ŚAKUNTALĀ: I don't trust it. Let my noble husband wear it!
(*Mātali enters.*)
MĀTALI: Good fortune! This meeting with your lawful wife and the sight of your son's face are reasons to rejoice.
KING: The sweet fruit of my desire! Mātali, didn't Indra know about all this?
MĀTALI: What is unknown to the gods? Come, Your Majesty! The sage Mārīca grants you an audience.
KING: Śakuntalā, hold our son's hand! We shall go to see Mārīca together.
ŚAKUNTALĀ: I feel shy about appearing before my elders in my husband's company.
KING: But it is customary at a joyous time like this. Come! Come!
(*They all walk around. Then Mārīca enters with Aditi; they sit.*)
MĀRĪCA (*looking at the king*):

> Aditi, this is king Duṣyanta,
> who leads Indra's armies in battle;
> his bow lets your son's thunderbolt
> lie ready with its tip unblunted. (26)

ADITI: He bears himself with dignity.
MĀTALI: Your Majesty, the parents of the gods look at you with affection reserved for a son. Approach them!
KING: Mātali, the sages so describe this pair:

> Source of the sun's twelve potent forms,
> parents of Indra, who rules the triple world,
> birthplace of Viṣṇu's primordial form,
> sired by Brahmā's sons, Marīci and Dakṣa. (27)

MĀTALI: Correct!
KING (*bowing*): Indra's servant, Duṣyanta, bows to you both.
MĀRĪCA: My son, live long and protect the earth!
ADITI: My son, be an invincible warrior!

ŚAKUNTALĀ: I worship at your feet with my son.
MĀRĪCA:

Child, with a husband like Indra
and a son like his son Jayanta,
you need no other blessing.
Be like Indra's wife Paulomī! (28)

ADITI: Child, may your husband honor you and may your child live long to give both families joy! Be seated!
(*All sit near Mārīca.*)
MĀRĪCA (*pointing to each one*):

By the turn of fortune,
virtuous Śakuntalā, her noble son,
and the king are reunited—
faith and wealth with order. (29)

KING: Sir, first came the success of my hopes, then the sight of you. Your kindness is unparalleled.

First flowers appear, then fruits,
first clouds rise, then rain falls,
but here the chain of events is reversed—
first came success, then your blessing. (30)

MĀTALI: This is the way the creator gods give blessings.
KING: Sir, I married your charge by secret marriage rites. When her relatives brought her to me after some time, my memory failed and I sinned against the sage Kaṇva, your kinsman. When I saw the ring, I remembered that I had married his daughter. This is all so strange!

Like one who doubts the existence
of an elephant who walks in front of him
but feels convinced by seeing footprints,
my mind has taken strange turns. (31)

MĀRĪCA: My son, you need not take the blame. Even your delusion has another cause. Listen!
KING: I am attentive.

MĀRĪCA: When Menakā took her bewildered daughter from the steps of the nymphs' shrine and brought her to my wife, I knew through meditation that you had rejected this girl as your lawful wife because of Durvāsas' curse, and that the curse would end when you saw the ring.
KING (*sighing*): So I am freed of blame.
ŚAKUNTALĀ (*to herself*): And I am happy to learn that I wasn't rejected by my husband without cause. But I don't remember being cursed. Maybe the empty heart of love's separation made me deaf to the curse . . . my friends did warn me to show the ring to my husband . . .
MĀRĪCA: My child, I have told you the truth. Don't be angry with your husband!

You were rejected when the curse
that clouded memory made him cruel,
but now darkness is lifted
and your power is restored—
a shadow has no shape
in a badly tarnished mirror,
but when the surface is clean
it can easily be seen. (32)

KING: Sir, here is the glory of my family!
(*He takes the child by the hand.*)
MĀRĪCA: Know that he is destined to turn the wheel of your empire!

His chariot will smoothly cross
the ocean's rough waves
and as a mighty warrior
he will conquer the seven continents.
Here he is called Sarvadamana,
Tamer-of-everything;
later when his burden is the world,
men will call him Bharata, Sustainer. (33)

KING: Since you performed his birth ceremonies, we can hope for all this.

ADITI: Sir, let Kaṇva be told that his daughter's hopes have been fulfilled. Menakā, who loves her daughter, is here in attendance.

ŚAKUNTALĀ (*to herself*): The lady expresses my own desire.

MĀRĪCA: He knows everything already through the power of his austerity.

KING: This is why the sage was not angry at me.

MĀRĪCA: Still, I want to hear his response to this joyful reunion. Who is there?

DISCIPLE (*entering*): Sir, it is I.

MĀRĪCA: Gālava, fly through the sky and report the joyous reunion to Kaṇva in my own words: "The curse is ended. Śakuntalā and her son are embraced by Duṣyanta now that his memory is restored."

DISCIPLE: As you command, sir!

(*He exits.*)

MĀRĪCA: My son, mount your friend Indra's chariot with your wife and son and return to your royal capital!

KING: As you command, sir!

MĀRĪCA: My son, what other joy can I give you?

KING: There is no greater joy, but if you will:

> May the king serve nature's good!
> May priests honor the goddess of speech!
> And may Śiva's dazzling power
> destroy my cycle of rebirths! (34)

(*All exit.*)

END OF ACT SEVEN AND OF THE PLAY
ŚAKUNTALĀ AND THE RING OF RECOLLECTION

Urvaśī Won by Valor

TRANSLATED BY DAVID GITOMER

CHARACTERS

Players in the prologue:
DIRECTOR: Director of the players and manager of the theater (*sūtradhāra*).
ASSISTANT: An actor named Māriṣa (*pāripārśvaka).*

Principal roles:
KING: Purūravas, the hero (*nāyaka*); ruler of Pratiṣṭhāna; battle companion of Indra; a royal sage of the lunar dynasty.
URVAŚĪ: The heroine (*nāyikā*); a nymph; celestial dancer and courtesan; born from the thigh of the sage Nārāyaṇa.
BUFFOON: Māṇavaka ("little man"); the king's brahman companion and confidant.
CITRALEKHĀ: A nymph; Urvaśī's friend and go-between.

Members of the royal household and the king's retinue:
QUEEN: Auśīnarī, chief queen and lawful head wife of King Purūravas; daughter of the king of Banaras; childless.
NIPUṆIKĀ: "The clever one"; personal maid to the queen.
CHAMBERLAIN: Lātavya; chief officer of the king's household; superintendent of the women's quarters (*kañcukī*).
CHARIOTEER: Driver of the king's chariot (*sūta*).
HUNTRESS: A tribal woman from the mountains (*kirātī*).
BOW-BEARER: A young female of Greco-Bactrian origin, em-

ployed to carry and care for the king's bow, arrow, hand-guard, etc. (*yavanī*, an "Ionian").

Various serving women.

Celestials:

RAMBHĀ, MENAKĀ, SAHAJANYĀ: Nymph companions of Urvaśī.

CITRARATHA: King of gandharvas (celestial musicians).
NĀRADA: A sage, sent as emissary from Indra's court.

Pupils of Bharata, creator of drama:
PALLAVA: Prakrit-speaking pupil.
GĀLAVA: Sanskrit-speaking pupil.

Inhabitants of Cyavana's hermitage:
ASCETIC WOMAN: Satyavatī, to whom Urvaśī has entrusted the raising of her son.
PRINCE ĀYUS: Son of Purūravas and Urvaśī.

Offstage voices:
TWO PANEGYRIST BARDS (*vaitālikau*)
MESSENGER OF THE GODS: Summoning Urvaśī to perform in heaven, Act Two.
A SINGER OFFSTAGE: In Act Four, the voice that sings the Māhārāṣṭrī Prakrit *anyokti* verses.
OMNISCIENT SAGE: Offering the gem of reunion to Purūravas, Act Four.
FEMALE SERVANT: Carrying the gem when the vulture steals it, Act Five.

Act One takes place on Golden Peak, the mountain of the demigods in the Himālayas, and in the sky nearby. Act Two is in the palace garden in Pratiṣṭhāna, at the confluence of the rivers Gaṅgā and Yamunā, and Act Three is on the roof of the palace at nightfall. Act Four takes place in the mountain grove of magic herb fragrances. The scene returns to the palace for Act Five. It is early spring in the first three acts. The season in Act Four is the beginning of the monsoon. Āyus has attained youth by Act Five, so it must take place about thirteen years after Act Three. One can suppose that Act Five occurs not long after Act Four.

ACT ONE

In scripture sages call him the cosmic person,
pervading, transcending earth and heaven,
the only lord confined by no realm;
ascetics seek liberation through him within,
where he is won by discipline and firm devotion—
may Śiva, immovable god, bring us final bliss! (1)

PROLOGUE

DIRECTOR (*looking backstage*): Māriṣa, come here, right away!
ASSISTANT (*entering*): Here I am, sir.
DIRECTOR: Māriṣa, the audience has often seen the plays of the old poets. Today I shall stage a truly new drama called *Urvaśī Won by Valor.* Tell the cast to be careful in their parts.
ASSISTANT: As you order, sir.
(*He exits.*)
DIRECTOR: Now, as for you worthy people, I make this request:

Out of kindness toward your servants
or respect for the good spirit embodied
in the foundation of the playhouse,
please listen with hearts attentive
to this work of Kālidāsa. (2)

VOICES OFFSTAGE: Help! Help!
DIRECTOR (*listening to a sound in the distance*): Ah, what's this?

No sooner have I made my request to you than I hear a sound in the sky like female ospreys in distress.
(*Thinking anxiously.*)

> A celestial courtesan, the issue of a sage's thigh,
> returning from service to Indra, lord of Kailāsa,
> has been abducted on the way by the gods' demon foes;
> now her company of nymphs is crying out pitifully. (3)

(*He exits; the prologue ends. Then a group of nymphs enters.*)

NYMPHS: Help! Help! Is there anyone who is on the side of the gods, anyone who knows his way in the sky?
(*Throwing aside the rear curtain, the king enters, mounted on a chariot, with his charioteer.*)
KING: Cease your crying! I am Purūravas, returning from my worship of the sun. Why are you calling for help?
RAMBHĀ: Because of a demon's scandalous crime.
KING: But how is that an offense to you?
MENAKĀ: Listen, great king. Our beloved Urvaśī is the delicate weapon Indra uses when he fears the force of some saint's austerities; she is heaven's ornament, eclipsing the goddess Śrī in beauty. While we were returning from Kubera's palace, some demon seized her and her friend Citralekhā and carried them off.
KING: Do you know in which direction the villain went?
SAHAJANYĀ: Northeast.
KING: Then you need not worry. I shall try to recover your friends.
NYMPHS: An act worthy of one born in the dynasty of the moon.
KING: But where will you wait for me?
NYMPHS: On Golden Peak, the mountain nearby.
KING: Charioteer, urge the horses on for a quick journey to the northeast quarter of the sky.
CHARIOTEER: As you command, sir.
(*He does this.*)

KING (*miming the effects of chariot speed*): Excellent! Excellent! With the speed of this chariot I could overtake Viṣṇu's mount Garuḍa even if he set out before me. How much easier it will be to catch a demon who has wronged generous Indra!

Dense clouds before me turn to powder
like dust on my chariot's path.
The spinning of the wheel seems to generate
a second set of spokes within spokes.
The wind's speed makes the horse's plume
motionless as if painted in a picture,
and my banner stands rigid on its flagstaff,
flying without crease from end to end. (4)

(*The king and the charioteer exit.*)
RAMBHĀ: Friends, let's go over to the spot we decided on.
(*They mime alighting on a mountain peak.*)
RAMBHĀ: Will the king remove the arrow from our hearts?
MENAKĀ: There's no doubt of it. Doesn't great Indra when he's threatened with battle bring Purūravas from earth with all honor, and place him in command of the army of victory?
RAMBHĀ: May he be victorious in every way!
SAHAJANYĀ (*after a moment*): Friends, take heart. The king's chariot Somadatta is appearing, its banner blazoned with a leaping deer. I know he hasn't failed in his mission.
(*All gaze upward. Then the king enters, with the charioteer and Urvaśī, her eyes closed in fear, clinging to Citralekhā.*)
CITRALEKHĀ: Take heart, dear friend. Take heart.
KING: Take heart, beauty. Take heart.

Timid girl, the fear the demon raised is gone;
Indra's might is the protector of the three worlds—
open your long eyes, as the lotus pond
opens its large blue flowers at dawn. (5)

CITRALEKHĀ: Her breathing is the only sign that she's alive. Even now she hasn't regained consciousness.
KING: She is terribly frightened.

Bound to life by a tendril stem,
her heart will not stop trembling—
see, it is shown by the sandal paste
smeared between her heaving breasts. (6)

CITRALEKHĀ: Friend, compose yourself. You're not behaving as a nymph should.
(*Urvaśī revives.*)
KING: Ah, your friend is returning to her natural state.

Like the night goddess released by darkness
when the hare-marked moon appears,
like the flame of a nocturnal fire
as it cuts through a screen of smoke,
this slender beauty seems almost freed
from the swoon that held her mind,
like the river Gaṅgā clearing again
after sand spills from her banks. (7)

CITRALEKHĀ: Dear friend, you can rest at ease. The depraved demons who defied the gods have been defeated.
URVAŚĪ (*opening her eyes*): By great Indra who sees all things with his supernatural power?
CITRALEKHĀ: Not by great Indra. By a royal sage whose splendor is as thrilling as great Indra's.
URVAŚĪ (*gazing at the king; to herself*): Then the demons have really done me a favor.
KING (*observing Urvaśī, who has returned to her natural state; to himself*): I understand why all the nymphs sent to seduce Sage Nārāyaṇa were shamed when they saw what he could produce from his thigh. But how can she be the creation of an ascetic?

In creating her, surely the luster-giving
moon was the progenitor,
or Love himself, who has only one mood,
the erotic, or flowering spring—

how could the ancient sage,
cold and dry from studying scripture,
his mind withdrawn from worldly things,
create this enchanting form? (8)

URVAŚĪ: Where could our friends be?
CITRALEKHĀ: The great king who saved us will know.
KING (*looking at Urvaśī*): They are broken-hearted.

By chance you were on the path of a man
whose eyes you fulfilled only once, beauty.
If parted from you even he would yearn;
how much more your long and loving friends? (9)

URVAŚĪ (*turns to Citralekhā and says aside*): How noble his words are! But is it any wonder that the nectar of soma comes from the moon?
(*Aloud to the king.*)
Yes, you understand why my heart hurries to see them . . .
KING (*gesturing*):

Slender beauty, those friends on
Golden Peak mountain see your face,
calm and shining once again,
like the moon freed from an eclipse. (10)

URVAŚĪ (*looking longingly at the king*): . . . sharing my pain, with eyes that seem to drink me in.
CITRALEKHĀ (*with a knowing intonation in her voice*): Oh, who?
URVAŚĪ: Our friends.
RAMBHĀ (*joyfully*): Here he is! Bringing Urvaśī and Citralekhā with him, the royal sage looks like the moon passing through the twin-starred constellation of spring.
MENAKĀ: Then both our desires have come true: our friend has been brought back to us and the king is uninjured.
SAHAJANYĀ: And no mean feat—demons are difficult to vanquish!
KING: Charioteer, here is the mountain peak. Bring the chariot down.

CHARIOTEER: As you command, sir.
(*He does this.*)
KING (*miming a jolt; to himself*): So! This rough landing has yielded a fine reward for me!

From the chariot's jolt my shoulder brushed
the shoulder of this nymph with hips like bows;
the touch of our bodies made my hair stand on end
as if the god of love had sprouted within me. (11)

URVAŚĪ (*bashfully*): Friend, move aside a little.
CITRALEKHĀ (*smiling*): I can't.
RAMBHĀ: Come, let's thank the king.
(*All draw near.*)
KING: Driver, stop the chariot!

Let this eager beauty
embrace her waiting friends
as resplendent spring
touches every waiting creeper. (12)

(*The charioteer does this.*)
NYMPHS: Congratulations on your victory, great king!
KING: And to you on this reunion with your friends.
URVAŚĪ (*getting down from the chariot, her hand supported by Citralekhā's*): Friends, embrace me tightly. I had no hope of ever seeing you again.
(*All rush to embrace her.*)
RAMBHĀ: May you protect the earth for a hundred aeons, great king!
CHARIOTEER: Sir, from the east comes the sound of chariots approaching with furious speed.

Now someone from the sky
wearing blazing golden armbands
descends on the mountain peak
like a cloud streaked with lightning. (13)

NYMPHS: Oh, it's Citraratha!
(*Then Citraratha enters.*)

CITRARATHA (*standing before the king*): Congratulations on the superiority of your valor, capable of aiding even great Indra.
KING: Greetings, king of the gandharvas!
(*Getting down from the chariot.*)
Welcome, dear friend.
(*They clasp one another's hands.*)
CITRARATHA: Friend, when Indra, lord of a hundred sacrifices, heard from Nārada that Urvaśī had been carried off by the demon, he entrusted the gandharva army with her recovery. Then, on the way, we heard the story of your victory from celestial singers and came here to see you. Please bring this lady and attend generous Indra with us. That great deed you undertook was a pleasing service to him.

> Long ago Urvaśī was first presented
> to storm-god Indra by Nārāyaṇa,
> and now by you who rescued her,
> breaking the demon's mighty grip. (14)

KING: You should not say that.

> It is by Indra's might alone
> that his allies vanquish enemies—
> when the lion roars in his mountain cave
> even the echo will stun elephants. (15)

CITRARATHA: That's fitting: modesty is the ornament of valor.
KING: This is not the time for me to see the lord of a hundred sacrifices. You yourself convey her to his presence.
CITRARATHA: As you wish, sir. This way, ladies.
(*The nymphs start to leave.*)
URVAŚĪ (*aside*): Citralekhā, friend, though he saved me, I'm unable to bid farewell to the king. You must be my mouth!
CITRALEKHĀ (*approaching the king*): Great king, Urvaśī wishes to bid you farewell in order to carry your fame as her dear companion to great Indra's realm.
KING: Farewell, until we meet again.

(*All the nymphs except Urvaśī and Citralekhā mime flying into the sky with the gandharvas.*)
URVAŚĪ (*miming the obstruction of her flight*): Oh, my pearl necklace is caught on the branch of a creeper.
(*She turns around.*)
Citralekhā, set it free, won't you?
CITRALEKHĀ (*smiling*): It is certainly stuck fast. This will be hard for me to untangle, but I'll do what I can!
URVAŚĪ: I'll hold you to your word!
(*Citralekhā mimes untangling it.*)
KING (*to himself*):

> Creeper, you favor me by contriving
> a moment's hindrance to her leaving;
> again I see her, turning back,
> casting sidelong glances toward me. (16)

CHARIOTEER: Sir,

> The demons who wronged lord Indra were hurled
> to the sea by the wind-god's magic in your weapon;
> now that swift arrow returns to your quiver
> like a great deadly serpent entering its hole. (17)

KING: Then bring the chariot around and I'll mount.
(*The charioteer does this. The king mimes mounting the chariot. Urvaśī exits, gazing down at the king with a sigh, with her friend and Citraratha.*)
KING (*looking in the direction Urvaśī has gone*): What my desire craves is impossible.

> Flying into the sky her father's footstep conquered,
> this divine nymph violently tears my mind
> from my body, like a wild goose
> tearing a thread from a lotus stalk's broken tip. (18)

(*All exit.*)

END OF ACT ONE

ACT TWO

(*The buffoon enters.*)

BUFFOON: Oh Lord! I'm bursting with the king's secret like a brahman stuffed with fabulous food at a feast. I can't keep my tongue in my head when people crowd around. So until my friend the king finishes hearing the petitioners, I'll wait outside the downstairs hall where hardly anybody ever comes.
(*He makes a round of the stage, then stands.*)
NIPUṆIKĀ (*entering*): The queen, daughter of the king of Banaras, has ordered me: "Nipuṇikā, ever since my husband returned from worshiping the sun, he seems desolate. You're a clever girl. Find out from his good friend Māṇavaka the cause of his distraction." Now how can I deceive this poor excuse for a brahman? But then, he keeps a secret about as long as dewdrops stay on grass in the desert. I'll find out where he is.
(*She makes a round of the stage, looking.*)
There's the little man, standing still and stupid as a monkey in a painting! I wonder why? I'll go up to him.
(*Approaching him.*)
Oh sir, I greet you.
BUFFOON: Be well, lady.
(*To himself.*)
When this mischievous servant girl comes around, the king's secret starts banging on my heart, trying to break out.
(*Aloud.*)
Aren't you supposed to be helping out with the music lessons, you clever girl? Why have you wandered over here?
NIPUṆIKĀ: To see you, sir, at the queen's bidding.

BUFFOON: What does my lady command?
NIPUṆIKĀ: The queen says, "The little man is always partial to me; he never neglects me when I suffer undeserved agonies."
BUFFOON: Nipuṇikā, did my friend the king behave badly toward the queen?
NIPUṆIKĀ: The master has addressed the queen by the name of some woman he longs for—that's why.
BUFFOON (*to himself*): What! The king himself broke the secret! Why should I go on torturing myself to keep it?
(*Aloud.*)
Did he address the lady as Urvaśī? The king's taken leave of his senses since he saw her. He's turned his back on ordinary pleasures, which bothers me as much as the queen.
NIPUṆIKĀ (*to herself*): I've forced my way into the fortress of the master's secret!
(*Aloud.*)
Then what am I to tell the queen, sir?
BUFFOON: Nipuṇikā, tell the queen that first I'll try to turn my friend away from this mirage, then I'll report the results to her in person.
NIPUṆIKĀ, As you command, sir.
(*She exits.*)
VOICE OF A BARD OFFSTAGE: Victory, divine one!

> As the sun beats back the forces of night
> beyond the last planet in his kingdom,
> you exert your authority untiringly
> to banish darkness from our hearts;
> as the lord of celestial lights
> rests briefly at the zenith of his arc,
> in the sixth watch of the royal day
> you do what gives you pleasure. (1)

BUFFOON (*listening to the sound in the distance*): The king's finished hearing the petitioners and is coming this way. I'll attend him.

(He exits; the prelude ends. Then the king enters, yearning, with the buffoon.)

KING:

After one glimpse
the beautiful nymph
abandoned heaven
and entered my heart—
the god of love
had pierced it first
with an arrow
perfectly aimed. (2)

BUFFOON (*to himself*): No wonder the poor daughter of the king of Banaras is miserable!

KING: My secret has been safe with you, hasn't it?

BUFFOON (*in despair, to himself*): I've been deceived by the servant girl. Otherwise, he'd never ask me about it!

KING: Why are you silent?

BUFFOON: I've been holding my tongue so well I can't even answer you.

KING: Very good. But where should I entertain myself now?

BUFFOON: Let's go to the kitchen!

KING: Why there?

BUFFOON: We'll watch them take what's been brought from the market and make it into all the five kinds of food—the kind you have to chew, the kind you don't have to chew, the kind you can lick, the kind you can suck, and the kind you can slurp. That's the stuff to make you forget your yearning!

KING: You'll be happy in the kitchen, surrounded by what you want. But how am I to enjoy myself when my desire is impossible to attain?

BUFFOON: This lady Urvaśī actually saw you in the flesh, didn't she?

KING: So?

BUFFOON: Well, then, I wouldn't say she's "impossible" to attain.

KING: You overestimate my charms.
BUFFOON: You've gotten me curious. Is this Urvaśī as perfect in beauty as I am in ugliness?
KING: Little man, consider it impossible to describe her in every detail. But listen to this summary.
BUFFOON: I'm listening.
KING:

> She is the ornament of her ornaments,
> the crowning jewel of her jeweled display.
> Friend, even the standard of perfection
> finds its ideal in her form. (3)

BUFFOON: So that's why you've taken up a vow like the crested cuckoo's. Since you crave only nectar from heaven, you refuse all other drinks.
KING: Friend, for the mind that is yearning there is no refuge but solitude. Lead the way to the pleasure grove.
BUFFOON (*to himself*): What kind of remedy is that?
(*Aloud.*)
This way, sir.
(*He makes a round of the stage.*)
See—as if the pleasure grove were urging him on, the southern wind rises to greet his guest.
KING (*looking*): Then this hospitable breeze is aptly named.

> Drenching the tender spring creeper
> with potent drops of nectar
> while swaying the regal jasmine
> in courtly tremulous dance,
> this breeze blows passion and propriety,
> so he seems like a lover to me. (4)

BUFFOON: And your two attachments are like his.
(*He makes a round of the stage.*)
Here's the gate to the pleasure grove. Come in, sir.
KING: After you.
(*The two enter the grove.*)

KING (*gazing before him*): Friend, I wasn't thinking right when I suggested the pleasure grove as a remedy for my distress.

I want to rush into the garden
to relieve the fiery pain,
but for one already lost in a flood
this is swimming against the stream. (5)

BUFFOON: What do you mean?
KING:

First Love's five arrows destroyed my mind
when I could not turn it from this wild craving;
now winds from the sandal hills torment me further
as they fragrantly waft through the mango grove,
stripping withered leaves, and revealing tender buds. (6)

BUFFOON: Oh, stop wailing. Soon Love himself will help you achieve your desire.
KING: I must take to heart the words of a brahman like you!
(*They make a round of the stage.*)
BUFFOON: Sir, don't you see spring becoming incarnate in the beauty of the pleasure grove?
KING: Yes, I see it in every tree.

Here is the amaranth, dark along the sides
and pink as a woman's nail at the tip;
there is the young aśoka in deepest crimson
about to burst forth into bloom;
on the mango a new blossom is covered
with gray-brown pollen dust barely formed—
between the infant bud and youth's bloom
stands the goddess of spring in splendor. (7)

BUFFOON: Here's a bower of pearl-white creepers. It seems to welcome you with a shower of blossoms jostled loose by bees butting against them. And here's a jeweled marble bench underneath. Why don't you sit down?
KING: As you like.

(*They sit.*)

BUFFOON: Now you're comfortable. You can entice your eyes with these delicate creepers and drive away your longing for Urvaśī.

KING (*sighing*):

> Friend, though the creepers of the grove
> are adorned with blossoms and bent in modesty,
> they cannot hold my eyes for long:
> I've been spoiled gazing at her beauty. (8)

Think of a way I can win my desire.

BUFFOON: I think I'll be as much help to you with Urvaśī as Indra's thunderbolt was to him when he went after Ahalyā—and you remember how badly that affair turned out! If you think I can help you, you're as unhinged as Indra.

KING: My great friendship makes me think you can manage this.

BUFFOON: Well, then, let me think. But don't break my concentration with your wailing again!

(*He mimes thinking.*)

KING (*indicating he feels an omen; to himself*):

> Her full-moon face should prove hard to win,
> but Love has assisted with this omen, I think—
> when one's mind suddenly grows calm without cause,
> he all but finds the goal of his desire. (9)

(*He stands up, expectant with hope. Then Urvaśī and Citralekhā enter, by the skyway.*)

CITRALEKHĀ: Friend, you haven't told me where we're going and why.

URVAŚĪ: How can you ask me that now, after you made such fun of me on Golden Peak mountain when my necklace got caught and I couldn't get off the ground?

CITRALEKHĀ: Are you on your way to see the royal sage Purūravas?

URVAŚĪ: What I'm set on is shameless.

CITRALEKHĀ: But who was sent as your go-between?

URVAŚĪ: My heart.
CITRALEKHĀ: Then there's nothing more I can say against it.
URVAŚĪ: But you must show me a path where I won't meet any obstacle.
CITRALEKHĀ: Friend, don't worry. Hasn't the gods' preceptor taught us how to tie our hair in that magic knot called Aparājita so demons will be powerless against us?
URVAŚĪ: I remember precisely how to do it.
(*They descend to the path of the demigods.*)
CITRALEKHĀ: We've arrived at the royal sage's palace, the crown of Prayāga. It seems to be admiring itself in the sacred waters where the river goddesses Yamunā and Gaṅgā meet.
URVAŚĪ (*looking*): You might say it looks like a bit of heaven brought to earth.
(*After pondering.*)
Friend, where could he be—the king who shows compassion toward creatures in distress?
CITRALEKHĀ: This pleasure grove is like a spot in Indra's paradise garden. We'll learn where he is by coming down here.
(*They alight.*)
CITRALEKHĀ (*seeing the king; excitedly*): Friend, there he is, like the newly risen moon expecting the momentary arrival of his bride, the moonlight.
URVAŚĪ (*looking*): The great king looks even more handsome to me now than when I first saw him.
CITRALEKHĀ: That's only natural. Come! Let's move closer to him!
URVAŚĪ: I'll use the magic to make myself invisible so I can stand close to him and listen to what he's saying. He's over there in a secluded spot talking about something with a friend.
CITRALEKHĀ: As you like.
(*They move nearer the king and buffoon.*)
BUFFOON: Well, I've figured out a way to arrange a meeting with your beloved, since she's so hard-to-get.
(*The king remains silent.*)

URVAŚĪ: Who is this woman the king desires—who thinks so much of herself!

CITRALEKHĀ: Why do you act like a mere human?

URVAŚĪ: Suddenly I'm afraid to use my supernatural powers to find out.

BUFFOON: I'm telling you I've figured out a way to meet her.

KING: Then tell me.

BUFFOON: Fall asleep, sir—you'll meet her in a dream. Or draw a likeness of the lady Urvaśī that you can sit and look at.

URVAŚĪ (*excitedly*): Oh my faint heart, let his words revive you!

KING: Neither will succeed.

How can I fall asleep
to dream the dream which joins us?
The god of love never ceases
piercing my heart with his shafts,
and before I've captured
her fair face in a drawing,
surely my eyes, friend,
will be blind with tears. (10)

CITRALEKHĀ: Did you hear?

URVAŚĪ: I heard, but it wasn't enough for my heart.

BUFFOON: That's all I can think of!

KING (*sighing*):

She does not know the sharp, ceaseless pain in my heart,
or perhaps she knows my love by magic and scorns me;
since Love gives me only barren desires to taste,
let him end the torment of my life, and be satisfied. (11)

CITRALEKHĀ: Did you hear?

URVAŚĪ: Oh no, how awful he thinks I am! But I can't appear before him and reply to his verse with another. Instead I'll use magic to write a letter on birchbark and send it to him.

CITRALEKHĀ: I approve.

(*Urvaśī mimes writing and tossing the letter.*)

BUFFOON (*seeing it*): Aagh! Aagh! What's this? Something

that looks like the castoff skin of a snake has fallen right in front of us!
KING (*considering it*): It's a letter written on birchbark.
BUFFOON: Could it be that the invisible Urvaśī heard your wailing and sent this writing to show that her passion's just as strong as yours?
KING: There is nothing our desires cannot imagine.
(*He takes the letter and reads it to himself; excitedly*)
Friend, your guess was a happy one!
BUFFOON: Sir, I want to hear what's written there.
CITRALEKHĀ: Excellent, little man! You're quite the sophisticate!
KING: Listen.
(*He reads.*)

If, as you imagine,
my lord,
my heart can't feel
anguished passion,
why do fair breezes
of paradise grove burn
as I toss on my bed
of crushed coral blossoms? (12)

URVAŚĪ: Oh, what will he answer?
CITRALEKHĀ: Didn't he answer when the hair on his arms sprang up like the down on a lotus stalk?
BUFFOON: Thank God! You've been revived, just like me when I'm famished and a feast offering comes my way.
KING: Revived? Why do you merely say "revived?"

The verse my love inscribed on the bark
declares delicate intent,
betrays passion strong as mine—
friend, it's as if we'd really met,
my wondering gaze
with her intoxicating eyes. (13)

URVAŚĪ: Now I know we share love equally.

KING: Friend, the sweat from my fingers might smudge this writing from my love's own hand. Please keep it safe in your possession.

BUFFOON (*taking it*): After the lady Urvaśī has shown you your desires in blossom, will she now cheat you of the fruit?

URVAŚĪ: Friend, until I make my timid heart strong enough, you must appear before the king and say what I would say.

CITRALEKHĀ: I will.

(*She removes the veil of invisibility and approaches the king.*)

Victory! Victory, great king!

KING (*excitedly*): Welcome, Citralekhā. Fair one,

> You don't delight me this way,
> separated from your friend,
> like Yamunā river without the Gaṅgā
> if first one's seen their confluence. (14)

CITRALEKHĀ: But don't we see the row of rain clouds first, then the streak of lightning?

BUFFOON (*turning to the king and speaking aside*): What? She isn't Urvaśī—only her friend?

CITRALEKHĀ: Urvaśī bows before the king and makes a request.

KING: What does she command?

CITRALEKHĀ: She says, "The great king was my refuge in the crisis with the demons. Now afflicted by Love, who attacked me at the sight of you, I'm more in need of your compassion."

KING: Fair one,

> You say she is lovesick but don't you see
> the pain Purūravas endures for her sake;
> love's affliction is shared by us both—
> two burning hot brands ready to be fused. (15)

CITRALEKHĀ (*approaching Urvaśī*): Friend, come. Since Love is more pitiless to your beloved than to you, I've become his go-between.

URVAŚĪ (*removing the veil of invisibility*): How quickly you abandon me!
CITRALEKHĀ (*smiling*): In a moment we'll see who's abandoning whom. Meanwhile, pay your respects.
URVAŚĪ (*bashfully*): Victory! Victory, great king!
KING: Beauty,

When you proclaim "victory"
the glory that is Indra's
now comes to me
along with you, his servant. (16)

(*Taking her hand, he seats her.*)
BUFFOON: Shouldn't you also pay your respects to the king's dear brahman friend?
(*Urvaśī bows, smiling.*)
BUFFOON: Be well, lady.
MESSENGER OF THE GODS (*offstage*): Citralekhā, hasten Urvaśī to heaven.

Sage Bharata has commanded
that you nymphs
give a performance
based on the eight dramatic moods,
for today Indra, lord of the winds,
with his friends the guardian gods,
is of a mind to see
your graceful gesture language. (17)

(*All listen. Urvaśī mimes dejection.*)
CITRALEKHĀ: You heard the words of the gods' messenger. You must ask the king's permission to leave.
URVAŚĪ: I cannot find the words.
CITRALEKHĀ: Great king, she is subject to another's will. With your permission, she doesn't want to offend the gods.
KING (*choosing his words with difficulty*): I do not wish to obstruct a command of lord Indra. But please remember . . . this person.

(*Urvaśī, miming the pain of separation, exits with her friend.*)
KING (*sighing*): Friend, my eyes seem useless now.
BUFFOON (*wanting to show him the letter*): But you can . . .
(*He breaks off in the middle of the speech; to himself.*)
Oh no! Oh no! I was so amazed at the sight of Urvaśī I didn't notice I'd carelessly let the birchbark letter drop out of my hand!
KING: What were you going to say?
BUFFOON: Uh, don't get depressed. Urvaśī's completely stuck on you. She can't let go of a passion that's gone so far.
KING: That's what I'm hoping, even at her departure.

> She is not the mistress of her body
> but only of the heart she gave to me—
> this trust was signed in sighs betrayed
> by the trembling rise and fall of her breast. (18)

BUFFOON (*to himself*): My heart's quaking because now he's sure to ask for the birchbark letter!
KING: With what shall I distract my eyes now?
(*Remembering.*)
Ah, bring me the birchbark letter!
BUFFOON (*miming dejection*): Oh dear, it's not anywhere to be seen. It's disappeared along with Urvaśī.
KING: An idiot like you is always careless. Well, look for it, fool!
BUFFOON (*getting up*): It should be someplace around here . . . or here . . .
(*He mimes searching for it. Then the queen, daughter of the king of Banaras, enters with her retinue.*)
QUEEN: Nipuṇikā, you clever girl, did you tell me the truth when you said you saw my husband enter this bower of creepers with his companion Māṇavaka?
NIPUṆIKĀ: Have my reports ever proven false, mistress?
QUEEN: Well then, I'll hide in the creepers and listen to find out whether you reported his private conversations correctly.
NIPUṆIKĀ: As you like, mistress.
QUEEN (*making a round of the stage*): Nipuṇikā, what's this?

The southern wind has blown some old rag-like thing right in front of us.

NIPUṆIKĀ (*considering it*): Mistress, it's a birchbark letter. The writing can be made out as it turns over in the wind. Oh dear, it's caught on the edge of your toe-ring. Let's see. Shall I read it?

QUEEN: First read it to yourself. Then I shall listen, if it's fit for my ears.

NIPUṆIKĀ (*doing so*): It looks like the same scandal I was telling you about. My guess is it's a poem from Urvaśī to the master. And that it came into our hands through the little man's carelessness.

QUEEN: Well then, I must certainly learn its contents!

(*Nipuṇikā reads the verse previously read by the king.*)

QUEEN: With this as my offering, I'll see the nymph's lover!

(*Accompanied by her retinue, she makes a round of the stage, arriving at the bower of creepers.*)

BUFFOON: Friend! What's that I see fluttering in the breeze on the toy mountain next to the pleasure grove?

KING (*rising*). I revere you, southern breeze, friend of spring.

> Carry away the perfume of pollen from blossoming
> creepers that spring has gathered—
> what will you do with a stolen letter
> written by my love's own tender hand?
> Since you loved the beautiful monkey Añjanā,
> you should know how a man pained by desire
> is sustained by mementos that divert the mind. (19)

NIPUṆIKĀ: Mistress, it's this very same birchbark letter they're searching for.

QUEEN: I see that.

BUFFOON: I've been tricked! It was a peacock's tail feather with the brownish-red color of a faded kesara flower.

KING: I am slain!

QUEEN (*approaching*): Husband, there is no need to be agitated. Here is the birchbark letter.

KING (*flustered*): Oh, it's the queen! Welcome, my queen!

BUFFOON (*turns to the king and says as an aside*): Right now, it's more like "ill-come."
KING (*aside*): Friend, what's the next move?
BUFFOON: What does the thief answer when he's caught with the goods?
KING: Fool, this is no time for joking!
(*Aloud.*)
My queen, this is not what I'm searching for. I happen to be looking for a transcription of the minutes from a meeting of the council of ministers!
QUEEN: Is it proper to conceal your youthful charms and the good fortune they earn you?
BUFFOON: Lady, you must feed him some sweets right away to alleviate this attack of bilious madness brought on by the midday sun.
QUEEN: Nipuṇikā, the brahman sustains his friend very nicely.
BUFFOON: Lady, certainly you see that everyone is sustained by delicious food.
KING: Fool, are you doing everything you can to prove me guilty?
QUEEN: The guilt is not yours, sir. It is I who am the offending party in this case, since it is not me you want to see standing before you. Nipuṇikā, come. Let us go.
(*Miming anger, she starts to go.*)
KING:

Though I've wronged you, be kind;
give up this anger, beauty—
when his mistress is enraged
how can the servant be guiltless? (20)

(*He falls to his knees.*)
QUEEN (*to herself*): I should not be so easily moved as to accept this contrition. But I'm afraid that my softheartedness will turn anger to remorse later.
(*Leaving the king, the queen exits with her retinue.*)

BUFFOON: The queen left churned up as a monsoon river. Come on, get up.
KING (*getting up*): It wasn't wrong of her to do that.

Even a hundred sweet words from a lover
will not enter a woman's heart
if their sentiment is not authentic;
the expert jeweler knows the fake
and scorns its tawdry luster. (21)

BUFFOON: Anyway, her being out of the way is very convenient for you. If you have a pain in the eye you can't bear to stare into a light.
KING: Don't say that. I still have the same respect for the queen, though my heart's gone out to Urvaśī. But since falling on my knees has no effect on her, I'll have to rely on patience.
BUFFOON: Your patience will take care of itself. Meanwhile, a famished brahman relies on you, sir, for his life. It's time to bathe and eat.
KING (*gazing upward*): Yes, it is past midday.

Tormented by heat, a peacock sits down
in the cool water trough beneath a tree;
the bee splits open the tip of a red bud
and hides himself in its dark cavity;
a duck abandons the lake's burning water
and rests in the shade of shore lotuses,
and a parrot caged in the pleasure house
begs for water, exhausted. (22)

(*All exit.*)

END OF ACT TWO

ACT THREE

(*Two pupils of the sage Bharata, the creator of drama, enter.*)

FIRST PUPIL: Pallava, my friend, our teacher took you along to carry his seat when he went to great Indra's palace, while I had to stay back and keep watch at the fire god's sanctuary. Did our teacher's play please the celestial assembly?

SECOND PUPIL: Gālava, I can't say if it pleased them or not. But Urvaśī got completely absorbed in her role in "Lakṣmī's Bridegroom Choice," the play composed by the goddess of speech herself—especially in the scenes where she had to portray the various dramatic moods. However . . .

FIRST PUPIL: What? You sound like you're trying to say there was a flaw in her performance.

SECOND PUPIL: Well, yes. At one point she slipped and flubbed a line.

FIRST PUPIL: What happened?

SECOND PUPIL: It was where Menakā, as Varuṇa's wife, asks Urvaśī, who was playing the part of Lakṣmī, "The world-protector gods have come together along with Viṣṇu and the greatest men of the three worlds. Which of them has your love and devotion?"

FIRST PUPIL: What did she say?

SECOND PUPIL: She was supposed to choose Viṣṇu and answer "Puruṣottama," but instead the word "Purūravas" came out of her mouth.

FIRST PUPIL: The body always conforms to its destiny. I hope our teacher wasn't angry with her.

SECOND PUPIL: He laid a curse on her. But Indra was kinder.

FIRST PUPIL: What happened?
SECOND PUPIL: The teacher's curse was this: "Because you violated my teaching, you will lose your place in heaven." But when great Indra, smasher of citadels, saw Urvaśī's face lowered in shame he said, "I owe a favor to my battle companion, the royal sage to whom you are devoted. You shall remain on earth with Purūravas, according to your wish, until he beholds an heir."
FIRST PUPIL: Indra does understand the ways of the heart.
SECOND PUPIL (*gazing up at the sun*): All our talk has made us miss the hour of our teacher's bath. Come on! Let's attend to him.
(*They exit; the interlude ends. Then the chamberlain enters.*)
CHAMBERLAIN:

In the morning of life
every householder strives
to win the world's wealth and power;
later his sons
will take up his burden,
leaving him free to rest—
now my old age
is imprisoned in service,
wearing down the body daily.
Alas, how painful
is my jurisdiction—
the chambers of the palace women! (1)

(*Making a round of the stage.*)
The daughter of the king of Banaras is undertaking a vow. In this regard she has instructed me, saying, "For the sake of my vow, I've abandoned jealous pride and entreated the king through the clever Nipuṇikā. You are to make the same entreaty in my name." Ah, I see that the king has finished his evening prayer recitation.
(*Making a round of the stage, looking.*)
What delightful scenes the end of day brings in the palace!

Peacocks like sculpted forms on perches
fall still as the drowse of night approaches;
gray pigeons on the turrets are obscured
by incense smoking from lattice windows,
and pious old women of the harem,
bearing with devotion their brilliant flames,
set out twilight's auspicious lamps
at altars strewn with flower offerings. (2)

(*Looking offstage.*)
Ah, His Majesty is coming this way.

Circled by torches in the hands
of tall serving women, he advances
like the primeval winged mountain,
its slopes blazing with flowers
glittering on branches of high trees. (3)

I'll keep my vigil here so he'll see me as he passes.
(*Then the king enters with his female retinue, as described, and with the buffoon.*)
KING (*to himself*):

With little pain I passed the day
shielded by duties from longing;
now during the night's long watches
there is nothing to distract my mind. (4)

CHAMBERLAIN (*approaching*): Victory! Victory, my lord! The queen entreats you as follows: "There will be a splendid view of the moon tonight from the roof of the Palace of Jewels. I wish to keep a vigil there in my lord's company while the moon unites with his favorite wife, the constellation Rohiṇī."
KING: Inform the queen that I will honor her wish.
CHAMBERLAIN: Yes, sir.
(*He exits.*)
KING: My friend, is the queen really undertaking all these preparations because of a vow?
BUFFOON: Oh, I suppose she felt sorry for snubbing you

when you fell at her feet, and now she wants to wipe away her mistake under the pretext of performing a vow.
KING: You're right, no doubt.

They scorn our prostrations, but later
their minds always burn with remorse—
when lovers humbly seek reunion
proud women feel secretly ashamed. (5)

Lead the way to the roof of the Palace of Jewels.
BUFFOON: Come this way, sir. Ascend by these gleaming marble stairs, gently rising like the waves of the Gaṅgā, toward the Palace of Jewels, a delightful spot to watch the nightfall.
KING: After you.
(*All mime climbing stairs.*)
BUFFOON (*looking out*): Look, sir, moonrise must be nigh—we can see the eastern quarter's lovely face as her veil of darkness is lifted away.
KING: You have expressed it beautifully.

Rising behind the eastern mountain
the half-hidden moon with its new beams
dispels the darkness like a lover returning;
as if to greet him, the evening sky
binds disheveled black curls and shows
the glowing face that captivates my eyes. (6)

BUFFOON: Oh lord! The king of all us brahmans has risen, splendid as a big white sugarball candy—with a chunk bitten off!
KING (*smiling*): To a glutton everything looks like food.
(*He joins his palms in reverential salute and bows.*)
Lord of the night,

You enter the sun to mark the time of holy rites;
your nectar propitiates ancestors and gods;
you wax full at night to dispel thick darkness—
I bow to you shining on Śiva's matted locks! (7)

BUFFOON: Now, with the permission of your ancestor the moon, who puts words in the mouth of a good brahman like me, be seated! Then I can take a load off my feet also.

KING (*at the buffoon's bidding, he sits down; looking at the retinue*): When the moon reveals everything clearly, these torches only repeat its light. You may retire.

RETINUE OF SERVING WOMEN: As you command, my lord. (*They exit.*)

KING (*gazing at the moon*): My friend, the queen will not arrive for an hour, so while we're alone I'll explain my condition.

BUFFOON: It's quite obvious. But since you saw how strong Urvaśī's passion is, the bonds of hope should give you strength to control yourself.

KING: That's true, but my heart's yearning is so strong.

> Like a flooding river's fury growing
> as its torrent breaks on jagged rocks,
> love's power increases hundredfold
> when obstacles bar the joy of union. (8)

BUFFOON: Even though your arms are wasted away from pining, you somehow look splendid. So I'd say a meeting with your love is not far off.

KING (*indicating he feels an omen*): Friend,

> As you ease my torment with words of hope
> my right arm inspires me with its throbbing. (9)

BUFFOON: You know that the words of a brahman never prove false.

(*The king stands up, expectant with hope. Then Urvaśī, in the costume of a woman on her way to a tryst, and Citralekhā enter by the skyway.*)

URVAŚĪ (*looking at herself*): Do you like my trysting outfit? See, I've put on a dark blue muslin bodice with just a few ornaments, so I won't be seen in the moonlight.

CITRALEKHĀ: I can't find words to praise it. But I'm thinking how wonderful it would be to see it through Purūravas' eyes.

URVAŚĪ: Then Love himself commands you to take me where that handsome man lives.
CITRALEKHĀ: But we've already arrived at your lover's place. Doesn't it look like the gleaming peak of Mount Kailāsa transformed into a palace?
URVAŚĪ: Then use your magic power to find out where the thief of my heart is hiding, and what he's doing.
CITRALEKHĀ (*thinking; to herself*): Hmmm . . . I'll have some fun with her for a bit.
(*Aloud.*)
Dear, he's in a den of pleasure, reveling in some woman's love.
(*Urvaśī mimes dejection.*)
CITRALEKHĀ: Silly, it's your love he's enjoying—in his imagination.
URVAŚĪ (*with a sigh of relief*): My heart is selfish enough to be suspicious.
CITRALEKHĀ: There's the royal sage on the roof of the Palace of Jewels with only his brahman friend for company. Come on! Let's go nearer.
(*They alight.*)
KING: My friend, the pain of love swells as the night advances.
URVAŚĪ: My heart trembles, not knowing about whom he's talking. Let's hide and listen to him talk freely until our doubt is cleared.
CITRALEKHĀ: As you like.
BUFFOON: Don't they prescribe cool moonbeams filled with nectar, like these?
KING: My friend, this disease is not treatable with such remedies.

> No bed of fresh flowers or moonbeams will cool me,
> or sandal paste smeared on my body, or garlands of gems:
> only that girl of heaven can relieve love's pain—
> but our private talk about her may lighten it. (10)

URVAŚĪ: My heart, I see you've won your reward by abandoning me and becoming his.

BUFFOON: Sure, I do the same thing: when I can't get my favorite fruit salad of yogurt and mangoes, I make myself feel better by calling for it out loud while I'm craving it.
KING: I feel that way too, my friend.
CITRALEKHĀ: Listen! Aren't you satisfied yet?
KING:

> My shoulder rubbed against hers
> when the chariot jolted on landing.
> This single limb has fortune;
> the rest of my body is earth's burden. (11)

URVAŚĪ: Why should I hesitate any longer?
(*She rushes up to the king.*)
Citralekhā, my friend, though I'm standing right in front of him, the great king seems indifferent to me.
CITRALEKHĀ (*smiling*): You are too hasty, dear. You forgot to remove the invisibility charm.
VOICE FROM OFFSTAGE: Come this way, mistress.
(*All listen to the distant sound. Urvaśī and her friend are dejected.*)
BUFFOON: Oh no, oh no! The queen's getting close—be careful what you say!
KING: Make sure you don't let anything out either!
URVAŚĪ: What do we do now?
CITRALEKHĀ: Don't be upset. The two of us are hidden. I see that his chief queen is dressed for performing a vow. She won't stay long.
(*Then the queen enters, with a retinue bearing oblations.*)
QUEEN (*gazing at the moon*): Nipuṇikā, our lord, the deer-marked moon, looks splendid when he unites with the constellation Rohiṇī.
MAID: But my master and mistress look even more beautiful together.
(*The two make a round of the stage.*)
BUFFOON (*seeing them*): Hey, the queen looks wonderful today! I don't know whether it's because she's bringing me sweets for the oblation, or because she's dropped her anger on account of this vow she's staging for your benefit.

KING (*smiling*): Both are possible. But the second seems more likely.

Her bodice is white,
her only ornaments
the auspicious signs
of a married woman's fortune,
and blades of ritual grass
embellishing her hair;
she's abandoned her pride
on the pretext of a vow—
her beauty shows
she's softened toward me. (12)

QUEEN (*approaching*): Victory! Victory, husband!
RETINUE: Victory! Victory, master!
BUFFOON: Be well, lady.
KING: My queen, welcome.
(*Taking her hand, he seats her.*)
URVAŚĪ: Friend, this woman is rightly addressed as "queen." She's no less commanding than Indra's wife Śacī.
CITRALEKHĀ: It's true. And that you say it shows you're not jealous.
QUEEN: I must carry out a particular vow that concerns you, husband. You'll only have to put up with the bother for about an hour.
KING: You must not say that. It is a favor, not a bother.
BUFFOON: I wish she'd bother us like this more often—as long as she brings sweets for the oblation!
KING: What is the name of the queen's vow?
(*The queen glances at Nipuṇikā.*)
NIPUṆIKĀ: Master, it is called "Propitiation of the Beloved."
KING (*looking at the queen*): If that is so,

By that vow you vainly crush
a fragile lotus flower body—
why appease a slave
who longs to please you, fair one? (13)

URVAŚĪ: His respect for her is very great.
CITRALEKHĀ: How naive you are! When these city men fall in love with other women, they become overly polite to their wives.
QUEEN: Husband, it is the power of the vow that makes you speak this way.
BUFFOON: Don't protest, sir! It wouldn't be right to contradict the good wishes you've already expressed so well!
QUEEN: Girls, bring the oblation so that I may worship the moonbeams fallen here on the Palace of Jewels—the feet of the moon god.
RETINUE: As the queen commands. Here is the oblation.
QUEEN (*miming worship of moonbeams with offerings of blossoms, etc.*): Girls, give the little man the sweets from the oblation.
RETINUE: As the queen commands. Māṇavaka, this is for you.
BUFFOON (*taking the dish of sweets*): Be well, lady. May your rite of abstinence bear much fruit!
QUEEN: Husband, please come here.
KING: I am ready.
(*Falling to her feet, with hands reverentially joined and opened in supplication, the queen dramatically mimes worship of the king.*)
QUEEN: As the divine mating of the moon with Rohiṇī is my witness, I do propitiate my husband with these words: From this day I shall form a bond of affection with the woman who seeks union with my husband, the woman my husband yearns for.
URVAŚĪ: Oh, how do I know she really means me? But my heart feels calm again and confident.
CITRALEKHĀ: Now that you have the permission of that faithful and generous woman, my friend, nothing more will bar the way to union with your beloved.
BUFFOON (*turns to the king and says as an aside*): The queen's like a frustrated fisherman who's glum when the fish escapes, but tells everyone how much merit he's won for sparing its life.
(*Aloud.*)

Lady, has the king become such a stranger that you can let him go like this?

QUEEN: Fool! I wish to soothe my husband's love-tormented body even at the cost of my own happiness. Decide from this whether I love him or not!

KING:

You have the power
to give me away
or make me your slave;
yet surely I'm not
as you suspect me,
timid lady. (14)

QUEEN: You may or may not be. The "Propitiation of the Beloved" vow is completed as prescribed. Come, girls! Let us go!

KING: Love, I am certainly not propitiated if you abandon me now and go away.

QUEEN: Husband, I have never before violated the conditions of a vow.

(*The queen exits with her retinue.*)

URVAŚĪ: Friend, the royal sage does love his wife. But I cannot take back my heart.

CITRALEKHĀ: What? Are you going to give up and go back to heaven?

KING (*taking a seat*): The queen could not have gone very far.

BUFFOON: Oh, say whatever you feel like. She thinks of you as an incurable patient she's given up on. She'll let you have anything you want.

KING: If only Urvaśī—

URVAŚĪ: —would be fulfilled today.

KING:

If only my hidden beloved would let
the sound of her anklet touch my ears,
or approach me gently from behind
and cover my eyes with her lotus hands;

if she'd alight on this terrace now
but shyly hesitate from sudden fear,
then slowly she'd be led to my side
by her ever-resourceful companion. (15)

URVAŚĪ: My friend, now I'll fulfill his desire.
(*Approaching from behind, she covers the eyes of the king. Citralekhā makes a sign to the buffoon not to say anything.*)
KING (*showing that he has felt her touch*): Friend, it is she, the beauty born from Nārāyaṇa's thigh.
BUFFOON: How do you know?
KING: How could I not know?

My body afflicted by the god of love
would not find bliss at another's touch,
as the white water lily will open
only for moonbeams, not for scorching sunrays. (16)

URVAŚĪ (removing her hands, she moves around to face him and approaches a few steps): Victory! Victory, great king!
KING: Beauty, welcome.
(*He invites her to share his seat; they sit.*)
CITRALEKHĀ: Has our friend found happiness?
KING: Can't you see I've found it?
URVAŚĪ: The queen has given the king away, so I come openly to be united with him. Don't think me an intruder, my friend.
BUFFOON: How did you know about the queen's vow? Have you been here since nightfall?
KING (*gazing at Urvaśī*):

If you may touch me only because
the queen has given me away,
by whose approval did you steal
my heart at our first meeting? (17)

CITRALEKHĀ: She has no answer to that, friend, but listen now to my urgent request.
KING: You have my attention, lady.

CITRALEKHĀ: When spring is over, I must attend the sun god during the hot season. You, friend, must make sure that my dear Urvaśī doesn't become homesick for heaven.
BUFFOON: Why should she miss heaven? The gods don't eat or drink there. They just sit around and stare unblinking as fish.
KING: Fair one,

Could anyone cause her to forget
the indescribable joys of heaven?
Yet no other woman will have a slave
such as I, Purūravas, will be to her. (18)

CITRALEKHĀ: I'm obliged to you, sir. Dear Urvaśī, be brave now and send me away.
URVAŚĪ (*embracing Citralekhā*): Friend, don't forget me.
CITRALEKHĀ (*smiling*): Now that you and he have each other, it is I who'll have to beg that of you.
(*She exits, bowing to the king.*)
BUFFOON: How fortunate you are in fulfilling your desire!
KING: But she is fortune itself to me.

Mine alone is the white silk parasol
of sovereignty over all the earth;
my edict stones shine in the glow
of bowing vassal kings' jeweled crowns;
yet this mastery does not confer
the contentment I feel today, friend,
in finding lovely servitude
at Urvaśī's delicate feet. (19)

URVAŚĪ: Nothing I could reply would be dearer than this.
KING (*taking Urvaśī by the hand*): What they say is true: When you win your desire, everything becomes the opposite of what it was.

The same moonbeams delight my body,
the same shafts of Love are kind to me—
whatever seemed harsh and angry, beauty,
favors me now in union with you. (20)

URVAŚĪ: Great king, I offended you by delaying so long.
KING: No, don't say that.

> That happiness is sweeter
> which follows upon suffering,
> like the perfect rest that shade trees
> give to burning travelers. (21)

BUFFOON: Sir, we've enjoyed the moonbeams, nightfall's delight. Now it's time for you to retire to the inner chambers.
KING: Then show your friend the way.
BUFFOON: Come this way, lady.
(*All make a round of the stage.*)
KING: Here now is my wish.
URVAŚĪ: Tell me.
KING:

> When my heart's desire was unattained
> the weary night grew a hundredfold;
> now if this night of our union, fair brow,
> lingered as long, I'd be blessed. (22)

(*All exit.*)

END OF ACT THREE

ACT FOUR

A SINGER OFFSTAGE:

Heartbroken, parted
from the friend she loves,
a distraught nymph
weeps with her companion
on the bank of a lake
where the touch of sunlight
has opened day-lotuses. (1)

(*Citralekhā and Sahajanyā enter during the entrance song, performing a dance accompanied by hand clapping. Then Citralekhā moves forward with deliberate steps and looks up to the sky.*)

A loving pair
of wild geese,
each consumed by grief
for a dear companion,
laments on the lake,
tearful eyes fluttering. (2)

SAHAJANYĀ (*distressed*): Friend, Citralekhā, your face, pale as a withered lotus, betrays a sickness of heart. Tell me what troubles you so that I can share your pain.

CITRALEKHĀ (*pitifully*): I was performing my duty in the nymphs' customary worship of the sun god. When Urvaśī's usual turn arrived at spring festival time and she did not come, I began to miss my dear friend terribly.

SAHAJANYĀ: I know the love you have for one another. What did you do?

CITRALEKHĀ: In meditation I used my magic power to find news of her. I saw that something terrible had occurred.

SAHAJANYĀ: What was it?

CITRALEKHĀ (*pitifully*): Urvaśī had persuaded the royal sage to entrust affairs of state to his ministers and had taken him to spend some time at play in the grove of magic herb fragrances near Kailāsa's peak.

SAHAJANYĀ (*as if to praise Urvaśī*): In places like that we find true pleasure. What happened there?

CITRALEKHĀ: The king was watching a sylph named Udayavatī play in the sand dunes on the banks of the Mandākinī River. When he stared too long Urvaśī flew into a rage.

SAHAJANYĀ: How could she bear it? Her love had become so intense. Something like this was bound to happen. What then?

CITRALEKHĀ: Her husband tried to appease her but she refused to listen. Then, because sage Bharata's curse had rendered her mortal and ignorant, she slipped into the grove of Śiva's son Kumāra, forgetting the divine ordinance that women are forbidden to enter it. And as soon as she set foot there, she was transformed into a creeper at the edge of the forest.

SAHAJANYĀ (*grief-stricken*): It is said that nothing is beyond the reach of fate, so even passion like this can undergo strange transformations. And now?

CITRALEKHĀ: The king has gone mad searching for his love in that grove, passing days and nights imagining he sees Urvaśī everywhere.

(*Looking at the sky.*)

There can be no remedy for him now: when black rain clouds arise even perfected souls fall prey to love's longing.

A SINGER OFFSTAGE:

A loving pair
of wild geese,
consumed by grief
for a dear companion,
laments on the lake,
wet with endless tears. (3)

SAHAJANYĀ: Such excellent men as he do not suffer long. A

means for their reunion will surely be found, and this means will also be the antidote for Urvaśī's curse.
(*Looking toward the eastern sky.*)
Come. We must perform our worship of the sun god as he begins to rise.
A SINGER OFFSTAGE:

Burning with worry, yearning
for the sight of her friend,
the goose finds diversion
among the lake's opened lotuses. (4)

(*They exit; the prelude ends.*)

The elephant lord,
starkly altered
by madness
in his love's desertion,
penetrates the grove,
adorning his massive body
with flowers and new sprouts
broken from the trees. (5)

(*Purūravas enters during the entrance song, performing a dance accompanied by hand clapping. Then, in the manner of a madman, he fixes his gaze on an imaginary object.*)
KING (*enraged*): Damn you, wicked demon! Stop! Stop! Where are you going with my beloved?
(*Looking.*)
What's this? He's taken off from the mountaintop and flown into the sky. He's showering me with arrows.
(*He picks up a lump of dirt and runs to hurl it; stops suddenly, moves forward with deliberate steps and looks up to the sky.*)
A SINGER OFFSTAGE:

The young goose
shakes his wings,
grief for his love
sealed in his heart—
tearful eyes fluttering
he laments on the lake. (6)

KING (*deliberates, then speaks pitifully*):

This is a young cloud bound in storm armor,
not a haughty fiend who stalks the night;
this is the gods' faraway rainbow,
not a bent bow discharging arrows;
this is a pounding rainfall,
not a volley of missiles,
and this is a streak of gold lightning,
not Urvaśī my love. (7)

(*He falls, fainting, then moves forward with deliberate steps; sighs.*)

I thought some night-walking fiend
was stealing my fawn-eyed love.
Then I saw the black rain cloud
pouring forth fresh lightning. (8)

(*Pitifully worrying.*)
Then where could she have gone?

If in anger she's used her magic
to hide, her anger will not last;
or if she's flown off to heaven,
her heart will pity me again. (9ab)

(*Angrily.*)

Not even the gods' demon foes
can steal her when I am near;
then what fate now decrees her
banished from the realm of my eyes? (9cd)

(*He moves forward with deliberate steps and looks up to the sky, then sighs and speaks tearfully.*)
Oh, grief draws grief in tow for those whom fortune shuns.

Rain clouds rising to shield the world
from the sun relieve summer's fierce heat—
now in this pain of my love's desertion
beautiful days seem to mock my grief. (10)

(*A dance called carcarī, "wandering in passion," follows.*)

Cloud, withdraw! Why have you started
this endless downpour that covers the skies?
Yet if I see my love while roaming the earth
I'll endure whatever you do. (11)

(*After performing a carcarikā, a version of the same dance, the king ponders.*)
It's no use ignoring the pain growing in my heart. Even sages proclaim that the king alone controls time. The king? Then why shall I not forbid the arrival of the rainy season?
(*Laughing, he rises and repeats.*)
Even sages proclaim that the king alone controls time! Well, then. I forbid it!
(*A carcarī dance follows.*)
A SINGER OFFSTAGE:

In spring heaven's wish-tree dances
waving clusters of buds like hands in the wind—
bees hum, drunk from its fragrance
and singing cuckoos respond. (12)

(*The king dances, acting out the verse.*)
KING: Or rather I shall not forbid it, since the signs of the rainy season may act as my royal accouterments.
(*Laughing, he dances again to the song "In spring heaven's wish-tree dances."*)
And how is that?

This lightning-streaked cloud becomes
my gold-threaded canopy;
blossom sprays of nicula trees fan me
like the royal fly whisks of yak tail;
peacock bards sing my praise more piercingly,
inspired by the dark skies' quenching of summer;
the mountains are merchants proffering treasures
from caravans of streams on rain-splashed ridges. (13)

But what use is boasting of royal paraphernalia now? First I'll seek my love in this grove.
(*A carcarī dance again, to a repetition of the last verse.*)

A SINGER OFFSTAGE:

Bereft of his mate, flooded with grief
he stumbles, sluggish in love's desertion—
in a mountain grove aflame with blossoms
the elephant lord slackens his stride. (14)

(*After the song, the king makes a round of the stage with deliberate steps, looking excitedly.*)
KING: Oh, this strengthens my resolve!

Red-lined white blossoms filled with rain
on this tender kandali plant
make me think of her eyes,
brimming with tears of anger. (15)

How am I to find out whether she has passed this way?

If she'd alight, barely touching the earth
in sandy forest places wet with rain,
I could trace the red-lac impressions
of heel prints deep from the weight of her hips. (16)

(*With deliberate steps he makes a round of the stage, looking excitedly.*)
By this clue I can make out the path of that jealous woman.

Stained by tears that stole the tint of passion
as they fell from the lips of my slender beauty,
this bodice, dark green as a parrot's belly,
was loosened by the fitful rage in her walk. (17)

Yes, I'll take it!
(*Makes a round of the stage; considers the "bodice," tearfully.*)
What's this? Only a patch of new grass scattered with fireflies that glow in daylight during the rainy season. Tell me then, where in this grove will I find news of my beloved?
(*He sees something.*)
Ah, here's a peacock on the slope of this wet green hill. He's mounted a rocky slab steaming from the rain.

He watches the clouds, as gusts
of the coming storm whip up his crest.
The peacock cranes his neck to the sky
and raises his happy cry—kekā! (18)

(Approaching.)
I'll question him.
A SINGER OFFSTAGE:

Though once he dispatched his rivals quickly,
the elephant lord knows now the pain of desertion—
yearning for the sight of his stolen beloved,
the pride of the herd is struck dumb. (19)

(A carcarī dance follows.)
KING:

Peacock, I beg you to tell me this thing:
while roaming the grove did you see my love?
Listen! A wild goose gait and a face like the moon—
by the signs that I've told you you'll know her. (20)

(He performs a carcarikā dance, then sits, placing his palms together in reverential greeting.)

O blue-necked bird, in this grove
the long white neck
of my love is raised in longing.
O white-eyed bird, the sight of
her long blue eyes
would be worthy of your waiting. (21)

(He performs a carcarikā dance, then looks.)
What's this? He doesn't answer, but starts to dance!
(A carcarī dance again.)
What's the reason for his joy? Ah, I know.

Gentle winds part tail feathers, black
and glossy as lightning-streaked clouds;
because my love has disappeared,
the peacock's plumage has no rival.

Her thick hair is adorned with flowers,
the ribbon loosened for sweet love play—
if she were here now, would a peacock
dare to compete? (22)

All right, then. Why should I ask a creature who delights in the misfortunes of others?
(*He moves forward with deliberate steps and looks up to the sky.*)
Ah, here's a cuckoo sitting on a branch of the rose-apple tree, her passion inflamed as dark rain clouds bring an end to the hot season. Her kind are the cleverest of birds. I'll question her.
A SINGER OFFSTAGE:

Hiding in a sylph's grove,
he bursts into
a flood of painful tears—
joy banished from his heart,
the elephant lord roams,
measuring the sky. (23)

(*A carcarī dance follows.*)
KING: Hello, dear bird,

Cuckoo, sweetly chattering,
my love's wandering freely—
tell me if you've seen her
in Indra's paradise garden. (24)

(*After dancing to this verse, he approaches, executing turns as he comes, and falls to his knees.*)
Lady,

Impassioned suitors call you
the go-between for the god of love,
an unfailing weapon, clever
in breaking a woman's fierce pride—
murmuring bird, if this is so,
then fetch my love, or lead me to her. (25)

(*Leaning to the left and shaking his head, he executes a few turns; speaks to the sky.*)
What did you say? "Why has she gone away, abandoning a man so in love with her?" Listen, lady.

She is enraged, though I cannot recall
even once I gave her cause for rage:
in this way women rule their lovers,
unleashing fury at perfect devotion. (26)

(*He sits down, anxious and confused, then rises to his knees and recites the previous verse, "She is enraged, though I cannot recall," while looking up.*)
What's this? She's cut off our conversation to look after her own affairs. But such behavior is well known.

"Great pain suffered by someone else
is only a trifle"—the proverb is true;
so the cuckoo ignores my wretched plea
and, blind from love, sucks a ripe fruit
as if it were her mate's sweet lip. (27)

Even so, I'm not angry with her, for her voice is like my love's. Be happy, lady. Let us press on.
(*Rising, with deliberate steps he makes a round of the stage, looking.*)
Ah, to the right of this avenue of trees the tinkling sound of an anklet announces my love's footsteps. I'll follow it.
(*Makes a round of the stage.*)
A SINGER OFFSTAGE:

His face weary from love's desertion,
his eyes filled with endless tears,
his gait faltering from unbearable pain,
the elephant lord wanders in the grove—
though his whole body burns with grief,
his mind knows still greater anguish. (28)

(*To a repetition of this song, the king performs a dance to the six directions. Immediately after he moves forward with deliberate steps and looks up to the sky.*)

Bereft of his love,
scorched by grief,
eyes filled with tears,
the pride of the herd
wanders in a daze. (29)

KING (*pitifully*): Oh, no! Misery!

Seeing the sky black with clouds,
he yearns to mate on Mānasa lake—
this is a royal goose honking,
not her delicate anklet tinkling. (30)

These birds are longing for Mānasa. Before they fly off I must obtain news of my love.
(*He approaches, executing turns as he comes, and falls to his knees.*)
Hey there! King of waterbirds,

Before you depart for Mānasa lake
drop these lotus stalks you'll eat on the way,
and gather more when you've spoken to me.
Save me from grief with news of my love—
a good king hears his petitioners
before seeing to his own affairs. (31)

(*He looks, with his head bent to one side.*)
Ah, from the way he looks up he seems to say, "My mind is filled only with longing for the journey; I did not see her."
(*The king sits; he does gestures of a carcarī dance.*)

Damned goose! Why do you hide it? (34a)

(*He acts out the preceding line of verse, then rises.*)

Goose, if you did not see my curve-browed love
passing by on the shore of the lake,
how is it, thief, you've copied to perfection
the gait of her alluring walk? (32)

(*Again a carcarī.*)

Trailing your gait, I've noticed it. (34b)

(*Performing a carcarikā, the king approaches, placing his palms together in reverential greeting.*)

Goose, give back my mistress,
the one whose gait you stole.
Anyone convicted of stealing a part
must by law return the whole. (33)

(*Again a carcarī.*)

When did you learn the amorous gait
only her full, rolling hips can teach? (34cd)

(*The carcarī dance continues. Repeating the verse "Goose, give back my mistress," the king then walks with deliberate steps and represents the verse in gestures; laughs out loud.*)
He's flown off out of fear, thinking "The king will punish a thief." I'll plunge into this place, and emerge in another space!
(*With deliberate steps, he makes a round of the stage, looking.*)
Ah, here is a ruddy drake with his love. I'll question him.
(*The dance called "The Crouching Hunter," involving crooked and difficult movements, follows immediately.*)
A SINGER OFFSTAGE:

When sprouts have flowered on the trees, (35a)

(*The dance called "The Robust Potter," involving vigorous and rounded movements.*)

it's enticing there with rings and murmurs. (35b)

(*A carcarī dance.*)

Maddened by separation from his love,
the elephant lord wanders in the grove. (35cd)

(*After a dance in both slow and fast tempos, he does a carcarī.*)

KING:

Yellow-headed ruddy drake,
were you splashing in the lake?
Tell me that you did not see
my love splashing in the lake. (36)

(*Performing a carcarikā, he approaches and falls to his knees.*)

A royal chariot driver questions you, drake,
since you're named for the chariot wheel—
a beauty with hips round as wheels abandoned me
and wild chariots of desire race through my mind. (37)

He calls "whoo whoo." He must not know who I am.

My mother's father and father's father
are the deities sun and moon,
but greater than lineage is this honor—
both Urvaśī and the goddess earth
have chosen me lord and husband. (38)

What's this? He remains silent. I'll have to scold him.
(*He falls to his knees.*)
You should know what it's like for me.

Thinking your mate is far away
you weep, overcome by longing,
though her body is only hidden
by a lotus leaf near the shore.
If such strong love
makes you fear this parting,
why do you turn away, denying news
to me whose grief is real? (39)

(*He sits down.*)
The force of my perverse fortune prevails! I'll plunge into this place and emerge in another space!
(*He takes a step and stops.*)
Yes. I won't go yet.
(*With deliberate steps, he makes a round of the stage, looking.*)

Ah,

The buzzing of this bee
within the red lotus arrests me—
the sound of passion her mouth makes
when I bite her lower lip. (40)

I'll make my request to the bee enjoying this lotus, so that I won't feel any regret after I've left.
(*He assumes the initial "square" pose of classical Indian dance, feet level, but with only one arm extended at a right angle to the body.*)
A SINGER OFFSTAGE:

As the mood of love grows heavy,
passion swells between them;
the young goose splashes on the lake
under the love god's sway. (41)

(*The king sits down in full "square" pose, with both arms extended at right angles to the body, then places palms together in reverential greeting.*)
KING:

Bee, you would say that her eyes are bewitching,
but you cannot have seen my love's precious body—
had you tasted the honeyed perfume of her sighs
you would find no pleasure in this white lotus. (42)

(*With deliberate steps, he makes a round of the stage, looking.*)
Here is the elephant king, resting his trunk on a kadamba branch, with his mate standing by his side. I'll obtain a full report of my love from him. I'll approach him softly.
(*The dance called "The Crouching Hunter."*)
A SINGER OFFSTAGE:

In the grove
he burns with grief,
deserted by his mate. (43a)

(*The dance called "The Robust Potter."*)

The elephant lord
fans bees away
from his rut-wet cheek. (43b)

(*After the dance the king looks around.*)
KING: But perhaps this is not the right time to approach him.

Let him enjoy now
the sap sweet as wine
and tender sprouts
of this Sallaki branch
broken off by his mate
and offered with her trunk. (44)

(*Assuming the classical dance pose for accosting, he looks again.*)
Ah, he has finished eating. Good. I'll go near and question him.
(*A carcarī dance follows immediately.*)

Great elephant, you destroy huge trees
with playful strokes. Listen, answer my question!
Did you see my love as she passed in this grove?
The moon is blemished by a hare-shaped scar
and cannot outrival the luster of her face. (45)

(*Taking two steps, he approaches the "elephant" from the front.*)

Drunken elephant, have you seen
the new moon crowned with jasmine flowers?
Lord of the herd, did you chance to glimpse
the splendor of divine, everlasting youth? (46)

(*Listening with excitement.*)
Aha! Your thundering roar revives me with news of my love. And because we are alike I have great affection for you.

They call me the king of kings
and you the emperor of elephants;
your flowing musk is a gift to bees
as my charity is to supplicants;

among jewels of women my Urvaśī
is most loved, as your mate is in the herd—
you are like me in every way, but may you
be spared the anguish of love's desertion. (47)

Be happy, sir.
(*With deliberate steps, he makes a round of the stage, looking.*)
Here is the delightful hill called Fragrant Caves Mountain. Celestial nymphs are fond of it. If only I might find my precious beloved nearby!
(*He makes a round of the stage and looks.*)
What's this? Darkness has fallen. But no matter—I'll be able to see by the lightning flashes. What? Even the clouds have lost their lightning as a result of my sins. But I refuse to turn back without questioning this mountain.
A SINGER OFFSTAGE:

Hiding in the dense grove,
he tears earth with hard, sharp hooves.
Watch how wildly the boar runs,
pursuing his own purpose. (48)

KING:

Swelling hill, on your smooth chest may rest
a smooth-limbed nymph with swelling breasts.
Broad-hipped mountain, do her lovely hips lie
enclosed in the grove of Love's seraglio? (49)

What's this? I fear he doesn't hear because of the distance. Very well. I'll go near and question him.
(*A carcarī dance follows.*)

Waterfalls washing bright crystal stones,
peaks crested with flowers in profusion,
alluring with demigods' high sweet singing:
earth-bearing mountain, show me my love! (50)

(*Performing a carcarikā, he approaches, palms together in reverential greeting.*)

Lord of every earth-bearing mountain,
have you seen the woman I deserted,
a nymph, a beauty in every limb,
dwelling on the edge of your lovely grove? (51)

(*His words return as an echo; he listens to the distant sound with excitement.*)
What? He said he saw her with my very words. Well, then. I will look for her.
(*He looks up to the sky, then speaks sadly.*)
What's this? Only an echo creeping forth from within the cave.
(*He falls down, fainting; rises, sitting dejectedly.*)
Ah, I am weary. I'll sit here on the bank of this mountain river and enjoy the wind from the waves.
(*With deliberate steps, he makes a round of the stage, looking.*)
Seeing this river newly churned up from the monsoon rains, why do I feel desire?

Her frowning brow becomes a wave,
her girdle bells these flustered birds;
she drags along the foam like a skirt
loosened in her angry haste;
crookedly she surges forward,
roiling in the wake of my neglect—
surely this is the jealous Urvaśī
transformed into a raging river. (52)

Very well. I shall propitiate her.
(*The dance called "The Crouching Hunter" follows.*)

Let my bowing appease you, beloved river beauty;
these flustered birds mimic you, paining me cruelly.
A yearning stag waits on your bank, stream goddess,
enduring the buzzing of angry black bees. (53)

(*A carcarī dance follows "The Crouching Hunter."*)

A SINGER OFFSTAGE:

His billowy arm whipped up by the eastern wind,
the ocean lord partners a storm cloud in sinuous dance;
conch shells of saffron color decorate his body
and the cranes' shrieking jangles like ankle bells;
his watery costume is the blue of lotuses
appliquéd with crocodiles, sharks, and elephants;
his hands of flood tide beat time on the shore
as the new rains pour down, and shut out the sky. (54)

KING (*performing a carcarikā, he approaches and falls to his knees*):

All my passion is bound to you,
my words are sweet as a lover's can be;
my mind cannot even bear the thought
of severing your trust in my fidelity—
then for what trifling sin, capricious lady,
do you choose to abandon me, your slave? (55)

What's this? She remains silent. Perhaps this really is a river, not Urvaśī at all. Otherwise how could she abandon Purūravas and flow to a tryst with the ocean? Good things are not won by despairing. So, then. I will go to the exact spot where my lovely-eyed nymph disappeared from my eyes.
(*He makes a round of the stage, looking.*)
I'll ask the spotted deer sitting here for news of my love.

A SINGER OFFSTAGE:

All around the great blossoming tree
the garden enchants with buzzing bees
and the warbling calls of mating cuckoos—
burned by the fire of his love's desertion,
Indra's Airāvata, king of elephants,
aimlessly wanders in paradise grove. (56)

KING: (*falling to his knees*):

The hide of this black spotted deer
appears like a sidelong glance
cast by the goddess of the grove
for a glimpse of her radiant forest. (57)

(*Observing.*)

The hart gazes only at his doe approaching,
hindered as she walks by her nursing fawn. (58)

(*After he acts out the preceding verse in dance, he dances a carcarī.*)

Her divine beauty is forever young;
her delicate frame bears the weight
of swelling breasts and ample hips,
giving her the gait of a wild goose—
if you see my deer-eyed love in these woods
that glisten like the sky,
then give me news and rescue me
from the sea of love's desolation. (59)

(*He approaches, palms together in reverential greeting.*)
Hey there, lord of the deer,

Have you seen my love in the grove? Listen!
I will tell you the mark that betrays her—
as she softly blinks her large brown eyes,
my blessed love has the look of your doe. (60)

(*Observing.*)
What's this? He shows no regard for my words, but goes on looking at his wife. Oh, this is my fate! Fit fate! The force of perverse fortune prevails, and provides instances for insult! So I'll plunge into this place and emerge in yet another space!
(*He makes a round of the stage, looking.*)
Oh, I see a sign of her path!

My love adorned her hair with the flower
that proclaims the end of summer's heat—
a fresh blossom of the red kadamba
with its ring of stamens still uneven. (61)

(*He makes a round of the stage, looking.*)
But what is this glinting brilliant scarlet in the cleft of this rock?

It spreads a glow, so it cannot be flesh
from an elephant killed by some lion,
nor could it be a cinder spark
on the rain-drenched forest floor—
no, this is a ruby whose fire equals
the passionate red of aśoka blossoms
lifted by a ray of the toiling sun
as if by his outstretched hand. (62)

Yes! I'll take it.
(*He mimes taking it.*)
A SINGER OFFSTAGE:

His hope bound to his lover,
his eyes filled with tears,
his face drawn thin with grief,
the elephant lord roams in the forest. (63)

(*With deliberate steps, he approaches and takes the jewel.*)
KING (*to himself*):

This gem should be set in her hair,
perfumed with coral flowers—
since my love can't be found,
why should I stain it with tears? (64)

(*He tosses it aside.*)
VOICE OFFSTAGE: Child, take it! Take it!

The red lac washed from Pārvatī's feet
has hardened to a ruby in this cleft;
the man who wears this jewel accomplishes
instant reunion with his beloved. (65)

KING (*listening to the distant sound*): Who gives me this order?
(*He looks up to the sky.*)
Some omniscient sage roaming the forest like a deer takes pity on me. Sir, I am grateful for this advice.
(*He takes the jewel.*)

O Gem of Reunion,

If you will end my separation
in reunion with that deep-naveled beauty,
I will wear you as my crest-jewel, sir,
as Lord Śiva wears the new moon. (66)

(*He makes a round of the stage, looking.*)
Why does the sight of this creeper fill me with desire? It has not even blossomed yet. But it is only right that my heart delights in it.

Like my delicate Urvaśī's tear-washed lips,
the creeper's sprouts are moist with rain;
like a deserted woman shunning ornaments,
unflowering she mourns the departed season—
droning bees look elsewhere for honey,
and she seems to wait in anxious silence;
the wrathful woman who scorned my prostration
now burns with penitent remorse. (67)

I'll woo this creeper who mimics my love with an embrace.

Seeing you, creeper, my heart has decided
that if fate decrees I win her once more,
I'll bring only delight to that wandering girl
and she'll resolve never to leave me again. (68)

(*Performing a carcarikā, he approaches and embraces the creeper. Then Urvaśī enters, stepping into the place of the creeper. The king keeps his eyes closed in embrace, and shows that he has been touched.*)
Oh, my body is blissfully soothed, as if from the touch of Urvaśī's limbs. But I have no more faith.

Whatever I take to be my love
quickly turns out to be otherwise;
if I open my eyes very slowly now
I might still believe this touch is hers. (69)

(*Slowly he opens his eyes.*)
What? It is really Urvaśī!
(*He falls down, fainting.*)

URVAŚĪ: Awake, great king!
KING (*regaining consciousness*): Love, today I am returned to life.

I was drowning, wrathful lady,
in the abyss of your desertion
when fortune gave you back to me
like breath restored to a dead man. (70)

URVAŚĪ: Forgive me, great king. It was my anger that reduced you to this terrible condition.
KING: There is no need for you to propitiate me. The very sight of you has appeased both my body and soul. But tell me, how could you remain separated from me for such a long time?
(*He dances a carcarī.*)

Peacock, cuckoo, goose, ruddy drake;
bee, elephant, mountain, river, deer—
while wandering weeping in the forest
was there anyone I did not ask about you? (71)

URVAŚĪ: Yes, I know. I could see everything you did with the senses I retained hidden inside.
KING: Love, I don't understand.
URVAŚĪ: Listen, great king. In former times, Śiva's son Kumāra took a vow of eternal chastity. While living on the outskirts of the grove of magic herb fragrances, near the marshes called "untainted," he set a boundary here.
KING: What sort of boundary?
URVAŚĪ: It was this: "Whatever woman trespasses on this place shall be transformed into a creeper. Without the jewel formed from the red lac on my mother Pārvatī's feet, she cannot be released from that state." Then, because sage Bharata's curse had rendered me mortally ignorant, I slipped into the grove, forgetting the divine ordinance that women are forbidden to enter it. And as soon as I set foot there, I was transformed into a creeper at the edge of the forest.
KING: Love, now everything makes sense.

When I slept exhausted from passion in our bed
you thought of me as traveling abroad;
how could you suffer this long separation
were you not entangled in heaven's decrees? (72)

And this is the instrument of our reunion. When I learned its power I regained you, as you said.
(*He shows her the jewel.*)
URVAŚĪ: Oh! It is the Reunion Gem! That is why, with just your embrace, great king, I'm restored to my natural state.
KING (*placing the jewel on his forehead*):

Dusted with the fiery glow
of the ruby set on my forehead,
your face wears the splendor
of a lotus tinged by dawn's light. (73)

URVAŚĪ: Love, you speak sweetly. But we have been gone from Pratiṣṭhāna a long time. At any moment your subjects will begin to complain. Come, then. Let us go.
KING: As you say, lady.
(*Both rise.*)
URVAŚĪ: Now, how do you wish to go?
KING:

Your walk is alluring, lady, but take me home
on this cloud you will change to a sky-going chariot,
with flashes of lightning for glittering banners
and stripes of bright rainbows adorning the sides. (74)

(*He dances a carcarī.*)
A SINGER OFFSTAGE:

Reunited with his mate,
bristling with royal joy,
the young goose roams the sky
in a chariot his love bestowed. (75)

(*They exit to this song.*)

END OF ACT FOUR

ACT FIVE

(*The buffoon enters, excitedly.*)

BUFFOON: Oh Lord! Thank God! After frolicking a long time with Urvaśī around paradise grove and who-knows-where-else, my dear friend has finally returned. Once more he rules, delighting his subjects by supervising the royal affairs. Except for the lack of an heir, he's got nothing at all to grieve about. And today, since there's a special phase of the moon, he's come down with his queens for a ritual bath where holy Gaṅgā and Yamunā meet. He's just finished and entered the pavilion. So while he's being dressed, I'll get first crack at his perfumes and garlands.
(*He makes a round of the stage.*)
FEMALE VOICE OFFSTAGE: Oh no! Oh no! I was carrying our lovely nymph's crest-jewel in a palm-leaf basket covered with a silk cloth. Some vulture, taking it to be flesh, swooped down and snatched it away!
BUFFOON (*listening to the distant sound*): This is terrible. She's speaking of my friend's prized ruby, the Gem of Reunion. Because of this commotion he's gotten up from his seat before they've finished fixing his hair and jewels. I'll attend him.
(*He exits; the prelude ends. Then the king enters with the charioteer, the chamberlain, a huntress, and the retinue.*)
KING: Huntress!

Where is that thief,
that bird who brings death on himself,
the first to steal
from the house of his own protector? (1)

HUNTRESS: Look! He's circling there. He seems to tint the sky red with the jewel he holds in his beak by a gold chain.
KING: I see him.

> By the golden chain that hangs from his beak
> the bird bears the gem in his speeding rounds.
> Like the whirling firebrand's illusory wheel,
> he streaks a circle in passionate red. (2)

But what should be done?
BUFFOON (*approaching*): Sir, there's no need for compassion in this case. The offender must be punished.
KING: You're right. Bring me my bow and arrow.
SERVANT: As you command, master.
(*He exits.*)
KING: I don't see the bird.
BUFFOON: The wretched creature has veered off to the south.
KING (*turning around and looking*): Now I see him.

> With the jewel's sprouting luster
> he's made an ear pendant
> like a spray of aśoka blossoms
> for the sky's lovely face. (3)

GREEK BOW-BEARER (*entering with a bow in her hand*): Master, here are your bow and hand-guard.
KING: What use is a bow now? The vulture has passed beyond arrow range.

> That precious gem shines far away
> where the soaring bird has carried it,
> like limbs of the red planet at night
> coupled with a fragment of dark cloud. (4)

(*Looking at the chamberlain.*)
Lātavya, tell the city guards on my authority to hunt down the savage bird this evening while he's roosting in his tree.
CHAMBERLAIN: As you command, lord.
(*He exits.*)

BUFFOON: Sit down for now, sir. Where could a burglar go to escape your punishment?

KING (*sits down, as does the buffoon*):

It is not because of the ruby's price
that I love the jewel he snatched away—
it is the Gem of Reunion, friend,
that reunited my love and me. (5)

(*Then the chamberlain enters holding the jewel and an arrow.*)

CHAMBERLAIN: Victory! Victory, lord!

The bird you condemned was pierced through
by your anger delivered in this deadly arrow;
meeting the fit punishment for his offense,
the vulture fell out of the sky with the crest-jewel. (6)

(*All mime amazement.*)

CHAMBERLAIN: To whom shall I give the jewel after it has been rinsed?

KING: No. Huntress, have it purified with fire and placed in a casket.

HUNTRESS: As you command, master.

(*She exits, taking the jewel.*)

KING: Lātavya, do you know whose arrow this is?

CHAMBERLAIN: I see it's marked with a name, but my eyes aren't strong enough to make out the letters.

KING: Then bring me the arrow.

(*The chamberlain does so. The king reads to himself the syllables of the name-inscription and mimes "the condition of having offspring."*)

CHAMBERLAIN: If you will excuse me, I have some business to attend to.

(*He exits.*)

BUFFOON: What are you pondering, sir?

KING: Just listen to the name of the arrow's dispatcher.

(*He reads.*)

This arrow belongs to the scion
of Īla's line, born of Urvaśī:
the bow-wielder's name is Prince Āyus,
dispatcher of his enemies' lives. (7)

BUFFOON (*with great delight*): Fortune favors you with an heir!
KING: Friend, how can this be? Except for the time of the sacrifice in the Naimiṣa forest, we have not been separated. Nor did I notice the changes of pregnancy in her. Where could a son have come from? And yet,

Though the nipples of her breasts became dark
and her complexion pale as a lavalī leaf,
for only a few days her body seemed altered,
and an unexplained weariness rose in her eyes. (8)

BUFFOON: You shouldn't imagine that these divine women have the ways of humans. They can conceal what they do with their supernatural powers.
KING: It may well be as you say. But why should she hide a son from me?
BUFFOON: Oh, she was probably thinking, "The king will neglect this old lady."
KING: Enough of your jokes. Think of an explanation.
BUFFOON: Who can guess the secrets of the gods?
CHAMBERLAIN (*entering*): Victory! Victory, lord! An ascetic woman has arrived from Cyavana's hermitage with a young boy. She wishes to see you.
KING: Show them both in without delay.
CHAMBERLAIN: As you command, lord.
(*He exits; reenters with the young prince, who carries a bow, and the ascetic woman.*)
CHAMBERLAIN: This way, good lady.
(*The three make a round of the stage.*)
BUFFOON (*observing*): Could this be the warrior prince whose name was on the arrow that killed the vulture? He looks very much like you, sir.

KING: He may be the one. And that is why

My eyes fall on him and tears begin to well;
my mind feels quiet joy, my heart the paternal bond;
I start to tremble; now royal reserve has fled—
I know I must embrace him fiercely with these arms. (9)

CHAMBERLAIN: Reverend mother, please stand here.
(*The ascetic woman and the prince stand in the place indicated.*)
KING: I salute you, reverend mother.
ASCETIC WOMAN: Most fortune-blessed majesty, may you perpetuate the lunar race!
(*To herself.*)
Can this be? Even without being told, the royal sage recognizes Āyus as his own son.
(*Aloud.*)
Child, pay homage to your esteemed father.
(*The prince places his palms together, holding the bow between them.*)
KING: Long life to you!
PRINCE (*to himself*):

He is my father, and I am his son—
as soon as this dawns, love springs from my heart;
but imagine the devotion those sons must feel
who as babies played on their fathers' knees! (10)

KING: What is the purpose of your coming, reverend mother?
ASCETIC WOMAN: Listen, great king. This boy Āyus was entrusted to my care by Urvaśī not long after he was born. Beginning with the birth-ceremony, the performance of the rites for a prince of the warrior lineage has been carried out in full by the holy Cyavana. After receiving his religious training, he was thoroughly educated in the martial sciences.
KING: Then he has never been an orphan.
ASCETIC WOMAN: Today, while he was out searching for flowers and firewood with the other boys he did something forbidden by the hermitage.

BUFFOON: What was that?
ASCETIC WOMAN: They say he shot an arrow at a vulture holding some meat in its beak while it was resting on the top of a tree.
(*The buffoon looks at the king.*)
KING: And what happened then?
ASCETIC WOMAN: When the holy Cyavana received the news, he instructed me to return my charge. Therefore I wish to see Urvaśī.
KING: Then please be seated, reverend mother.
(*The ascetic woman sits on a seat brought by a servant.*)
KING: Lātavya, summon Urvaśī.
CHAMBERLAIN: As you command, lord.
(*He exits.*)
KING (*looking at the prince*): Come. Come, child.

It is said that the touch of a son
thrills every limb of the body—
come, then, and gladden me now,
like a moonbeam melting a moonstone. (11)

ASCETIC WOMAN: Son, delight your father.
(*The prince approaches the king and clasps his feet.*)
KING (*embracing the prince and placing him on a small seat near his feet*): Child, honor your father's dear friend, this brahman. Don't be afraid.
BUFFOON: Why should he be afraid? Anyone who lives in a hermitage knows what a monkey looks like.
PRINCE (*smiling*): Uncle, I honor you.
BUFFOON: Be well, sir!
(*Urvaśī and the chamberlain enter.*)
URVAŚĪ (*looking at the prince*): Who is that youth with the bow sitting there? The king himself is tying up his topknot. Oh, Satyavatī is here. That must be my little son Āyus! But he has grown so big!
(*She makes a round of the stage.*)

KING (*seeing Urvaśī*): Child,

> The woman who gave you birth approaches,
> unable to take her eyes from you;
> she shows a mother's natural love
> in the flow of milk that soaks her bodice. (12)

ASCETIC WOMAN: Son, come. Rise to meet your mother.
(*The prince rises to meet Urvaśī.*)
URVAŚĪ: I ask your blessing, honored mother.
(*She kneels at her feet.*)
ASCETIC WOMAN: Daughter, may your husband honor you.
PRINCE: Mother, I bow to you.
URVAŚĪ (*embracing the prince and lifting up his face*): Child, may you always please your father.
(*She approaches the king.*)
Victory! Victory, great king!
KING: Welcome to the mother of my son! Please share my seat.
(*He gestures for her to do so. All sit in order of rank, after Urvaśī.*)
ASCETIC WOMAN: Āyus has received his religious training and is now grown to full youth. So, in the presence of your husband, I'm returning the boy you entrusted to me. I wish to be dismissed now, as my duties in the hermitage have been interrupted.
URVAŚĪ: As soon as I fulfill my long-frustrated desire to see you I must begin to grieve at your parting. But it is not right for me to obstruct sacred duty. Good lady, go that we may see you again.
KING: Mother, please convey my respects to the holy Cyavana.
ASCETIC WOMAN: I will.
PRINCE: Good lady, if you are really returning, please take me to the hermitage also.
KING: Child, your student days are over; the first stage of life is behind you now. It is time to pass on to the second stage, and devote yourself to worldly affairs.

ASCETIC WOMAN: Child, follow your teacher's words.
PRINCE: Then you must do something for me.

> Send me my peacock, the fledgling Jewelthroat,
> when the plumage of his tail is full grown—
> I remember how he'd sleep in my lap,
> nestling blissfully as I rubbed his crest. (13)

ASCETIC WOMAN (*laughing*): I'll do just that. Be well, all of you!
(*She exits.*)
KING: Fair wife,

> Today I become the best of fathers
> through this worthy son of yours,
> like Indra, smasher of citadels,
> father of Jayanta born of Paulomī. (14)

(*Urvaśī remembers and weeps.*)
BUFFOON: Why is your face suddenly covered with tears?
KING (*agitatedly*):

> Beauty, why do you cry as I find great joy
> in attaining the assurance of my dynasty?
> The tears that fall on your high swelling breasts
> only repeat the adornment of your pearl strands. (15)

(*He wipes away her tears.*)
URVAŚĪ: Listen, great king. At first I had forgotten, overcome with joy at the sight of our son. Now at the mention of Indra's name, the memory of a pledge pains my heart.
KING: Tell me what the pledge was.
URVAŚĪ: The heart you captured owes prior allegiance to Indra.
KING: What do you mean?
URVAŚĪ: Indra said: "When my dear friend beholds the face of the heir you have borne him, you must return to my side once again." I was afraid of being separated from you, so as soon as he was born I secretly entrusted him to the care of the lady Satyavatī, to be educated in the hermitage of holy Cyavana.

Today she has returned Āyus to me, considering him grown fully capable of pleasing his father. This, then, is the measure of our living together.

(*All mime despair.*)

KING (*sighing*): Oh, how hostile is fate to happiness!

As soon as finding a son revives me,
I learn I must lose you again, slender wife—
no sooner does the first monsoon cloud
give the tree relief from the burning sun
than lightning fire strikes it down. (16)

BUFFOON: Your good fortune has dragged a chain of misfortunes along with it. Now I guess you'll have to put on bark clothes and go to the ascetics' grove.

URVAŚĪ: This has all happened because fate is cruel to me, but you must be thinking that I arranged for our son to be restored after completing his education so that I could return to heaven.

KING: You must not say that—

Your subjection demands this easy desertion
and cannot do what it finds most dear;
obey the edict of your master, while I,
entrusting the kingdom to Āyus your son,
resort to groves where deer herds wander. (17)

PRINCE: Father, you should not yoke a calf to a cart meant for a bull.

KING: My son,

An elephant in rut, though a calf,
quickly subdues the rest of the herd;
the venom from an infant snake's fangs
takes effect without delay;
a true overlord, even in youth,
is endowed by nature to guard the earth—
be it known: not by age but by birth
is your eminence equal to the task. (18)

Lātavya, tell the council of ministers on my authority to prepare a royal consecration for Āyus.

CHAMBERLAIN: As you command, lord.

(*He exits, pained. All mime being dazzled by a great light.*)

KING (*looking at the sky*): Why is there lightning when the sky is cloudless?

URVAŚĪ (*looking*): Oh, it's holy Nārada!

KING: Yes, holy Nārada.

> With matted locks the color of sulfurous yellow
> and a sacred thread pure white, like the crescent moon,
> he appears to be a moving heavenly tree of wishes,
> golden-branched, and richly decked with ropes of pearls.
> (19)

Bring an offering to our guest.

URVAŚĪ (*receiving the offering*): Here is the offering for our holy guest.

(*Nārada enters.*)

NĀRADA: Victory to the protector of all that lies between heaven and the nether world!

KING (*taking the offering from Urvaśī and pouring it at Nārada's feet*): Holy one, I salute you.

URVAŚĪ: Holy one, I reverence you.

NĀRADA: May this couple never be separated!

KING (*to himself*): If only it were so!

(*Aloud, embracing the prince.*)

Child, salute the holy one.

PRINCE: Holy one, Āyus, son of Urvaśī, pays you homage.

NĀRADA: May you live long!

KING: Please be seated.

NĀRADA: Of course.

(*He sits; all sit following him.*)

KING (*politely*): Holy one, what is the purpose of your coming?

NĀRADA: King, listen to the message of great Indra.

KING: You have my attention.

NĀRADA: Generous Indra has seen everything with his supernatural power and knows of your resolve to go to the forest. Therefore he instructs you—

KING: What does he command me?

NĀRADA: These are his words: "We have been informed by the sages who see past, present, and future that there is about to be a conflict between the gods and the demons. As you have been a great companion in battle to us, you are not to lay down your weapons. Urvaśī, moreover, will be your lawful wife and helpmate as long as you live.

URVAŚĪ (*turning to the king; aside*): Oh, it's as if an arrow had been removed from my heart!

KING: I am subject to the will of the lord of the gods.

NĀRADA: And that is proper:

Indra, lord of Vasus, should see to your affairs
and you should undertake what he desires,
as the sun strengthens fire, and daily the fire
rekindles the sun with its flames. (20)

(*He looks up to the sky.*)
Rambhā, bring the materials which Indra himself has supplied for the consecration of Crown Prince Āyus as heir to the kingdom.

RAMBHĀ (*entering*): Here are the materials for his consecration.

NĀRADA: Seat His Highness on the gold throne.

RAMBHĀ: Here, child.
(*Seats the boy.*)

NĀRADA (*pouring a pitcher over the prince's head*): Rambhā, perform the remainder of the rite.

RAMBHĀ (*performing it as instructed*): Child, pay homage to the holy sage and your parents.
(*The prince pays homage by prostrating to them in order of rank.*)

NĀRADA: May you be well, sir!

KING: May you bear the yoke of our dynasty!
URVAŚĪ: May you always please your father!
(*Two bards are heard offstage.*)
FIRST BARD: Victory, young prince!

Like Brahmā's son, the immortal sage Atri,
and Atri's son, the cool-rayed moon;
like the moon's son, the wise planet,
and my lord the king, the planet's son—
may you follow the way of your father,
practicing virtues prized among men!
In a lineage of such eminence
this blessing is virtually fulfilled. (21)

SECOND BARD:

Shared by your father, the noblest of the noble,
and you, whose courage and strength are unshakable,
the splendor of sovereignty now shines more brightly,
like Gaṅgā's waters shared by Himālaya and the sea. (22)

RAMBHĀ (*approaching Urvaśī*): Dear friend, how fortunate you are to see the splendor of sovereignty bestowed on your son while you remain with your husband!
URVAŚĪ: Surely the good fortune belongs to us all.
(*She takes the prince by the hand.*)
Come, child, you must pay your respects to your elder mother, the senior queen.
KING: Stay. We will all go together to the lady in a while.
NĀRADA:

The royal splendor of crown prince Āyus
calls to mind the war god Kumāra, Śiva's son,
when Indra, lord of storms, installed him
commander-in-chief of heaven's armies. (23)

KING: Generous Indra has favored me.
NĀRADA: Is there anything more you wish him to do for you?
KING: If Indra is pleased with me, why should I wish more?

Still, let us say this:

It is rare to find a happy alliance
when things are mutually opposite—
let wealth unite with the goddess of speech
that hearts of truth may prosper! (24)

(*All exit.*)

END OF ACT FIVE AND OF THE PLAY
URVAŚĪ WON BY VALOR

Mālavikā and Agnimitra

TRANSLATED BY EDWIN GEROW

CHARACTERS

Players in the prologue:
DIRECTOR: Director of the players and manager of the theater (*sūtradhāra*).
ASSISTANT: Assistant director (*pāripārśvika*).

Principal roles:
KING: Agnimitra, the hero (*nāyaka*); ruler of Vidiśā.
MĀLAVIKĀ: The heroine (*nāyikā*); a maid in the retinue of Queen Dhāriṇī.
BUFFOON: Gautama, the king's comical brahman companion (*vidūṣaka*).
NUN: Kauśikī, a nun (*parivrājikā*) in the retinue of Queen Dhāriṇī.
QUEEN: Dhāriṇī, chief queen of King Agnimitra.
IRĀVATĪ: Junior queen of King Agnimitra.

Members of the king's retinue:
MINISTER: Vāhataka, the prime minister (*amātya*).
CHAMBERLAIN: Maudgalya, chief officer of the king's household (*kañcukī*).
DOORKEEPER: Jayasenā, female usher at the door to the king's chambers (*pratīhārī*).
GAṆADĀSA: Dancing master; tutor of Mālavikā; patronized by the queen.

HARADATTA: Dancing master; rival of Gaṇadāsa; patronized by the king.

Various maidservants:
BAKULĀVALIKĀ: Maid to the queen and friend of Mālavikā.
KAUMUDIKĀ: Maid to the queen.
NIPUṆIKĀ: Maid to Irāvatī.
MADHUKARIKĀ: Keeper of the king's garden.
SAMĀHITIKĀ: Maid to the nun.
TWO GIRLS: Jyotsnikā and Rajanikā, sent as tribute to the king by the prince of Vidarbha.

Male servant:
SĀRASAKA: A hunchback, attendant to the queen.

Offstage voices:
VOICE OFFSTAGE: From the area or dressing room behind the curtain (*nepathye*), out of sight of the audience. Mainly that of a character about to enter the stage.
BARDS OFFSTAGE: Keepers of the royal calendar and panegyrists to the king (*vaitālikau*).

All five acts take place in the palace of Agnimitra; the season is spring.

ACT ONE

Our lord omnipotent is source of all reward,
yet wears a single skin of antelope.
Our lord commingles with the lovely goddess Śrī,
yet is the saint of world-renouncing saints.
Our lord bears this universe in his eight forms,
yet suffers in himself no pride.
May Śiva dispel the darkness from our sight
that we may view our path aright! (1)

PROLOGUE

DIRECTOR (*looking toward the dressing room*): Māriṣa, come here!
ASSISTANT (*entering*): Sir, I am here.
DIRECTOR: The learned assembly has told me to produce a play suitable for the spring festival—something called *Mālavikā and Agnimitra* by Kālidāsa. Let the musical prelude begin!
ASSISTANT: Not so fast! Why ignore works of celebrated poets like Bhāsa, Saumilla, and Kaviputra to bestow honor on a modern writer?
DIRECTOR: Your remark cannot survive examination. Listen:

Not all is justified by the name of old,
nor is the new poem never extolled—
wise men examine, then select the best from both,
but fools merely parrot others' quotes. (2)

ASSISTANT: You, sir, are the authority, of course.

DIRECTOR: Hurry then!

> I wish to fulfill the assembly's command,
> accepted with bowed head—
> henceforth I am the clever servant
> of Queen Dhāriṇī. (3)

(*They exit; the prologue ends.*)

BAKULĀVALIKĀ (*entering*): Queen Dhāriṇī commands me to ask dancing master Gaṇadāsa how Mālavikā is doing in her study of the chalika dance. So now I'm on my way to the theater.
(*She walks about; a second servant girl enters bearing a jewel in her hand. Bakulāvalikā sees her.*)
Hello Kaumudikā! What are you looking at? You pass right by and don't even see me!
KAUMUDIKĀ: Oh Bakulāvalikā! Don't be angry. I can't take my eyes off this lovely serpent ring I got from the queen's jeweler.
BAKULĀVALIKĀ (*examining the ring*): It's worth looking at. The halo of rays on the ring seems to make your finger bloom.
KAUMUDIKĀ: Where are you off to, friend?
BAKULĀVALIKĀ: The queen wants me to ask Gaṇadāsa how well Mālavikā is learning her lessons.
KAUMUDIKĀ: Then, the king did see her, though she was cleverly kept out of sight.
BAKULĀVALIKĀ: Yes, indeed; he saw her in a picture of the queen and her retinue!
KAUMUDIKĀ: How did it happen?
BAKULĀVALIKĀ: Well, the queen went to the picture gallery. She stopped to admire a painting whose colors were still fresh. Just then the king arrived.
KAUMUDIKĀ: Yes, then?
BAKULĀVALIKĀ: After the usual greetings, the king sat next

to the queen. Noticing in the picture a young lady among the queen's attendants, the king asked—

KAUMUDIKĀ: What?

BAKULĀVALIKĀ: "My queen, what is the name of that unprecedented beauty seated there beside you?"

KAUMUDIKĀ: Aha! He needs little instruction in the fine points of physiognomy! What then?

BAKULĀVALIKĀ: The queen ignored the question and the king, a bit worried now, asked her again and again. When the queen said nothing, little Princess Vasulakṣmī piped up: "Papa, this is Mālavikā."

KAUMUDIKĀ (*smiling*): Such innocence! Tell me the rest.

BAKULĀVALIKĀ: What rest? The real Mālavikā was immediately whisked away from the king's usual haunts.

KAUMUDIKĀ: Friend, you have your work to do. And I must bring this ring to the queen.

(*She exits.*)

BAKULĀVALIKĀ (*walking around, looking*): The dancing master's leaving the theater. I'll present myself to him.

(*She approaches.*)

GAṆADĀSA (*entering*): Surely the traditional calling of each man is a thing of honor; and certainly respect is not paid in vain to ours:

For ancient sages consider drama
the visible and pacific sacrifice of the gods;
its two modes are shown by Śiva himself
in the body he divides with Umā;
actions of men, born of nature's three strands,
are there displayed in many moods—
and though men have many different tastes,
the play is the one delight of all. (4)

BAKULĀVALIKĀ (*approaching*): Greetings, sir.

GAṆADĀSA: My girl, may you long prosper.

BAKULĀVALIKĀ: Sir, the queen sends me to ask, "Mālavikā must be giving you a lot of trouble learning her lessons?"

GAṆADĀSA: Young lady, you may tell the queen that my pupil is clever as well as intelligent:

Whatever manner of portrayal
I demonstrate to her,
she shows me back again,
perfected in technique. (5)

BAKULĀVALIKĀ (*to herself*): I see that she has already surpassed Irāvatī.
(*Aloud.*)
Your pupil is blessed, since she pleases her teacher so well.
GAṆADĀSA: Ah, but her talent is rare! May I ask where the queen found such a jewel?
BAKULĀVALIKĀ: The queen has a half-brother of lower caste, Vīrasena, who was posted by the king to a frontier fort near the Narmadā river. It was he who sent Mālavikā as an offering to his sister, asking that the girl be employed at some artistic task.
GAṆADĀSA (*to himself*): Her beauty and her behavior both suggest that the girl is not made of common stuff.
(*Aloud.*)
I also have been honored by the gift.

The teacher's art achieves new power
in the shape of this special girl
as cloud-born water in the oyster shell
induces a perfect pearl. (6)

BAKULĀVALIKĀ: Sir, where is your pupil now?
GAṆADĀSA: She is enjoying the breeze in the window overlooking the long pond. I let her rest after practicing the dance of five aspects.
BAKULĀVALIKĀ: Then will you, sir, please excuse me? I'll freshen her enthusiasm with news of her teacher's satisfaction.
GAṆADĀSA: Go see your friend: I'll take a moment and go to my own house.

(*They exit; the prelude ends. King Agnimitra enters, with his attendants to one side, followed by his minister bearing a message.*)

KING (*looking at the minister, who is reading the message to himself*): Vāhataka, what is the latest project of King Vidarbha?

MINISTER: My lord, it appears to be his own destruction.

KING: Let's hear the message.

MINISTER: He is replying to your earlier letter about his cousin Mādhavasena: "I have been addressed by Your Honorable Person in the following terms"—you will recall that you sent him this message—"Your uncle's son, Prince Mādhavasena, who had been promised to us in marriage was set upon and seized by your frontier guards as he approached my borders. You ought, in consideration of my dignity, to release him, along with his wife and sister!"

Vidarbha replies to this: "But surely, you are aware of what constitutes proper royal conduct when the parties are of equal dignity; Your Honor ought in this matter to be impartial. Mādhavasena's sister was lost in the commotion of the encounter; I am making efforts to find her. But if Your Honor wishes Mādhavasena to be released, hear my conditions:

If you'll release my brother-in-law, Mauryasaciva,
then I'll set free your son-to-be, Mādhavasena." (7)

KING (*angrily*): This fellow is ignorant of his own rank. Does he now seek to barter with me by exchange of treaties? Vāhataka, Vidarbha is my natural enemy and vexes me. Order the army division under General Vīrasena to proceed with the plan agreed on previously. It is time to obliterate this upstart who has the nerve to stand against me.

MINISTER: As my lord commands!

KING (*hesitating*): But what do you think?

MINISTER: My lord's plan conforms to the precepts of politics:

"An enemy new in his kingdom
is like a newly planted tree:
easy to topple, for he's not
taken root in his people." (8)

KING: The words of the pundit are trustworthy. Let the commander then bestir himself, fixing well their message in his mind.
MINISTER: So be it.
(*He exits. The king's attendants occupy themselves with their several tasks.*)
BUFFOON (*entering*): The king did entrust me with a small request: "Gautama," he said, "devise some means whereby I may behold Mālavikā—rather than the picture which I saw by chance." I have done just that. I must tell him so.
KING (*seeing the buffoon*): Ah! Here comes my other minister for "external affairs."
BUFFOON (*approaching*): May you prosper!
KING (*with a nod of the head*): Sit here.
(*Buffoon sits.*)
Has the eye of your wisdom perceived a scheme that will work?
BUFFOON: Ask rather about the success of the scheme.
KING: What?
BUFFOON (*in his ear*): Just this . . .
KING: Well done, my friend! And cleverly begun! Though success is always difficult, we have hope in this affair.

A king avoids much peril, and attains
his ends with the help of friends—
a man with perfect eyes sees nothing
in the night without a light. (9)

VOICE OFFSTAGE: Enough boasting! Only in the king's presence will my superiority be recognized.
KING (*listening*): Friend, a flower blooms on the tree of your excellent policy.
BUFFOON: And you will soon see the fruit.
(*The chamberlain enters.*)
CHAMBERLAIN: My lord, the minister reports that your commands have been carried out. But now Haradatta and

Gaṇadāsa,

Each seeking to condemn the other,
both masters of the dancer's art,
now sue to see you—two of the drama's
moods, each playing out his part. (10)

KING: Let them enter.
CHAMBERLAIN: As the king commands.
(*He exits; reenters with the two dancing masters, Haradatta and Gaṇadāsa.*)
This way gentlemen.
HARADATTA (*looking at the king*): How difficult of approach is the king's majesty!

I am no stranger, nor his enemy,
yet I tremble to approach his side.
Before my eyes his aspect changes
new each moment, like the sea. (11)

GAṆADĀSA: Great indeed is this brilliance which has the form of man!

His guardian of the door invites my entrance
and trusted servants lead me to the Lion throne.
No one bars my way; and yet I'm restrained
by splendors I dare not look upon. (12)

CHAMBERLAIN: The king! Advance and honor him!
BOTH (*approaching*): Victory to the king!
KING: Welcome to you!
(*He looks at the servants.*)
Seats for them.
(*Both sit on chairs brought by the servants.*)
Why are you two dancing masters in attendance here during the usual time for teaching?
GAṆADĀSA: King, hear! I learned my science from the master Sutīrtha; Your Majesty gave his patronage; the queen took me into her retinue!

KING: I know that. So?
GAṆADĀSA: I was insulted in front of very important people by this Haradatta. He said I was not worthy to take the dust from his feet!
HARADATTA: King, he was the first to speak:
(*Mimics.*)
"Between this gentleman and myself there is just one difference. He is a pond; I am the ocean." Will Your Majesty consent to test us in theory and in practice? Only the king is sufficiently judicious.
BUFFOON: Well put.
GAṆADĀSA: That is the main point! Will Your Majesty listen attentively—
KING: Wait a minute! The queen would think me partial. This affair should only be pursued before her and the learned Kauśikī.
BUFFOON: Well put.
BOTH TEACHERS: Whatever pleases the king.
KING: Maudgalya, mention this to the queen, and call her here; summon the learned Kauśikī too.
CHAMBERLAIN: As the king commands.
(*He exits; reenters with the queen and the nun, Kauśikī.*)
This way, my lady.
QUEEN (*to the nun*): Reverend nun, what's your opinion of this quarrel between Haradatta and Gaṇadāsa?
NUN: You needn't worry about the defeat of your party. Gaṇadāsa is not about to be bested by this opponent.
QUEEN: It may be so; but the king's support is an advantage.
NUN: But you too carry an august title, Chief Queen.

> A fire burns hotter
> in the heat of noon;
> and the night's embrace
> highlights the pallid moon. (13)

BUFFOON: Hear! Hear! Cometh Queen Dhāriṇī, preceded by her Prime Ministress!

KING: I see her—

> Auspiciously adorned,
> followed by ascetic Kauśikī—
> the triple Veda incarnate
> along with its philosophy! (14)

NUN (*approaching*): Victory to the king!
KING: I welcome you, my good woman.
NUN:

> For one hundred autumns,
> may you husband both Dhāriṇīs:
> your queen and the earth herself;
> their progeny precious, their patience alike. (15)

QUEEN: May my noble lord be victorious!
KING: Welcome my queen.
(*To the nun.*)
Good lady, take this seat.
(*All sit down.*)
These two gentlemen, Haradatta and Gaṇadāsa, are quarreling over their dancing expertise. Please accept the task of questioning them.
NUN (*smiling*): Such flattery. Would you have a valuable gem examined in a village when you were near the city?
KING: No, no! You are justly known as the learned Kauśikī. In any case the queen and I are partial.
TEACHERS: The king is right: you have not taken sides, and so are able to distinguish qualities from faults.
KING: Then let the dispute begin.
NUN: Your Majesty, the art of dance lies chiefly in its practice. What is the use of trading opinions? Does the queen agree?
QUEEN: If you ask me, I don't like the whole quarrel. It is displeasing.
GAṆADĀSA: No! Don't think me likely to dishonor you with my abilities.

BUFFOON: My lady! The ram fight commences! For the first time they will earn their salaries.
QUEEN: Aren't you the lover of quarrels!
BUFFOON: No, no, no. There's no peace for one rutting elephant so long as the other is unconquered.
KING: Have you sufficiently observed the grace of their bodily movements?
NUN: Yes.
KING: Then what else must they prove to us?
NUN (*smiling*): That's the point!

Some artists are born, their art innate,
but can't like some a pupil educate.
He whose art both pupil and himself inspires
alone is "teacher," for he shows his art entire. (16)

BUFFOON: Did you two hear the lady's words? In a nutshell the decision depends on showing us your teaching.
HARADATTA: That's agreeable to us.
GAṆADĀSA: My queen, the matter is settled!
QUEEN: If a stupid pupil ruins good instruction, is it the fault of the teacher?
KING: Queen, it so happens that it is. The teacher's acceptance of such a pupil shows insufficient discrimination.
QUEEN (*to herself*): What now?
(*Looking at Gaṇadāsa; aloud.*)
Don't further the king's fancies, which are the cause of all this bother. Withdraw from the whole affair. It's pointless.
BUFFOON: Yes, of course, the queen is right. Dear Gaṇadāsa! Why risk your dignity as royal dancing master? Go on! Just gorge yourself on the sweet fruits of service to Sarasvatī! Why bother with quarreling? It's so uncomfortable!
GAṆADĀSA: Yes, that is surely the queen's meaning. But listen to this timely verse:

Should I be afraid to quarrel and lose my job,
and bear the barbs of others silently?
Is my learning nothing but a livelihood?
Am I a merchant dealing in the wares of wit? (17)

QUEEN (*to Gaṇadāsa*): Your pupil just began her studies; it isn't proper to test instruction that hasn't yet been mastered.
GAṆADĀSA: But that is why I insist!
QUEEN: All right! Let the two pupils perform before the nun alone.
NUN: That wouldn't be proper! Accepting the judgment of a single person, even one who is ominiscient, would likely lead to error.
QUEEN (*to herself*): Stupid woman! Do you take me for a sleepwalker? I am wide awake!
(*She turns away in vexation; the king indicates the queen to the nun.*)
NUN:

Why do you hide
your face from him without reason?
Even righteous wives
express their anger in good season. (18)

BUFFOON: But her anger is justified. Her dependents have to be protected.
(*To Gaṇadāsa.*)
How fortunate you are to be rescued by the queen's pretense of anger! Some aren't quite up to showing off their teaching, though they be clever enough otherwise!
GAṆADĀSA: Queen! Hear him! Everyone will think so!

If you won't allow me to show
how well I can impart my art
even when my skills are mocked,
then I'm lost. Why won't you take my part? (19)

QUEEN (*to herself*): What's the use?
(*Aloud.*)
The teacher has authority over his students.
GAṆADĀSA: I'm worrying for nothing. The queen agrees.
(*To the king.*)
Will the king tell me which form of dance I am to direct?
KING: Whatever the august judge commands.

NUN: The queen seems preoccupied. I am worried.
QUEEN: Speak without fear. I am the mistress of my retinue.
KING: "And of me," she might add.
QUEEN: Dear lady, speak.
NUN: The chalika dance of Śarmiṣṭhā, based on a lyrical quatrain, is considered difficult to execute. We will see how each teacher directs the same passage, and learn how their teaching skills differ.
TEACHERS: As the good lady commands.
BUFFOON: Let the two parties send a messenger to His Majesty as soon as the theater is ready for a musical recital. Otherwise, not even the sound of the drum will rouse us.
HARADATTA: Yes sir.
(*Rises. Gaṇadāsa looks at the queen.*)
QUEEN (*to Gaṇadāsa*): I am not opposed to your victory. May you prevail!
(*Teachers begin to leave.*)
NUN: A moment, gentlemen.
TEACHERS (*turning around*): We are here.
NUN: Let me speak as the judge. Each of your students in turn should enter from backstage to demonstrate her facility in each dance posture.
BOTH: You need not tell us that.
(*They exit.*)
QUEEN (*to the king*): If my noble lord were to show as much cleverness in arranging affairs of state, we would all prosper.
KING:

> You misunderstand, my angry one!
> You think it's all a game!
> But men of equal merit
> will contest each other's fame! (20)

(*Backstage, the sound of a drum. All listen.*)
NUN: Hurry! The music has begun. Indeed—

> The ruffle of the peacock drum intoxicates the soul—
> it rises from the stable middle tone and resounds so deep
> that peacocks take it for the thunder of the clouds
> and stretch their necks to imitate the sound. (21)

KING: My queen, let us be members of the audience.
QUEEN (*to herself*): The coarseness of this nobleman.
BUFFOON (*in a stage whisper, to the king*): Go quickly or the queen will raise more objections.
KING:

The hurried passion of the drumbeat drives me on—
it is the sound of my desire reaching satisfaction. (22)

(*All exit.*)

END OF ACT ONE

ACT TWO

(*The arrangements for the musical performance are ready. The king is revealed seated, accompanied by the buffoon, the queen, and the nun, each with attendants according to rank.*)

KING: Sister! Of the two teachers, whose performance are we to see first?
NUN: Since they are equal in the weight of their knowledge, Gaṇadāsa deserves precedence by the weight of his years.
KING: Maudgalya, tell them. Then go about your business.
CHAMBERLAIN: As the king commands.
(*He exits.*)
GAṆADĀSA (*entering*): My lord! Here is Śarmiṣṭhā's four-part chalika composition in moderate rhythm; would it please your lordship to observe it?
KING: Sir, I am most respectfully attentive.
(*Gaṇadāsa exits; the king turns to the buffoon.*)
Friend:

My eyes are eager for a vision
of the girl waiting backstage.
They lose restraint, they rush headlong
to seize the curtain's cloth! (1)

BUFFOON (*to the king*). Nectar for the eye is near and already attracts the bee! You may drink now, but don't get drunk!
(*Mālavikā enters, her teacher carefully regarding her movements; the buffoon whispers.*)
Look, your excellency! Sweetness itself pales before her image!

KING (*to the buffoon*): Friend, at first

My heart suspected in her portrait
some forgery of beauty.
But now I think the painter dozed
and failed to do his duty. (2)

GAṆADĀSA: Child, be confident and do not fear!
KING (*to himself*): In every attitude her beauty is blameless:

Her long eyes, the autumn-moon glow of her face,
arms curving gently from her shoulders,
a delicate chest with firm high breasts,
torso lustrous as with polish,
her hips ample, yet hands could encompass her waist;
her toes are curved, and the shape of her body
fulfills the ideal in her teacher's mind. (3)

MĀLAVIKĀ (*having finished the preliminary dance, she sings the lyric*):

My lover loves me not.
O heart, abandon hope!
What now?
My left eyelid's a-flutter!
Might he, so long away,
come back to me?
My lord! Thy servant
longs for thee. (4)

(*She dances in accord with the mood of each phrase.*)
BUFFOON (*to the king*): Friend, the verse is a pretext; she offered herself to you!
KING: Friend, my heart believes it:

It is I who am the object of this disguised complaint—
She can't declare her love before the angry queen,
so she hides her passion in the movements of the dance
and sings: "My love, believe me devoted to you!" (5)

(*At the end of the song Mālavikā begins to leave.*)

BUFFOON: Young lady, wait! Didn't you forget something?
GAṆADĀSA: Stay, child, you may leave once your performance is corrected.
(*Mālavikā stops, waits.*)
KING (*to himself*): Oh, her loveliness grows more lovely in each new condition:

More lovely than her dance
this stance erect and motionless—
left arm akimbo,
bracelets silent on her wrist,
the other arm languid
like a fruit-dark branch,
eyes fixed on flowers
that lie crushed at her feet. (6)

QUEEN (*to Gaṇadāsa*): Do you take even Gautama's words to heart?
GAṆADĀSA: Queen, don't belittle him; the subtle views of Gautama often reflect royal inspiration.

Even dimwits are enlightened
by a wise man's company;
when paṅka nuts touch muddy water,
miraculously it clears. (7)

(*Looking at the buffoon.*)
We will hear what you have to say.
BUFFOON (*looking at Gaṇadāsa*): First ask Kauśikī for her opinion; then I'll tell you the fault I saw!
GAṆADĀSA: My good woman: Judge it as you saw it: good or bad.
NUN: Everything I saw was flawless.

The meaning was set forth
with gestures and interwoven words,
dance steps followed time,
truth was in every mood,

the portrayal was gentle
and seemed natural to her limbs;
emotion wrought emotion from the matter—
it was a very work of passion. (8)

GAṆADĀSA: What does the king think?
KING: Our partisan confidence is somewhat slackened.
GAṆADĀSA: (*to the king*): I am today truly a dancing master:

That teaching is the best
which you as judge require:
it comes like gold unblemished
from your testing fire. (9)

QUEEN: Your fortune prospers in the homage of the judges.
GAṆADĀSA: The queen's patronage alone is my prosperity.
(*Looking at the buffoon.*)
Gautama, now tell us what's on your mind.
BUFFOON: On the occasion of a pupil's first recital, one must first propitiate a brahman. This you forgot to do.
(*All laugh; Mālavikā smiles.*)
NUN: Oh, the researcher is deeply versed in procedure.
KING (*to himself*): At last my eye has found its true object:

Now that I've seen her smile,
lips half hiding lovely teeth
like an unfolding lotus
whose filaments peek out, half seen. (10)

GAṆADĀSA: Imposing brahman! This is not her first offering in the theater. Otherwise, how would we not have honored you, worthy as you are?
BUFFOON: I'm just a silly cātaka bird: I want a drink even when it thunders in a rainless sky. Fools are always hoping for some sign of a wise man's pleasure. Well, the young lady has recited beautifully; I will offer her this small token of my satisfaction.
(*Draws a bracelet from the king's arm.*)
QUEEN: Wait a minute! Why are you giving this prize? You haven't seen her rival's skills.

BUFFOON: I'm giving it, of course, because it belongs to someone else.
QUEEN (*looking at the teacher*): Good sir! Has your pupil finished her performance?
GAṆADĀSA: (*to Mālavikā*): Child, you may leave now.
(*Mālavikā exits, with the teacher.*)
BUFFOON (*to the king*): So far and no further has the power of my intellect been able to serve you.
KING: A minor qualification indeed!

Her disappearance from our midst
is the sunset of my eyes' great fortune—
the end of my heart's great festival,
a prison confining my self-control. (11)

BUFFOON (*to the king*): Like a sick pauper you want the medicine and think the doctor will give it free!
HARADATTA (*entering*): King! Now please favor my production with your attention.
KING (*to himself*): What reason remains for our looking more!
(*Affecting politeness, aloud.*)
We are indeed eager!
HARADATTA: I am flattered.
A BARD OFFSTAGE: Victory to the king! The hour of noon is upon us! For

Swans laze with half-closed eyes
in the shade of the lotus leaves.
House pigeons shun rooftops
shimmering with heat.
A peacock pursues the water wheel
thirsty for its breeze.
The seven-steeded sun
enflames all with his rays
like you, O king, your qualities ablaze. (12)

BUFFOON: Help! The brahman's meal time has arrived! Your Highness' physicians consider it unhealthy to deviate from any routine.

(*Looking at Haradatta.*)
Haradatta! What do you say?
HARADATTA: I have no reason to speak.
KING: Then we will see your performance tomorrow. Take your ease.
HARADATTA: As the king commands.
(*He exits.*)
QUEEN: Let the royal prince attend to his ritual bath.
BUFFOON: Madam, I would prefer that you hurry the food and drink.
NUN (*standing up*): Health to your highness.
(*She exits with the queen.*)
BUFFOON: Friend, Mālavikā is unexcelled in beauty, and skill.
KING: Friend,

The playful god dipped his arrow of love
in poison sharp
when he sought to perfect her beauty
with skill and grace. (13)

Enough, friend, I need compassion!
BUFFOON: And so do I! The pit of my stomach burns like a cooking pot in the market.
KING: Please pursue my affairs as eagerly as you do food.
BUFFOON: I'll do my best. But Mālavikā can be seen only when the queen permits. She's moonlight hidden in a drift of cloud. And you! You're like a vulture wheeling round the slaughterhouse looking for raw meat and a little anxious too. The man who expects success must be patient. And that would please me.
KING: But I can't wait!

I have no repose but a girl with gentle eyes—
My heart cannot but all my concubines despise. (14)

(*All exit.*)

END OF ACT TWO

ACT THREE

(*A servant of the nun enters.*)

SAMĀHITIKĀ: My mistress sends me to get a citron from the king's pleasure grove! So I must find Madhukarikā, the guardian of the grove. Here she is, looking at the golden aśoka tree. I'll approach her.
(*The guardian enters. Samāhitikā approaches.*)
Madhukarikā, are your forest duties pleasant?
MADHUKARIKĀ: Ah! Samāhitikā. Welcome, friend.
SAMĀHITIKĀ: My mistress waits upon the queen and must not approach with empty hands. So she sends me to get a citron from you.
MADHUKARIKĀ: The citrons are nearby. First, tell me about the quarrelsome dancing masters! Whose recital did your mistress prefer?
SAMĀHITIKĀ: Both were learned in the texts and both were skilled in practice; still Gaṇadāsa came out ahead because of his excellent pupil, Mālavikā.
MADHUKARIKĀ: Have you heard any gossip about Mālavikā?
SAMĀHITIKĀ: The king is eager to have her; but out of respect for Queen Dhāriṇī's feelings he's somehow controlling himself. And poor Mālavikā these days seems to wither like a jasmine vine, plucked and then abandoned. I don't know any more. I must go now.
MADHUKARIKĀ: Take the citron on this branch.
SAMĀHITIKĀ (*takes the citron with a gesture*): And may you obtain the sweet fruit of service to a worthy master.
(*She begins to leave.*)
MADHUKARIKĀ: Friend, we'll go together. I'll tell the queen

that the golden aśoka tree, so late in blooming, now shows signs of pregnancy.

SAMĀHITIKĀ: It is a timely duty.

(*They exit; the interlude ends. The king enters, showing the effects of unrequited love, with the buffoon.*)

KING (*looking down at himself*):

My body wastes away, unrequited
by the joy of her embrace;
tear-filled my eyes,
for failing to glimpse her face.
But you, my heart, are ever near
that girl with antelope eyes.
Why then so close to joy
do you suffer so and cry? (1)

BUFFOON: These moanings do not flatter your royal composure! I have seen Bakulāvalikā, and I gave her Your Highness' message.

KING: What did she say?

BUFFOON: She was honored by your commission. But, poor Mālavikā is too well guarded by the queen. She cannot easily be approached, like the jewel in the cobra's hood. I'm still trying.

KING: O Love! I'm writhing in these bonds of yours and . . . and you strike me such a blow! I cannot bear another moment. Oh!

(*Amazed.*)

From a weapon made of hope
comes a pain that crushes hearts!
Is your flowered arrow, Love,
both cruel and tender, sweet and harsh? (2)

BUFFOON: I told you we've made a start in this affair. Control yourself!

KING: Where shall I spend the rest of the day? My heart shuns its usual occupations.

BUFFOON: Just now Nipuṇikā brought a present of red

amaranth blossoms from Queen Irāvatī, who invites you to come play on the swing with her. Sweet in their first flowering! Harbingers of the new spring season! And you promised her anyway! Let's go to the pleasure grove.

KING: I cannot.

BUFFOON: What?

KING: Friend, women are too clever. The lady will notice that my heart is elsewhere, even as I fondle her. So I think,

It is better to end habitual affairs.
There are many occasions to cut them off—
the court we pay to spirited women,
however once intense, should not lack passion. (3)

BUFFOON: You must not so suddenly slight the civilities due the ladies of the harem!

KING (*reflecting*): Then lead the way to the pleasure grove.

BUFFOON: This way.

(*Both move off.*)

Look closely! The grove hastens your entrance; the new shoots are like beckoning fingers, unsteady in the gentle wind . . .

KING (*gesturing the wind's touch*): Ah! Noble spring!

The soft southern breeze, sweet with mango
is the hand of the god of spring;
his voice, the cuckoo distraught with pity
who coos: can we bear love's sting? (4)

BUFFOON: Enter and take your pleasure.

(*Both enter.*)

Look carefully: the goddess of the grove, to entice you in, wears a dress of spring flowers that would shame the conceits of young women.

KING: I look with amazement.

A black and tawny kurabaka flower
shames their careful mascara!
Their red lac-lipstick pales
before the scarlet aśoka!

The tilaka-ritual tamed by tilaka blooms
whose unguent is a swarm of bees!
So does the spring goddess belittle
cosmetic rites of young women! (5)

(*Both describe in gesture the beauty of the grove.*)

MĀLAVIKĀ (*entering, with a distracted air*): I'm ashamed of seeking a husband whose feelings are unknown to me. Where will I find the strength to explain all this to my kind friends? How long will the god of love make me bear this pain which has no remedy?

(*She goes a few steps.*)

Where am I?

(*She portrays reflection.*)

Ah, yes, my queen told me to take her place in the ceremony to calm the birth pangs of the golden aśoka tree. The poor lady fell from a swing through Gautama's carelessness and injured her foot. And if the aśoka does bloom before the fifth night, the queen promised to give me something that would fulfill a wish.

(*She pauses, looks around.*)

I seem to have arrived first at the ritual ground. While I wait for Bakulāvalikā to bring the foot-ornaments, I'll sit alone and lament my fate!

BUFFOON (*seeing her*): Hey! Hey! Here's a morsel of sugar candy for one who's soured on rum.

KING: What?

BUFFOON: Mālavikā is here—her clothing unadorned, her face anxious, and she's alone!

KING (*happily*): Mālavikā?

BUFFOON: Yes!

KING: My life is again bearable!

And my distressed heart rejoices
when I hear you say it's she—
I am a thirsty traveler, who hears
a waterbird's call near a tree-hidden stream. (6)

BUFFOON: She is coming out of the grove of trees.

KING (*joyfully looking*): I see her:

> Broad hipped,
> slender-waisted,
> bosom full and bold;
> my life itself advances,
> casting sidelong glances. (7)

Friend, her loveliness excels its former state—

> Her cheeks are pale as stalks of cane;
> her ornaments are few—
> an early jasmine vine whose buds are rare
> and leaves still new. (8)

BUFFOON: She will soon be adorned the way you are, with lovesickness.
KING: Your friendship gives you foresight.
MĀLAVIKĀ: This aśoka imitates my longing: she too yearns for her gay spring flowering, and has not yet put on her finery. I'll rest on this stone bench in the tree's cool shade.
BUFFOON: Did you hear Mālavikā say that she yearns?
KING: Ah! But the implication is unverified; for

> The wind from the southern mountain,
> fragrant with amaranth pollen,
> fresh with scents of budding flowers,
> often incites an aimless longing. (9)

(*Mālavikā sits.*)
Friend, we are now hidden in the bower.
BUFFOON: I think I hear Irāvatī not far away.
KING: The elephant who finds a lotus pond does not worry about crocodiles.
(*He continues looking out.*)
MĀLAVIKĀ: O heart, give up this pointless passion! Why do you torment me?
(*The buffoon looks at the king.*)
KING: Friend, how devious is love!
(*Aside to the buffoon, though addressed to Mālavikā.*)

You won't reveal the cause of your desire
and my thought no certain truth attains—
yet, nymph of the lovely thighs, I think
I am the object of these sweet complaints. (10)

BUFFOON: You will soon doubt less. Here comes stealthy Bakulāvalikā armed with your message of love.

KING: Will she remember our request?

BUFFOON: Will the daughter of a slave forget so imposing a message? Even I remember it!

BAKULĀVALIKĀ (*entering with foot-ornaments in her hands*): Is my friend well?

MĀLAVIKĀ: Bakulāvalikā is here! Friend, welcome. Sit down.

BAKULĀVALIKĀ (*sitting*): The queen has chosen you for the ceremony because you are a faithful servant. Give me your foot so that I may decorate it with an anklet and red lac.

MĀLAVIKĀ (*to herself*): Oh heart! heart! Take no pleasure in these tokens of power! How can I get myself out of this? Otherwise this ornament will be for my funeral.

BAKULĀVALIKĀ: What are you thinking about? The queen awaits the blossoming of the golden aśoka.

KING: Is she being dressed up only for the aśoka's blossoming?

BUFFOON: As if you didn't know: do you think the queen would dress her in harem garments on my account?

MĀLAVIKĀ: Friend, pardon me.

(*She offers her foot.*)

BAKULĀVALIKĀ: I think of your foot as my own body.

(*She begins to mime the adornment of the foot.*)

KING:

My friend, consider the tip of her foot,
where the fresh lac flashes:
anew in her toe sprouts the tree of love
that Śiva burned to ashes! (11)

BUFFOON: The foot is suited to its high office.

KING: Ah! true! true!

Toenails shining with lac red as new sprouts,
the girl's foot with equal justice might strike
the aśoka tree thirsting to flower
or her lover bent low with recent guilt. (12)

BUFFOON: The lady will strike you, for you have often sinned.
KING: I take the words of a prescient brahman to heart.
(*Irāvatī enters, intoxicated, with a servant girl.*)
IRĀVATĪ: Nipuṇikā, my girl, I have heard often that tipsiness is quite becoming to the feminine sex. Is that saying true?
NIPUṆIKĀ: It was formerly a mere saying; now it is true.
IRĀVATĪ: You flatter me. Tell me how did you learn that the king has already gone to the swing?
NIPUṆIKĀ: Observing his unshakable affection for your ladyship.
IRĀVATĪ: You serve me well. Now tell me the truth.
NIPUṆIKĀ: I heard it from noble Gautama, who is greedy for the spring festival offerings. Hurry, your ladyship!
IRĀVATĪ (*pacing about in accordance with her state of mind*): My heart hurries to meet the king. But my feet make no progress. I've had a bit too much to drink.
NIPUṆIKĀ: We have arrived at the swing.
IRĀVATĪ: Nipuṇikā! The king is not here!
NIPUṆIKĀ: Look around! He's probably hiding—one of his pranks. Let's go over to the aśoka, near the stone bench strewn with flowers of the priyaṅgu creeper.
IRĀVATĪ: All right.
NIPUṆIKĀ (*looking around*): Look, your ladyship, while we sit here ants are biting off the mango bud.
IRĀVATĪ (*suspiciously*): What do you mean?
NIPUṆIKĀ: Bakulāvalikā is adorning Mālavikā's feet under the aśoka.
IRĀVATĪ (*showing alarm*): Mālavikā doesn't belong here! What do you make of it?
NIPUṆIKĀ: The queen, who fell from the swing and injured her foot, must have ordered Mālavikā to perform the aśoka

blossom ritual. Why else would the queen entrust her very own pair of anklets to a servant?

IRĀVATĪ: That is a great honor for her.

NIPUṆIKĀ: Why isn't the king here?

IRĀVATĪ: Friend, my feet can't go any further. My mind is troubled. I must find the truth behind my suspicions.

(*She contemplates Mālavikā, then reflects; to herself.*)

My heart is right to tremble.

BAKULĀVALIKĀ (*showing a foot to Mālavikā*): Does the streak of lac please you?

MĀLAVIKĀ: Friend, I'm ashamed to praise it on my own foot. Tell me who taught you the art of cosmetics?

BAKULĀVALIKĀ: I'm a pupil of the king.

BUFFOON (*to the king*): Hurry, go claim your tuition fee.

MĀLAVIKĀ: You don't seem proud of it.

BAKULĀVALIKĀ: But now that I've found two feet worthy of my studies, my pride stirs.

(*Looking at the red lac; to herself.*)

Well, I've done what I was sent to do.

(*Aloud.*)

I've finished painting one foot. It needs only my own breath to dry it. Or perhaps the wind will do it.

KING: Friend, look! look!

> My breath might have dried her foot wet with lac!
> The first chance to serve her! What held me back? (13)

BUFFOON: Don't despair! You'll have other occasions for that sort of thing.

BAKULĀVALIKĀ: Your foot shines like a hundred-petaled red lotus.

(*Confidentially.*)

May you be constantly at the king's side!

(*Irāvatī glances at Nipuṇikā.*)

KING: My wish too!

MĀLAVIKĀ: Friend, do not say what cannot be said.

BAKULĀVALIKĀ: I speak only what must be said.

MĀLAVIKĀ: Am I so dear to you?

BAKULĀVALIKĀ: Not only to me!
MĀLAVIKĀ: To whom else?
BAKULĀVALIKĀ: To the king himself, who fancies himself an expert where quality is concerned.
MĀLAVIKĀ: You speak falsely. The king doesn't even notice me.
BAKULĀVALIKĀ: You don't notice the truth! Which, in any case is clear enough from the wasted and pale limbs of the king.
NIPUṆIKĀ: The bitch learned that line beforehand.
BAKULĀVALIKĀ: Remember the old adage: passion knows passion best.
MĀLAVIKĀ: Is that your opinion too?
BAKULĀVALIKĀ: Not mine alone; these words sweet with affection come from the king's own lips.
MĀLAVIKĀ: Friend, I wonder about the queen; my heart is afraid.
BAKULĀVALIKĀ: Stupid! Who would not ornament herself with a fresh mango blossom even though it might attract a swarm of bees?
MĀLAVIKĀ: Will you remain a faithful friend even in my hour of peril?
BAKULĀVALIKĀ: My name is Bakulāvalikā, is it not? Like a "garland of bakula flowers," I become more fragrant when bruised.
KING: Well said, Bakulāvalikā!

> Your flattery has sharpened her intent;
> you've answered rightly her denials;
> your words confirm Mālavikā's sweet passion—
> so depends the life of love on the envoy's wit! (14)

IRĀVATĪ (*to Nipuṇikā*): Girl! See! Mālavikā's fortune, as well as her foot, has been prepared by Bakulāvalikā.
NIPUṆIKĀ: Well, yes! How will the king fare now that the tree has succumbed?
IRĀVATĪ: My heart is rightly suspicious. When I understand the meaning of all this I'll decide what to do.

BAKULĀVALIKĀ: The other foot is now anointed. Let me put on the two anklets.
(*She does so in gesture.*)
Friend, arise! Perform the command of the queen! May the aśoka bloom!
(*Both rise.*)
IRĀVATĪ (*to Nipuṇikā*): Did you hear? By the queen's command! Indeed! Indeed!
BAKULĀVALIKĀ: Look! Standing before you, the first bloom of passion ready for enjoyment!
MĀLAVIKĀ (*joyously*): The king?
BAKULĀVALIKĀ (*smiling*): No, not the king. This cluster of sprouts hanging from the aśoka. Make it an ornament for your ear.
(*Mālavikā shows disappointment.*)
BUFFOON: Did you hear that?
KING: Friend, can lovers be satisfied with so little?

Polite meetings with an indifferent love
hold no joy for me,
but when two impassioned lovers despair to meet,
death itself is sweet! (15)

(*Mālavikā, who has arranged her garland of fresh buds, kicks the tree.*)

She plucked its buds for her ear,
then repaid it with a gentle kick—
I might have been the one she struck,
she might have taken the bud from me,
but I'm cheated by a tree! (16)

MĀLAVIKĀ: This aśoka is perverse, for it accepts my command to bloom, yet it shows no flowers. I hope our little ceremony won't be for nothing.
BAKULĀVALIKĀ: Friend, it would not be your fault. The tree is worthless if it accepts the honor of your foot and still is slow to bloom.
KING: Aśoka!

> You're blessed by the touch of her foot,
> tender as a new lotus shoot,
> and anklets that echo its moves—
> if you don't burst forth in bloom
> vain will be the pregnant thirsts
> that playful lovers share with you. (17)

Friend, I want to approach them; make some remark as a pretext.

BUFFOON: Let's go. I'll make fun of her.

(*They both approach.*)

NIPUṆIKĀ: Queen! The king comes!

IRĀVATĪ: As my heart suspected.

BUFFOON (*approaching*): Young lady! Do you think it proper to strike the aśoka with your left foot?

BOTH (*in agitation*): Heavens! The king!

BUFFOON: Bakulāvalikā! You're quite knowledgeable; why didn't you restrain the young lady from committing this impropriety?

(*Mālavikā shows fear.*)

NIPUṆIKĀ: Your ladyship, look! Gautama's up to something!

IRĀVATĪ: How else could the penniless brahman make a living?

BAKULĀVALIKĀ: Please sir! She's performing the queen's command; the transgression is not really hers! Please forgive her!

(*She makes Mālavikā fall before the king, and does so herself.*)

KING: If so, then you have not sinned. Arise, young lady.

(*Taking her by the hand, he raises her.*)

BUFFOON: Quite properly done! It's really Dhāriṇī to whom you are paying your respects.

KING (*laughing*):

> My smiling and graceful maiden,
> your left foot shows no mark—
> though it be tender as a new sprout
> and has struck against the harsh tree bark. (18)

(*Mālavikā expresses shame.*)

IRĀVATĪ: My noble lord has a heart like soft butter.
MĀLAVIKĀ: Bakulāvalikā, come! We must tell the queen that her command is fulfilled.
BAKULĀVALIKĀ: His Majesty must excuse you first.
KING: Please. You may go. Yet hear one request suited to the occasion.
BAKULĀVALIKĀ: Listen attentively. We await Your Majesty's command.
KING:

For many seasons too this humble soul
has not borne the flower of happiness;
fulfill his longings with a touch—
he needs no other tenderness. (19)

IRĀVATĪ (*approaching suddenly*): Go on! Go on! Fulfill them all! The aśoka hasn't flowered; but this one blooms and bears fruit all at once!
(*All look at Irāvatī in confusion.*)
KING (*aside*): Friend, what recourse have we now?
BUFFOON: What? The strength of our legs.
IRĀVATĪ: Bakulāvalikā! You have done well. Mālavikā! Carry on! Fulfill the longings of our royal prince!
BOTH: Queen, forgive us! Who are we to claim the king's affection?
(*They exit.*)
IRĀVATĪ: Men are scoundrels! I didn't even recognize the trick. I'm naive as a deer, enchanted by the hunter's horn.
BUFFOON (*to the king*): Sir, think of some reply. Even a burglar caught in the act would say "I'm just practicing window repair!"
KING: My dearest! Mālavikā means nothing to me. While waiting for you, I thought only to amuse myself as best I could.
IRĀVATĪ: Oh, likely, likely! And you found such an agreeable way of passing the time! I shouldn't have interrupted with my unfortunate lament!
BUFFOON: You misconstrue the natural good manners of our

king. Does it matter if he stops a moment in idle conversation with the queen's servant? Only you see a fault!

IRĀVATĪ: Oh! It's a "conversation," is it? Why do I trouble myself?

(*In anger she begins to leave.*)

KING (*following*): Forgive me!

(*Irāvatī moves with difficulty, her feet entangled in her loosened girdle.*)

My darling, disrespect to a lover isn't becoming.

IRĀVATĪ: Wretch! Faithless heart!

KING:

> "A wretch!" With such harsh words
> do you disdain your constant love?
> Even your girdle, fallen at your feet,
> entreats you, my pet, to forgive. (20)

IRĀVATĪ: This damned thing's on your side!

(*Seizing the girdle, she tries to strike the king with it.*)

KING: My Irāvatī now,

> Angry and tearful, would strike me cruelly
> with a golden girdle fallen from her hips,
> like a swollen cloud about to punish
> Mount Vindhya with her thunderbolt. (21)

IRĀVATĪ: Will you insult me a second time?

(*She seizes the girdle with her hand.*)

KING (*grasps her hand, along with the garment*):

> Do you now withhold punishment,
> from the penitent sinner?
> Your coquetry increases his delight
> at this display of anger. (22)

I accept your pardon.

(*He falls at her feet.*)

IRĀVATĪ: These are not the feet of Mālavikā, which slake your thirst for joy!

(*She exits, with her servant girl.*)

BUFFOON: Get up! Her blessing has been given.
KING (*rising, looking after Irāvatī*): What? Has she gone?
BUFFOON: She didn't forgive your sins, but luckily friend, she did leave. Let's get out of here quickly! Or else, like Mars in retrogression she'll return.
KING: Oh, the inconstancy of love!

She spurns me,
yet my heart feels her not unkind
for it's smitten with another—
for a while I'll put her angers out of mind. (23)

(*All exit.*)

END OF ACT THREE

ACT FOUR

(*The king enters, restless, with a doorkeeper.*)

KING (*to himself*):

Drawn first to her on rumor's path,
my hope took root;
then she reached vision's realm,
and sprouts of love sprang up;
at last, touched by her hand,
my flesh thrilled and put forth buds.
Now may this tender love tree
gratify my taste for fruit. (1)

(*Aloud.*)
Gautama! Gautama!

DOORKEEPER: Victory to the king! Your Majesty, Gautama is not here.

KING (*to himself*): Ah! I sent him to get news of Mālavikā.

BUFFOON (*entering*): May my lord prosper.

KING: Jayasenā, find Queen Dhāriṇī and inquire about her injured foot.

DOORKEEPER: As the king commands.

(*She exits.*)

KING: Gautama, what news of our young friend?

BUFFOON: Well, the cat's caught the pigeon.

KING (*dejectedly*): What happened?

BUFFOON: Her mistress, red-eyed with anger, has thrown the wretched girl into the underground storeroom—or should I say into the jaws of death?

KING: The queen has learned of our meeting.

BUFFOON: Yes.
KING: Who is so unfriendly as to want to make the queen angry with us?
BUFFOON: Well, listen! The nun told me that yesterday Lady Irāvatī went to inquire about Queen Dhāriṇī's injured foot.
KING: Yes, yes.
BUFFOON: The queen asked whether she had seen her "beloved consort," to which Irāvatī replied, "Why do you refer to him so politely? Were you not aware that he is 'consort' also to certain persons of your domestic staff?"
KING: Without probing too deeply, I suspect she refers to Mālavikā.
BUFFOON: Then at the queen's urging, Irāvatī disclosed your indiscretion.
KING: She appears unusually vexed. Tell me the rest.
BUFFOON: What else is there to tell? Mālavikā and Bakulāvalikā resemble two snake maidens, their feet bound, transported into a hell, where the sun's rays never reach.
KING: Oh! How terrible!

> The sweet-throated cuckoo and the bee
> intent on the blossoms of the mango tree
> have in the hollow trunk been caught
> by sudden wind and rain's onslaught. (2)

Friend, is there any escape?
BUFFOON: Queen Dhāriṇī has told the guard of the storeroom, Mādhavikā, not to let either of them out, unless shown the queen's own signet ring.
KING (*sighing resignedly*): Friend, can anything be done?
BUFFOON (*reflecting*): There is one possible stratagem.
KING: What is it?
BUFFOON (*looking about*): Some one may be listening. I'll whisper.
(*He whispers.*)
So.
(*He instructs the king.*)
KING (*joyously*): Excellent! May it work!

DOORKEEPER (*entering*): Your Majesty, Queen Dhāriṇī is sitting on a couch in the breezeway enjoying some of the nun's stories. Her foot is anointed with red lac and a servant is rubbing it.
KING: The time is propitious for entering.
BUFFOON: You go ahead. I must not approach the queen with empty hands.
KING: Make Jayasenā party to our secret.
BUFFOON: I will.
(*He whispers.*)
And that's the way it is.
(*He exits, after informing her.*)
KING: Jayasenā! Show me the way to the couch in the breezeway.
DOORKEEPER: This way, Your Majesty.
(*The queen is revealed lying on a couch with the nun and attendants according to rank.*)
QUEEN: Noble Lady, that's a good beginning. What next?
NUN (*looking about*): I'll continue later. Here comes His Majesty, the Lord of Vidiśā.
QUEEN: Ah! My husband.
(*Tries to stand.*)
KING: Please! Please! Don't trouble yourself with civilities!

My softly speaking queen!
Don't disturb your foot for me!
That foot and I are much the same,
disposed, we both, on a bed of pain—
and deprived of the sudden anklet's noise;
nor should you, my queen, disturb my joys. (3)

QUEEN: May the noble lord be victorious!
NUN: May the king conquer.
KING (*acknowledging the nun, then sitting*): My queen, is the pain bearable?
QUEEN: Today it is better.
(*Enter the buffoon, much agitated, his thumb bound up in his sacred thread.*)

BUFFOON: Save me! Save me, Your Majesty! I've been bitten by a snake!
(*All are shocked.*)
KING: How awful! Where were you going?
BUFFOON: To the grove to get some flowers for an offering to the queen.
QUEEN: Oh! Oh! Oh! Is it I who put this brahman's life in danger?
BUFFOON: As I reached for a cluster of aśoka blossoms, death in the form of a cobra came out of a hollow in the tree to bite me!
(*Shows the snake bite.*)
NUN: The usual remedy is an incision of the bite. It should be done right away!

> Incision of the bite, or burning,
> or letting blood from the wound—
> these three give life back
> to those whom snakes attack. (4)

KING: This is a task for the poison specialist. Jayasenā! Bring Dhruvasiddhi here quickly.
DOORKEEPER: As the king commands.
(*He exits.*)
BUFFOON: Oh! I am seized by evil death!
KING: Be calm! Be calm! Sometimes the bite has no poison.
BUFFOON: Calm! My limbs are already in convulsions!
QUEEN: A portent of misfortune. Support the brahman!
(*Attendants agitatedly support him.*)
BUFFOON (*looking at the king*): Sir! I have been your companion since your youth. Please keep that in mind, and safeguard the welfare of my childless wife.
KING: Don't be afraid, Gautama. Soon the physician will treat you. Be brave.
DOORKEEPER (*entering*): King, the doctor Dhruvasiddhi says, "Bring Gautama to me."
KING: Then have the eunuchs carry him to the august doctor.
DOORKEEPER: I will.

BUFFOON (*looking at the queen*): My queen, I may live, I may not. Forgive me if I have sinned against you! It was in service to the king!

QUEEN: May you live long.

(*The buffoon and the doorkeeper exit.*)

KING: The timid fellow doubts even Dhruvasiddhi—whose very name assures success.

DOORKEEPER (*entering*): Victory! Dhruvasiddhi says, "In order to perform the water-pot ritual I need something marked with the sign of a snake. Find it."

QUEEN: My ring has the mark of a snake. Take it and give it back afterwards.

(*Gives the ring; the doorkeeper takes the ring, remains standing near.*)

KING: Jayasenā, inform me quickly whether the operation is successful.

DOORKEEPER: As the king commands.

(*She exits.*)

NUN: My heart declares that Gautama will be cured of the poison.

KING: May it be so.

DOORKEEPER (*entering*): Victory to the king! Gautama's convulsions have ceased. He is again healthy.

QUEEN: And luckily I am free from blame.

DOORKEEPER: My lord, your minister Vāhataka wishes you to know that there is much royal business to be transacted; he requests the favor of an audience.

QUEEN: My prince, may your undertakings be successful!

KING: My queen, this place is now in the open sun. But your foot requires shade. So let the couch be moved elsewhere.

QUEEN: Servants! Do as the king directs.

ATTENDANTS: Yes, Your Majesty.

(*The queen, the nun, and their attendants exit.*)

KING: Jayasenā, take me to the pleasure grove by the secret path.

DOORKEEPER: This way, my lord.

KING: Jayasenā, has Gautama finished his preparations?

DOORKEEPER: Yes, indeed.
KING:

Though the strategem assures our rendezvous,
My heart trembles, and is full of fears. (5)

BUFFOON (*entering*): Prosperity to the king! The auspicious ceremonies are complete.
KING: Jayasenā, you have much to occupy yourself elsewhere.
DOORKEEPER: As the king commands.
(*She exits.*)
KING: Gautama, the storeroom guard Mādhavikā is shrewd. Didn't she suspect anything?
BUFFOON: It *was* the queen's signet ring. What could she suspect?
KING: I don't mean the ring. She might have asked why the two girls were being released, or why you were appointed to do it, instead of one of the queen's retinue.
BUFFOON: I was asked. But though I'm slow-witted, my mind rose to the occasion.
KING: Tell me.
BUFFOON: I said, "The king has been informed by his astrologers that his governing star is in an inauspicious conjunction. It is, therefore, necessary that all the prisons be opened."
KING (*joyously*): Yes, what next?
BUFFOON: Then I said that the king was freeing the girls at the queen's request, for she did not wish to hurt Irāvatī's feelings, and I was acting for the king. Mādhavikā fell for it. Our goal is achieved.
KING (*embracing the buffoon*): You are indeed my friend!

Sharp wits alone cannot assure success
The road must also pass through sympathy. (6)

BUFFOON: Hurry! I left Mālavikā and her friend in the cottage near the pond to come back for you.
KING: I'll pay my respects to her. Go ahead.
BUFFOON: Come!

(*He moves around.*)
Here's the cottage.

KING (*showing fear*): Look! Here comes Irāvatī's servant, Candrikā, with a bouquet of flowers in her hand. Let's hide behind this wall.

BUFFOON: Ah! Yes, Candrikā the moonbeam; she must be avoided by thieves and lovers alike.

(*Both hide.*)

KING: Gautama, how does our friend pass the time while she waits for me? Come. Let's go to the window and look.

BUFFOON: All right.

(*Both, hidden, look on as Mālavikā and Bakulāvalikā enter.*)

BAKULĀVALIKĀ: Friend, bow to the king!

MĀLAVIKĀ (*joyously*): Namas te! Where is the king?

KING: She must be referring to my picture.

MĀLAVIKĀ (*looking at the door, dejectedly*): You're playing tricks on me.

KING: Friend, both the girl's joy and her dejection are delightful. Consider how

> The white lotus opens with the rising sun,
> but must wait for dusk to close—
> this lovely girl's face conveys
> contrary beauties in one glance. (7)

BAKULĀVALIKĀ: I'm talking about the king's portrait.

BOTH (*bowing*): Victory to the king!

MĀLAVIKĀ: My longing for the king wasn't satisfied in the commotion of our meeting. But now at least his perfect form appears in the picture.

BUFFOON: Did you hear? The lady says you aren't as pretty as your picture! Fool! Such vanity! You're as proud of your beauty as an empty box is of its jewels.

KING: My friend, though inquisitive, females are shy by nature. Consider:

> Their mind's eye conjures up
> details of each past rendezvous.
> Yet when their lover comes to visit
> their glances will not rest on him. (8)

MĀLAVIKĀ: At whom is the king looking with such a longing glance?
BAKULĀVALIKĀ: That's Irāvatī at the king's side.
MĀLAVIKĀ: Friend, it seems ungallant of the king to ignore his other consorts and fix his gaze on one alone.
BAKULĀVALIKĀ (*to herself*): She imagines it's the real king in the picture! I will tease her.
(*Aloud.*)
Friend, Irāvatī is the king's favorite.
MĀLAVIKĀ: Why then do I give myself all this trouble?
(*She turns away in vexation.*)
KING: Friend, look—

The pouting lip! As her face turns away
vexed, her rouge is broken by a frown—
she's learnt her lessons well, the little tease,
to feign such anger at her friend's misdeeds! (9)

BUFFOON: Be ready to calm her down.
MĀLAVIKĀ: And Gautama serves him here too!
(*Tries to turn away.*)
BAKULĀVALIKĀ (*restraining Mālavikā*): You're not angry now?
MĀLAVIKĀ: If you think my reasons for anger are old and withered, this refreshes them nicely.
KING (*approaching*):

These scenes are merely pictures
and not a cause for anger, lotus face!
And now I stand before you, visible,
intent on you alone, your slave. (10)

BAKULĀVALIKĀ: Victory!
MĀLAVIKĀ (*to herself*): Why did I find the king's picture so vexing?
(*With ashamed face she makes obeisance. The king shows the hesitation of a lover.*)
BUFFOON (*to the king*): You seem rather unmoved.
KING: It's because our friend is not trustworthy.
BUFFOON: What reason have you to distrust her?

KING: Listen:

In dreams she came, but vanished without trace;
and then from nowhere, rushed to my embrace:
why should my heart trust her when it exhibits
all the wounds of love from her elusive visits? (11)

BAKULĀVALIKĀ: Friend, you have often deceived the king. You must make yourself worthy of his trust.

MĀLAVIKĀ: I'm more to be pitied—in my dreams the king would not embrace me!

BAKULĀVALIKĀ: The girl deserves an answer, my king!

KING:

The five-arrowed god bears witness
to the dedication of my soul.
What answer? She's my mistress—
I'll serve her secretly. (12)

BAKULĀVALIKĀ: We are satisfied.

BUFFOON (*moving about, in confusion*): Bakulāvalikā! Look! A deer is trampling the shoots of a young aśoka tree. Come, we'll shoo him away.

BAKULĀVALIKĀ: Come.

(*Sets out.*)

KING: Will my friend stand watchful guard over us?

BUFFOON: Am I not a descendant of Gotama himself?

BAKULĀVALIKĀ (*moving about*): Gautama, sir! I'll hide. You guard the door.

BUFFOON: Fine.

(*Bakulāvalikā exits; the buffoon looks about.*)

Here is a crystal bench. I'll sit on it.

(*He sits.*)

How pleasant is the feel of this fine stone!

(*He drops off to sleep; Mālavikā remains, in great alarm.*)

KING:

Lovely girl! My touch startles you!
Such fear becomes you not; trust me!
Be instead a jasmine vine and cling
to your fragrant mango tree. (13)

MĀLAVIKĀ: I cannot, for fear of the queen.
KING: Fear nothing, my dear.
MĀLAVIKĀ (*with a smile*): I have seen the great courage of my lord, who fears nothing—even Irāvatī!
KING:

But, ruby-lips, in our Baimbika clan,
courtesy is the family vow—
may your long-eyed glances fall on me;
for I live only if you allow! (14)

Please favor the person who has long been fond of you.
(*He tries to embrace her; Mālavikā avoids him with a gesture.*)
KING (*to himself*): Ah! How charming the amorous vexation of young women!

Trembling she slaps my hand
that tries the girdle of her dress;
her arms become a shield for breasts
pressed in my hot embrace—
though I long to drink the nectar
of her long-eyed glance,
she turns away—these are but moves
in passion's charming game. (15)

(*Enter Irāvatī and Nipuṇikā.*)
IRĀVATĪ: Friend, did you hear Candrikā right? Does noble Gautama rest alone on the porch of the lake house?
NIPUṆIKĀ: Why else would I tell you?
IRĀVATĪ: Let's go there to see our king's companion, freed from danger . . .
NIPUṆIKĀ: You did not seem to finish.
IRĀVATĪ: Yes, and to honor the king's picture.
NIPUṆIKĀ: Why can't you be nice to the real king instead?
IRĀVATĪ: Silly! He isn't as nice as his picture. His heart belongs to someone else. I only wish to cleanse my offense toward him.
NIPUṆIKĀ: Come this way, then, my queen.
(*Both approach.*)

MAIDSERVANT (*entering*): Victory to Queen Irāvatī! Queen Dhāriṇī says, "I am no longer disposed to jealous anger. Mālavikā and her friend were put in chains only to encourage respect for you. If you now approve, I wish to favor my lord, the king. Tell me your wish."

IRĀVATĪ: Guardian, tell the queen it's not for me to give her orders. She has shown affection for me by punishing her servant; by whose favor if not hers will I prosper?

MAID: I'll tell her.

(*She exits.*)

NIPUṆIKĀ (*moving and looking about*): My queen! Who else but noble Gautama is lying here on the doorstep of the lake house, fast asleep like an ox in the market place.

IRĀVATĪ: Oh, no! The poison continues to work its change!

NIPUṆIKĀ: The color of his face seems healthy enough. Wasn't he treated by doctor Dhruvasiddhi? We need not fear the worst.

BUFFOON (*in his sleep*): My dear Mālavikā. . .

NIPUṆIKĀ: Did you hear? What is this cheat up to now? He fills his belly with the candies of our good wishes, all the while dreaming of Mālavikā!

BUFFOON: . . . more beautiful than Irāvatī . . .

NIPUṆIKĀ: How grotesque! I'll give this snake-fearing brahman something to fear. Here's a crooked stick shaped like a snake. I'll hide behind this wall.

IRĀVATĪ: The wretch deserves worse than a snakebite!

(*Nipuṇikā throws the stick at the buffoon.*)

BUFFOON (*waking suddenly*): King! King! Ayeee! A snake's landed on me!

KING (*approaching in haste*): Friend, nothing to fear, nothing to fear!

MĀLAVIKĀ (*following*): My lord, don't rush so! He said a *snake*.

IRĀVATĪ: Oh no! The king himself is running to him.

BUFFOON (*ironically, with loud laughter*): What? It's just a stick of wood? Oh my! Hmmm! It appears that my snakebite—though inflicted by ketaki thorns—has taken a definite turn for the worse.

BAKULĀVALIKĀ (*entering in great haste through the curtain*): My lord! Don't enter. There's a second snake here with a very crooked disposition!
IRĀVATĪ (*rushing suddenly up to the king*): Does the royal couple find their daytime tryst propitious for love-making?
(*All look at Irāvatī, confused, astounded.*)
KING: My dear, your courtesy is unprecedented.
IRĀVATĪ: Bakulāvalikā! Your messenger service for lonely hearts works round-the-clock.
BAKULĀVALIKĀ: Is it my fault then? Is it the croaking of the frogs that causes the rain?
BUFFOON (*to Irāvatī*): No! No! The very sight of you has made the king forget all about your disrespectful behavior. Are you ready to accept his gracious pardon?
IRĀVATĪ: I am angry, but what can I do?
KING: Your anger is groundless, my dear; it does not become you,

> Never, even for a moment, has your face
> shown signs of anger without cause—
> Speak, my sylph! Would the moon of the starry night
> eclipse unless the time was right? (16)

IRĀVATĪ: Groundless! Yes, you are right for once. I would really look silly to be angry just because my lot of happiness has passed to someone else.
KING: You misunderstand, my dear! I see no real cause for anger:

> Two guilty servants came to me to plead
> at festival that none be punished, but be freed! (17)

IRĀVATĪ: Nipuṇikā, go tell Queen Dhāriṇī we now know whose side she's on.
NIPUṆIKĀ: I will.
(*She exits.*)
BUFFOON (*to himself*): Ayeee! Calamity threatens! No sooner is the baby pigeon freed from its cage than it flies again into the paws of the cat!

NIPUṆIKĀ (*entering; to Irāvatī*): My queen, I met Mādhavikā by chance and this is what happened . . .
(*Whispers the rest.*)
IRĀVATĪ (*to herself*): So! The plots of that rascal brahman are discovered!
(*To the buffoon.*)
You are indeed the king's minister of extraneous affairs!
BUFFOON: My dear! If I ever spoke a diplomatic word, may I forget the holy Gāyatrī!
KING (*to himself*): How will I ever get out of this thicket of trouble?
DOORKEEPER (*entering*): My Lord, Little Princess Vasulakṣmī has been frightened by a monkey, while chasing a ball. She's in the queen's lap trembling like a wind-blown creeper and she won't calm down.
KING: Another royal calamity! Must children be so timid?
IRĀVATĪ (*with agitation*): Hurry, my noble lord! Console her! She must not relapse into shock!
KING: I will revive her.
(*He hurries off.*)
BUFFOON: Bravo, monkey! Bravo! You've rescued us from a bit of a problem!
(*The king and the buffoon exit; then Irāvatī, Nipuṇikā, and the doorkeeper.*)
MĀLAVIKĀ: Friend, when I think of the queen my heart trembles. I don't know whether I can bear to go on living.
VOICE OFFSTAGE: Marvelous! Even before the fifth night the golden aśoka is covered with its passion flowers! I must tell the queen!
(*Both, listening, are joyous.*)
BAKULĀVALIKĀ: Take heart, friend! The queen keeps her promises.
MĀLAVIKĀ: Let's follow the guardian of the pleasure grove!
BAKULĀVALIKĀ: Let's.
(*All exit.*)

END OF ACT FOUR

ACT FIVE

(*Madhukarikā, the guardian of the pleasure grove, enters.*)

MADHUKARIKĀ: I have made an altar by the aśoka tree and adorned it. I'll tell the queen that my work is finished.
(*She walks about.*)
Ah! The fates are kind to Mālavikā; just as Queen Dhāriṇī became angry with her, the news of the aśoka's blooming made her calm again. Where is the queen?
(*She looks around.*)
Ah! Who's that coming out of the courtyard? It's the hunchback, Sārasaka, one of the queen's servants, carrying a jewel! I'll question him.
(*Enter Sārasaka, as described; she approaches him.*)
Sārasaka! Where are you going?
SĀRASAKA: Madhukarikā, it's time to pay the learned brahmans their sacrificial fee. I'm bringing it to the king's priest.
MADHUKARIKĀ: For what ritual?
SĀRASAKA: As soon as she heard that her son Vasumitra had been appointed by the commander-in-chief to protect the sacrificial war horse, the queen made an offering of eighteen gold pieces, hoping to protect her son's life.
MADHUKARIKĀ: Where's the queen now? What is she doing?
SĀRASAKA: She's in the temple listening to the scribes read a message from her brother Vīrasena about events in Vidarbha.
MADHUKARIKĀ: What is the news of the Vidarbhan king?
SĀRASAKA: He has been captured by our king's forces under Vīrasena, and his kinsman Mādhavasena has also been freed. Mādhavasena has sent an ambassador to the king with valuable gifts of jewels, horses, and craftsmen.

MADHUKARIKĀ: Go then about your business. I'll wait upon the queen.
(*Both exit; the interlude ends.*)
DOORKEEPER (*entering*): The queen is occupied with the aśoka ceremony and asked me to tell the king that she wants to inspect its flowering beauty in his royal company. And so I'm waiting for the king, who is in his audience chamber.
(*She walks about.*)
BARDS OFFSTAGE: Give thanks that the king's staff of authority rests heavily on the heads of his enemies!
FIRST BARD: O king!

> Like embodied Love delighting in gentle cries of doves,
> you spend the spring in river gardens of Vidiśā;
> your enemies bend low, with trees on Varadā's banks,
> mere tethers for your army's elephants. (1)

SECOND BARD:

> Two heroes went among the Krathakaiśika;
> two deeds of valor are famed in sages' tales—
> you stole away Dame Fortune from Vidarbha's king,
> and Kṛṣṇa's iron arms kidnaped Rukmiṇī. (2)

DOORKEEPER: The king arrives, his route announced by shouts of victory; I'll wait beside this pillar of the main porch.
(*Stands aside. The king enters with the buffoon.*)
KING:

> I think of my beloved, at my approach alarmed,
> I hear of King Vidarbha, humbled by my arms.
> My heart takes pleasure and yet suffers pain—
> a lotus burned by sun, and cooled by rain. (3)

BUFFOON: In my view, Your Majesty will soon be entirely happy.
KING: How so?
BUFFOON: They say Queen Dhāriṇī today told the learned Kauśikī: "My good lady, if you are proud of your cosmetic

skills, then adorn Mālavikā in marriage finery." And she did dress Mālavikā with particular care. So it seems the queen may satisfy your wishes.

KING: My friend, we could have guessed as much from Dhāriṇī's behavior—once her envy cools, she shows great respect for my views.

DOORKEEPER (*approaching*): Victory to the king! The queen wishes to contemplate the flowering beauty of the golden aśoka in Your Majesty's company.

KING: Is the queen there now?

DOORKEEPER: Yes, she has quit the harem with appropriate ceremony, and waits for you with her own servants, among them Mālavikā.

KING (*looking at the buffoon with joy*): Jayasenā, lead the way.

DOORKEEPER: This way, my lord.

(*She moves off.*)

BUFFOON (*looking about*): Friend, in the pleasure grove the spring seems more advanced.

KING: It's just as you say.

The youthful season comes of age—
the mango tree is covered with fruit;
amaranth blossoms everywhere,
and longing fills the heart. (4)

BUFFOON: Look! The aśoka has put on a robe of flowers!

KING: Reluctantly it bloomed; now it wears a beauty incomparable. Look:

The flowers of all aśokas that hope for spring
have come to her, the first to slake her thirst. (5)

BUFFOON: Don't lose heart! Even though we're here, Queen Dhāriṇī has allowed Mālavikā to come along.

KING (*joyfully*): Friend, look:

Seconded by my respectful love, the queen there stands
like Earth herself, royal fortune in her lotus hands. (6)

(*Enter Queen Dhāriṇī, Mālavikā, the nun, and attendants according to rank.*)

MĀLAVIKĀ (*to herself*): I know why I wear these ornaments. Still my heart trembles like water on the lotus pad. My left eye quivers and will not stop.

BUFFOON: Friend, Mālavikā is lovely in her marriage garment.

KING: I gaze on her:

> In dazzling silks that drape discreetly
> she imitates, her ornaments rare,
> a night in spring, when moonlight overwhelms
> the stars still pale from winter's cold. (7)

QUEEN (*approaching*): Victory to the king!

BUFFOON: May Your Ladyship prosper!

NUN: The king be victorious!

KING: My lady, I salute you!

NUN: May your will be accomplished.

QUEEN (*with a smile*): My noble lord, I have made this aśoka tree a place where you can meet and advise the younger generation.

BUFFOON: Ah! She pays you homage!

KING (*shyly walking around the aśoka*):

> This tree's indeed a fit locale
> for honors such as queens may give:
> struck and humbled in these springtime rites
> it pays respect with flowers at your behest. (8)

BUFFOON: My lord, you may now gaze confidently upon her youthful . . .

QUEEN: Upon . . .?

BUFFOON: Upon the youthful— hm! —beauty of the aśoka's flowers.

(*All sit down.*)

KING (*looking at Mālavikā; to himself*): Worst of all is separation in her presence!

I'm the cakravāka bird;
my love's my lonely mate:
The queen who disapproves our match
is night who makes us wait. (9)

CHAMBERLAIN (*entering*): Victory to the king! Your minister sends a message:
(*Reads.*)
"Among those sent from Vidarbha as tribute were two girls, skilled in the arts, who were not shown to you before, being excessively fatigued by the journey. They are now ready for an audience. I await your orders."
KING: Bring them in.
CHAMBERLAIN: As the king commands.
(*He exits; reenters with the two girls.*)
This way, my ladies.
FIRST GIRL (*to the other, alone*): Friend Rajanikā, though this royal house is unfamiliar, my heart was calm as I entered.
SECOND GIRL: Jyotsnikā, mine too! There is a proverb: the feelings of the heart portend pain or pleasure.
FIRST GIRL: I hope so.
CHAMBERLAIN: The two ladies may approach.
(*Both do so. Mālavikā and the nun, seeing the girls, look at each other.*)
BOTH GIRLS (*bowing*): Victory to the king and queen!
KING: Sit down, both of you.
(*Both sit.*)
In what arts are you skilled?
BOTH: My lord, we are trained in singing.
KING: Queen, will you take one of them?
QUEEN: Mālavikā, come here. Which one would please you as a companion?
BOTH (*seeing Mālavikā*): Oh! my heavens! The king's daughter!
(*They fall to their knees.*)
May you be victorious!
(*They break out in tears, with Mālavikā; all look on astounded.*)
KING: Who are you two? And who is she?

BOTH: My lord, she is the daughter of our sovereign!
KING: Explain yourselves!
BOTH: My lord, Your Majesty's forces released Prince Mādhavasena from prison during the conquest of Vidarbha. This is Mālavikā, his younger sister.
QUEEN: She the daughter of a king! I have defiled sandalwood by using it for sandals!
KING: How did she get here, in this condition?
MĀLAVIKĀ (*sighing, to herself*): By the command of fate.
SECOND GIRL: Listen, my lord. When Prince Mādhavasena fell into the hands of his kinsman, his sister was spirited away by the faithful minister, Sumati, leaving behind all the retinue.
KING: This much I heard. We know nothing else.
NUN: I will tell the rest, unlucky wretch that I am.
BOTH GIRLS: Is it the voice of the noble Kauśikī?
MĀLAVIKĀ: It is.
BOTH: We hardly recognize her in the dress of an ascetic. Lady, we greet you.
NUN: Welcome to both of you.
KING: Are they from your personal retinue?
NUN: They are.
BUFFOON: Will you finally tell the rest of the story?
NUN (*weakly*): Listen: I am the younger sister of Sumati, the minister of Mādhavasena.
KING: Understood. Then?
NUN: After Mādhavasena had been captured, Sumati escaped with Mālavikā and myself, and in hopes of finding Your Excellency, took up with a caravan bound on foot for Vidiśā.
KING: Then?
NUN: The merchants continued on the road and into the next forest.
KING: Yes?
NUN: Then:

> A band of shouting tribesmen fell upon us;
> their chests were bound by thongs of arrowed quivers;
> peacock feathers in their hair hung to their heels—
> with bows in hand, their rush was difficult to stop. (10)

(*Mālavikā expresses fear.*)
BUFFOON: My sweet, fear nothing. The nun speaks of things long past.
KING: What next?
NUN: No sooner had the attack begun than the thieves put the soldiers of the caravan to flight.
KING: The rest must be painful.
NUN: My dear brother—

> While trying to rescue the princess, has since
> repaid with his life what he owed to his prince. (11)

FIRST GIRL: Oh! Sumati is dead!
SECOND GIRL: And our princess is reduced to this condition?
(*The nun cries.*)
KING: Being human, we must in time give up our mortal bodies. Do not grieve for the excellent Sumati, whose death was fruitful in his master's service. What happened then?
NUN: I fell unconscious, and when I came to, the girl had disappeared.
KING: You have lived through a great calamity.
NUN: Then I cremated the body of my brother, and in the sadness of recent widowhood, as it were, came to this country and donned these ascetic clothes.
KING: Such is the way of the honorable. And then?
NUN: From the forest dwellers the princess came to Vīrasena, from Vīrasena to the queen; and I saw her again only when I entered the queen's retinue. That is the end of my story.
MĀLAVIKĀ (*to herself*): What will the king say now?
KING: Oh how calamities dishonor us!

> This girl, virtuous, pure, and good,
> fit to be a queen,
> we called our slave—we used a silken cloth
> our pots to clean. (12)

QUEEN: My good woman, it was highly improper not to tell us about the noble birth of Mālavikā!
NUN: No ill is intended! I kept the secret for a good reason.

QUEEN: What reason?
NUN: Listen: while her father was alive, she and I once went on a pilgrimage. A certain soothsayer told her that she would find a worthy husband only after living as a servant for a year. I thought that this prophecy—which was bound to happen in any case—was fulfilled by her service to the queen; and so I waited, and think I did well.
KING: You were right to wait.
CHAMBERLAIN (*entering*): The minister begs leave to convey this news, which was overlooked in the press of other matters: the Vidarbhan operation has been successfully concluded in accordance with your previous directives. I await an expression of Your Majesty's wishes.
KING: Maudgalya, I desire to establish a dyarchy for the two brothers Yajñasena and Mādhavasena.

> Let them rule the northern and southern
> banks of the Varadā
> dividing the kingdom as the sun and moon
> divide the night and day. (13)

CHAMBERLAIN: My lord, I will inform the assembly of ministers.
(*The king approves with a motion of his hand; the chamberlain exits.*)
FIRST GIRL (*to Mālavikā*): Princess, your brother is lucky to win as fiefdom half the kingdom!
MĀLAVIKĀ: I think he has already been rewarded, for he is freed from danger to his life.
CHAMBERLAIN (*entering*): Victory to the king! Your minister salutes the auspicious decision of Your Majesty, which is also approved by the assembly:

> The kings will each share half the royal burden
> like two horses bearing the chariot's yoke,
> and will bring harmony from competition,
> under Your Majesty's benignant goad. (14)

KING: Then tell the assembly to inform General Vīrasena and let it be done.
CHAMBERLAIN: As the king commands.
(*He exits; reenters bearing a gift and a message.*)
Your Majesty's command is accomplished. Meanwhile a message and a gift have been received from your royal father, General Puṣpamitra. May Your Highness be pleased to read it.
(*The king accepts the gift, places it on his head, then conveys it to his retinue. He unwraps the message.*)
QUEEN (*to herself*): Oh, at last my heart's main interest! I'll hear some news of my son, Vasumitra, if they ever finish paying respects to one another. He was given such a heavy responsibility by the general.
KING (*sitting, reads*): "Prosper! General Puṣpamitra, from the army of sacrifice, to his son Agnimitra, his own life, in Vidiśā: I embrace you affectionately and inform you that the sacrificial horse has been set free to roam for a year. As the officiant of the royal sacrifice, I appointed Vasumitra to the animal's protection, with one hundred subordinate princes. While roaming on the right bank of the Indus, the horse was set upon by a force of Greeks; a great battle ensued between the two armies."
(*The queen shows despair.*)
How did such a thing happen?
(*Reads again.*)

> "The great bowman Vasumitra tamed our foes
> and saved the horse they tried to steal by force." (15)

QUEEN: My heart is relieved.
KING (*continuing*): "And now my grandson and I, like Sagara and Aṁśumant, will sacrifice the rescued horse. Let your excellency and ladies of the court, bearing no ill will, proceed without delay to the celebration of the sacrifice."
I am delighted.
NUN: Fortunate are the parents who prosper by the victory of a son!

(*To the queen.*)

Thanks to your husband, you stand
first among heroes' wives;
Thanks to your son, the title
"Mother of Heroes" is your device. (16)

QUEEN: Good lady, I am pleased: the son is like the father!
KING: Maudgalya, does the young elephant not imitate the chief of the herd?
CHAMBERLAIN:

The son's display of valor is not enough
to strike my mind with awe;
the father sowed this seed of victory
like Ūrujanman the fire within the sea. (17)

KING: Maudgalya, in celebration of this victory, release all prisoners, including the brother-in-law of Yajñasena.
CHAMBERLAIN: As the king commands.
(*He exits.*)
QUEEN: Jayasenā, go! Tell the ladies of the harem—first of all Melakā—the news of my son's victory.
DOORKEEPER: I will.
(*She begins to leave.*)
QUEEN: Wait a moment!
DOORKEEPER: Yes?
QUEEN (*aside, to the doorkeeper*): And tell Irāvatī what I promised Mālavikā if the aśoka bloomed, and also tell her about Mālavikā's noble birth. I implore Irāvatī's permission not to break faith with Mālavikā.
DOORKEEPER: As the queen commands.
(*She exits; reenters.*)
I have become as it were a jewel box bearing the congratulations of the ladies of the harem at your son's victory.
QUEEN: I am not surprised. Their nobility is not inferior to mine.
DOORKEEPER (*aside, to the queen*): My queen, Irāvatī replies, "Most seemly are the words of your highness, who in any

case enjoys authority. Promises given must not be otherwise."

QUEEN (*to the nun*): With your approval, good lady, I wish to give Mālavikā in marriage to the king as was intended by the noble Sumati.

NUN: You are still her mistress, my lady.

QUEEN (*taking Mālavikā by the hand*): Will the royal prince accept this token of my satisfaction, appropriate to our good fortune?

(*The king remains silent, ashamed, shy; with a smile.*)

Does His Highness disdain me?

BUFFOON: Noble lady, it is not unusual for the groom to be a bit shy.

(*The king looks askance at the buffoon.*)

Or perhaps he will accept Mālavikā only after Your Highness has given her the title "Queen."

QUEEN: That title is hers by birth. Why repeat it?

NUN: Not so, not so! My precious lady,

> Do uncut jewels, freshly mined
> deserve setting in a golden band? (18)

QUEEN (*remembering; to the nun*): Excuse me. With all this talk of nobility, the proprieties have been forgotten: Jayasenā! Go and bring a pair of fine cloths for the bride.

DOORKEEPER: As the queen commands.

(*She exits; reenters with the two garments.*)

My queen, here they are.

QUEEN (*embracing Mālavikā*): Now will the king accept her?

KING: My queen, I find no words to respond to your command.

NUN: At last! He accepts her!

BUFFOON: Such is his respect for Queen Dhāriṇī.

(*The queen looks to her attendants.*)

ATTENDANT (*approaching Mālavikā*): Victory to the queen.

(*Dhāriṇī regards the nun.*)

NUN (*to the queen*): In this behavior, Your Majesty, I find nothing remarkable.

The faithful wife does not refuse her lord
the rival he esteems;
a great river conveys to the mighty ocean
the waters of lesser streams. (19)

NIPUṆIKĀ (*entering*): Victory to the king! Queen Irāvatī sends this message: "If my lapse of conduct gave some offense to the king, please understand that it was from my natural regard for him, and let me receive at least a pardon from His Majesty, whose desires have been fulfilled."

QUEEN: Nipuṇikā, the king will certainly know how to reply to her message.

NIPUṆIKĀ: As the queen commands.

(*She exits.*)

NUN: My lord, if you will give me leave, I will convey to Mādhavasena the joyful news; for his purposes are much furthered by alliance with you.

QUEEN: My lady, must you leave us?

KING: I will commend you highly in my letter to His Highness.

NUN: This humble person has reached happiness in the warmth of your kindness.

QUEEN: Command me, king! How else may I serve your pleasure?

KING: What else can be enjoyed? This alone I do request, my angry one:

While your auspicious glance remains upon me
let no foes rise against us now or ever again;
the benefits of rule shall shower on the people—
plenty and wealth, as long as Agnimitra reigns! (20)

(*All exit.*)

END OF ACT FIVE AND OF THE PLAY
MĀLAVIKĀ AND AGNIMITRA

Notes

NOTES TO THE INTRODUCTION

Kālidāsa's World and His Plays

1. In Tibetan, Tāranātha, *rGya-gar-chos-'byuṅ,* trans. Lama Chimpa and Alaka Chattopadhyaya, pp. 114–16; I have followed this translation, with minor revisions. Tāranātha places Kālidāsa during the period of the philosopher Nāgārjuna, c. second–third century A.D. Another source of the Kālidāsa legend is Ballāla's *Bhoja Prabandha.* In this late sixteenth-century work the poet is portrayed as a courtier of King Bhoja of Dhāra and is credited with the solution of many riddles; see trans. by Louis Gray (see also note 22 below). One variant of the legend combines his skill at riddles and his obsession with courtesans into a tale of his tragic death.

Once, the king of Ceylon announced a riddle and offered a large reward for its solution. The riddle was "'that on a flower flowers are born' is heard but not seen" (*kusume kusumotpattiḥ śrūyate na ca dṛśyate*). Kālidāsa heard it from a courtesan and composed the solution in one line: "O girl, how is it that on the lotus of your face there are two blue lotuses of eyes?" (*bāle tava mukhāṁbhoje katham indīvaradvayam*). The courtesan, in her greed for the reward, killed the poet, but the skill of the line revealed her crime. See R. V. Tullu, "Traditional Accounts of Kālidāsa."

2. N. R. Subbanna, *Kālidāsa Citations.* The most recent comprehensive bibliography of texts, translations, and critical studies on Kālidāsa is S. P. Narang's *Kālidāsa Bibliography;* an annotated selection of primary and secondary sources is in K. Krishnamoorthy's *Kālidāsa,* pp. 147–52.

3. S. N. Dasgupta and S. K. De, *A History of Sanskrit Literature: Classical Period,* pp. 122–23.

4. *Meghadūta* 27, 30; all quotations are based on the critical edition of S. K. De.

5. *Meghadūta* 33–36.

6. B. S. Miller, "Kālidāsa's Verbal Icon: Aṣṭamūrti Śiva."

7. Stella Kramrisch, *The Presence of Śiva,* ch. 8.

8. Daniel H. H. Ingalls, "Kālidāsa and the Attitudes of the Golden Age."

9. J. C. Heesterman, *The Ancient Indian Royal Consecration,* pp. 224 ff.

10. *Manu* 7.3–7; chapter 7 is devoted to the duties of kings.

11. This is alluded to throughout Kālidāsa's plays; it is made explicit in the dialogue between Duṣyanta and Indra's charioteer Mātali at the opening of Act Seven of the *Śākuntala*.

12. Kālidāsa describes Raghu's son Aja in these terms in the opening verses of canto eight of the *Raghuvaṁśa*. *Rājādhirājarṣi* is the epithet of Candragupta II in the Udayagiri cave inscription composed by the court poet Vīrasena; D. R. Bhandarkar, *Inscriptions of the Early Gupta Kings*, 3:256.

13. See A. L. Basham, *The Wonder That Was India*, pp. 83 ff.

14. Ingalls, "Kālidāsa and the Attitudes of the Golden Age"; for summaries of earlier arguments on Kālidāsa's dates, see A. A. Macdonell, *A History of Sanskrit Literature*, pp. 320–27; A. B. Keith, *The Sanskrit Drama*, pp. 143–47; Dasgupta and De, *History*, pp. 118–26. Dasgupta, in his editorial notes (pp. 728–46), presents an ingenious argument for dating Kālidāsa to the post-Mauryan period, on the basis of legal concepts in his works, but the conclusions are overdrawn.

15. *Epigraphia Indica* (1900–1901; rpt., Delhi: Archaeological Survey of India, 1981), 6.7, v. 37.

yenāyoji naveśmasthiramarthavidhau vivekinā jinaveśma |
sa vijayatāṁ ravikīrtiḥ kavitāśritakālidāsabhāravikīrtiḥ ||

See R. C. Majumdar, et al. *History and Culture of the Indian People*, 3:234–37. It has been argued that the poet Vatsabhaṭṭi was indebted to Kālidāsa's *Meghadūta* in two verses (10, 11) of his Mandasor inscription of A.D. 472, thus offering even earlier evidence of Kālidāsa's work; see Georg Bühler, *Die indischen Inschriften und das Alter der indischen Kunstpoesie*, p. 18; Bhandarkar, *Inscriptions*, pp. 163–76, 322–32.

16. Bāṇabhaṭṭa, *Harṣacarita* 1.16:

nirgatāsu na vā kasya kālidāsasya sūktiṣu |
prītir madhurasāndrāsu mañjarīṣv iva jāyate ||

17. Bhandarkar, *Inscriptions*, pp. 203–20; analyzed pp. 148–63.

18. *Raghuvaṁśa* 4.28 ff.

19. A. S. Altekar, *The Coinage of the Gupta Empire*, pp. 90 ff.

20. The earliest sources of the Vikramāditya tradition are Jain works, on which later works, such as *Siṁhāsanadvatriṁśaka*, are based. See Majumdar, *History and Culture*, 2:154–57; D. C. Sircar, *Indian Epigraphy*, pp. 251–58, 331, and *Ancient Malwa and the Vikramāditya Tradition*, N. R. Banerjea, "Ujjayinī and Kālidāsa: Analysis of the Archaeology," pp. 113–18.

21. J. F. Fleet, *Inscriptions of the Early Gupta Kings and Their Successors*, Chammak and Siwani copper-plate inscriptions of Pravarasena II; text, p. 237, l. 15; p. 246, ll. 15–16.

22. The earliest known account connecting Kālidāsa with Vikramāditya is given by Bhoja, the eleventh-century royal patron and writer. In his *Śṛṅgāra*

Prakāśa, Bhoja reproduces a verse which is explained as referring to an embassy of Kālidāsa from Vikramāditya to a king, Kuntaleśa. Kuntala was a neighboring state conquered by the Vākāṭaka king Pṛthvīsena, and is not unlikely that the epithet belongs to him and his descendants. A sixteenth-century commentary on the Prakrit epic poem *Setubandha,* which describes the victory of Rāma over Rāvaṇa, says that the poem was composed by King Pravarasena and later revised by Kālidāsa, at the suggestion of Vikramāditya. See V. Raghavan, *Bhoja's Śṛṅgāra Prakāśa,* pp. 765–71.

The Kashmirian poet Kṣemendra cites a poem called *Kunteśvaradautya,* apparently now lost, and attributes it to Kālidāsa; *Aucityavicāracarcā,* 20.64. See also A. S. Altekar, "The Vākāṭakas," pp. 174–80. Altekar notes: "The literary tradition which associates Kālidāsa with King Bhojarāja can also be satisfactorily explained if we assume that he was first a tutor and then a protégé of Pravarasena II. The Vākāṭaka kingdom included Bhojadeśa or Bhojakaṭaka, which figures as a province of the kingdom in the Chammaka copper plates. Just as Pravarasena was known as Kuntaleśa, because of the recent conquest of Kuntala, he may also have been known as Bhojapati, because of the inclusion of Bhojakaṭaka in his kingdom. Very probably the Bhoja country or Berar was the home province of Vākāṭakas. Later on literary tradition confused Pravarasena, the king of Bhojadeśa, with king Bhoja, the king of Malwa, confusion which led to the mistake of Kālidāsa being regarded as a protégé of the Paramāra ruler Bhoja, who was indeed both a celebrated writer himself and also a famous patron of men of letters, but lived about six centuries later than Kālidāsa" (pp. 176–77). See V. V. Mirashi, "The Rāṣṭrakūṭas of Kuntala and the Date of Kālidāsa," pp. 78–92.

23. The evidence relating to *Devīcandragupta* is analyzed by V. Raghavan in *Bhoja's Śṛṅgāra Prakāśa,* pp. 843–65.

24. Bhandarkar, *Inscriptions,* pp. 234–42.

25. *Ibid.,* pp. 244–47; Altekar, *Coinage of the Gupta Empire,* ch. 6.

26. George Grierson, "Bhakti Marga," 2:539; Ananda K. Coomaraswamy, *Yakṣas,* pp. 1:27–28.

27. Bhandarkar, *Inscriptions,* pp. 255–57.

28. Majumdar, *History and Culture,* 3:431 ff.; Altekar, *Coinage of the Gupta Empire,* pp. 203–6; see p. 128 and pl. 8.8, a coin of Candragupta II in which the altar looks like a Śivaliṅga with its base.

29. In addition to the inscriptions and coins to which I have already made reference, literature and sculpture provide vivid examples. See B. S. Miller, "Bhartrihari's Poems" in *The Hermit and the Love-Thief;* J.A.B. van Buitenen, *Two Plays of Ancient India;* James Harle, *Gupta Sculpture;* Pratapaditya Pal, *The Ideal Image: Gupta Sculptural Tradition and Its Influence;* Joanna Williams, *The Art of Gupta India;* Stella Kramrisch, "Figural Sculpture of the Gupta Period." For summaries of Western notions of what is classical in literature and art, see "Classicism" in A. Preminger et al., eds., *Princeton Encyclopedia of Poetry and Poetics,* pp. 136 ff.

30. See, for example, Keith, *The Sanskrit Drama,* pp. 80–90; Bhāsa, *Plays Ascribed to Bhāsa,* ed. C. R. Devadhar; Balwant Gargi, *Folk Theater of India;* Kapila Vatsyayan, *Traditional Indian Theatre: Multiple Streams.*

31. Van Buitenen, *Two Plays of Ancient India* includes translations of the *Mṛcchakaṭika* and the *Mudrārākṣasa.* Fragments of the *Devīcandragupta* are difficult to appreciate without technical knowledge of Sanskrit drama and Gupta history.

32. References to Bharata's *Nāṭyaśāstra* (*NŚ*) are cited from the text and translation of M. Ghosh. On the dating of the extant text, see S. K. De, "The Problem of Bharata and the Ādi-Bhārata," pp. 156–76; S. A. Srinivasan, *On the Composition of the Nāṭyaśāstra;* Ghosh's introduction, *NŚ,* pp. lxxix–lxxxii. Good discussions of basic forms, theories, and examples will be found in Keith *The Sanskrit Drama,* and Sylvain Lévi, *Le Théâtre Indien.* See also G. K. Bhat, *Bharatanāṭyamañjarī;* Dhanaṁjaya, *Daśarūpa* (*DR*).

33. On Greek tragedy, see Helen Bacon, "Aeschylus"; cf. J. A. B. van Buitenen, "The Classical Drama," in E. C. Dimock, et al., eds. *The Literatures of India;* Sudhir Kakar, *The Inner World: A Psycho-analytic Study of Childhood and Society in India,* pp. 17, 28, 47; Minakshi L. Dalal, *Conflict in Sanskrit Drama.*

34. See *Vik* 2.17; Edwin Gerow's article in this volume and his "Dramatic Criticism" in Dimock, *The Literatures of India,* pp. 129–36; cf. Northrop Frye on fictional modes in *Anatomy of Criticism.*

35. *NŚ* 1.1–129, 4.269; see F. B. J. Kuiper, *Varuṇa and Vidūṣaka: On the Origin of the Sanskrit Drama,* pp. 36–37.

36. *NŚ* 1.106–9.

37. *Malāv* 1.4. The variant reading *kāntam* is more common than *śāntam;* see Gerow's note on the text.

> devānām idam āmananti munayaḥ śāntaṁ kratuṁ cākṣuṣaṁ
> rudreṇedam umākṛtavyatikare svāṅge vibhaktaṁ dvidhā |
> traiguṇyodbhavam atra lokacaritaṁ nānārasaṁ dṛśyate
> nāṭyaṁ bhinnarucer janasya bahudhāpy ekaṁ samārādhanam ||

The three *guṇas* are *sattva* (purity), *rajas* (passion), and *tamas* (darkness).

38. *NŚ* 27.1–17, 49–70.

39. *NŚ* 36.80–81; see V. Raghavan, "Sanskrit Drama in Performance," in R. van Meter Baumer and J. Brandon, eds., *Sanskrit Drama in Performance,* p. 43.

40. *Kumārasaṁbhava* 7.90.

> tau saṁdhiṣu vyañjitavṛttibhedaṁ
> rasāntareṣu pratibaddharāgam |
> apaśyatām apsarasāṁ muhūrtaṁ
> prayogam ādyaṁ lalitāṅgahāram ||

Saṁdhi refers to the sections of the plot (*NŚ* 21). *Vṛtti* refers to the style of drama (*NŚ* 22). *Rasa* means the flavor or mood of an aesthetic experience (*NŚ* 6); the rasas are classically eight in number (*NŚ* 6.15). *Aṅgahāra* is *āṅgikābhinaya* (*NŚ* 4.19 ff.) *Rāga* literally means "color" or "passion"; it refers to the melodic mode which is the basis for improvisation in Indian music. The word does not have this technical meaning in the *NŚ*, where the term *jāti* is used instead, but by Kālidāsa's time, it was a technical term (*Śāk* 1.4+, 1.5, 5.103+; *Mālav* 2.8, quoted in the next note). *Prayoga* means performance; it is a term Kālidāsa uses in his prologues.

41. *Mālav* 2.8:

aṅgair antarnihitavacanaiḥ sūcitaḥ samyagarthaḥ
pādanyāso layam anugataḥ tanmayatvaṁ raseṣu |
śākhāyonir mṛdur abhinayas tadvikalpānuvṛttau
bhāvo bhāvaṁ nudati viṣayād rāgabandhaḥ sa eva ||

For a more detailed discussion of Mālavikā's dance, see Kapila Vatsyayan, *Classical Indian Dance in Literature and the Arts,* pp. 213–17, 234–36.

42. *Vik,* Act 3, *praveśaka*. In the dialogue between the two students, one speaks Sanskrit and the other Prakrit.

43. Vāmana, author of *Kāvyālaṁkārasūtravṛtti* and believed to have been a minister of Jayāpīḍa, king of Kashmir A.D. 779–813, introduced this distinction. See Raghavan, *Bhoja's Śṛṅgāra Prakāśa,* pp. 73–81.

44. See *NŚ* 8–13; Bharatha Iyer, *Kathakali: The Sacred Dance Drama of Malabar,* for a discussion of *abhinaya* in the living traditions of Kathakali and Kūṭiyāṭṭam; Pragna Thakkar Enros, "Producing Sanskrit Plays in the Tradition of Kūṭiyāṭṭam," and V. Raghavan, "Sanskrit Drama in Performance," in Baumer and Brandon, *Sanskrit Drama in Performance.* Despite major differences between the dance drama in Kerala and classical Sanskrit drama (as we know it from the plays, from the *Nāṭyaśāstra,* and from a description of a production in a late eighth-century A.D. work from Kashmir entitled *Kuṭṭanīmata,* summarized by Raghavan, "Sanskrit Drama in Performance," pp. 16–17), there is a common emphasis on *abhinaya.* Although no play of Kālidāsa's is in the repertoire of the ritual theater of Kerala, the performance manuals for various plays, which have been handed down for centuries from generation to generation of Cakyars, supplement our textual knowledge of ancient performance style. I am indebted to Rukmini Devi for discussing this relationship with me one morning at Kalakshetra in January 1982.

45. See *Paintings from Ajanta Caves,* UNESCO World Art Series (New York Graphic Society, 1954); also Yazdani, *Ajantā.*

46. *Śāk* 1.20; this verse is classed by the commentators as *svabhāvokti,* "speaking of a thing as it is." See Daniel H. H. Ingalls, *An Anthology of Sanskrit Court Poetry,* sec. 35.

47. Such an incident is narrated in Iyer, *Kathakali,* as told to him by the Kathakali actor Kunju Kurup. One hears similar stories from dancers of Bharata Nāṭyam and other traditional schools.

48. The assistant director (*pāripārśvika*) is described in the *Nāṭyaśāstra* following the description of the director (*sūtradhāra*), *NŚ* 35.74–75. The qualities of the actress (*nāṭakīyā*) are given in general terms and in terms of her role as courtesan or other heroine; *NŚ* 34.25–70, 35.81–87,101.

49. *NŚ* 5.

50. *NŚ* 14.1–35.

51. *NŚ* 20.13–40. These introductory monologues or dialogues, called *viṣkambhaka* or *praveśaka,* compress into a short narrative or dialogue parts of the plot that are not enacted on stage, but that are essential for an understanding of the main action.

52. *Śāk* 7.34.

53. W. F. Wertheim, *East-West Parallels: Sociological Approaches to Modern Asia,* ch. 2, "Society as a Composite of Conflicting Values."

54. For an introduction to the norms of Sanskrit *kāvya* see Miller, *Hermit and the Love-Thief;* Ingalls, *Sanskrit Court Poetry;* Edwin Gerow, "The Sanskrit Lyric: A Genre Analysis," in Dimock, *The Literatures of India,* pp. 144–56; Louis Renou, "Sur la structure du kāvya."

55. *NŚ* 18.1–61. See L. Nitti-Dolci, *Les Grammairiens Prākrits,* ch. 2; R. A. Singh, "Inquiries into the Spoken Languages of India, From Early Times to Census of 1901," pp. 7 ff; S. M. Katre, *Prakrit Languages and Their Contribution to Indian Culture,* pp. 25–27; M. M. Deshpande, *Sociolinguistic Attitudes in India: An Historical Perspective.* See also P. Thieme, "Das indische Theater," pp. 45–47, where Thieme stresses the stylized realism and shadow-play origins of dramatic multilingualism; cf. J. A. B. van Buitenen, "The Classical Drama" in Dimock, *The Literatures of India,* pp. 81–85.

56. Lévi, *Théâtre Indien,* vol. 2, appendix: "Il ne faut pas s'imaginer toutefois que la variété des prācrits entraîne une inextricable confusion de langages. La plupart ne diffèrent que par certains caractères morphologiques ou phonétiques régulièrement fixés et limités à un petit nombre; le sanscrit en est toujours la base, et les prācrits ne sont guère que des prononciations spéciales du sanscrit."

57. *Śāk* 1.3–4. The Sanskrit verse contains the figure *parikara,* in which the many adjectival qualifications reinforce the distinctiveness of summer; see Edwin Gerow, *A Glossary of Sanskrit Figures of Speech,* p. 203. The Prakrit song, by contrast, contains a single image, whose effect is felt musically.

subhagasalilāvagāhāḥ pāṭalasaṁsargisurabhivanavātāḥ |
pracchāyasulabhanidrā divasāḥ pariṇāmaramaṇīyāḥ ||3||

īsīsicuṁbiāiṁ bhamarehiṁ suumārakesarasihāiṁ |
odaṁsayaṁti daamāṇā pamadāo sirīsakusumāiṁ ||4||

Other songs in the plays occur at *Śāk*, 3.13, 4.12, 4.16, 5.1, 6.2, 6.3; *Mālav* 2.4.; *Vik* 2.12 and throughout Act Four. There is also an epigrammatic Prakrit verse at *Śāk*, 6.1.

58. This is also true of the *Mṛcchakaṭika*, the *Mudrārākṣasa*, and the plays of Bhāsa. It is noteworthy that in all three dramas of Bhavabhūti, with over 800 verses, there are only 2 Prakrit verses (*Mālatīmādhava* 6.10, 11); that there is no Prakrit-speaking buffoon in the plays; and that throughout the *Uttararāmacarita*, there are only a few lines by the ascetic boy Saudhātaki in the *viṣkambhaka* to Act Four and short speeches by Sītā and Kausalyā.

59. Relevant to understanding the relationship between hero and heroine and the nature of secondary characters is Clifford Geertz's statement on the conception of the individual in Balinese society, in "From the Native's Point of View," p. 31:

> The Western conception of the person as a bounded, unique, more or less integrated motivational and cognitive universe; a dynamic center of awareness, emotion, judgement and action organized into a distinctive whole and set contrastively both against other such wholes and against a social and natural background is, however incorrigible it may seem to us, a rather peculiar idea within the context of the world's cultures. Rather than attempt to place the experience of others within the framework of such a conception, which is what the extolled "empathy" in fact usually comes down to, we must, if we are to achieve understanding, set that conception aside and view their experience within the framework of their own idea of what selfhood is.

See also Louis Dumont, *Homo Hierarchicus: Essai sur le système des castes;* Kakar, *The Inner World.*

60. The relation among these pursuits is widely debated in Indian literature of the classical period. The clearest debate is found in chapter 2 of the *Kāma Sūtra*. For a succinct statement on them as "attitudes" toward the world, see Karl Potter, *Presuppositions of India's Philosophies*, pp. 5–11; also Richard Robinson, "Humanism versus Asceticism in Aśvaghoṣa and Kālidāsa."

61. See *NŚ* 6.31 (*vibhāvānubhāvavyabhicārisaṁyogād rasaniṣpattiḥ*).

62. On *nāṭaka*, see *NŚ* 20.10–11.; Gerow's article in this book; Frye, "The Mythos of Summer: Romance" in *Anatomy of Criticism*, and Northrop Frye, *The Secular Scripture: A Study of the Structure of Romance*, pp. 103, 107, 147; Henry Wells and H. H. Anniah Gowda, *Shakespeare Turned East.*

63. *Mālav* 1.1+ (*kālidāsagrathitavastu mālavikāgnimitraṁ nāma nāṭakam*). Except for the restriction that a *nāṭikā* should have only four acts (*DR* 3.43–48; *NŚ* 20.59–62 is likely an interpolation) the definition of this subgenre (*uparūpaka*) describes the play well; see Gerow's article, note 21; Keith, *The Sanskrit Drama*, p. 350.

64. *Ṛg Veda* 10.71.1, 3, 4. See W. Norman Brown, "The Creative Role of the Goddess Vāc in the Ṛg Veda," pp. 393–97; Stella Kramrisch, "The Indian Great Goddess," pp. 247–49.

65. *Ṛg Veda* 10.125.

66. See M. Christopher Byrski, *Concept of Ancient Indian Theatre,* p. 142; cf. Kuiper, *Varuṇa and Vidūṣaka.*

67. *Meghadūta* 101.

68. Miller, *Hermit and the Love-Thief,* p. 87.

69. See *Kumārasaṁbhava* 6.87, 7.19–20; *Śāk* 4.4–5; *Mālav* 3.5–12.

70. The later Sanskrit poet Bilhaṇa defines her as "the precious vessel for tasting the drama of erotic love." See his *Caurapañcāśikā,* v. N24(c) in the Miller ed.:

śṛṅgāranāṭakarasottamaratnapātrīm

71. Devangana Desai, *Erotic Sculpture of India: A Socio-Cultural Study,* pp. 99–100; cf. *Meghadūta* 78; *Kāma Sūtra* 3.26.

72. *Mālav* 3.5–12; see Coomaraswamy, *Yakṣas;* Odette Viennot, *Le Culte de l'Arbre dans l'Inde Ancienne.*

73. *Mālav* 3.5; cf. *Kalikā Purāṇa* 55.24.

74. *Ṛg Veda* 10.95; *Śatapatha Brāhmaṇa* 3.4.1.22, 11.5.1. This interpretation of the myth is that of D. D. Kosambi, *Myth and Reality: Studies in the Formation of Indian Culture,* pp. 42–57.

75. *Padma Purāṇa* (Sṛṣṭikāṇḍa) 12.62–86; *Matsya Purāṇa* 24.10–32; *Viṣṇudharmottara Purāṇa* 1.129–37. See S. S. Janaki, "The Vikramorvaśīya of Kālidāsa: A Study of the Poet's Sources."

76. According to Kosambi, this is an inversion of the more ancient taboo against males' entering the groves of the goddess. *Myth and Reality,* p. 76.

77. In Velankar's critical edition, which follows the commentators Raṅganātha and Koṇeśvara, there are 31 stanzas in Māhārāṣṭrī and Apabhraṁśa. Out of these 11 Apabhraṁśa verses are addressed by the king to objects and animals of nature, while the remaining 20, as the commentators suggest, are descriptive of the king's state. In those editions of the play where commentators reject the propriety of the king speaking anything but Sanskrit, his verses addressed to various aspects and creatures of nature are in Sanskrit and the responses from nature provoked by the Apabhraṁśa verses are absent. See D. Gitomer's notes on the text.

78. *Vik* 4.8, 11, 20, 24, 34, 36, 45, 50, 53, 59, 71.

79. These *anyokti* verses occur at *Vik* 4.1–6, 12, 14, 19, 23, 28, 35, 41, 43, 48, 54, 63, 75; see Gitomer note to *Vik* 4.1.

80. The verses quoted are *Vik* 4.10, 11, 14.

ayam ekapade tayā viyogaḥ
priyayā copanataḥ suduḥsaho me |
navavāridharodayād ahobhir
bhavitavyaṁ ca nirātapatvaramyaiḥ ||

jalahara saṁhara ehu ko paiṁ āḍattao
aviraladhārāsāra disāmuhakaṁtao |
e maiṁ puhavi bhamaṁte jai pia pekkhimi
tavve jaṁ ju karīhisi taṁ tu sahīmi ||

daiārahio ahiaṁ duhio
virahāṇugao parimaṁtharao ।
girikāṇaṇae kusumujjalae
gaajūhavaī taha jhīṇagaī ॥

81. *Śatapatha Brāhmaṇa* 13.5.4.13.

82. That this is no ordinary antelope is clear from Kālidāsa's references and metaphors. It bears suggestive resemblance to the antelope form of Prajāpati that Stella Kramrisch elucidates in her book *The Presence of Śiva,* pp. 3–5.

83. Durvāsas is the embodiment of Śiva's fury. In the play he may be seen as the dark side of Duṣyanta; he represents the furious sentiment (*raudrarasa*), in contrast with the heroic (*vīrarasa*). The myth of his birth appears in several places in Purāṇic literature, e.g. *Śiva Purāṇa* (*Śatarudrasaṁhitā*) 19. In the *Mahābhārata* (1.67), he shows his pleasure at Kuntī's hospitality and gives her a *mantra* to invoke the god of her choice in order to obtain offspring.

84. *Meghadūta* 24; see Majumdar, *History and Culture,* 2:95 ff.

85. *Padma Purāṇa* 12.3.

86. *Mbh* 1.68.

87. See G. K. Bhat, *The Vidūṣaka;* S. K. De, "Wit, Humor, and Satire in Sanskrit Literature," pp. 257–89; Keith Jeffers, "Vidūṣaka versus Fool"; Kuiper, *Varuṇa and Vidūṣaka,* pp. 200–36. According to Kuiper, the relation between *nāyaka* and *vidūṣaka* reflects the Vedic antagonism between Indra, who is the guardian deity of the *nāyaka* (*NŚ* 1.82–95), and Varuṇa. The *vidūṣaka* impersonates Viṣṇu and "purifies" the king by taking on himself the latter's impurity. This scapegoat function could only be performed by a brahman.

88. The director (*sūtradhāra*) is defined as one who knows the rules (*sūtras*) of performance and directs their execution; *NŚ* 35.65–74, 98. In texts on architecture, the term *sūtradhāra* applies to the master builder, who knows the rules of structure and design.

89. *Atharva Veda* 6.130 is generally interpreted as a love charm; the female speaker asks the gods to send *smara* to make that man burn for her (*dévāḥ prá hinuta smarám asaú mā́m ánu śocatu*). *Smara* is described as being related to the nymphs who are chariot conquering, and belonging to the chariot conquering (*rathajítāṁ rāthajiteyīnām apsarásām ayáṁ smaráḥ*).

90. See *Avimāraka* in Bhāsa, *Plays Ascribed to Bhāsa,* ed. C. R. Devadhar, pp. 109–90; Bhavabhūti, *Uttararāmacarita,* ed. S. K. Belvalkar; Bilhaṇa, *Caurapañcāśikā,* ed. Miller; Jayadeva, *Gītagovinda,* ed. Miller. See also Miller, "The Divine Duality of Rādhā and Krishna."

91. See Ananda Coomaraswamy, "Recollection, Indian and Platonic"; Karl Potter, ed. *Indian Metaphysics and Epistemology: The Tradition of Nyāya-Vaiśeṣika up to Gaṅgeśa,* pp. 172–73, 219, 258, 297–98, 312–13.

92. *NŚ* 7.54–55. Similar definitions are found in the *Viṣṇudharmottara, Śṛṅgāraprakāśa,* and other texts. In Mammaṭa's *Kāvyaprakāśa* (10.199),

smaraṇa is an *alaṁkāra,* defined as the recollection of an object as it was experienced, when a similar object is seen (*yathānubhavam arthasya dṛṣṭe tatsadṛśe smṛtiḥ* । *smaraṇam*); a simile is implicit in this. In the *Sāhityadarpaṇa* (10.27), Viśvanātha modified the definition, replacing Mammaṭa's restricted relation between visual perception (*dṛṣṭa*) and recollection with a more general concept of perception (*anubhāva*) as the source of recollection, so that a recollection of an object arising from the perception of something like it is termed *smaraṇa* (*sadṛśānubhāvād vastusmṛtiḥ smaraṇam ucyate*).

93. See Raniero Gnoli, *The Aesthetic Experience According to Abhinavagupta,* text pp. 16 ff.; trans. pp. 74 ff.

94. The same verse is cited by Henry David Thoreau when he discusses aesthetic experience in "Monday" of *A Week on the Concord and Merrimack Rivers,* p. 175. It is the notion of recollection in Kālidāsa's plays that has led to the claim by Lacchmidhar Kalla, in *The Birthplace of Kālidāsa,* that the *Śākuntala* is an allegorical dramatization of *pratyabhijñā.* For a thorough refutation of this idea, see R. K. Kaw, *The Doctrine of Recognition (Pratyabhijñā Philosophy),* pp. 43–49.

95. See Wells and Gowda, "The Power of Recollection," in *Shakespeare Turned East.*

Sanskrit Dramatic Theory and Kālidāsa's Plays

1. See E. Gerow, "Kālidāsa" in the *Encyclopaedia Britannica,* 15th ed.

2. Aśvaghoṣa is usually dated in the first century A.D., which presumes Kālidāsa's date to be later than that. For a contrary opinion, see Dasgupta in S. N. Dasgupta and S. K. De, *A History of Classical Sanskrit Literature,* p. 735. I prefer to ignore the "Bhāsa problem." Those who accept the Trivandrum plays as genuine would be able to point to another Kālidāsa predecessor, but I doubt that they are earlier than the fourth century A.D.

3. Dasgupta and De, *History,* pp. 630–50, esp. pp. 642–44.

4. Ibid., bibliography.

5. E.g., *Suparṇādhyāya, Viṣṇudharmottara Purāṇa,* Pāṇini, Kauṭilya.

6. Dasgupta and De, *History,* p. 552.

7. Early works on poetics contain pointed criticisms of Kālidāsa's style, and his plays are less preferred as models of plot and dramatic structure than are the *Priyadarśikā* and *Ratnāvalī* of Harṣa, and the *Veṇīsaṁhāra* of Bhaṭṭa Narayaṇa. See Mammaṭa, *Kāvyaprakāśa* 7.198, 250. In Venkatacarya's edition of Dhanaṁjaya's *Daśarūpaka* there are 38 citations from Kālidāsa's works in approximately 360 from all authors; see index, pp. 327 ff.

8. *NŚ* 18, 20; *DR* 2.

9. *NŚ* 19; *DR* 1.

10. *NŚ* 6, 7; *DR* 4; see E. Gerow, *Indian Poetics.*

11. The erotic, the heroic, the disgusting, the furious, the comic, the

marvelous, the horrible, the pathetic. Later is added the peaceful. Of these, of course, the chief in terms of actual poetic examples is the erotic (*śṛṅgāra*), with the heroic and comic also represented. The others are rare.

12. *DR* 3, from which the work takes its title.

13. *DR* 3.1 ff.

14. *DR* 3.22–24; there are many variant accounts of this theory; see A. B. Keith, *The Sanskrit Drama*, pp. 345 ff.

15. *DR* 3.38.

16. *DR* 3.33.

17. *DR* 3.39–40.

18. *DR* 3.54–56; see also Dasgupta and De, *History*, pp. 494–500.

19. The *bhāṇa*, a monologue form, is preserved in four old examples, known as *Caturbhāṇī*, ed. Kavi and Sastri; see Dasgupta and De, *History*, pp. 248–55 and 761–62. The *vyāyoga* is a one-act play of heroic *rasa*, represented by several Bhāsa plays; *DR* 3.60–62. There are too few examples of the five remaining types (*samavakāra, īhāmṛga, ḍima, utsṛṣṭikāṅka,* and *vīthī*) to know what is intended by their definitions; *DR* 3.57–76.

20. See the doggerel quoted by Sten Konow in *Das Indische Drama*, p. 94;

kālidāsasya sarvasvam abhijñānaśakuntalam (*sic*) ।
tatrāpi ca caturtho'ṅko yatra yāti śakuntalā ||

A variant is cited by E. Gerow in "Plot Structure and the Development of *Rasa* in the Śakuntalā," part 1, p. 564.

21. *Mālav* 1.2. Perhaps because of this inconsistency, it is later included in the *uparūpaka* called *nāṭikā* (little *nāṭaka*), introduced in the *Daśarūpaka* as a mixture of *nāṭaka* and *prakaraṇa*. The usual example is Harṣadeva's *Ratnāvalī;* see note 63 to Miller's article.

22. Acharya ed. (Nirnaya Sagar Press), p. 4; also colophon, p. 141. In the prologue of the Northern Recension, this term is used, but *nāṭaka* is found elsewhere and is adopted in the edition of Velankar. *T(r)oṭaka* is among the *uparūpakas* in Viśvanātha's *Sāhityadarpaṇa* (6.273), but it is not known as such earlier; see *NŚ* 19.86, *DR* 1.40. It is said to be a form of *nāṭaka* in five acts, in which the heroine is a goddess, divine and human characters meet, and music plays a prominent part.

23. See S. Konow, *Indian Drama* (Ghosal trans.), pp. 50–51; Sylvain Lévi, *Le Théâtre Indien*, pp. 145–46.

24. J. A. B. van Buitenen, *Two Plays of Ancient India*, pp. 67–68.

25. Ibid., pp. 20–21, quoting *DR* 2.1–2.

26. *DR* 3.49.

27. In Viśākhadatta's *Mudrārākṣasa* the hero himself engineers the imbroglio; in the first four acts of the *Mṛcchakaṭika*, Vasantasenā plays the role of arranging Cārudatta's visit and the reconciliation.

28. Which is not to say less popular; these "lower" forms (melodrama, etc.) monopolize popular culture in the West. But the higher forms, in India

at least, though quite elitist in other ways, still presume the "popular" verities.

29. See E. Gerow, "Ūrubhaṅga of Bhāsa."

30. Lévi, *Théâtre Indien,* pp. 179–80.

31. Ibid., pp. 122–23; Keith, *Sanskrit Drama,* pp. 310–11; *DR* 2.8–9.

32. See C. Byrski, "Sanskrit Drama as an Aggregate of Model Situations," in R. van Meter Baumer and J. Brandon, eds. *Sanskrit Drama in Performance.*

33. *DR* 1.24.

34. See Gerow, "Plot Structure," on which this summary is based.

35. Dasgupta and De, *History,* pp. 138 ff.; *Ṛg Veda* 10.95.

36. Lévi, *Théâtre Indien,* p. 181.

37. Ibid., p. 177.

38. E.g., in Abhinavagupta's masterful commentary on the *rasasūtra* of the *Nāṭyaśāstra,* and in the works of the Bengali Vaiṣṇava theologians.

39. Byrski, "Sanskrit Drama as an Aggregate of Model Situations," pp. 145–46.

40. Listed in note 11 above.

41. See Ānandavardhana, *Dhvanyāloka,* ed. Krishnamoorthy. For bibliography on this text, see Gerow, *Indian Poetics.*

42. The same analogy and the same "aesthetic" terminology occur in Chinese critical writings; see James J. Y. Liu, *Chinese Theories of Literature,* p. 103.

43. *Rām* 1.2.9 ff.; see B. Stoler Miller, "The Ādikāvya: Impact of the *Rāmāyaṇa* on Indian Literary Norms."

44. See, e.g., *DR* 4.35.

45. See E. Gerow, "Rasa as a Category of Literary Criticism," in Baumer and Brandon, *Sanskrit Drama in Performance,* pp. 226–57.

46. Expressed in his commentaries on the *Nāṭyaśāstra* and the *Dhvanyāloka;* see bibliography in E. Gerow, *Indian Poetics;* see esp. K. C. Pandey, *Abhinavagupta,* and J. L. Masson and M. Patwardhan, *Aesthetic Rapture.*

47. It is, however, included in the Baroda critical edition.

48. See Gerow, "Plot Structure."

49. *Poetics* 1447a.16, 1448a.2ff.

50. *Ethics* 1104b.4ff., 1174b.14ff.

51. *Poetics* 1448b.15, 1452a.1ff., 1455a.17.

52. See Aśvaghoṣa's elaborate defense of his (Buddhist) poetry in the final two verses of *Saundarananda.* In effect, Buddhism allows only didactic poetry.

53. See Abhinavagupta, *Abhinavabhāratī,* commentary on *rasasūtra.*

54. A sophisticated analysis of "plot" will involve the notion of one *rasa* itself used as complication to another *rasa.* The subordinate *rasa* functions as a "transient" mood (*vyabhicāribhāva*); these transient moods in aggregate

(usually 33) provide the material of the "drama" and a background against which the one chief *rasa* is felt as dominant. *DR* 4.8 ff.; *Dhvanyāloka* 2, 3 passim.

55. See, e.g., *Ratnāvalī, Mālatīmādhava.*

56. By contrast, the *satī* figures, such as Damayantī, Sāvitrī, Sītā, in their various ways act to preserve their mates' integrity; see Lévi, *Théâtre Indien,* pp. 179–80.

57. See E. Gerow, "The Persistence of Classical Esthetic Categories in Contemporary Indian Literature," in E. C. Dimock et al., eds., *The Literatures of India,* pp. 212–27.

The Theater in Kālidāsa's Art

1. *NŚ* 1. Translations from *NŚ* generally follow Ghosh, but in some cases have been edited slightly.

2. M. L. Varapande, *Traditions of Indian Theatre,* p. 61 in a chapter on the Nāgārjunakoṇḍa amphitheater, an anomalous structure. See also note to translation of *NŚ* 2 on the playhouse.

3. Clifford R. Jones, "Temple Theaters and the Sanskrit Tradition."

4. *NŚ* 2.17, 80–82, 82–85. A number of articles appeared in the *Indian Historical Quarterly* (1932) vol. 8 and (1933) vol. 9, attempting to reconstruct the playhouse from the descriptions in *NŚ*. The first piece, D. R. Mankad's "Hindu Theatre," was essentially accepted, but refuted in certain key details by V. Raghavan, M. Ghosh, and A. K. Coomaraswamy. One controversy centered on the placement of the *nepathya* doors. An excellent conspectus of the issues relating to the playhouse is found in the introduction to G. K. Bhat's *Bharatanāṭyamañjarī,* an abridged text and translation of *NŚ*.

5. Farley Richmond, "Suggestions for Directors of Sanskrit Plays," in R. van Meter Baumer and Brandon, eds., *Sanskrit Drama in Performance,* pp. 74 ff. The article contains a concise summary of Sanskrit stagecraft and the problems of interpreting the *NŚ*.

6. *NŚ* 2.46–50.

7. See the notes to Richmond, "Suggestions for Directors," and the introduction to Bhat's *Bharata.*

8. *NŚ* 2.69–71, 82–85.

9. *NŚ* 5.11–12; see Paul Thieme, "Das indische Theater," pp. 44 f., 49 f., and Bhat, *Bharata,* pp. xlvii-l.

10. *NŚ* 2.63–65. Adya Rangacharya, *Drama in Sanskrit Literature,* p. 215 speculates on the association of elephants with the guardians of the directions, and in general with Indra and kingship. In a playhouse attached to a palace, the royal party would have occupied the entire audience area in a prescribed arrangement. See Mankad, "Hindu Theatre," p. 497 insert, and Bhat, *Bharata,* pp. xlii–xliv. Bhat's interpretation (p. xliv) is the most help-

ful: "The *raṅgaśīrṣa* area, it must be remembered, is used for seating the musicians throughout the performance. The doors also are located here; so that the entrance and exit of characters is continually done in this very area. As such, the *mattavāraṇī* area could more profitably be used to play some scenes or parts of acts, to compensate for the limited back-stage area that was available. This would accord also with Bharata's zonal divisions of the stage (*kakṣyā-vibhāga*)."

11. *NŚ* 2, 3. Christopher Byrski in *Concept of Ancient Indian Theatre* discusses the connection between the *NŚ* and Vedic religion; see also F.B.J. Kuiper, *Varuṇa and Vidūṣaka.*

12. *NŚ* 3.89–93.

13. *NŚ* 1.70; on *jarjara,* see F.B.J. Kuiper, "The Worship of the Jarjara on the Stage."

14. *NŚ* 5.

15. *NŚ* 5.114.

16. *NŚ* 5.16, note to translation.

17. The *nāndī* is not well specified in *NŚ*. To rectify prescription with practice, Viśvanātha's *Sāhityadarpaṇa* explains the difference between the *pūrvaraṅga* and the *raṅgadvāra;* see the Sanskrit text (Nirnaya Sagar Press edition) 6.21–26 and translation of Ballantyne and Mitra 6.281.

18. V. Raghavan, "Kudiyattam—Its Form and Significance as Sanskrit Drama," and "Sanskrit Drama in Performance," in Baumer and Brandon, *Sanskrit Drama in Performance,* p. 43.

19. *NŚ* 27.87 ff.

20. *NŚ* 2.18–21.

21. The *Kuṭṭanīmata* of Dāmodaragupta contains a description of the *abhinaya* for the first act of Harṣa's play *Ratnāvalī* when performed by an all-female troupe. See also *NŚ* 35.28–32.

22. *NŚ* 35.84–86.

23. *NŚ* 35.86–87.

24. *NŚ* 35.9–11; *NŚ* 35.79. See also G. K. Bhat, *The Vidūṣaka.*

25. *NŚ* 35.88–90.

26. *NŚ* 23 is on costumes and makeup.

27. *NŚ* 23.15–41.

28. *NŚ* 23.45–48.

29. *NŚ* 23.117–18 ff. on costumes of the three types.

30. *NŚ* 23.73 ff., 35.107 ff.

31. *NŚ* 35.24.

32. *NŚ* 23.83.

33. *NŚ* 23.84–85.

34. *NŚ* 35.26–27.

35. *NŚ* 13.4 ff.

36. *NŚ* 13.171–76 as analyzed by Vatsyayan, *Classical Indian Dance,* p. 306. *Avahittha sthāna* is described at *NŚ* 13.164–65.

37. *NŚ* 9.60–63.
38. *NŚ* 9.204.
39. *NŚ* 10.24. The best source for tracing a complex movement is Mandakranta Bose, *Classical Indian Dancing: A Glossary.* This is a complete catalogue to all major manuals on dance and drama, with relatively clear explanations of the postures. References to the *NŚ* are for the Gaekwad edition, so some searching is necessary.
40. See *NŚ* 13.88–92.
41. *NŚ* 11.59–60; cf. 9.92.
42. *NŚ* 23.182 ff.
43. *NŚ* 13.152 ff.
44. *Utplutis* are a category of jumping *karaṇas* which are listed in the later *Saṅgītaratnākara,* 7.756 ff.
45. Raghavan, "Sanskrit Drama in Performance," p. 32, referring to *NŚ* 4.108.
46. *NŚ* 11.30 ff.
47. *NŚ* 13.92–95.
48. *NŚ* 14.2–3. Determination of the exact size of the stage would help in establishing a correct translation.
49. *NŚ* 14.4–7.
50. *NŚ* 14.9–10.
51. Vatsyayan, *Classical Indian Dance,* p. 249, analyzes an even more complicated zonal treatment in Act Four of *Mālavikāgnimitra.*
52. *NŚ* 26.85 ff.
53. *NŚ* 9.26.
54. Viśvanātha, *Sāhityadarpaṇa,* 6.139 (Ballantyne and Mitra 6.425) *DR* 1.126.
55. *NŚ* 26.88, note to translation.
56. *NŚ* 26.83–85.
57. *NŚ* 14.62–65.
58. Vatsyayan, *Classical Indian Dance,* p. 251, gives the technical terms for the gestures suggested by Rāghavabhaṭṭa in his commentary on the *Śākuntala.*
59. *NŚ* 7.7–27. See also Gerow's article in this volume.
60. *NŚ* 7.27–93.
61. *NŚ* 7.94 ff.
62. See Richmond, "Suggestions for Directors," pp. 102–4.
63. *NŚ* 7.93.
64. Raghavan, "Sanskrit Drama in Performance," p. 36.
65. *NŚ* 7.60.
66. *NŚ* 7.103.
67. *NŚ* 7.102.
68. *NŚ* 7.57.
69. *NŚ* 7.21.

70. *NŚ* 7.101.
71. *NŚ* 7.26.
72. *NŚ* 7.27.
73. *NŚ* 7.67.
74. *NŚ* 7.53.
75. *NŚ* 21.89.
76. *DR* 1.79/1.42.
77. *NŚ* 7.32.
78. *NŚ* 7.105.
79. *NŚ* 7.90.
80. *NŚ* 27.49 ff.
81. *NŚ* 27.59.
82. *NŚ* 27.55, 62, 63.
83. *NŚ* 27.4–5.
84. *NŚ* 27.17.

NOTES TO THE PLAYS

In each case, discussions about the text on which the translation is based and about its sources are followed by a series of notes on textual details. These notes are keyed to act and verse, and the significant word or phrase is repeated for identification where necessary. Prose passages are indicated by a plus sign (+), so that 1.2+ refers to Act One, prose following verse 2.

Notes are not marked in the body of the translation. They are meant to be used after the reader has studied introductions and translations and wants further commentary on certain words, phrases, ideas, and passages, as well as on textual variants. Sources cited here in abbreviated form may be found in the bibliography.

Śakuntalā and the Ring of Recollection (Abhijñānaśākuntala)

Recensions of the Text

This translation of *Abhijñānaśākuntala* is based on the text and commentary of Rāghavabhaṭṭa, called *Arthadyotanikā,* reedited by Narayan Ram Acharya Kavyatirtha (Bombay: Nirnaya Sagar Press, 1958). This is the twelfth edition of the text and commentary, first edited by N. B. Godbole and K. P. Parab in 1883 and revised by various hands, including M. R. Kale, who added an English translation and extensive notes in 1898.

The text established by Rāghavabhaṭṭa is the most widely accepted text of the so-called Devanagari Recension of the play, which was first edited by Otto Boehtlingk (Bonn: H. B. Koenig, 1842) and later reedited and annotated by M. Monier Williams (Oxford: Clarendon Press, 1876). Rāghavabhaṭṭa probably wrote his commentary in the last quarter of the fifteenth century; although there are citations of the play in critical literature from the tenth century, this is the earliest complete commentary known. See P. K. Gode, "The Date of Rāghavabhaṭṭa, the Commentator of Kālidāsa's *Abhijñānaśākuntalam* and Other Works"; T. G. Mainkar, "The Arthadyotanikā," in *Studies in Sanskrit Dramatic Criticism* pp. 38–53; Edwin Gerow, "Plot Structure and the Development of *Rasa* in the Śakuntalā." Gerow's analysis is largely based on Rāghavabhaṭṭa's interpretation of the play in terms of the plot theory of the *Nāṭyaśāstra;* the main points are summarized by Gerow in this volume.

The quality of Rāghavabhaṭṭa's commentary is generally high. He goes far beyond the simple glosses on words and phrases to offer interpretations of concepts, as well as citations of variant readings and attempts to justify his choice of particular readings. His text includes 194 verses, in contrast to 221 in the longer text of the so-called Bengali Recension, fixed by the commentary of Candraśekhara, which is the basis of Richard Pischel's edition in the Harvard Oriental Series; this is a revision, edited by Carl Cappeller, of Pischel's earlier edition (Kiel: Schwers, 1877). Pischel based his decision in favor of the Bengali text on the supposed purity of the Prakrits and on the fact that two verses (Pischel 3.31, 36) not found in Act Three of the Devanagari text are found in Viśvanātha's *Sāhityadarpaṇa* and other sources.

Recent research has revealed several more verses from the Bengali text in anthologies and treatises from the eleventh to the seventeenth century, among which are four verses quoted anonymously in Bhoja's *Śṛṅgāra Prakāśa*. See N. R. Subbanna, *Kālidāsa Citations,* pp. 219–24. But this only shows that the Bengali text already existed in some form before the fourteenth century, when Viśvanātha wrote his work on poetics. The anonymous verses may well have been incorporated into the inflated text by an editor familiar with Bhoja's work; it is difficult to know. Apart from these verses, and several others that appear in various anthologies, no substantial portion of the Bengali text appears in secondary literature, despite numerous citations of the play in works on poetics, beginning with the *Abhinavabhāratī* in the tenth century.

Of the two other recensions that were once distinguished, it is now clear that the Kashmiri version is an eclectic text, closely dependent on the Bengali text, with an obviously interpolated interlude before Act Seven. This version was first edited by Karl Burkhard, "Die Kaçmīrer Çakuntalā-Handschrift," *Sitzungberichte der Wiener Akademie der Wissenschaften* (1884), 107:479–640. The edition is based on a single Kashmiri birchbark manuscript in Śāradā script, procured by George Bühler in 1877 in Kashmir during a tour in search of Sanskrit manuscripts. This manuscript is now in the Government Collection at the Bhandarkar Oriental Research Institute, Poona (no. 192 of 1875–76); see Georg Bühler, "Detailed Report of a Search of Sanskrit Manuscripts in Kashmir, Rajputana, and Central India," *Journal of the Bombay Branch of the Royal Asiatic Society* (1877), vol. 12, no. 24a. According to V. Raghavan this manuscript was missed by P. K. Gode in his *Descriptive Catalogue of the Nāṭaka Mss. in the B.O.R.I.*, vol. 24. The manuscript is the basis of the edition S. K. Belvalkar was preparing for the Sahitya Akademi at the time of his death. Published posthumously, in 1965, it is essentially a transcription of the manuscript and differs little from Burkhard's text.

An edition based on Maithili manuscripts, with the commentaries of Śaṅkara and Narahari, edited by R. Jha (Darbhanga: Mithila Institute, 1957), makes claims for independence, but it seems to be a mixture of the common Bengali text and the Kashmiri version.

The South Indian text is a version of the Devanagari Recension. It is most commonly associated with the commentary of Kāṭayavema, who probably lived in the fifteenth century and is the only commentator to have analyzed all three plays.

In addition to the extra verses, many of which are similar to others found in both texts, and considerable variation in the rendering of the Prakrits and in the stage directions (both being aspects of dramatic literature that were probably highly fluid in ancient India), the most prominent difference between the two recensions is the so-called śṛṅgāric elaboration that occurs in the final scene of Act Three in the Bengali Recension (Pischel 3.29–38). This prolonged erotic dialogue between the king and Śakuntalā adds nothing to the *rasa* of the act, but one can imagine its insertion into the play to please some patron. The verses are not among the best in the play (3.31, 36 are cited at *Sāhityadarpaṇa* 6.202, but not attributed to Kālidāsa) and the entire dialogue shows a lack of subtlety.

The readings of the Devanagari text seem more elegant in most cases, but in many it is impossible to decide which is more "original." A good example for comparison is 1.8; especially in the last line the readings give the verse a different flavor. The Devanagari reading is:

dhāvantyamī mṛgajavākṣamayeva rathyāḥ |

The Bengali reading is more direct, without the figurative reference to the antelope:

dhāvanti vartmani taranti nu vājinas te |

Rāghavabhaṭṭa's choice among variants is often determined on the basis of postclassical literary canons, and in some places he proposes "improvements" on Kālidāsa's text; but these are documented in the commentary and are not adopted in Acharya Kavyatirtha's edition of the text. A selection of Rāghavabhaṭṭa's observations on variant readings is discussed by Mainkar in *Studies in Sanskrit Dramatic Criticism;* readers of Sanskrit may consult the *Arthadyotanikā* itself (e.g., 1.2, 13, 17, 18, 21, 27; 2.6, 9, 10; 3.7, 8, 12; 4.5, 6, 13; 5.3, 11).

A. Scharpé, in his *Kālidāsa Lexicon,* part 1 (1954), reproduces the readings of Carl Cappeller's edition of the Devanagari text (Leipzig: H. Haessel, 1909), combined with those of Pischel's revised edition. For those wishing to compare the two texts and multiple variants, this is a useful publication.

Sources of the Play

The most obvious source for Kālidāsa's drama is the story of Duḥṣanta Paurava and Śakuntalā in the first book of the *Mahābhārata* (1.62–69). It is narrated to establish the origin of the Kuru dynasty through the birth of Bharata. The narrative is introduced by verses in praise of Duḥṣanta's dharmic nature and a vivid description of him hunting wild animals in the forest with his army. The violent slaughter of thousands of animals continues until the king comes upon Kaṇva's hermitage and meets Śakuntalā. She is alone, since Kaṇva has gone out to gather flowers. She herself relates the story of her parentage in elaborate detail, as she heard it from Kaṇva. Learning that she is the daughter of a king, Duḥṣanta proposes marriage, but before she will lie with him, she extracts a vow that if she bears a son, he must be recognized as heir apparent to the kingdom. He agrees, lies with her, and departs. After a pregnancy of three years' duration, she gives birth to a son. When the boy is six years old, Kaṇva decides to send the mother and child to the king.

In the epic, Śakuntalā is rejected by the king, who feigns ignorance of their marriage—the device of the ring and Durvāsas' curse are absent here. After Śakuntalā departs, a voice from the sky announces that she has spoken the truth and the king recognizes his wife and son, claiming that had he done so without divine intervention, the people would have been suspicious.

In addition to descriptive passages, the epic version consists of speeches by only three characters—Duḥṣanta, Śakuntalā, and Kaṇva. The cast of minor characters is introduced in the play by Kālidāsa to define dramatic structures and relationships. Notable are the buffoon and Śakuntalā's two companions, as well as the policemen, the fisherman, Mātali, and Mārīca.

The device of the ring, while not in the *Mahābhārata* version, may have been borrowed from a related story, the "Kaṭṭhahāri Jātaka," translated by E. B. Cowell as "The King and the Stick-Gatherer." In this story Brahmadatta, the king of Banaras, meets a forest girl while wandering in the woods and marries her, after which she conceives the Bodhisattva. The king gives her his signet ring, telling her "If it be a girl, spend this ring on her nurture; but if it be a boy, bring ring and child to me." When she brings her son to the king, he rejects her out of shame. She performs an "act of truth," saying, "If this child is yours, may he stay in mid-air; but if not, may he fall to earth and be killed"; then she seizes the boy and tosses him into the air. The Bodhisattva, seated cross-legged in midair, declares that he is the king's son and thus forces the king to recognize his mother and himself.

The *Bhāgavata Purāṇa* (9.20.8–22) and the *Padma Purāṇa* (3.1–6, Svarga Kāṇḍa) both contain versions of the story. The former is directly derived from the *Mahābhārata,* while the latter is more elaborate, mixing the epic version with the elements drawn from Kālidāsa's play.

In the epic version of the story it is Śakuntalā herself whose words and actions dominate the relationship, while in Kālidāsa's drama, the king, Kaṇva, and various minor characters play much larger roles. The divine voice (*vāk*) speaks in the epic to publicly validate the king's secret marriage with Śakuntalā; in the drama, it speaks only to Kaṇva to let him know that his daughter is pregnant. This shift, like many other details in the play, is necessitated by the demands of classical aesthetics. According to the critic Bhoja, the curse of Durvāsas functions to remove a flaw (*doṣa*) in the original story and allows the poet various means to develop the *rasa;* see his *Śṛṅgāra Prakāśa,* 2:460 in the Josyer ed.

Notes on the Text and Translation

The notes that follow are mainly intended to elucidate points in the text that may not be sufficiently clear to the English reader. For more exhaustive treatment of variant readings, the student of Sanskrit is referred to the notes of Acharya Kavyatirtha, A. Scharpé, and Richard Pischel. Good notes on grammatical and lexical problems are found in the editions of M. R. Kale and M. Monier Williams. A detailed discussion of Rāghavabhaṭṭa's commentary is found in Edwin Gerow's article "Plot Structure and Development of *Rasa* in the Śakuntalā."

Kālidāsa's concern with the nature of sacred law and religious duty (*dharma*) comes into sharper focus when we see how often his notions of law and duty have parallels in the Hindu law books, especially the *Mānava Dharmaśāstra*. All references in the notes are to Bühler's English translation, *The Laws of Manu* (*Manu*). This concern is amplified in the *Śākuntala* by the settings of the sacred forest (*dharmāraṇya*) the hermitage (*āśrama*), and the ascetics' grove (*tapovana*), in which the action begins and ends. The language and imagery of religious austerity (*tapas*) intensify the erotic passion of the lovers, especially in the torment of separation, and thus help to produce the aesthetic experience of love (cf. *Kumārasaṁbhava* 5, translated by B. Stoler Miller in "Kālidāsa's Verbal Icon: Aṣṭamūrti Śiva").

Act One

1.1+ *Śakuntalā and the Ring of Recollection* . . . This is not a literal rendering of the Sanskrit compound *Abhijñānaśākuntala,* whose exact form and meaning are controversial even among Sanskrit critics and commentators. The word *abhijñāna* means "recognition," or "recollection"; it is used in the play to refer to the ring Duṣyanta gives as a token to Śakuntalā (this sense is clear at 4.1+ and 5.21+). A more exact translation of the title might be "[The drama of] Śakuntalā [remembered] through the ring of recollection," where the entire compound refers to the implied word *nāṭaka* (drama), and a word like *smṛta* (remembered) may be supplied according to a rule of Sanskrit grammar governing elision in compound words.

1.3 To plunge in fresh waters . . . This verse belongs to a type of Sanskrit poetry devoted to descriptions of the seasons, of which the *Ṛtusaṁhāra* is the most famous collection. See Daniel H. H. Ingalls, *Court Poetry,* sec. 9. Such verses also abound in the Prakrit anthologies.

1.4 Mimosa . . . here *śirīṣa*. The translation of plant names is difficult in most cases, since Sanskrit may have many names for different varieties of flowers and plants, such as mimosa, lotus, or jasmine, for which English offers few alternatives. I have also rendered *śamī* (1.16; 4.4) and *keśara* (1.17+) as "mimosa" according to context and commentaries.

1.5 Duṣyanta . . . The name appears in variant forms in Sanskrit and Prakrit. Pischel uses the Sanskrit form Duḥṣanta, which is also adopted in the critical edition of the *Mahābhārata,* it being the most common reading of southern manuscripts. Duṣyanta is the more common form in northern texts of the epic and the drama and is used by Rāghavabhaṭṭa. The Śaurasenī form is usually Dussanta, while the Māgadhī varies greatly.

1.6 The wild bowman Śiva . . . As *pinākin,* Śiva is armed with the bow *pināka* and arrows of time and destiny. See Stella Kramrisch, *The Presence of Śiva,* pp. 27–51. Another reference to Duṣyanta's extraordinary skills as a bowman occurs in the opening verse of Act Three.

1.7 The graceful turn of his neck . . . This verse is referred to by Abhinavagupta in the *Abhinavabhāratī* as an example in his discussion of aesthetic perception of emotions like fear; see Raniero Gnoli, *The Aesthetic Experience According to Abhinavagupta;* text p. 15, trans. pp. 65 ff.

1.9+ Hermitage . . . Although I translate *āśrama* as "hermitage," its inhabitants are not in fact "hermits" living solitary existences; usually they are sages who retire to forest sanctuaries where they practice religious austerities in the company of disciples. They generally live in communities that are organized like extended families. See Romila Thapar, "Renunciation: The Making of a Counter-Culture?" So Kaṇva is identified as the "master" (*kulapati,* 1.11+) or "father" (Pkt. *tāda;* Skt. *tāta*) of the community.

It is interesting to note the existence of a temple built in a village called Kansuāñ near Kota, in eastern Rajasthan. According to its inscription, the temple was built in A.D. 738 by the brahman prince Śivagaṇa, "knowing that this blessed hermitage of Kaṇva (*kaṇvāśrama*) takes away all sin." See Michael Meister, "Forest and Cave: Temples at Candrabhāgā and Kansuāñ." The inscription is reminiscent of Duṣyanta's attitude toward the place: "The sight of this holy hermitage will purify us" (*puṇyāśramadarśanena tāvadātmānaṁ punīmahe,* 1.12+).

The inhabitants of an āśrama are known by various titles, among which Kālidāsa frequently uses *tapasvin* (ascetic) and *ṛṣi* (sage); also *vaikhānasa,* which indicates a particular kind of sage who leads a more isolated, though not a solitary, life—thus I render it "monk."

1.11 Dynasty of the moon . . . The compound word *Puruvaṁśa* refers to one of the two great dynasties of Hindu mythology, the lunar and the solar. Puru is the progenitor of the lunar dynasty and Ikṣvāku is the progenitor of the solar. The blessing "May you beget a son to turn the wheel of your empire!" includes the notion of the *cakravartin* or universal king; see A. L. Basham, *The Wonder That Was India,* pp. 83 ff.

1.12 Scarred arm . . . Literally, scarred by the bowstring. The verse is somewhat ironical, since the king has been hunting animals of the hermitage, violating his duty to protect them.

1.12+ Somatīrtha . . . A place of pilgrimage (*tīrtha*) on the coast of Gujarat, near the temple of Somanāth. Its name is explained by the myth that here Soma, the moon, was cured of consumption inflicted on him by the curse of his father-in-law, Dakṣa (*Mbh* 9.34.38 ff.).

1.13 Iṅgudī . . . The nuts of the iṅgudī plant are pressed for lamp oil and ointment by forest dwellers; cf. 2.10; *Raghuvaṁśa* 14.81.

1.14 Yet my arm is quivering . . . The quivering arm is a conventional sign of good omen; it is used by Kālidāsa specifically as an omen of love; see *Raghuvaṁśa* 12.90.

1.15+ Anasūyā and Priyaṁvadā . . . The two friends have clearly differentiated personalities, appropriate to their names. Anasūyā ("without envy") is serious and decisive; it is she who narrates the story of Śakuntalā's birth. A female of the same name is known from epic and Purāṇic sources; e.g., *Rām* 2.109–11; *Viṣṇu Purāṇa* 1.10; She is, like Aditi, a daughter of Dakṣa; she marries the sage Atri and is the mother of three sons, one of whom is Durvāsas, the embodiment of Śiva's fury who figures so prominently in the plot. In the forest, she teaches Sītā *tapas*. Kālidāsa doubtless intended these literary associations, and his audience would have appreciated the overtones they give to the character. Priyaṁvadā ("sweet talker") has no such mythology, but the name is an epithet of Pārvatī in the *Kumārasaṁbhava* (5.28). Anasūyā is a śakti, Priyaṁvadā is more playful—it is she who placates Durvāsas in Act Four, according to the instructions of Anasūyā.

1.18+ Jasmine creeper who chose the mango tree in marriage . . . By using the word *svayaṁvaravadhū*, Kālidāsa is suggesting that Śakuntalā too may follow the practice whereby princesses choose their own husbands—that her choice and marriage are made in secret rather than publicly reduces it in status and necessitates the long process of "purification." See *Raghuvaṁśa* 6.1 ff. for Kālidāsa's description of the *svayaṁvara* of Indumatī.

1.18+ Could her social class be different from her father's? . . . If in fact Śakuntalā shared the social rank (*varṇa*) of Kaṇva, she would belong to the priestly class (*brāhmaṇa*) and would therefore be a forbidden wife for the king, who belongs to the warrior class (*kṣatriya*); see *Manu* 3.13 ff. But as the daughter of the royal sage (*rājarṣi*) Viśvāmitra, she also belongs to the warrior class and is suitable to be the king's wife.

1.21+ Special guest . . . The duty toward a guest (*atithidharma*) is fundamental in Hinduism; see *Manu* 3.99–116. The motif of the guest is important in the drama, since much of the plot turns on the honor accorded to Duṣyanta here and the neglect of Durvāsas in Act Four.

1.23+ Even in her religious life, she is subject to her father . . . see *Manu* 9.2, 3.

Act Two

2.0 Greek women . . . *Yavanī* is the word used for the women who bear the king's bow and arrows—probably Greeks from Asia Minor (*yavanadeśa*) who settled in Bactria; see *Vik* 5.3 ff.

2.2+ When a straight reed is twisted into a crooked reed . . . Since the *vidūṣaka* is normally hunchbacked (*kubja*), his claim to have been twisted by following the "play of the crooked ones" (*kubjalīlā*) is ironical.

2.3+ Hunting is said to be a vice . . . See *Manu* 7.47, 50, where hunting is one of the most pernicious of the ten vices of kings. The brahman buffoon's objection to hunting is subjective, not legalistic, but the general argues to refute Hindu law.

2.5 See *Raghuvaṁśa* 9.49.

2.7 The fiery heat of the sunstone (*sūryakānta*) is a frequent subject of comparison in Sanskrit poetry; see Bhartrihari's poem no. 65 in Miller, *Hermit and the Love-Thief,* p. 54.

2.14 ff. The two ascetic boys (*ṛṣikumārau*) belong to the hermitage family of Kaṇva. Because they articulate dharmic values, they speak Sanskrit. By contrast, the king's own son speaks Prakrit (7.14+), as is appropriate to the spontaneous desire he expresses.

2.16+ Triśaṅku . . . The mythic king who was left hanging between heaven and earth in the struggle of Viśvāmitra with the gods; see *Rām* 1.56–59.

Act Three

3.2 This act begins and ends with the king alone, deep in thought, so that his encounter with Śakuntalā in the bower is like a fantasy, a mirage; terms that the king uses when he is tormented by separation (6.10, 16).

3.9+ Twin stars of spring serve the crescent moon . . . The pair of stars called Viśākhā form one of the constellations associated with the moon. According to Rāghavabhaṭṭa, the reference is to Śakuntalā's two friends and their concern for her in her emaciated state.

3.20 The king invokes the *gāndharva* form of marriage, a secret marriage of mutual consent that is permitted for the warrior class (*kṣatriya*) by Hindu law. *Manu* (3.32) says, "The voluntary union of a maiden and her lover one must know as the *gāndharva* rite, which springs from desire and has sexual intercourse for its purpose."

3.21+ Red goose, bid farewell to your gander! . . . The *cakravāka* is the ruddy goose or sheldrake; fabled to be inseparable by day, the female birds and their mates are doomed to be parted every night. See 4.16; *Mālav* 5.9; *Vik* 4.34 ff.; *Meghadūta* 80; *Raghuvaṁśa* 8.56; see also Salim Ali, *The Book of Indian Birds,* no. 217.

Act Four

4.4 Like fire in mimosa wood . . . *Agnigarbhāṁ śamīm iva.* The image refers to the myth of Agni's entry into the śamī tree to save himself from being consumed by the fire of Śiva's seed, which he carried at the request of the gods; *Mbh* 13.84. In Vedic ritual śamī wood is used to make the lower or "female" of the two sticks used for kindling the sacred fire. As Rāghavabhaṭṭa points out, the verse contains a pun on the word *tejas,* refering both to "semen" and "fiery energy." As Gerow notes, *garbha* may also refer to the *garbha-saṁdhi* of the plot, which is in this act.

4.6 Indian critics consider Act Four to be the core of the play and this verse to be its essence; three other verses in the act (18, 19, 20) are also highly praised, but not universally. Bhoja cites this verse as an example of *vipralambha* (love-in-separation) in *Śṛṅgāra Prakāśa,* 3:58. See Gerow article, note 20.

4.7 The way Yayāti honored Śarmiṣṭhā . . . Though she was the daughter of the king of the demons, and accompanied his senior wife Devayanī as her maid, Śarmiṣṭhā won the love of Yayāti and married him in a *gāndharva* rite, after which she gave birth to three sons, the youngest of whom was Puru; *Mbh* 1.70 ff.

4.8 The meter in this verse is *triṣṭubh,* but the cadence of each *pāda* is more regular than is normal in Vedic prosody. However, the meter gives the scene an archaic quality, appropriate to the marriage rite that is being reenacted, with the bridegroom absent.

Act Five

5.2 Abhinavagupta comments on this verse in the *Abhinavabhāratī;* see Gnoli, *Aesthetic Experience,* text pp. 16 ff., trans. pp. 74 ff. The idea of the final line is repeated at *Raghuvaṁśa* 7.15; "the mind indeed is conscious of a relationship from another life" (*mano hi janmāntarasaṁgatijñam*).

5.9 See *Raghuvaṁśa* 5.5 ff.

5.12 This verse is also found among Bhartrihari's poems, no. 63; see Miller, *Hermit and the Love-Thief,* p. 54.

Act Six

6.1 The verse is meant to be ironical, pointing to the fact that brahmans also kill animals, but are not despised for doing so; see *Manu* 10.46–48.

6.1+ Death's dog . . . Yama, the god of death, is accompanied by two four-eyed dogs who guard the way of the dead.

6.22+ A wealthy merchant sea captain named Dhanamitra has been lost in a shipwreck and the laws say that since the brave man was childless, his accumulated wealth all goes to the king . . . This law is a dramatically stylized version of a law of inheritance found in Kauṭilya's *Arthaśāstra* (3.5.28), which says that a man's property lapses to the king if there is no suitable heir. The version in the Hindu lawbooks is similar; see *Manu* 9.189. S. N. Dasgupta, in *A History of Sanskrit Literature,* pp. 733 ff., wrongly argues that Kālidāsa is following Mauryan law here and so must have lived in the Śuṅga period rather than in the Gupta period, when brahmanic law was in force. The "rite to ensure the birth of a son" (*puṁsavana*) is an ancient life-cycle ritual (*saṁskāra*) which is known from the *Atharva Veda* (6.77.7–3). It is one of several gestation rites performed in the third month of pregnancy.

6.25 See *Raghuvaṁśa* 1.66, 67.

6.28 A wild goose can extract the milk and leave the water untouched . . . The Indian *haṁsa* is fabled for its ability to separate milk, and Soma, from water when these are mixed.

Act Seven

7.6 Parivaha . . . This is the name of the sixth of the seven winds whose paths divide the atmosphere, according to Hindu cosmology. The sixth wind came into being by the second of Viṣṇu's cosmic strides. The myth relates that the demon Bali, usurper of Indra's power, grants three paces of land to Viṣṇu when he comes to him in the guise of a dwarf. Then Viṣṇu assumes his cosmic shape and traverses earth, atmosphere, and heaven. The Parivaha wind bears the three streams of the heavenly Ganges and the seven stars of the Great Bear. Rāghavabhaṭṭa's commentary cites the *Siddhānta-śiromaṇi,* an astronomical work by Bhāskarācārya, written in 1150 A.D., as well as the *Viṣṇu Purāṇa* and the *Vāmana Purāṇa*.

7.8+ What mountain do I see stretching into the eastern and western seas . . . *Pūrvāpara* is used to described Himālaya in the opening verse of *Kumārasaṁbhava*.

7.9 Mārīca, the descendant of Brahmā . . . Kaśyapa, as a son of Marīci and grandson of Brahmā, is called Mārīca. Because of his prominent role in creation, he also bears the epithet Prajāpati (lord of creatures, divine creator), even though he is not one of the original Prajāpatis mentioned in Hindu mythology; see *Manu* 1.35. Mārīca married Aditi, as well as twelve other daughters of Dakṣa, and fathered both gods and demons. Aditi bore Indra, the king of the gods.

7.12+ Aśoka tree . . . A symbol of fertility and love, it bears flowers of scarlet hue that are thought to bloom when touched by the foot of a beautiful girl; see *Mālav* 3.5 ff. Sītā was imprisoned in an aśoka grove by Rāvaṇa; thus the tree is also associated with her torment and chastity.

7.16 A hand with fine webs connecting the fingers . . . This is one of the signs of a *cakravartin,* a king who turns the cosmic wheel; see note to 1.11.

7.20+ Śakunta . . . The boy's confusion is based on the ambiguity of the phrase *saundalāvaṇṇam* in Prakrit; it may mean, as Sanskrit *śakunta-lāvaṇyam,* "the beauty of the śakunta bird." Or it may refer directly to the name Śakuntalā, if understood, as Sanskrit *śakuntalāvarṇam,* "the nature of Śakuntalā."

7.20+ Aparājitā . . . Means "the invincible one." It is an epithet of the goddess Durgā and the name of a wish-granting herb growing on the mountain of the goddess; see *Kālikā Purāṇa* 64.95–96; *Vik* 2.9 ff. where *aparājita* refers to the magic knot of invisibility tied in the hair.

7.27 This verse recounts the genealogy and creative power of Mārīca and Aditi, who, as direct descendants of the self-created Brahmā, are equally divine; see note to 7.9.

7.33 The seven continents . . . According to Indian mythical geography, the earth consists of seven islands, surrounded by seven seas. The legendary Bharata, celebrated for his dharmic rule, was called "The Sustainer." He created an empire of such great extent that all of India came to be called Bhārata, or Bharatavarṣa.

Urvaśī Won by Valor (Vikramorvaśīya)

Recensions of the Text

This is a translation of the critical edition of the *Vikramorvaśīya* as constituted by H. D. Velankar (New Delhi: Sahitya Akademi, 1961). The ongoing controversy surrounding the Prakrit verses and unusual stage directions in Act Four make the choice of a text a difficult one. In the end, this longer version containing the disputed material was selected not out of an overwhelming conviction of its greater authenticity, but from a desire to share with a wider audience this unique record of a Sanskrit drama in performance.

Velankar has described the manuscript groups and editions based on them in his introduction. A clearer presentation of issues surrounding the authenticity of the Prakrit verses in Act Four is found in T. G. Mainkar's "The Prakrit Verses in the Fourth Act of the Vikramorvaśīyam." Briefly, the play exists in two recensions named after the scholars who critically edited them: the shorter Southern Recension found in manuscripts known as the Pandit group, and the longer Northern Recension preserved in manuscripts of the Bollensen group. The latter is essentially adopted by Velankar for his edition, but in the case of problematic readings he generally follows Pandit.

As is often the case, the play's commentators were its first editors. A commentator may make use of the text known in his region of the subcontinent, frequently attempting to "purify" it according to the canons of poetics, or he may conflate several available versions. In the case of the *Vikramorvaśīya,* the Southern Recension is associated with Kāṭayavema, an intelligent and learned critic who lived around 1400 A.D., according to Mainkar, and the Northern primarily with Raṅganātha, by general agreement a somewhat lesser scholar who flourished about 250 years after Kāṭayavema.

The longer manuscripts of the Northern Recension, critically edited initially by Bollensen (St. Petersburg, 1846), suffer somewhat from guilt by association with the later, inferior commentator. In the only other critical edition until Velankar, that of S. P. Pandit in the Bombay Sanskrit Series, analyses from the two commentators are juxtaposed in the notes by the editor, to the great detriment of Raṅganātha. Pandit largely follows the southern manuscripts and Kāṭayavema, who includes no *chāyās* (Sanskrit translations) of the Prakrit verses, presumably because either he did not know those verses or he deemed them unworthy of inclusion.

For the most recent critical edition, Velankar states that he was "particularly lucky in getting a manuscript of one more commentary . . . by one Koṇeśvara . . . written in Bengali characters [and] exhaustive, sometimes even more helpful than that of Raṅganātha, particularly in the fourth act, where it gives all the Prakrit stanzas and explains them in detail, giving quotations from different sources in support of its explanations" (p. xxxiii). The discovery of this manuscript would seem to offer hope for shifting the evidence in favor of the Northern Recension. Unfortunately, nowhere does Velankar specifically show how he used Koṇeśvara to interpret the Act Four material where Raṅganātha proved insufficient. Nor does he address the inconsistent and mechanical manner in which Raṅganātha has cited texts on poetics (*alaṁkāraśāstra*) in explanation of the unusual stage directions in Act Four. (See my article in the introduction and the notes to Act Four.) Since the publication of Velankar's edition, Koṇeśvara's commentary has become available and needs further study.

The argument based on commentatorial support (or lack of it) for the expanded version of the fourth act is but one weapon in the battle over the genuineness of the material. It is an important debate, for if there were ever enough conclusive evidence for one side to win, the verdict might alter the understanding of what constitutes the classical norm in Sanskrit drama. Opponents of the Prakrit (actually Apabhraṁśa) verses, for instance, say that the dramaturgical manuals specify that the king, being an *uttamapātra* (character of the high, as opposed to middle or low, degree) must speak only Sanskrit; see *NŚ* 18.31, *DR* 2.97. Raṅganātha pleads insanity as the king's motivation for singing the less elevated language, a situation also mentioned in the śāstras (see *NŚ* 18.32 ff. and *DR* 2.99), pointing likewise to the king's use of peculiar prose and excessive alliteration in verse when he does speak Sanskrit. (See notes to Act Four for examples.) Interestingly, by *NŚ* 18.42, nymphs may speak Sanskrit because of their association with the gods, but no such play is known. All the nymphs in *Vikramorvaśīya* speak Prakrit.

Another objection is that the verses have no intrinsic connection with the events of the act, that they were, in fact, independent Prakrit and Apabhraṁśa lyrics inserted by some imaginative director to help create the world of madness that Purūravas finds in the grove (and within himself). This is the conjecture of, among others, V. Raghavan in "Music in Ancient Indian Drama." When offstage voices recite (or sing) verses which indirectly describe the king's desolate condition by way of comparison to an elephant in rut or a forsaken wild goose—the *dhruvās* described by the *Nāṭyaśāstra*, 32.407 ff.—it is difficult to determine the degree of specificity to the particular situation of the drama.

Pandit sees the verses as either generally descriptive of love-in-separation and therefore only vaguely related to the narrative, or as repetitive of the adjacent Sanskrit verses, or as interruptive of "the free and natural flow of the sentiments as expressed in the Sanskrit passages" (p. 9). One might add that these verses and the stage directions also sometimes seem disruptive even of the *action* as it is described in the Sanskrit passages. Velankar, of course, is at pains to point out specific references in the Prakrit verses to things and events in the Sanskrit prose which are *not* exploited in the Sanskrit verse. Mainkar cautiously points out that both phenomena occur. He notes that the lake setting of the Prakrit verses hearkens back to the *Śatapatha Brāhmaṇa* version of the story rather than Kālidāsa's own treatment. (See the section on sources.) It should be pointed out, however, that the term *kaccha,* accepted by all editors, at 4.71+ does imply a watery locale.

Even if the problem of the appropriateness of the material is solved, the question of its authenticity remains. The verses sung by the offstage voices describing the condition of the king or of the two lovers, termed *anyokti* by Velankar, are composed in a standard lyric Prakrit of drama called Māhārāṣṭrī. When the king sings about himself (*pratyukti*), the language is Apabhraṁśa, which has a long history of use in poetry but is not sanctioned by the *Nāṭyaśāstra,* is not mentioned by Abhinavagupta in his discussion of change of language owing to alteration of condition, and is not employed by imitators of this act; cf. Bhavabhūti, *Mālatīmādhava* (Act Nine), *Uttararāmacarita* (Act Three).

S. N. Ghosal, in his *The Apabhraṁśa Verses of the Vikramorvaśīya from the Linguistic Standpoint,* attempts to determine whether Kālidāsa could have written the kind of Apabhraṁśa found in the play, or whether the verses must be assigned to another era. He reviews the earlier linguistic studies of Richard Pischel, who examines but rejects the verses as not genuine, and of Ludwig Alsdorf, *Apabhraṁśa Studien.* Ghosal subjects the verses to a historical and metrical analysis, reconstructs them, and provides translations and a glossary. His conclusion is that the verses are genuine; he seems to have proved only that they are contemporaneous with Kālidāsa, not that Kālidāsa actually wrote them. Mainkar compares these verses with the certainly genuine Prakrit verses in this and the other Kālidāsa dramas and finds them wanting in subtlety and imagination; cf. *Śāk* 1.4, 3.13, 4.12, 5.1, 6.1, 6.2, 6.3; *Mālav* 2.4; *Vik* 2.12.

In part, no doubt, because he wanted to criticize the translations, Ghosal chose as one of his texts the edition of M. R. Kale. Kale basically follows the Northern Recension for most of the text, though he quotes from both Raṅganātha and Kāṭayavema in his original commentary and notes. On the other hand, he relegates the extra material of Act Four to an appendix, in the manner of Pandit, and quotes Pandit's reasons for doing so. Kale's edition contains many typographical errors and, though its notes are of immense value to the student and translator, should not be considered a reliable starting point for a historical linguistic study.

Another method of establishing the authenticity of a particular version of a text and locating it in time is to find references in works on poetics and dramaturgy, where verses or incidents may be cited as positive or negative examples of figures of speech, creation of aesthetic mood, or treatment of dramatic situations. Citations for the Sanskrit material of Act Four abound in *alaṁkāraśāstra* (see Mainkar, "The Prakrit Verses," p. 109, and N. R. Subanna, *Kālidāsa Citations,* pp. 39–54), but no author quotes any of the additional Prakrit passages. One would especially expect citation of one of the initial songs (*dhruvā*) at the opening of Act Four by Abhinavagupta as illustration for his commentary on *NŚ* 32. (See Subanna, *Kālidāsa Citations,* pp. 227–35, for a discussion of the implications of the distribution of *Vikramorvaśīya* citations in *alaṁkāraśāstra.*)

Manuscripts which contain the additional verses invariably contain the additional stage directions as well. While further checking in the dramaturgical manuals may yield some discoveries, my search so far has uncovered little that is helpful in interpreting the unusual stage directions in Act Four. Such stage directions are also missing from such well-known imitations of the act as those mentioned above by Bhavabhūti, dated to c. 700 A.D. by A. B. Keith, *Sanskrit Drama,* p. 278; cf. Sten Konow, who argues for a date of late seventh to early eighth century, *Das indische Drama,* p. 79.

If the term *toṭaka* or *troṭaka* does indeed denote a "musical play" or one in which "music with dances and songs plays a prominent part," as is the conjecture of A. K. Warder in *Indian Kāvya Literature,* 3:138, then the unusual stage directions would appear to be appropriate, if not genuine. Warder argues that there are two recensions, a musical recension (the Northern), styled *toṭaka,* and a dramatic recension, called by the standard term *nāṭaka.* The problem with this argument is that the commentators themselves define the term *toṭaka* only as a five-act drama in which human and divine characters interact; it is not clear that the designation "musical play" found in some manuscripts is essential to the definition. Moreover, the term is used in the *Nāṭyaśāstra* as a meter (16.41) and in the *Daśarūpaka* as a subdivision ("quarreling") of the *saṁdhi* (juncture) called *garbha* (1.77). Only in later texts, such as the *Sāhityadarpaṇa* (7.273), is *toṭaka* considered a type of play, one of the eighteen *uparūpakas,* or minor varieties. (See Gerow's article in the introduction.)

A real weakness of Velankar's edition is his dependence on Pandit's text. "In reconstituting the text, I have generally followed the careful selection of readings made by Pandit, especially where I found that the readings were supported by a clear majority of his manuscripts" (p. xxxiv). Pandit's edition, of course, follows the Southern Recension set by Kāṭayavema, the recension which does not include the additional fourth-act material

Velankar wants to retain. The resulting text is a conflation of the best of both worlds, but is true to neither.

Even without the additional material, the sustained monologue in madness and passion found in the fourth act of the *Vikramorvaśīya* is an anomaly. (Bhavabhūti gave Mādhava an on-stage companion; actually the third act of *Uttararāmacarita,* with its invisible Sītā haunting the desolate Rāma, has a greater affinity to the *Vikramorvaśīya.*) It is quite possible that Kālidāsa wrote the shorter version, fully knowing and intending that, according to contemporary practice, a director or theatrical company would realize his vision with the addition of Prakrit songs and dance movements. If he were associated with the permanent troupe of a royal court, he would have doubtless participated in the creation of those songs and dances himself.

Sources of the Play

The story of the love between the mortal king Purūravas and the celestial nymph Urvaśī has its origins in an eighteen-verse dialogue hymn from the *Ṛg Veda* (10.95), which inspired numerous versions in the Purāṇas and in the fable literature. The way in which Kālidāsa wove together a number of these variations and transformed them into an intense evocation of the madness of love-in-separation reveals the nature of classicizing processes in the Gupta age, as well as the poet's skill, sensitivity, and innovation. The *Kālidasā Bibliography* of Satya Pal Narang, pp. 161–62, lists thirteen articles on the sources of the play. Kale (pp. 24 ff.) gives a brief account and appends to his edition the texts of most of the relevant sources, without translation. Velankar also includes a well-organized interpretive description of the sources in his introduction (p. xxxviii). The most thorough treatment of the subject, however, is to be found in S. S. Janaki's "The Vikramorvaśīya of Kālidāsa—A Study of the Poet's Sources."

The Vedic hymn presupposes a floating body of stories about the pair, suggested by scattered references elsewhere in the Veda, and by the hymn's own vagueness: the author appears to have written a dialogue epitomizing events with which he assumes his audience to be familiar. The nymph Urvaśī has fallen in love with King Purūravas and become pregnant by him. Interpreting certain verses in the light of later versions, it seems that Urvaśī agrees to remain on earth with her lover only if a number of conditions are met. When the immortals arrange matters so that Purūravas cannot but violate the conditions, Urvaśī remains unyielding in her determination to return to her heavenly home. The hymn, then, consists of a dialogue alternating the pathetic pleas of Purūravas with Urvaśī's rather cold remembrance of their affair and adamant refusal, even when he threatens to kill himself, to remain by his side. Finally she seems to agree to send him the child she will bear, but leaves him with a warning against the love of women: "There can be no friendship with women; their hearts are the hearts of jackals." The name of this son, Āyus (which means "life" or "vitality"), is not mentioned here, but does occur elsewhere in the *Ṛg Veda* in association with that of Urvaśī. Moreover, there seems to be, throughout the ritual texts, a strong connection of Āyus especially, but of Purūravas and Urvaśī as well, with fire and with producing fire from fire sticks. See Janaki, "Sources," p. 13.

All subsequent versions of the story seek to soften the character of Urvaśī, first by making her abandonment of Purūravas less absolute. Two secondary Vedic accounts, *Bṛhaddevatā* 7.140–47 and the *Vedārthadīpikā,* Ṣaḍguruśiṣya's commentary on the *Sarvānukramaṇī* (10.95), make it clear that in the oldest version Urvaśī refuses to spend even one night with her mortal lover after the conditions are violated. In the *Śatapatha Brāhmaṇa* (5.1–2) she not only concedes a single night at the end of the year, but she also suggests that he ask the gandharvas who will come to take her away how to become a gandharva like them, and so remain united with her forever. They instruct him to worship the fire sticks, which elsewhere in the *Brāhmaṇa* and other ritual texts are called Purūravas and Urvaśī, the fire itself being known as Āyus. The Brāhmaṇa version also contains the first description of Purūravas wandering in separation.

Both epics mention the couple, but the *Rāmāyaṇa* references do not seem to have contributed to Kālidāsa's treatment. They do, however, allude to the story of the creation of fire (see Araṇyakāṇḍa 48.18 and Uttarakāṇḍa 56.12.29), as does the *Mahābhārata* (Ādiparvan 63–69). There the king brings the three sacrificial fires to earth along with Urvaśī, who bears him six sons, Āyus being the eldest. The kṣatriya Purūravas also contests arrogantly with brahmans and is consequently cursed. No curse, however, is directed at Urvaśī, and there is no story of separation and reunion.

The device of the curse becomes another way of making Urvaśī's character less harsh, by removing from her the blame for abandoning Purūravas. The motif of the curse, however, is first introduced in the *Vedārthadīpikā* as a way of explaining why Urvaśī happens to be on the earth, where she initially meets Purūravas. This change in the use of the curse is undoubtedly the reason for *two* curses in Kālidāsa's version, the first banishing Urvaśī from heaven to Purūravas' side when she speaks her line incorrectly in the heavenly play (see the interlude to Act Three), and the second causing her separation from Purūravas as a consequence of entering Kumāra's grove. It is also the *Vedārthadīpikā* which makes explicit the conditions which seem to be suggested in the hymn: that Urvaśī keep her pet rams (or lambs) constantly by her side and that she never see Purūravas naked. Interestingly, though the Purāṇas are rich in potential source material, Kālidāsa did not draw from those that maintain or elaborate the device of the curse.

Of the thirteen Purāṇas which contain Purūravas-Urvaśī narratives, then, only three need concern us here. Dating is difficult; Velankar wants to follow P. V. Kane, *History of Dharmaśāstra,* 5:852–55, 876–78 and 899–901, in assigning the *Matsya Purāṇa* to the third century, that is, before Kālidāsa; Janaki cites the article of her mentor, Dr. V. Raghavan, "Gleanings from the *Matsya Purāṇa,*" pp. 80 ff., wherein, she says, are "exhaustive references to prove the acquaintance of the Purāṇa text with Kālidāsa" ("Sources," p. 17). The *Padma* is by general agreement post-Kālidāsa, but since its version of the story is nearly identical with that of the *Matsya,* its date is not important. The *Matsya* version (24.10–32), because its narrative clearly intends to be a love story, drops Urvaśī's stipulations for remaining on earth. Introduced are the rescue from the demons (Act One), giving cause for Urvaśī's grateful love, and the performance of the play "Lakṣmī's Bridegroom Choice," with Urvaśī's slip in the dialogue and consequent banishment to earth (see Act Three interlude). The king's separation from Urvaśī and mad wandering in the Kumāra grove (Act Four) are laid to a curse placed on the king by the personified *puruṣārthas* ("goals of man") Kāma (Desire) and Artha (Worldly Gain), whom the king has snubbed in favor of Dharma (Duty) when the three visit him together.

The *Viṣṇudharmottara Purāṇa* (1.129–37) contains the most detailed account of the story and, as it is late, seems to have been influenced by rather than to have influenced the *Vikramorvaśīya.* Rambhā replaces Citralekhā as Urvaśī's friend and go-between. The tryst in the royal pleasure garden (Acts Two and Three in the play, but reduced to one episode in the Purāṇa) is an element not found in the *Matsya.* Yet this Purāṇa also contains elements of the *Śatapatha Brāhmaṇa* version: Urvaśī lays down stipulations for her stay on earth, but the conditions are said to be imposed at the insistence of Nārada under threat of a curse. Again, Purūravas is forced to violate the conditions by the gandharvas, who want Urvaśī back in heaven. As regards this awkward combination of the *Brāhmaṇa* and Kālidāsa versions, Janaki tends to view the former as original and the latter as interpolated; Velankar implies he believes the opposite to be true.

Another later version of the story is found in Somadeva's *Kathāsaritsāgara.* The two meet in Indra's Nandana grove, where Purūravas is worshiping Viṣṇu. Because of the king's great devotion he is given the nymph. Later, as a reward for slaying a demon, Purūravas is summoned to heaven, where he witnesses a dance by the nymph Rambhā. When he laughs at a flaw in her performance, her guru causes him to be separated from Urvaśī. Reunion is accomplished through the king's propitiation of Kṛṣṇa at Badarikāśrama. Though the story has a marked medieval devotional flavor, it is possible that it preserves certain elements which predate and influence Kālidāsa, such as the prominence of the Nandana grove setting.

Lastly, it should be pointed out that the device of the *saṁgamanīya maṇi* (gem of reunion) appears to be pure invention on Kālidāsa's part. See Velankar's introduction, pp. xlv-xlvi, and S. G. Kantawala, "The

Saṁgamanīya Gem Episode in the *Vikramorvaśīyam.*" As a plot device it parallels the ring in *Śākuntala,* but rather than serving as an emblem of the power of memory in the aesthetic-erotic experience, it becomes (literally) the glittering center, passionate red, of Kālidāsa's web of Śaivite cosmology. (See Miller's article in this volume.)

Urvaśī's jealous rage drives her into the grove of Śiva's son, Kumāra (also called Kārttikeya or Skanda), a place forbidden to women. When the curse which this activates (again, an innovation of Kālidāsa) transforms her into a creeper, a traditional image in Sanskrit poetry for the delicate sinuousness of the female form, the antidote for the curse is announced to her lover by the mysterious voice of an unseen sage who is *mṛgacārī,* either "wandering like a deer" or "wandering in the form of a deer." The deer, like the antelope, is an animal associated with Śiva; some commentators and modern writers identify the sage as Śiva himself. The antidote turns out to be a red jewel formed from the hardened red lac (presumably washed) from the feet of Pārvatī, Śiva's consort. Red lac is a kind of makeup invariably associated with fertility (see Act Three of *Mālavikāgnimitra*) and the auspicious preparations for marriage. The opposition and union of the ascetic (the chaste grove) and the erotic (the creeper, and gem) are at the heart of Śaiva mythology; see Wendy O'Flaherty, *Asceticism and Eroticism.*

The third new element of Kālidāsa's version is the *Indrānugraha,* the remission of the first curse (Urvaśī's banishment to earth until Purūravas sees a son) by Indra. When Nārada, the sage who is Indra's emissary, announces that the curse has been lifted and that Urvaśī may remain on earth, he likens the consecration of Āyus as crown prince to the installation of Śiva's son Skanda as the commander-in-chief of heaven's armies. In this regard we should recall that Kālidāsa's telling of the Śiva-Pārvatī story is called *Kumārasaṁbhava,* "The Birth of Kumāra"; the purpose of their union was to produce a son who could defeat the demon army. When Nārada makes his comparison at 5.23, Kālidāsa is joining the Indra mythology of kingship and war to his Śaivite vision of the generative in art.

Notes on the Text and Translation

In these notes I have attempted not to duplicate matters discussed in the introduction. There will therefore be, for example, no additional explanations of stage directions and stagecraft. For readers who know Sanskrit, full technical discussions of problems involving language, grammar, aesthetics, and allusions to other texts are included in the notes to the editions of Pandit, Kale, and Velankar. Though some discussion of textual matters is inevitable, the aim here is to explain what might be unfamiliar to the English reader, to uncover some aspect of the original that the translation has failed to convey, or to justify the choice of an unconventional rendering.

Act One

1.1 The benedictory verse (*nāndī*) invokes the deity in order to ward off any possible obstacles to the performance. It should also contain hints about the events of the drama about to be played. As the commentators explain, "in ancient scripture" refers to the Vedic origin of the story; "earth and heaven" alludes to the union of a mortal man with a celestial woman; "by . . . firm devotion" evokes the trial of separation, etc.

1.1+ *Urvaśī Won by Valor* . . . The title of the play is open to various syntactic interpretations; the *-īya* suffix, in the sense of "a work about," may be affixed to various types of compounds, including *dvandva* (coordinate) compounds; see Pāṇini 4.3.88. The title could mean "[The Play About] Urvaśī and Valor." But "Urvaśī [Won by] Valor," the common translation, seems more appropriate. Urvaśī *is* won by valor when Purūravas rescues her from the demon. The Gandharva king Citraratha makes much of Purūravas' *vikrama* (valor, heroism; see 1.13+ passim) and cites it as a correspondence between Purūravas and his counterpart Indra. Some commentators maintain that Vikrama was another name for Purūravas, but this is probably based on the grammatical necessity explained above; the identification is not made explicit in the text. It is possible that the play was first performed as part of a spring festival at the court of Kālidāsa's patron Vikramāditya. (See Miller's article.) It would be an obvious eulogistic technique to identify one's royal patron with the legendary ancient king by repeated mention of his signature, *Vikrama,* early in the performance. Does the play also celebrate a historical elevation of the son of a secondary, younger queen to the rank of crown prince (*yuvarāja*)?

1.2 Good spirit embodied in the foundation of the playhouse . . . Both Raṅganātha and Kāṭayavema interpret *vastupuruṣa* as "plot and hero." But *puruṣa* is an uncommon term for the *nāyaka* (hero) of a drama, and the architectural term *vāstupuruṣa* ("man in the foundation") immediately evokes the myth of the demon, subdued by the gods, who falls to earth, becomes the maṇḍala-like site plan of temples and other buildings, and must be propitiated before the building is used. Hence Kālidāsa must have strongly intended the suggested sense to be understood. See the work of Stella Kramrisch, *The Hindu Temple* and "Īśānaśivagurudevapaddhati: Kriyāpāda chapters 26–27."

1.3 A celestial courtesan, the issue of a sage's thigh . . . The nymphs, as the folk-etymology which derives their name from *ap,* "water" suggests, were originally water divinities who came to be associated with the heavenly court as dancers and actresses. As Menakā says immediately below, they were often dispatched by the gods to distract ascetics from gaining too much power through the practice of austerities. The birth of Urvaśī from the thigh of the sage Nārāyaṇa in just such a disturbance is recounted in various Purāṇas. (Pandit states that this ancient seer is not the same as the god Viṣṇu, also called Nārāyaṇa, but that the two were later identified.)

1.3+ Rambhā . . . Her name means "plantain," thought to be a beautiful shape for a woman's thighs in the vocabulary of Sanskrit poetry. Many legends are associated with this nymph, including: the *Kathāsaritsāgara* version of the Purūravas-Urvaśī story (see note on sources); an abduction by Rāvaṇa, the glamorous villain of the *Rāmāyaṇa;* and an incident in which she is turned to stone by Viśvāmitra when sent to seduce him from practicing austerities.

1.3+ Menakā is another well-known nymph, also sent to seduce Viśvāmitra; the mother of Śakuntalā. Sahajanyā has no particular legends associated with her. Citralekhā is known as the portrait painter of the gods.

1.3+ Golden Peak . . . This northern hill of the Himālayan range forms a border to the region of *kiṁnara* and *kiṁpuruṣa* demigods; see note to 4.50. Note that the place where Purūravas and Urvaśī meet is also the site of Duṣyanta's reunion with Śakuntalā, *Śāk* 7.8 ff.

1.3+ Born in the dynasty of the moon . . . See verse 5.21 and note to *Śāk* 1.11.

1.4+ Chariot Somadatta . . . banner blazoned with a leaping deer . . . Both the chariot's name and the device on Purūravas' banner relate to his lunar lineage. The moon is said to be the source of the divine nectar soma; the moon is variously described as "deer-marked," "hare-marked," etc.

1.7+ Royal sage . . . See Miller's article and *Śāk* 2.14.

1.8 Who has only one mood, the erotic . . . referring to the aesthetic mood (*rasa*) of *śṛṅgāra*.

1.10+ Sharing my pain, with eyes that seem to drink me in . . . Urvaśī's shy comment is grammatically applicable to her friends or the king.

1.12 Resplendent spring . . . *Śrīrivārtavī*. This prefigures the dominant motif of Act Two, the descent or incarnation of Śrī in the pleasure garden in springtime. Śrī is the goddess Lakṣmī, but in a general sense is often used to personify beauty-and-fortune (considered a single entity).

1.12+ Congratulations . . . *Diṣṭyā*. This is the standard congratulatory formula in Sanskrit dramas. It consists of the instrumental case of the word "fortune," the name of the person congratulated in the nominative, the reason for congratulation in the instrumental, and the present tense of the verb "to increase." *diṣṭyā mahārājo vijayena vardhate*, "by fortune the great king increases with/by victory." The formula is variously translated "congratulations," "your fortune increases," "what luck!" etc., according to context and speaker.

1.13+ Nārada . . . Appears as Indra's emissary in Act Five.

1.14 Cf. *Śāk* 7.3.

1.18 The sky her father's footstep conquered . . . Here Kālidāsa is clearly identifying the sage Nārāyaṇa with Viṣṇu. In another incarnation, as the dwarf Vāmana, he bested the demon Bali by encompassing the universe in three steps. The second step was the sky.

1.18 Tearing a thread . . . Do wild geese really break open the tips of lotus stalks and extract the filaments for food? Or is this extremely common image (cf. 4.31, though the translation has been simplified there to "lotus stalks") merely a *kavisamaya* (poetic convention)?

Act Two

2.0 He's turned his back on ordinary pleasures, which bothers me . . . The buffoon is the king's companion and therefore sympathetic; also he has nothing to do when the king is uninterested in diversions.

2.1 In the sixth watch . . . The day and night were each divided into eight parts. This act takes place in the sixth watch of the day—late morning, usually a time for rest. Most of the business was conducted during the cooler early morning hours.

2.2+ The five kinds of food . . . These are not listed in the original, but have been supplied from Kāṭayavema's commentary.

2.3+ You crave only nectar from heaven . . . The *cātaka,* or crested cuckoo, is mythically said to drink only rainwater; see *Śāk* 7.7. Here the buffoon uses the word *rasa,* which means "juice," "essence," "flavor," "love," or aesthetic mood. The use of the term and the image recall Urvaśī's divine origin, but also allude to Kālidāsa's ubiquitous subtext on art and aesthetic experience, not so fully developed or so self-conscious here as in *Śākuntala.*

2.3+ What kind of remedy is that? . . . The buffoon remembers his promise to dissuade the king from this "path," as well as seeing the folly of leading the lovelorn king to such a sensuous place. The king himself realizes this at 2.4+.

2.3+ Hospitable breeze is aptly named . . . *Dakṣiṇa* means both "southern" and "polite."

2.4 Tender spring creeper; regal jasmine . . . The parallel, of course, is with Urvaśī and the queen. From this it is also understood that the queen is past the first bloom of youth.

2.8+ Indra, Ahalyā . . . Indra desired Ahalyā, wife of the sage Gotama, and the first woman created by Brahmā. He was cursed for pursuing her by having his body covered with a thousand vaginas, which were later turned into eyes. The translation is a bit expanded to make the sense clear.

2.8+ Indra's thunderbolt . . . Though the reading is supported by a number of manuscripts, Velankar is the only editor who chooses the sensible *vajjo* (Skt. *vajra,* thunderbolt) over *vejjo* (Skt. *vaidya,* doctor).

2.9+ The crown of Prayāga . . . The text says "the crown of Pratiṣṭhāna," but this is obviously not the historical Pratiṣṭhāna, which is

Paithan on the Godāvarī, but the historical Prayāga at the confluence of the Gaṅgā and Yamunā—present-day Allahabad.

2.10 Cf. *Śāk* 6.22.

2.11+ You're quite the sophisticate! . . . The remark is meant ironically.

2.19 Añjanā was a celestial cursed to monkey birth. The wind god loosened her garment, became enamored of her, and desired to make love to her. He preserved her chastity but nonetheless begot a son on her, the famous Āñjaneya, also known as Hanumān, companion and devotee of Rāma.

2.19+ "Ill-come" . . . The word-play is translated literally. *Svāgatam* is a familiar expression meaning "well-come"; the buffoon turns it around and coins *durāgatam*.

2.19+ By delicious food . . . Velankar has adopted a substantially different reading here from Kale and Pandit: *sarvaḥ āśvāsitaścitrabhojanena* rather than *āśvāsitaḥ piśāco'pi bhojanena* ("Even a ghost/goblin is sustained by food!").

2.20+ Soft-heartedness . . . Pandit and Kale here read *adākṣiṇyakṛtāt*. Velankar's *dākṣiṇyakṛtāt* follows Kāṭayavema and is superior.

2.20+ Churned up . . . *aprasanna,* literally "uncalmed," "unpropitiated." The concept of propitiation is central to the understanding of Indian social psychology, especially in the classical dynamics of love—as will be seen in the queen's vow in the next act. The queen is *aprasanna* like a monsoon river because she has reddened (like a muddy river) through anger. The buffoon says "get up" because the king is on his knees.

2.21 Sentiment . . . *Rasa,* refers to *śṛṅgārarasa,* the sentiment of erotic love.

2.21 Tawdry luster . . . *Kṛtrimarāga,* literally "artificial redness," or "artificial passion."

2.21+ Her being out of the way . . . An expanded translation of *etat* from *avigaṇayya* in the commentary.

2.21+ Don't say that . . . The king's display of respect for the queen shows his *dākṣiṇya* (courtesy, politeness), considered an important quality in a royal lover; see *DR* 2.8.

Act Three

3.0 Until he beholds an heir . . . Many manuscripts add the Prakrit *tui* (Skt. *tvayi*), "in you," the locative case being used idiomatically to mean "born from you." The real point of Indra's alteration of the curse is to alleviate his friend Purūravas' childless condition, which we know from the buffoon's remark at the opening of Act Five, as well as Purūravas' own initial reaction to the sight of Āyus. His reaction would have been different had Queen Auśīnarī already produced an heir.

3.2 Harem . . . The *antaḥpura* or women's apartments (literally, "inner chamber") are not simply a harem in the sense of a pool of women kept for the king's pleasure. Rather they are the entire inner section of the palace (although the *catuḥśālā* of the *Veṇīsaṁhāra* seems to be accessible from the outside) where all the women live. The apartments are usually served by old women and administered by an elderly man such as the chamberlain here.

3.3 Primeval winged mountain . . . In Indian myth mountains are represented as primeval winged creatures whose flights darkened the earth and even heaven. Indra asked them to restrict their movements and when they refused he angrily cut off their wings, forcing them to be immovable. The king is hyperbolically compared with a mountain moving on outstretched wings. See *Ṛg Veda* 2.12.2.

3.3+ Keep my vigil . . . *Pratipālayāmi.* Note that the queen uses the same word a minute later in her vow at 3.4+. This seems to be a deliberate technique on Kālidāsa's part. Rather than calling the second passage a "bad echo" of the first, I am inclined to see the first as a kind of anticipation of a more important occurrence of the word in an upcoming passage, here the queen's request. There are several other instances of this in the play. See note to 5.6+.

3.9+ A woman on her way to a tryst . . . Technically Urvaśī is not such a woman (*abhisārikā*), since her meeting is not secret—Indra has permitted her to pursue the affair with Purūravas. See *NŚ* 22.219.

3.9+ Your magic power . . . Urvaśī seems to have lost at least some of her own *prabhāva* when she was evicted from heaven. That also seems to be the implied explanation (4.2+ and 4.71+) for her stumbling into Kumāra's grove.

3.9+ Some woman's love . . . *Manorathalabdha* is omitted from the translation of Citralekha's speech. It can mean either "won by desire" or "won in imagination." Urvaśī takes the former, negative (for her) construction. "In his imagination" has been added to Citralekhā's next speech to make the point a bit clearer. Cf. Bakulāvalikā's teasing of Mālavikā, *Mālavikāgnimitra* 4.8+.

3.9+ My heart is selfish enough to be suspicious . . . *Adakṣiṇaṁ saṁdegdhi me hṛdayam.* I reject the possible translation "it confuses my unskilled heart"—unlikely in the case of a courtesan; but she *may* be innocent with regard to love (see note to 3.14+).

3.12 The auspicious signs of a married woman's fortune . . . The queen is dressed simply and modestly in accordance with the purity of her vow. All married women are thought to possess *saubhāgya,* a wealth of beauty and good fortune which derives solely from their married condition. Emblematic of this condition are the gold thread which is tied around the bride's neck at the time of marriage and the *kuṁkuma* (turmeric with lime) which is worn in the center of the forehead. Nosering, bangles, or a necklace of glass beads are also sometimes considered necessary for a married woman to wear. While her husband is alive she must never appear without these. When her husband dies, the *saubhāgya* departs and she may not wear any of these ornaments.

3.12+ The queen glances at Nipuṇikā . . . She is embarrassed to name her vow, or pretending to be embarrassed.

3.13 Against Kale's translation and the commentaries, Vidvan H. V. Nagaraja Rao of the Mysore Oriental Research Institute thinks that the body (*gātram*) referred to is the king's, not the queen's. (There is no pronoun in the Sanskrit.) While it is true that the observance of the vow involves a fast which would no doubt work a hardship on the queen, the king is also being pained by the loss of face he must endure. The paradox of the delicacy of a warrior's body in amorous affairs is not without precedent: Viṣṇu's nails are strong enough to rip open the demon Hiraṇyakaśipu's stomach, yet delicate enough to break on Lakṣmī's breast during love-making. The second couplet of the verse might also serve to substantiate this view.

3.13+ That you can let him go like this . . . The phrase has been added to "Lady, has the king become such a stranger?" (*bhavati, kimudāsinastatrabhavān*) to make the sense clearer. The buffoon here stupidly feigns ignorance of what has been going on. The Pandit-Kale reading is very different: *bhavati, kiṁ tādṛśaḥ priyastatrabhavān,* "Lady, is the king so beloved [to you that you give him away to another to satisfy his desire]?" The queen's answer could be a response to either question.

3.14 The sentiment of the entire verse rings false, from the disavowal of his affair with Urvaśī to the flattering vocative *bhīru,* "timid lady." The king is saying what is expected of him. Velankar takes no notice of the missing *mātra* in the second half of the first line. Kale supplies *vā,* thereby rectifying the meter and clarifying the sense.

3.14+ The royal sage does love his wife . . . Now Urvaśī says what is expected of her and it also rings false. Actually, though Urvaśī is a celestial courtesan, she may never have *loved* anyone, and love may make her take everything positively, at face value.

3.16+ To be united with him . . . Depending on whether the Prakrit *se* is rendered as the masculine genitive pronoun (Skt. *asya*) or the feminine (Skt. *asyāḥ*), *praṇayavatī* will either mean a "friend" of the queen or a "lover," "suitor" of the king.

3.17+ Unblinking as fish . . . The gods have no eyelids. See *NŚ* 23.155: "The director should not have [the actors portraying gods] refrain from blinking their eyelids"—even though the gods don't blink.

Act Four

As the note on the text of this play explains in greater detail, the longer of two available recensions was chosen for this translation. Though the authenticity of the additional material is questioned, there can be no doubt for anyone who has studied the dramaturgical manuals and the larger corpus of Sanskrit drama that the stage directions in the Northern Recension represent something of the way in which the playwright's text was developed in performance. While considering the notes that follow, the reader should keep in mind the general description of the stage directions, particularly the points concerning zonal division and portrayal of animals.

No note is given when (a) the translation has been expanded to explain the term; (b) the term has not been located in the dramaturgical manuals; (c) the term has been found to have a number of meanings in different texts and there has been no compelling reason to select one over the others; (d) the explanation is musical, involving scales and time signatures; or (e) the explanation is in a secondary source which has accepted without further investigation Kale's interpretation of Raṅganātha's frequently unreliable commentary.

4.1 A singer offstage . . . The text gives most of these Prakrit *anyokti* stanzas with no indication of who sings them. I have added the designation "a singer offstage" to clarify. The singer, or singers, may have stood with the seated musicians between the two doors to the *nepathya* (in the manner of Kathakali).

4.1+ Entrance song . . . This is a *dhruvā,* a type of song to which the *Nāṭyaśāstra* devotes all of chapter 32. *Dhruvās* figure prominently in the preliminaries (*pūrvaraṅga*). (See *NŚ* 32.483.) About them Bharata says, "Just as a well-built dwelling does not become beautiful without color, so without song the drama gives no joy" (*NŚ* 32.482). He advises the use of songs wherever appropriate (*NŚ* 32.481). The particular type of *dhruvā* here is a *praveśikī* or entrance song.

4.1+ Dance accompanied by hand clapping . . . *Prāveśikī ākṣiptikā.* Velankar says that since according to *NŚ* 32.23–24 *ākṣiptikā* is a type of *dhruvā,* it must stand for the word *dhruvā* when considered with the previous word *praveśikī*. The only other reference to anything like the word *ākṣiptikā* is much later in *NŚ* 32, the chapter on *dhruvās,* and the superior Calcutta text (at 32.188) reads *kṣiptakā* there. Further, if Velankar means to understand *ākṣiptikā* as *ākṣepikī,* as one of the three types of *dhruvās* (*praveśikī,* "for an entrance," *ākṣepikī,* "for suggestion," *naiṣkrāmikī,* "for an exit"), he must justify a *praveśikī* and an *ākṣepikī* occurring in the same context; see *NŚ* 32.449. In the face of this confusion I am more inclined to accept the commentator Raṅganātha's citation from Bharata, which describes the *ākṣiptikā* as a sung entrance-dance with hand clapping. As Raghavan (*Bhoja's Śṛṅgāra Prakāśa,* p. 586) confirms, however, the passage is not found in the *Nāṭyaśāstra*. *Ākṣiptaka* is also the name of an *aṅgahāra* (complex of poses); see *NŚ* 4.180–82.

4.1+ With deliberate steps . . . *Dvipadikayā.* The *dvipadikā,* like the *dvipadī,* is a well-known Prakrit metrical form, "that which has two *pādas*" (hemistichs). Velankar, however, maintains that the term indicates "a mode of walking" (p. lxxxiii) and does not have reference to Prakrit meters. According to him, it never occurs "in direct connection, whether expressed or suggested with a Sanskrit or Prakrit stanza." He seems justified because even where there are verses adjacent to the term, they are *anyokti* stanzas, recited by someone other than the person to whom the stage direction refers. Moreover, many of the adjacent stanzas contain four, not two, *pādas*. Kale does cite from *NŚ* a *śuddhā dvipadikā* containing four *pādas,* but this goes against all later writers on Prakrit metrics.

Raghavan lists it as one of the twelve *uparūpakas* (minor dramatic forms) given in *Bhoja's Śṛṅgāra Prakāśa* (see pp. 542 ff.), and provides a number of examples where dances are named after the songs with which they are associated—*uparūpakas* often contain much dancing. *Dvipadī* is also a kind of *laya* (tempo) of a character's *gati* (gait). In this regard the commentator Rāghavabhaṭṭa has said that the actress's song at the opening of *Śākuntala* (1.4) is a *dvipadī,* which is a *laya*. Raghavan interprets this to mean that the song is in that *laya* or tempo. Finally, he cites Jagaddhara's comment on Mādhava's entrance in Act One of *Mālatīmādhava* of Bhavabhūti. There the commentator explains the stage direction *gamanamalasam* as *dvipadikā,* and quotes an authority to show that it signifies a slow and dragging gait.

4.1+ Looks up to the sky . . . *Diśo'valokya*. An unusual stage direction, in *Vik* it precedes an offstage Prakrit song, or later in the play the king's seeing something which might be above eye level.

4.2. This verse is an *ākṣepikī dhruvā;* see note to 4.1+. It is suggestive rather than directly expressive of what is on the stage. Note how the lake setting of the first verse remains in the second, but the nymphs have been metaphorically transformed into geese, which will serve as one of the animal motifs in the act. They may have been represented on the stage by dancers.

4.2+ Grove of magic herb fragrances . . . *Gandhamādanam vanam.* A primary association with this mountain grove is the curative properties of the medicinal herbs found there. It is mentioned at *Mbh* 7.114.63 ff., "a mountain overgrown with medicinal herbs of great efficacy." Hanumān, not knowing which herbs to pluck, tore off the entire mountain and brought it south for Lakṣmaṇa's cure.

4.3+ This verse is a *jambhalikā,* another type of *dhruvā* (see 4.1+). The meter is of the type called *avalambaka* (see Hemacandra 4.53–56) under which are subsumed *khaṇḍaka, khaṇḍadhārā, khaṇḍikā, khuraka, galitaka* and *bhinnaka*. Many of these terms are better known in later texts such as *Saṅgītaratnākara* than they are to the *Nāṭyaśāstra*. Raghavan's theory again is that they were dances associated with particular types of songs.

4.4 A *naiṣkrāmikī dhruvā,* or exit song—but not called such in the text. Both this verse and verse 4.75 are designated *khaṇḍadhārā* and both are used for exits.

4.5+ In the manner of a madman . . . Purūravas' clothing should be soiled (*NŚ* 23.123–24). Further, "Insanity (*unmāda*) is to be represented on the stage by laughing, weeping, crying, talking, lying down, sitting, running, dancing, singing, reciting something without reason, smearing the body with ashes and dust, grabbing at grass, dried-out floral offerings, dirty clothes, rags and broken pots to put as decoration on the body, along with many other senseless acts; imitation of others" (*NŚ* 7.83).

4.5+ Fixes his gaze on an imaginary object . . . *Ākāśabaddhalakṣya*. The term is not found in the *Nāṭyaśāstra* or the *Daśarūpaka,* but my definition (following Monier-Williams) can be defended on the analogy of *ākāśabhāṣita* (*NŚ* 26.83–85). Usually the character is meant to be conversing with a real character the audience must imagine offstage. Here Purūravas is seeing a cloud but imagining a demon.

4.10+ *Carcarī* . . . Kale rightly shows that this is another term which is well known from Prakrit metrics as the name of a kind of song. A partial translation of the commentary: "It is a song sung by an actor or actress under the influence of passion, and in a tone either low, middle, or of the highest pitch." Velankar relies on an argument similar to the one which he used to establish *dvipadikā* as a movement rather than a type of meter: since the term always occurs outside the context of both Sanskrit and Prakrit verses it cannot refer to anything like prosody, in spite of the fact that it has come to refer to a song through association.

As with *dvipadikā,* V. Raghavan has identified *carcarī* as one of the twelve *uparūpakas* of Bhoja (see pp. 543 ff.), *nāṭya-rāsaka*. It signifies a kind of ensemble dance very much resembling the familiar *rās-līlā* of Kṛṣṇa and the gopīs. The basic form is a circle dance involving women only or pairs of men and women (since Kṛṣṇa multiplied his form in order to dance with each cowherd girl). Many variations are possible, so that endless "wonderful geometric patterns" may be formed by the dancers.

The *carcarī* dance figures prominently in the first act of Harṣa's *Ratnāvalī,* where it is associated with the spring festival. Even though the fourth act of the *Vikramorvaśīya* takes place during the monsoon season, the *carcarī* would not be out of place as the king recreates in memory the characteristics of Urvaśī, whom he met and courted in the spring (and superimposes them on the animals and features of the landscape). We are fortunate in having an account of the *abhinaya* (mimed acting) in the first act of *Ratnāvalī* woven into the poem *Kuṭṭanīmata* of Dāmodaragupta. The dancing of the *carcarī* also occurs in the fourth act of the Prakrit drama *Karpūramañjarī*. However, Raghavan's exhaustive account of the *carcarī* does not mention the *Vikramorvaśīya*.

4.11+ It's no use . . . The two senses of *vṛthā* produce two interpretations of the speech. (a) "Why should I bother to disregard the pain growing in my heart—even sages proclaim that the king alone controls time?" Here

Purūravas knows he is the king. (b) "It's no use trying to ignore my pain anymore because only the king can alter time." Here Purūravas has in his madness forgotten for a moment that he is king. The "pain" is that which separated lovers undergo in the rainy season. According to Nagaraja Rao, the statement that (literally) "the king is the cause of time" can be traced to a remark of Bhīṣma to Yudhiṣṭhira in the Anuśāsana Parvan of the *Mahābhārata*. Purūravas is mad enough to take the statement literally.

4.16 Cf. *Śākuntala* 3.5. As a nymph Urvaśī need not actually touch the ground, but if she did, the weight of her buttocks would produce a heelprint.

4.21 This is one of the several Sanskrit verses in this act which employ what the aestheticians consider an ungraceful amount of syllabic alliteration:

nīlakaṇṭha mamotkaṇṭhā vane'smin vanitā tvayā |
dīrghāpāṅgā sitāpāṅga dṛṣṭā dṛṣṭikṣamā bhavet ||

This verse is actually cited at *Kāvyaprakāśa* 7.55 as an example of a sound hindering the suggestion of a certain aesthetic mood; here, the use of retroflex sounds hinders *śṛṅgāra rasa;* see also *Kāvyaprakāśa* 7.62 and 10.142, *Sāhityadarpaṇa* 7.8 (*pratikūlatva*). One can only think that Kālidāsa used the technique intentionally to portray Purūravas' madness.

4.22 *Matpriyāyā vināśād* literally means "because of the destruction of my love." *Vināśa* usually means "death"; to use the word would incur the poetic blemish (*doṣa*) of "inauspiciousness." But since Urvaśī is immortal anyway, it is used to show the king's madness, according to Raṅganātha.

4.23 Hiding in a sylph's grove . . . *Vidyādharakānanālīna*. *Ālīna* can mean "hiding in" or "sticking to." Purūravas wants to remain in the place where his love was last seen. *Ambaramānena* (Pkt. *ambaramāṇe*), "with the measure of the sky," is a difficult phrase. As the commentary suggests, it does by extension mean "very large," "broad," "powerful." My almost literal translation attempts to convey a creature who seems to measure the sky as he moves, but it could also convey that he is wandering aimlessly.

4.24 The two names of the cuckoo which Purūravas uses here, *parabhṛtā* and *parapuṣṭā,* refer to the female cuckoo's habit of laying her eggs in a crow's nest for the crow to hatch. The commentator attributes the repeated vocative in the original to the king's madness.

4.25 This verse explains why Purūravas called the cuckoo the cleverest of birds. The commentary cites several examples from other works of Kālidāsa (e.g., *Kumārasaṁbhava* 4.16) showing how the cuckoo's sweet song makes women who are offended by their lovers' dalliances with other women forget their wrath.

4.30 Mānasa Lake was produced by Brahmā from his mind (*manas*). It is a sacred place on Mount Kailāsa, and the place to which wild geese return every year at breeding season. That the call of the *rājahaṁsa* resembles the tinkling of an anklet is a standard *kavisamaya*. The commentator cites examples from *Kumārasaṁbhava* 1.34 and *Ṛtusaṁhāra* 3.1.

4.33 Anyone convicted of stealing a part must by law return the whole . . . Apparently an established legal principle according to Kāṭayavema, citing the *Yājñavalkya Smṛti* (Pandit, p. 117). The king is legally correct perhaps, but in the context of speaking to a goose, insane. *DR* 3.24 cites this as an example of *asatpralāpa,* "incoherent chatter," on which Dhanika comments, "Not the rhetorical fault of *asaṁgati* (lack of coherence), but the incoherent talk of persons just awakening, drunk, insane, or childish." The DR lists *asatpralāpa* as a subdivision of the dramatic form called *vīthī,* but the classification is confused.

4.34+ I'll plunge into this place and emerge in another space! . . . The king's prose here is mad and musical: yāvad*an*yamava*kā*śamava*gā*hiṣye. There are no stress accents in Sanskrit but a natural emphasis does seem to fall on the italicized heavy syllables. *Avakāśam* is an opportunity or time more than a physical place. *Avagāhiṣye* is literally "I will plunge" or "I will involve myself in."

4.34+ Ruddy drake . . . The *cakravāka,* sometimes translated sheldrake, is a reddish bird with a paler colored head; verse 36 below mentions *gorocana,* a yellow pigment prepared from the bile of cattle, which must refer to the head color. Couples of *cakravāka* birds are regarded as mourning a separation; see *Śāk,* note to 3.21+. As the *cātaka* typifies thirst (see note to 2.3+ above), the *cakravāka* typifies longing in love.

4.34+ "The Crouching Hunter" . . . *Kuṭilikā.* The commentary glosses the name as describing the dance. It mentions the *ardhamatalli karaṇa* (*NŚ* 4.89) which, if built up from its component parts, begins with *dolāpāda* (raising the foot in *kuñcita*—toes contracted, instep arched—then placing it on the ground in *añcita*—touching the ground with the heel, toes outstretched) but with the hands swinging (*recita,* built on *haṁsapakṣa*—three fingers extended, little finger raised, thumb bent), which makes it *skhalita karaṇa* (*NŚ* 4.147); finally, the left hand rests on the hip. This may be what the dance looks like, but since I am not sure that Raṅganātha is to be trusted here, I prefer to start from Pāṇini (4.4.18) *aṇ kuṭilikāyāḥ* which enjoins the taddhita suffix *aṇ* [= a] for the instrumental in the sense of "conveys away by stealth," "comes upon by stealth," as a hunter. The word also echoes the buffoon's staff and the general sense of crookedness.

4.35a+ "The Robust Potter" . . . The commentary only says "a particular dance" (*nāṭyaviśeṣa*). *Mallaghaṭī* could mean "having a wrestler's pot," but *malla* itself also means "drinking vessel," or "cup." Velankar thinks it might have been a dance involving the use of earthen pitchers "like the *garbā* in Gujarat" (p. lxxxvi).

4.37 The original contains word repetitions which, again, Raṅganātha attributes to the king's madness:

rathāṅganāman saṁtyakto rathāṅgaśroṇibimbayā |
ayaṁ tvāṁ pṛcchati rathī manorathaśatairvṛtaḥ ||

The etymology of *manoratha,* "desire," is "chariot of the mind" (*manas* + *ratha*); see Maurice Bloomfield, "The Mind as Wish-Car in the Veda," p. 282.

4.40+ "Square" pose . . . *Caturaśraka.* There are many gestures and other theatrical terms called *caturaśra* ("four-cornered"). Vatsyayan (*Classical Indian Dance,* p. 245) says that both *caturaśraka* and *ardhacaturaśraka* are *sthānas,* but I have been unable to locate them in the Bose catalogue. Elsewhere (p. 96) she says that *caturaśra* is the only *sthānaka* not found in either the *Nāṭyaśāstra* or the *Abhinayadarpaṇa,* but that it is found in the *Saṅgītaratnākara,* where it means the same as Bharata's *sauṣṭhava* and *caturaśra* of the body. Though these are distinct postures (see *NŚ* 11.89–93), perhaps Vatsyayan (or the *Saṅgītaratnākara*) presents them as alike on the basis of their both being a kind of "first position" in the Indian dance vocabulary.

4.43b Fans bees away from his rut-wet cheek . . . The translation supplied by Velankar in his notes—"with all the bees gone away from his cheek (for want of rut)"—cannot be correct, unless we are to accept some strange poetic convention that an elephant would cease to produce rut in separation. The presence of rut would rather emphasize the anguish of separation.

4.44+ Pose for accosting . . . *Sthānakena.* Like the derivatives of *caturaśra,* this term was difficult to deal with because of its very ubiquity. The commentator Raṅganātha seems to identify *sthānaka* with *ālāpa,* but like his citation for *ākṣiptikā* it seems to come from some Bharata other than the one whose name is attached to the *Nāṭyaśāstra.* I have based my translation on the list of twelve forms of verbal representation at *NŚ* 24.49 ff., among which is listed *ālāpa.*

4.49 Another verse with repetitive alliteration:

api vanāntaram alpabhujāntarā
śrayati parvata parvasu saṁnatā |
idam anaṅgaparigraham aṅganā
pṛthunitamba nitambavatī tava ||

Unlike 4.21 the sounds chosen would not necessarily be considered as hindering the erotic mood.

4.50 Demigods . . . Here the *kiṁnaras* of the Himālayas. They have human bodies and horses' heads; they are renowned for their singing.

4.51 This is a Sanskrit verse, but resembles a Prakrit one in its simplicity. Every editor and commentator has remarked on its similarity to *Rāmāyaṇa* (Araṇyakāṇḍa) 64.29–30. The original says only "seen the woman deserted by me." Because of the absence of an interrogative particle the syntax can also be declarative, and because of the presence of both first and second person instrumental pronouns ("by me" and "by you") the verse can serve as an echo which answers Purūravas' question positively. This is called a *trigata* in poetics; see *DR* 3.17 where, like the *asatpralāpa* of 4.33, it is cited as a subdivision of the minor dramatic form *vīthī;* no specimen exists of a *vīthī.*

4.52 Her frowning brow becomes a wave . . . This verse reveals Kālidāsa's mastery of the figure known as *utprekṣā,* a kind of metaphor, often extended, involving cause and effect (here the result of Urvaśī's jealous rage). The verse figures prominently, as does 4.67, in Ānandavardhana's argument at *Dhvanyāloka* 2.5 for the existence of the *rasavad alaṁkāra,* in which the evocation of aesthetic mood is used to support a figure.

4.54 In his madness Purūravas even confuses the river he is standing before with the ocean. *Meghāṅgena nṛtyati,* "dances with (or accompanied by) the limb of a cloud." Kale thinks this refers to a cloud reflected in the water, considered as a "limb" of the ocean, but these would presumably be "legs," not "arms." We already know from the first line that his "arm" is a wave. Further, it is unlikely that there would be any reflections if the ocean were agitated in a monsoon downpour. Velankar evasively translates this passage "the Ocean is dancing by the side of the clouds."

The original is actually two stanzas in different meters.

4.56 This is the single *anyokti* verse in Sanskrit. It is also composed in moric rather than syllabic meter, another feature which it shares with Prakrit verses. Velankar speculates that since this *gajānyokti* concerns Airāvata, Indra's elephant mount, Sanskrit is employed "due to his preeminence." Pandit gives the verse in his appendix along with the rejected Prakrit material.

4.57 *Kānanaśriyā,* "by the goddess of the grove." See note on Śrī, *Vik* 1.12.

4.59 In these woods that glisten like the sky . . . Literally, "in the forest brilliant as the sky" (*gaganojjvalakānane*). What does it mean? Vidvan Nagaraja Rao suggests that leaves in a thick forest would reflect blue when the sun shines on them. This is supported by the commentary's statement that the similarity is the deep blue color; but since the sun would not be shining in the rainy season, a comparison might be made on the basis of the shared dark-greenness of the forest and the monsoon sky, and the shared glittering of leaves wet with rain and the lightning flashes.

4.62 Ruby . . . The commentator identifies the jewel as a ruby (*padmarāga*), but Kālidāsa, despite all the references to the gem's redness, never names it as such. The last line of the original is expanded in translation to bring out the double meaning of *kara,* "ray" and "hand," a frequently exploited pun in Sanskrit.

4.64 *Naivenam* is an unnoticed error in the critical edition for *naivainam. Ina,* "lord," "master" is not correct here.

4.65 On the *saṁgamanīya maṇi,* see note on sources.

4.68 Ghosal (pp. 92 ff.) has a thorough discussion of this verse and the many variant readings, interpretations and suggested emendations of Bollensen, Pischel, Alsdorf, and Velankar. There are sharp differences among manuscripts in every line. In line c Pandit reads *raṇṇe viṇu* (Skt. *araṇyena vinā*), which with the verb *karimi* Kale translates as "remove her from the forest." Velankar's emendation is *rañjeviṇu* (Skt. *rañjayitvā*, "having pleased her"). At the end of the same line most editors choose *ṇibhantī*, but Raṅganātha provides a *chāyā* of *nirbhrāntim* and glosses it with *nirgatā* (so the word would mean something like "wandering forth") while Velankar translates his *chāyā* or *nirbhrāntām* as "absolutely certain." Both meanings are etymologically possible but not well established. *Kaantī*, or *kalantī* (at the end of line d) for Sanskrit *kṛtāntā*, *kṛtāntām*, or *kṛtāntam* is also open to a number of interpretations.

4.70 In Pandit and Kale, Purūravas addresses Urvaśī as *tanvī* "slender lady," "beauty"—it also means "creeper"—instead of *caṇḍī*, "wrathful lady."

4.71+ Urvaśī means that, as she will explain, she retained her senses when she was a creeper and could see what Purūravas was doing. Kale follows Pandit, reading for *antaḥkaraṇapratyakṣīkṛtam*—*abhyantarakaraṇayā* ("with my senses concealed within").

4.72 Were you not entangled in heaven's decrees . . . The translation is expanded to convey the import of the verse as explained by Kāṭayavema: *na kathaṁcidapi yattvayoktaṁ tattathaiva*, that is, "Had it not happened as you related [you would not have remained separated from me by choice]."

4.73 Of the ruby set on my forehead . . . There are a number of contradictions in the play itself as to who wears the jewel, and consequently some confusion among the editors on this point. Velankar's reading for the stage direction (*lalāṭe maṇiṁ niveśya*) has no personal pronoun attached to the word *lalāṭa* (forehead). There is also no personal pronoun in the next verse or in the relevant portion of the commentary.

What is probably intended is that the king puts the jewel on his forehead here (but not on his crest) to honor it and in accordance with verse 4.65. Later he gives it to Urvaśī as an ornament.

4.75 This is a *khaṇḍadhārā dhruvā*; it is the only *anyokti* verse in which an animal is presented in a patently human activity. The goose riding in an aerial chariot gives a fitting fairy-tale quality to the end of the act. It serves to integrate the animal realm of madness with the king's sane self. I have added the phrase "his love bestowed."

Act Five

5.0 Paradise grove . . . Some grove near the Gandhamādana of the previous act.

5.0 Lovely nymph . . . Velankar's problematic reading is *apsarovilāsavatī*, "possessed of the *vilāsa* (playful, seductive ways) of an apsaras." It is a senseless description for one who *is* an apsaras. I cannot find a commentatorial explanation for this reading. Kale translates the Pandit reading *abhyantaravilāsinī* "(worthy of being a crest-jewel) for the harem ladies." This makes more sense but still does not seem apt. My translation follows the critical edition but freely interprets the compound to keep the reference to Urvaśī.

5.0 Huntress . . . Another puzzle in Velankar's edition. The king calls out what seems to be a masculine name (Recaka) and is answered (after the verse) by a *kirātī* or female mountaineer, translated here simply as "huntress"—all the king's retinue appear to be female. In the Pandit-Kale text there is no name either in the stage direction or in the following vocative. The name Recaka itself is curious, being known primarily as a technical term in yoga for a type of breathing exercise (*prāṇāyāma*) or in dance for a type of movement; see *NŚ* 4.246.

5.2+ The offender must be punished . . . The *Arthaśāstra* 4.8.86.84 prescribes death by torture for thieves apprehended with royal property, but that text represents a harsh ideal of statecraft not necessarily always practiced.

5.4+ Burglar . . . *Kumbhīlaka* (or *kumbhīraka*, Pkt. *kumbhīlao*) specifically refers to the thief who commits the breaking-and-entering type of house burglary. The word is probably an original Prakrit term borrowed into Sanskrit.

5.6+ Of the arrow's dispatcher . . . Another example of "significant anticipation" (cf. note on 3.3+). The term *prahartur* will be used in the same inflection in the next verse ("dispatcher of his enemies' lives").

5.9+ Long life to you! . . . The boy's name, Āyus ("life," "vitality) gives opportunity for much word-play throughout this act. The king here voices the common salutation *āyuṣmān bhava*, literally "may you be possessed of [long] life."

5.10+ *Śāk* 7.14 is a parallel verse, but from the point of view of the father.

5.11+ The *pādapīṭha* is not necessarily a footstool, but a seat near the feet where the king might seat a favorite.

5.11+ Don't be afraid . . . because of the buffoon's grotesque appearance.

5.12+ And is now grown to full youth . . . The Sanskrit expression is *kavacadhara*, "wearing armor," but even before the period of the classical language it had become an idiom meaning simply "has attained youth." That it is an idiom is implied by Pāṇini's *vayasi ca*, 3.2.10; still, it is an especially well-chosen expression in the case of a kṣatriya boy.

5.12+ Grieve at your parting . . . Velankar's adoption of the reading *kāmaṁ cirasya prekṣya virahotkaṇṭhitāsmi*, "longing in separation" seems inappropriate with reference to Satyavatī's return to the āśrama. Moreover, it cannot refer at this point to Urvaśī's realization that she must leave her husband, for it is not until 5.14+ that we have the stage direction "Urvaśī remembers and weeps." Kale's translation of the Pandit reading is somewhat more natural: *cirasyāryāṁ dṛṣṭvā adhikataraṁ tṛṣṇāsmi,* "Having seen you, honorable lady, I am more desirous [that you remain]."

5.13 The translation has been amplified to highlight the peacock's youth, which is implicit in the image of its sleeping in Āyus' lap. "Fledgling" has been added.

5.14 Verses of Kālidāsa in *Śākuntala* (7.28) and *Raghuvaṁśa* (3.23) express the same comparison.

5.16+ Go to the ascetics' grove . . . In Kālidāsa's *Raghuvaṁśa* (3.70, 7.71) as well, the king retires when his son is old enough to be installed as crown prince.

5.18+ As a celestial, Urvaśī would be the first to recognize Nārada from his radiance. Nārada is an important sage who functions as a messenger of the gods.

5.19+ Lawful wife and helpmate . . . Nārada here raises Urvaśī's status from mere co-wife to *sahadharmacāriṇī,* a lawful and legitimate wife, like Auśīnarī.

5.19+ As long as you live . . . One wonders if the immortal nymph will simply return to heaven when Purūravas dies.

5.20 Raṅganātha tells us that it is well known from the Purāṇas that fire enters the sun in the day and at night the sun enters the fire. See *Raghuvaṁśa* 4.1 for a parallel verse.

5.20+ Of crown prince Āyus . . . A possible reference to the consecration of Prince Kumāragupta, son of Candragupta II (see Miller's article in the introduction) is seen in the Sanskrit expression *kumārasyāyuṣo,* used also at 5.7. *Kumāra* means "youth," "prince," as well as being a name of Skanda, Śiva's son (see 5.23).

5.22+ In Pandit's edition the prince gets up to go with Urvaśī to see Queen Auśīnarī when Nārada stops them, saying "you will go to her at the appropriate time." The king says nothing. Velankar does not notice this variant, but his own reading is more graceful. Conventionally one might expect the queen to be on stage for the play's ending; cf. *Mālavikāgnimitra.*

Mālavikā and Agnimitra (Mālavikāgnimitra)

Critical Apparatus

I have used three published editions of the play: that of C. Sankara Rama Sastri (Mylapore: Balamanorama Press, 1929), with commentary (modern) by Sahṛdayatilaka Rama Pisharody, published as vol. 12 of Sri Balamanorama Series; that of Narayan Ram Acharya, 9th ed. (Bombay: Nirnaya Sagar Press, 1950), with the commentary of Kāṭayavemabhūpāla; and that of Friedrich Bollensen (Leipzig: F. A. Brockhaus, 1879).

The third is the only so-called critical edition available; but it is very old and clearly does not cover all the manuscript traditions evidenced in the two Indian editions. Bollensen is also one of those early editors who carried the principle of *lectio difficilior* to the point of absurdity. His readings are often so contorted as to be better called *lectiones implacabiles*.

I have, consequently, tended to prefer the Balamanorama Press edition edited by Sastri, which is often wittier and more elegant than the Nirnaya Sagar Press version of Acharya. Pisharody's commentary to the Sastri edition has influenced my readings also to an appreciable extent, for it is an excellent and perceptive literary as well as grammatical commentary. In my notes I have signaled the occasional passages where the Acharya or Bollensen editions were preferred. I should emphasize that the principle of choice is not scientific at all, but is thoroughly eclectic—governed only by my feeling as to what gave a better sequential stimulus to the plot or the story line.

After the translation was essentially complete, the "critical" edition of the play by K. A. Subramania Iyer (New Delhi: Sahitya Akademi, 1978) was further consulted. No appreciable changes in the text have resulted. In fact this edition, though consulting some new manuscripts, is less reliable than its predecessors, and is not truly critical. It ignores Acharya's printed edition and the manuscript sources from which it stems, which often supply (in my view) the preferable reading (e.g., 1.4, variant *śāntam*; 1.19+ *chāyā: notthāpayiṣyati*; 3.0 *chāyā: ātmanaḥ prabhutvaṁ darśayati*; 5.12+ variant *yuktā pratīkṣā*). It also references the other printed texts in a sloppy fashion, ignoring them sometimes, referencing them sometimes—even in the *same* phrase—for no apparent reason (cf. p. 9, *l.* 13; p. 10, *l.* 12). The principles of selection are never explained, nor is there any discussion that would convince the reader that a thorough search for manuscripts had been undertaken. It is evident that such a search was not made, and that much, already known, has been missed.

The remarks of S. K. De on the play in Dasgupta and De, *A History of Sanskrit Literature,* pp. 136–38, can be consulted with profit.

Notes on the Text and Translation

I do not conceive of this as necessarily a "playable" translation; it is quite purposely literary. I sought to maintain the ethical tone of the Sanskrit original, which, even in Kālidāsa, never departs very far from the standpoint of cultured and elegant artificiality—an artificiality inherent in the uses of the language. I read in the Sanskrit a good deal of quasi-pompous irony, and this—the chief delight of the original harmony—would disappear entirely in a "colloquialized" translation.

I have also translated the set verses of the original in a somewhat more formal manner than the prose sections, often keeping a metrical scheme. I sometimes resort to rhyme, and to artificial usages which may increase the "Pracht und Glanz" of the translation.

At the same time, I have tried to give a literal translation, not embroidering or subtracting from the intended sense of the original—save possibly for a few epithets which are rendered otherwise or not at all. Occasionally I have used the excellent commentary of Pisharody to bring out a "meaning" not necessarily in the text itself, but one which probably ought to be there. The same commentary has sometimes been used to decide between different possible interpretations. Even the stage directions have not been augmented, though it would have suited my purpose sometimes to do so (viz. "ironically," "stoically," "resignedly," etc.).

Act One

1.1 Our path aright . . . *Nas* read by some Mss., though *vas* is the reading in all printed texts.

1.1+ Cannot survive examination . . . Acharya, *vivekagrastam.*

1.3+ *Chalika* dance . . . All read (Prakrit) *chaliam,* variously rendered in the *chāyās: chalikam, calitam, chalitam.* The term is mentioned in *Kāvyādarśa* 1.39 but one of its definitions is wholly unsuitable to the present context: *puṁnṛtyaṁ chalikaṁ prāhuḥ,* "*chalika* is a dance for males." See V. Raghavan, *Bhōja's Śṛṅgāra Prakāśa,* p. 556. (Also see note to 2.0 below.)

1.3+ Fine points of physiognomy . . . Free translation; *chāyā* reads *nanv ākṛtiviśeṣe ādaraḥ padaṁ karoti,* "respect for (her) distinctive visage makes a place (in his mind)."

1.4 Pacific . . . Acharya: *śāntam.*

1.6 Achieves new power . . . Is raised to a power: *guṇa*.

1.6+ Dance of five aspects . . . *Abhinaya:* the system of expressive gestures which in general constitutes the dancer's art of portrayal.

1.7 Mādhavasena . . . Agnimitra has apparently become involved in a dynastic quarrel within the Vaidarbha royal house, and has in effect taken sides by contracting a marriage alliance with Mādhavasena, Vaidarbha's paternal cousin. Mādhavasena and Vaidarbha, being sons of brothers, would be potential enemies in any division of the royal patrimony or power. Furthermore, Mādhavasena's alliance with Agnimitra, himself a powerful king, would considerably weaken Vaidarbha's position; hence, this latter's attempt on his cousin. But Agnimitra, by the same token, is now obliged to intervene to secure redress for his ally. Vaidarbha's "arrogance" is precisely that he ignores Agnimitra's obligatory involvement, and demands that he be a neutral. He also uses in reply Agnimitra's laconic term of address, *pūjya,* "honorable," which may also suggest condescension.

1.8 This declamation is attributed to Gaṇadāsa in other editions and Gaṇadāsa's to Haradatta.

1.12+ Worthy to take the dust from his feet . . . Literally: "He is not equaled even by the dust of my feet." A traditional expression of dutiful subservience is "to take the dust of [the master's] feet." To deepen the insult even this form of service was scorned by Haradatta.

1.12+ The queen would think me partial . . . The king is partial in the sense that Haradatta is in his retinue.

1.12+ What's your opinion of this quarrel . . . I.e., "How do you think it will come out?" (from commentary, Sastri ed.).

1.13+ Prime Ministress . . . *Chāyā: pīṭhamardikā,* a feminine (apparently intended ironically) of *pīṭhamarda,* a companion of the king, usually a servant aiding the king's amorous ventures.

1.14 Triple Veda incarnate along with its philosophy . . . The three older *saṁhitās* of the Veda (*Ṛg, Yajur,* and *Sāma*) are often called the *trayī,* "triple," short for *trayī vidyā,* "triplex wisdom": as the older "wisdom" in this sense is completed by the *adhyātmavidyā* ("knowledge of the supreme soul") in the Upaniṣads, so the queen, worldly, is followed by the ascetic nun.

1.15 Dhāriṇīs . . . "Dhāriṇī," the queen's name, means "earth."

1.15+ Dispute . . . *Vastu,* deleted Acharya.

1.15+ For the first time they will earn their salaries . . . Free translation. Literally: "Why should we pay them to no purpose?"

1.16+ What now? . . . *Chāyā: katham idānīm:* Acharya, Bollensen; *yathedānīm,* Sastri, "Just as in the present case."

1.18 Express their anger . . . Commentary, Sastri ed., takes *kāraṇakopāḥ* as predicated: "Wives, though they be imperious, express anger only when justified."

1.19+ "And of me" . . . A number of witticisms are possible here with the different readings. For the preceding line the Acharya ed. reads, *chāyā:*

prabhavati prabhur ātmanaḥ parijanasya, "A lord is master of his own retinue," which has two senses: I am not your (the nun's) master, and (less direct) I *am* master of Mālavikā (who is in my retinue). To this the king's *mama cēti brūhi* is probably a reply to the less direct "threat" of the queen's: She might as well have said she's master of me as well (i.e., I can't have my way). The Sastri reading, *chāyā: nanu prabhaviṣyāmy ātmanaḥ parijanasya,* "Am I not mistress of my own servants?" is more direct and therefore less likely, for it does not seem to be addressed to the nun at all. But the king's reply can, with some twisting of the grammar (apparently—Pisharody's commentary) be taken as a direct quote: "and she might have said, she's 'mistress of herself as well' " (the meaning would be conciliatory). But properly, of course, the reflexive pronoun would be "ātman" in all persons.

1.19+ Śarmiṣṭhā . . . Acharya only. See note on *chalika* at 2.0 below.

1.19+ Quatrain . . . *Catuṣpādam,* taken as referring to the usual classical metrical framework, where each stanza is built of four metrically similar sequences.

1.19+ Will rouse us . . . *Chāyā: notthāpayiṣyati:* Acharya.

1.20+ Audience . . . *Sāmājikāḥ,* Acharya and Bollensen.

1.21+ Objections . . . Following Bollensen.

Act Two

2.0 Śarmiṣṭhā's four-part *chalika* . . . According to Pisharody, Śarmiṣṭhā is the wife of Yayāti; they are parents of Puru; see Miller note to *Śāk* 4.7. The "moderate rhythm," is suitable to *śṛṅgāra rasa;* and the "four-part" or "quatrain" is a reference to the usual construction of Sanskrit verse into four quarters or pādas of often identical metric structure. The "chalika" is used "to suggest one's (sentimental) condition by representation of another's condition": but that definition perhaps fits the present situation too closely to be reliable.

2.4 The only stanza in the play not written in Sanskrit. According to Pisharody, each quarter illustrates a different sentiment: despondency, joy (the fluttering of the left eye in a woman indicates attainment of her wishes), reflection, and piteousness. Each sentiment would doubtless have been made the subject of *abhinaya,* as in the contemporary Bharata Nāṭyam.

2.7 Paṅka nuts . . . *Paṅkacchid: Strychnos potatorum,* the fruit of which is used for purifying foul water.

2.8 Limbs . . . *Śākhāyoni:* variously explained. I follow here Pisharody, who quotes Bharata: *āṅgikas tu bhavec chākhā; śākhā* is attested in the sense "limb of the body" or "body." Acharya takes it as a handheld device for keeping rhythm. Cf. Dasgupta and De, *A History of Sanskrit Literature,* p. 638.

2.9+ Homage of the judges . . . Doubtless said dryly.

2.9+ Researcher . . . Acharya: *prāśnikaḥ.*

2.10+ In a rainless sky . . . At this point Sastri interjects a line of the nun: *evam eva;* deleted Acharya.

2.10+ Belongs to someone else . . . Said mockingly; is there a play on *parakīyā,* intended, more or less in the spirit of the much later Bengali Vaiṣṇavas—a *woman* belonging to another?

2.13+ Must be patient . . . Acharya, *chāyā: anāturo bhūtvā.* Sastri, *anādara iva.*

Act Three

3.0 Waits upon the queen . . . Acharya, *chāyā: devī.*

3.0 Gossip . . . *Chāyā: kaulīna,* "gossip, rumor" (most likely pejorative).

3.0 Somehow controlling himself . . . Acharya, *chāyā: ātmanaḥ prabhutvaṁ darśayati.*

3.0 Signs of pregnancy . . . *Chāyā: dohada (nimittam).* The mysterious cravings that affect a woman in pregnancy are here attributed to the tree about to flower; a common conceit, apparently not compromised by the grammatical gender (masculine) of the tree. The aśoka ritual, which is the topic of this and the next act, is in its imagery clearly expressive of the theme, springtime as rebirth. The queen, representing perhaps the earth mother, and the notion of fructifying prosperity in the kingdom, give the spring season a "kick." A charming symbolism which Kālidāsa here has woven into his amorous intrigue.

3.2+ Amaranth . . . Acharya, Bollensen, *chāyā: kurabaka.*

3.3+ The grove hastens your entrance . . . Acharya, Bollensen, *chāyā: pramadavanam* is subject.

3.4 The involved syntax of this stanza is difficult to represent. In the Sanskrit it is the god of spring who is subject of both clauses; as the agent causing the wind to blow, and as the one asking, via the cries of the cuckoo about the hurts of love.

3.8+ She too yearns . . . In Sanskrit, *aśoka* is masculine.

3.9+ Pointless passion . . . Acharya, *chāyā: atibhūmilaṅghinas* added.

3.10+ Funeral . . . She fears perhaps that the tree will not bloom and the queen be angry, or that despite her beautification the king will still spurn her.

3.10+ On my account . . . Or Sastri, *chāyā; akāraṇād eva,* for no reason at all. Another possible witticism lies in the two Prakrit readings underlying the ambiguous *chāyā: devīmām (devī mām/devī imām):* "Do you think the queen would dress me for the ritual?" Probably forced. The king thought (hoped) *he* was the object of the ornamentation (Pisharody).

3.10+ Foot as my own body . . . Mālavikā asks pardon for the indelicate act of offering her foot to another of similar rank; Bakulāvalikā replies that in touching Mālavikā's foot, she touches "her own body."

3.12+ Irāvatī, the king's special favorite among his wives, has been displaced by the new passion for Mālavikā. The king's wives, while showing signs of jealousy over his affection, of course do not expect constancy in the modern sense of the term; the present intrigue has more to do with the question of rank in the harem. The king's chief queen, his *dhārmikapatnī*, Dhāriṇī, is supreme for all royal and official functions, and considers part of her responsibility making some provision for the king's fanciful interests in lesser wives. But Mālavikā is a servant girl, and is thus not only a rival for Irāvatī but a challenge to Dhāriṇī, her mistress.

3.12+ *Priyaṅgu:* a creeper putting forth blossoms at the touch of woman; also, panic seed.

3.13+ Wasted and pale limbs . . . Conventional sign of unrequited love.

3.13+ My heart is afraid . . . Acharya, Bollensen, *chāyā: na me hṛdayaṁ viśvasiti.*

3.14 Envoy . . . *Dūtī:* the female companion who serves as amorous go-between in arranging rendezvous, etc.

3.14+ Mālavikā's fortune, as well as her foot . . . Acharya, Bollensen, *chāyā: kāritam . . . padaṁ mālavikāyāḥ;* I presume and translate a pun on *padam,* hard to avoid, though the Prakrit appears elsewhere to use only *caraṇa (calaṇa)* in the sense "foot"; in the women's dialect, Sanskrit *pādam* would likely be *pāam.*

3.14+ Succumbed . . . Sastri; *nirvikārasyāpi* by Pisharody's commentary refers to the "indifferent" tree—ironic—and *a fortiori* how much better she has succeeded in arousing the longing of the king!

3.16 Cheated by a tree . . . I.e., he would have liked both to have given her the flower and to have been kicked.

3.19+ "I'm just practicing window repair!" . . . Literally: "I am an expert in broken walls" (*saṁdhicchede*); in other words, in the repair of broken walls. The Indian burglar, as evidenced in the famous scene in the fourth act of *Mṛcchakaṭika,* was a specialist at entry via easily breached, probably adobe foundations.

3.19+ I shouldn't have interrupted with my unfortunate lament! . . . *Chāyā: mandabhāginyaivaṁ na kriyate;* literally: "I wouldn't have behaved so, foolish wretch that I am."

3.21+ Grasps her hand, along with the garment . . . This stage direction in Acharya and Bollensen only.

3.22+ Like Mars in retrogression . . . A baleful portent.

Act Four

4.1 Buds . . . What is meant is goose pimples.

4.3+ I've been bitten by a snake! . . . Acharya; Sastri adds, *chāyā: mṛtyunā.*

4.4 This verse is attributed to the king by Bollensen (p. 54). The simple *śloka* form suggests that the verse may have been borrowed from a medical résumé text.

4.4+ Dhruvasiddhi . . . Literally: "certain-success".

4.6+ Moonbeam . . . A pun; *candrikā* means "moonbeam."

4.6+ Where is the king? . . . After this line, Sastri attributes a line to Bakulāvalikā: *chāyā: dvāragatā bhūtvā pṛṣṭhato drakṣyasi,* "If you'll go to the door, you'll see him behind you"; deleted Acarya, Bollensen.

4.7+ Bowing . . . Still looking at the picture.

4.12 Five-arrowed god . . . Kāmadeva, the Indian Cupid; his five flowered arrows are the five senses.

4.12+ Will my friend stand watchful guard over us? . . . The king generally addresses the buffoon with the term *vayasya,* "friend"; the ladies of the harem and the servant girls use a variety of other endearments, *sakhi, halā, huñjā,* which I have also translated "friend"; in contexts like this the distinction involved in the Sanskrit is needed to understand to whom the speech is addressed.

4.12+ Gotama . . . A legendary sage, famed for his powers of intellect; the authorship of the *Nyāyasūtras* (logic) is attributed to him. *Gautama,* the buffoon's name, does signify some presumed genealogical link, unlikely as that may seem.

4.14 Baimbika . . . Presumably, the king's clan name; other editions have different readings. There is a pun on "ruby-lips" (*bimboṣṭhī*).

4.15+ I only wish to cleanse my offense . . . After having angrily refused his plea for forgiveness.

4.15+ What is this cheat up to now? . . . Refers to the buffoon's usual role in arranging liaisons.

4.15+ Snake bite . . . Bollensen, *chāyā: sarpadaśanam.*

4.15+ A definite turn for the worse . . . Free translation; the buffoon's remark indicates he is fully aware he has been had.

4.15+ Entering in great haste through the curtain . . . The usual stage direction indicating great haste: *paṭākṣepa,* "throwing the curtain aside."

4.15+ A second snake . . . Referring, of course, to Irāvatī.

4.17+ Gāyatrī . . . Refers to *Ṛg Veda* 3.62.10., a verse used by every brahman in the course of his daily worship; hence the most familiar and generally known Vedic verse. The buffoon, not a distinguished Vedic scholar, is here making light of his own "wisdom."

Act Five

5.0 Sacrificial war-horse . . . The ancient horse-sacrifice (*aśvamedha*) is referred to: in an act of ritualized effrontery, a king, desirous of confirming his own power, sends his warhorse, accompanied by an army, wandering through the neighboring dominions. Any rival king will have to catch and kill the horse in order to put down the pretension: otherwise vassalage is admitted. The event referred to figures among the few bits of positive information that help to date this play, and lend to it at least a thin veneer of "historicity"—extremely rare among Sanskrit dramas. See note on *Mālav* 5.15.

5.0 Mādhavasena has also been freed . . . See note on Mādhavasena at 1.7 above.

5.1 Vidiśā . . . Agnimitra rules in Vidiśā (the modern Bilsa), a town on the banks of a river of the same name. The district is in Madhya Pradesh, about 30 miles northeast of Bhopal.

5.1 Varadā's banks . . . A river of Vidarbha.

5.2 Krathakaiśika . . . Two ancient lineages or tribes associated with the region of Vidarbha. Cf. Mallinātha on *Raghuvaṁśa* 5.39.

5.2 Rukmiṇī . . . The story is told in the *Harivaṁśa,* chapters 87–88 (Poona ed.).

5.5 The Sanskrit verse is an *utprekṣā* of the form "It is as if this aśoka bore the flowers of all the other aśoka trees—so complete and early is its blooming." Pisharody.

5.6+ My left eye quivers . . . In women, a good omen (in men, a bad omen).

5.7 Rare . . . Bollensen, *laghubhiḥ.*

5.7+ The younger generation . . . *Chāyā: taruṇījana.* Literally "young ladies."

5.8+ Upon the youthful—hm!—beauty . . . A grammatical play on the unreferenced feminine pronoun *imām;* though he clearly intends Mālavikā, the buffoon neatly sidesteps by coming up with another "feminine" object, the noun *śobhā,* "beauty."

5.9 Cakravāka bird . . . The Indian lovebird, thought to remain apart from its mate during the night and mourn (no pun intended); see note to *Śāk* 3.21+.

5.12+ No ill is intended . . . *Śāntaṁ pāpam.* Untranslatable: "(May) evil (be) appeased!" i.e., "Let no fault be seen (in my action)."

5.12+ You were right to wait . . . Acharya: *yuktā pratīkṣā.*

5.12+ Yajñasena . . . This is the first mention of the Vaidarbha king's proper name; he and Mādhavasena are not "brothers," but cousins; however, the term "brother" has been loosely used in India to indicate male relatives of the same generation, and this usage would not be out of place here. Bollensen (p. 250) rejects the reading on the odd ground that this sense is not found elsewhere in Kālidāsa (!).

5.14+ The king accepts the gift, places it on his head . . . A gesture of respect and obeisance.

5.15 This second military theme, introduced by Kālidāsa only to give Queen Dhāriṇī ample cause for rejoicing, and, thus, to remove whatever obstacle is left to Mālavikā's elevation, is taken by most scholars to establish in some sense our King Agnimitra's historicity. See Vincent Smith, *Oxford History of India* (3d ed.), pp. 138–39; E.J. Rapson, *Cambridge History of India,* 1:467–69. Puṣpamitra (Puṣyamitra), Agnimitra, and Vasumitra, are indeed the first, second, and fourth Śuṅga rulers, as recorded in Purāṇic lists.

5.15+ Aṁśumant . . . The story is told in *Rāmāyaṇa* 1.40 and elsewhere. The horse, which is the symbol of royal authority, is sacrificed to consecrate that authority, after roaming safely for one year.

5.16+ Good lady, I am pleased . . . The speech attributed to the queen in Bollensen and Acharya is given to the buffoon in Sastri.

5.17 The fire within the sea . . . The story is told in *Mbh* 1.169–71.

5.17+ Fortune . . . Viz., his victory, her son's life (Pisharody).

5.18+ Dhāriṇī regards the nun . . . To inquire whether anything remains undone (Pisharody).

SELECTED BIBLIOGRAPHY

ABBREVIATIONS

DR	*Daśarūpaka*. Dhanaṁjaya, *Daśarūpaka*.
Mālav	*Mālavikāgnimitra*, C. S. Rama Sastri edition; Gerow translation.
Manu	*Mānava Dharmaśāstra*, Jolly edition; Bühler, *Laws of Manu*.
Mbh	*Mahābhārata*, Poona edition.
NŚ	*Nāṭyaśāstra*. Bharata, *Nāṭyaśāstra*, Ghosh edition and translation.
Rām	*Rāmāyaṇa* of Vālmīki, Baroda edition.
Śāk	*Abhijñānaśākuntala*, edition with Rāghavabhaṭṭa's commentary; Miller translation.
Vik	*Vikramorvaśīya*, Velankar edition; Gitomer translation.

KĀLIDĀSA TEXTS

Abhijñānaśākuntala.

Devanagari Recension, with commentary of Rāghavabhaṭṭa, 12th ed. by N. R. Acharya. Bombay: Nirnaya Sagar Press, 1958.

Bengali Recension, ed. Richard Pischel, rev. Carl Cappeller. Harvard Oriental Series, no. 16. Cambridge, Mass.: Harvard University Press, 1922.

Kumārasaṁbhava.

With Vallabhadeva's commentary, ed. M. S. Narayana Murti. *Verzeichnis der orientalischen Handschriften in Deutschland* (Wiesbaden: Franz Steiner, 1980), supp. vol. 20, no. 1.

With Mallinātha's commentary, 13th ed. Bombay: Nirnaya Sagar Press, 1946.

Mālavikāgnimitra.

C. S. Rama Sastri, ed., with commentary by S. R. Pisharody. Madras: Balamanorama Press, 1929.

N. R. Acharya, ed., with Kāṭayavema's commentary, 9th ed. Bombay: Nirnaya Sagar Press, 1950.

Friedrich Bollensen, ed. Leipzig: F. A. Brockhaus, 1879.

K. A. Subramania Iyer, ed. New Delhi: Sahitya Akademi, 1978.

Meghadūta.
S. K. De, ed. Delhi: Sahitya Akademi, 1957.
With Mallinātha's commentary, 4th ed. Bombay: Nirnaya Sagar Press, 1911.
With Vallabhadeva's commentary, ed. E. Hulzsch. London: Royal Asiatic Society, 1911.
Raghuvaṁśa.
With Mallinātha's commentary, ed. and trans. G. N. Nandargikar. Reprint, Delhi: Motilal Banarsidass, 1982.
Ṛtusaṁhāra.
With the commentary *Maṇirāma,* 8th ed. Bombay: Nirnaya Sagar Press, 1952.
Vikramorvaśīya.
H. D. Velankar, ed. Delhi: Sahitya Akademi, 1961.
With Koṇeśvara's commentary, *Annals of the Bhandarkar Oriental Research Institute* (1958) 38:255–98; and two other commentaries, Hyderabad Sanskrit Academy Series, no. 14. Hyderabad: Osmania University, 1966.
With Kāṭayavema and Raṅganātha commentaries, ed. S. P. Pandit. Bombay Sanskrit Series, no. 16. Bombay: Central Book Depot, 1889.
M. R. Kale, ed. and trans., with editor's commentary. Bombay, 1889; 11th ed., Delhi: Motilal Banarsidass, 1967.
Kālidāsa Lexicon, ed. A. Scharpé. *Rijksuniversiteit te Gent, Werken uitgegeven door de Faculteit van de Letteren en Wijsbegeerte,* vols. 117, 120, 122, 134, 159, 160. Bruges, 1954, 1956, 1958, 1964, 1975.

For other editions and extensive bibliography, see S. P. Narang, *Kālidāsa Bibliography* (Delhi: Heritage Publishers, 1976).

SANSKRIT TEXTS AND TRANSLATIONS

Abhinavagupta. *Abhinavabhāratī,* commentary on Bharata's *Nāṭyaśāstra,* vols. 1–4, ed. M. R. Kavi. Gaekwad's Oriental Series, nos. 36, 68, 124, 145. Baroda, 1934–64. Text with Hindi and Sanskrit commentaries, ed. A. Madhusudan Shastri, 2 vols. Banaras: Banaras Hindu University, 1971, 1975.

Ānandavardhana. *Dhvanyāloka,* ed. and trans. K. Krishnamoorthy. Dharwar: Karnatak University, 1974.

Aśvaghoṣa. *Saundarananda,* ed. and trans. E. H. Johnston. 2 vols. London: Oxford University Press, 1928, 1932.

—— *Śāriputraprakaraṇa,* fragments ed. Heinrich von Lüders. *Sitzungsberichte der Berliner Akademie der Wissenschaften,* pp. 388–411. Berlin, 1911.

Atharva Veda Saṁhita, ed. R. Roth and W. D. Whitney. Berlin, F. Dummler, 1855–56. Trans. W. D. Whitney. 2 vols. Harvard Oriental Series, nos. 7 and 8. Cambridge, Mass.: Harvard University Press, 1905.

Ballāla. *Bhoja Prabandha*, ed. V. Pansikar. Bombay: Nirnaya Sagar Press, 1932. Trans. Louis Gray, *The Narrative of Bhoja*. New Haven, Conn.: American Oriental Society, 1950.

Bāṇabhaṭṭa. *Harṣacarita*, ed. P. V. Kane. 1918. Reprint, Delhi: Motilal Banarsidass, 1965. Trans. E. B. Cowell and F. W. Thomas. London: Royal Asiatic Society, 1897.

Bhāgavata Purāṇa. Gorakhpur: Gita Press, 1962. Trans. N. Raghunathan, *Srimad Bhāgavatam*. Madras: Vighneswara Publishing, 1976.

Bharata. *Nāṭyaśāstra*, ed. and trans. M. Ghosh. 2 vols. Trans. vol. 1, Calcutta: Manisha Granthalaya, 1956, 1967; trans. vol. 2, Calcutta: Asiatic Society, 1961. (For other editions of text, and commentary, see Abhinavagupta, *Abhinavabhāratī*.)

Bhāsa. *Plays Ascribed to Bhāsa*, ed. C. R. Devadhar. Poona: Oriental Book Agency, 1962. Trans. A. C. Woolner and L. Sarup, 2 vols. London: Oxford University Press, 1930–31.

—— *Avimāraka* in *Plays Ascribed to Bhāsa*, pp. 109–190. Trans. J. L. Masson and D. D. Kosambi, *Avimāraka: Love's Enchanted World*. Delhi: Motilal Banarsidass, 1970.

Bhaṭṭa Nārāyaṇa. *Veṇīsaṁhāra*, ed. Julius Grill. Leipzig, 1871. Trans. Francine Bourgeois. Paris: Institut de civilisation indienne, 1971.

Bhavabhūti. *Mahāvīracarita*, ed. T. Mall and A. A. Macdonell. London: Oxford University Press, 1928.

—— *Mālatīmādhava*, with the commentary of Jagaddhara, ed. R. G. Bhandarkar. Bombay: Central Book Depot, 1876. Trans. Michael Coulson, *Three Sanskrit Plays*, pp. 295–422. Harmondsworth: Penguin, 1981.

—— *Uttararāmacarita*, ed. S. K. Belvalkar. Poona: Oriental Book Agency, 1921. Trans. Belvalkar, *Rāma's Later History*. Harvard Oriental Series, no. 21. Cambridge, Mass.: Harvard University Press, 1915.

Bhoja. *Śṛṅgāra Prakāśa*, ed. G. R. Josyer. 4 vols. Mysore, 1963.

Bilhaṇa. *Caurapañcāśikā*, ed. and trans. B. Stoler Miller, *Phantasies of a Love-Thief*. New York: Columbia University Press, 1971.

Bṛhaddevatā, attributed to Śaunaka, ed. and trans. A. A. Macdonell. 2 vols. 1904. Reprint, Delhi: Motilal Banarsidass, 1965.

Caturbhāṇī, ed. M. R. Kavi and S. K. R. Sastri. Trichur, 1922.

Dhanaṁjaya. *Daśarūpaka*, with the commentary *Avaloka*, ed. T. Venkatacharya. Madras: Adyar Library, 1969. Trans. G. C. O. Haas. 1912. Reprint, Delhi: Motilal Banarsidass, 1962.

Harivaṁśa, Bengali Recension. Calcutta: Asiatic Society, 1839. Crit. ed. P. L. Vaidya. 2 vols. Poona: Bhandarkar Oriental Research Institute, 1969, 1971. Trans. M. N. Dutt, 2 vols. Calcutta, 1897.

Harṣadeva. *Priyadarśikā,* ed. R. V. Krishnamachariar. Srirangam: Vani Vilas Press, 1906. Trans. G. K. Nariman, A. V. W. Jackson, and C. J. Ogden. New York: Columbia University Press, 1923.

—— *Ratnāvalī,* ed. K. P. Parab and V. S. Joshi. Bombay: Nirnaya Sagar Press, 1888. Trans. P. Lal, *Great Sanskrit Plays.* New York: New Directions, 1964.

Hemacandra. *Kāvyānuśāsana,* ed. R. C. Parikh and V. M. Kulkarni. 2d ed. Bombay: Sri Mahavira Jaina Vidyalaya, 1964.

Jayadeva. *Gītagovinda,* ed. and trans. B. Stoler Miller, *Love Song of the Dark Lord.* New York: Columbia University Press, 1977.

Kālikā Purāṇa. Bombay: Venkateshvara Press, 1907.

Kāma Sūtra of Vatsyayana, ed. D. L. Gosvami, with a commentary called *Jayamaṅgala.* Banaras: Chowkhambha, 1929. Trans. R. Burton. 1883. Reprint, New York: E. P. Dutton, 1962.

Kathāsaritsāgara of Somadeva, ed. J. L. Sastri. Delhi: Motilal Banarsidass, 1970. Trans. C. H. Tawney, ed. N. M. Penzer, 10 vols. 1924. Reprint, Delhi: Motilal Banarsidass, 1968.

"Kaṭṭhahāri Jātaka," in *The Jātaka Together with Its Commentary,* ed. V. Fausbøll, vol. 1. London: Trubner, 1877. Trans. *The Jātaka, or Stories of the Buddha's Former Births,* ed. E. B. Cowell, vol. 1. Cambridge: Cambridge University Press, 1895.

Kauṭilya. *Arthaśāstra,* ed. and trans. R. P. Kangle, 2 vols. Bombay: University of Bombay, 1970, 1972.

Kṣemendra. *Aucityavicāracarcā.* Banaras: Chowkhamba, 1933.

Kuṭṭanīmata of Dāmodaragupta, ed. Madhusudan Kaul. Calcutta: Royal Asiatic Society, 1944.

Mahābhārata, crit. ed. V. S. Sukthankar, et al. Poona: Bhandarkar Oriental Research Institute, 1933–66. Trans. J. A. B. van Buitenen, vols. 1–3. Chicago: University of Chicago Press, 1973–78.

Mammaṭa. *Kāvyaprakāśa,* ed. R. D. Karmarkar, with commentary of Bālabodhinī, 7th ed. Poona: Bhandarkar Oriental Research Institute, 1965; also ed. V. G. Apate, Ānandāśrama Sanskrit Series, no. 66. Poona, 1929.

Mānava Dharmaśāstra, ed. Julius Jolly. London, 1887. Trans. Georg Bühler, *The Laws of Manu.* Oxford: Clarendon Press, 1886.

Matsya Purāṇa, ed. N. Apte. Ānandāśrama Sanskrit Series, no. 54. Poona, 1907. Trans. Sacred Books of the Hindus, no. 17. Allahabad, 1916

Padma Purāṇa, ed. V. N. Mandalika. Ānandāśrama Sanskrit Series. 4 vols. Poona: Ānandāśrama, 1893–94.

Rāmāyaṇa of Vālmīki, ed. G. H. Bhatt, et al. Baroda: Oriental Institute, 1960–75.

Ṛg Veda Saṁhitā, ed. F. Max Müller, with the commentary of Sāyaṇa. 6 vols. London, 1849–74. Trans. K. F. Geldner, *Der Rig Veda.* 4 vols. Harvard

Oriental Series, nos. 33–36. Cambridge, Mass.: Harvard University Press, 1951.

Saṅgītaratnākara, ed. V. C. Apte. Ānandāśrama Sanskrit Series, no. 35. 2 vols. Poona: Ānandāśrama, 1942.

Sarvānukramaṇī, attributed to Kātyāyana, with extracts from the *Vedārthadīpikā*, ed. A. A. Macdonell. Oxford: Clarendon Press, 1886.

Śatapatha Brāhmaṇa. Part 2 of *The White Yajur Veda*, ed. Albrecht Weber. Berlin and London, 1855. Trans. Julius Eggeling, 5 vols. Sacred Books of the East, nos. 12, 26, 41, 43, 44. Reprint, Delhi: Motilal Banarsidass, 1963.

Śūdraka. *Mṛcchakaṭika*, ed. K. P. Parab, rev. N. R. Acarya, 8th ed. Bombay: Nirnaya Sagara Press, 1950. Trans. J. A. B. van Buitenen, *Two Plays of Ancient India*. New York: Columbia University Press, 1968.

Śyāmilaka. *Pādatāḍitaka*, ed. G. H. Schokker. Indo-Iranian Monographs, no. 9. The Hague: Mouton, 1966. Trans. G. H. Schokker and P. J. Wolsley. Dordrecht: D. Reidel, 1966, 1976.

Viśākhadatta. *Mudrārākṣasa*, ed. K. H. Dhruva. Poona: Oriental Book Agency, 1923. Trans. J. A. B. van Buitenen, *Two Plays of Ancient India*. New York: Columbia University Press, 1968.

Viṣṇudharmottara Purāṇa. Bombay: Venkatesvara Press, 1912; ed. P. Shah. Gaekwad's Oriental Series, nos. 130, 137. Baroda: Oriental Institute, 1958, 1961.

Viṣṇu Purāṇa, ed. S. Gupta. Gorakhpur: Gita Press, 1967. Trans. H. H. Wilson. 5 vols. London: Trübner, 1864–77.

Viśvanātha, *Sāhityadarpaṇa*, ed. K. M. Sastri. Kashi Sanskrit Series, no. 145. Varanasi, 1967; also ed. Durgaprasad Dviveda, 5th ed. Bombay: Nirnaya Sagar Press, 1922. Trans. J. R. Ballantyne and P. D. Mitra, *The Mirror of Composition: A Treatise on Poetical Criticism*. Calcutta: Baptist Mission Press, 1875.

SECONDARY SOURCES

Ali, Salim. *The Book of Indian Birds*. Bombay: Natural History Society, 1964.

Alsdorf, Ludwig. *Apabhraṁśa Studien*. Leipzig: Deutsche Morgenlandische Gesellschaft, 1937.

Altekar, A. S. *The Coinage of the Gupta Empire*. Corpus of Indian Coins, vol. 4. Banaras: Numismatic Society of India, 1957.

—— "The Vākāṭakas." In *The Early History of the Deccan*, ed. G. Yazdani, part 3, pp. 174–80. London: Oxford University Press, 1960.

Aristotle. *Ethics*, ed. I. Bywater. Oxford: Clarendon Press, 1890.

—— *Poetics*, ed. R. Kassel. Oxford: Clarendon Press, 1965.

Bacon, Helen. "Aeschylus." In *Ancient Writers: Greece,* ed. T. James Luce. New York: Scribner's, 1983.

Banerjea, N. R. "Ujjayinī and Kālidāsa: Analysis of the Archaeology." In *MADHU: Recent Researches in Indian Archaeology and Art History,* ed. M. S. Nagaraja Rao. Delhi: Agam Kala Prakashan, 1981.

Basham, A. L. *The Wonder That Was India*. New York: Macmillan, 1954.

Baumer, R. van Meter and J. Brandon, ed. *Sanskrit Drama in Performance*. Honolulu: The University Press of Hawaii, 1981.

Bhandarkar, D. R. *Inscriptions of the Early Gupta Kings*. Revised from the 1888 edition of J. F. Fleet. *Corpus Inscriptionum Indicarum,* vol. 3. Delhi: Archaeological Survey of India, 1981.

Bhat, G. K. *Bharatanāṭyamañjarī*. Poona: Bhandarkar Oriental Research Institute, 1975.

—— *The Vidūṣaka*. Ahmedabad: New Order Book Co., 1959.

Bloomfield, Maurice. "The Mind as Wish-car in the Veda." *Journal of the American Oriental Society* (1919), 39:282–85.

Bose, Mandakranta. *Classical Indian Dancing: A Glossary*. Calcutta: General Printers and Publishers, 1970.

Brown, W. Norman. "The Creative Role of the Goddess Vāc in the Ṛg Veda." *Pratidānam: Indian, Iranian and Indo-European Studies Presented to F. B. J. Kuiper*. The Hague: Mouton, 1968.

Bühler, Georg. *Die indischen Inschriften und das Alter der indischen Kunstpoesie*. Sitzungsberichte der philosophisch-historischen Classe der Kaiserlichen Akademie der Wissenschaften zu Wien, vol. 122, no. 11. Vienna, 1890.

Byrski, Christopher. *Concept of Ancient Indian Theatre*. Delhi: Munshiram Manoharlal, 1974.

—— *Methodology of the Analysis of Sanskrit Drama*. Warsaw: privately printed, 1979.

Coomaraswamy, A. K. "Recollection, Indian and Platonic." *Journal of the American Oriental Society* (1944), vol. 64, suppl. no. 3; reprinted in *Coomaraswamy: Selected Papers,* ed. Roger Lipsey, 2:49–65. Princeton: Princeton University Press, 1977.

—— *Yakṣas*. 2 vols. Washington, D.C.: Smithsonian Institution, 1928, 1931; reprint, Delhi: Munshiram Manoharlal, 1971.

Dalal, Minakshi L. *Conflict in Sanskrit Drama*. Bombay and Delhi: Somaiya Publications, 1973.

Dasgupta, S. N. and S. K. De. *A History of Sanskrit Literature: Classical Period*. Calcutta: University of Calcutta, 1947.

De, S. K. "The Problem of Bharata and Ādi-Bharata." In *Some Problems of Sanskrit Poetics*. Calcutta: Firma Mukhopadhyay, 1959.

—— "Wit, Humor, and Satire in Sanskrit Literature." In *Aspects of Sanskrit Literature*. Calcutta: Firma Mukhopadhyay, 1959.

Desai, Devangana. *Erotic Sculpture of India: A Socio-Cultural Study.* Delhi: Tata McGraw Hill, 1975.

Deshpande, M. M. *Sociolinguistic Attitudes in India: An Historical Perspective.* Ann Arbor: Karoma Publishers, 1979.

Dimock, E. C., Jr., et al. *The Literatures of India.* Chicago: University of Chicago Press, 1974.

Dumont, Louis. *Homo Hierarchicus: Essai sur le système des castes.* Paris: Gallimard, 1966.

Fleet, J. F. *Inscriptions of the Early Gupta Kings and Their Successors.* 1888. Reprint, Banaras: Indological Book House, 1963.

Frye, Northrop. *Anatomy of Criticism.* Princeton: Princeton University Press, 1957.

—— *The Secular Scripture: A Study of the Structure of Romance.* Cambridge, Mass.: Harvard University Press, 1976.

Gargi, Balwant. *Folk Theater of India.* Seattle: University of Washington Press, 1966.

Geertz, Clifford. "From the Native's Point of View." *Bulletin of the American Academy of Arts and Sciences* (1974) 28:31.

Gerow, Edwin. *A Glossary of Sanskrit Figures of Speech.* The Hague: Mouton, 1971.

—— "Kālidāsa." In *New Encyclopaedia Britannica,* 15th ed. 1974.

—— *Indian Poetics.* In *A History of Indian Literature,* ed. Jan Gonda, vol. 5, fasc. 3. Wiesbaden: Otto Harrassowitz, 1977.

—— "Plot Structure and the Development of *Rasa* in the Śakuntalā." Pts. 1 and 2. *Journal of the American Oriental Society* (1979), 99(4):559–72; (1980), 100(3):267–82.

—— "Ūrubhaṅga of Bhāsa." *Journal of South Asian Literature,* issue on the *Mahābhārata,* ed. Arvind Sharma (forthcoming).

Ghosal, S. N. *The Apabhraṁśa Verses of the Vikramorvaśīya from the Linguistic Standpoint.* Calcutta: World Press, 1972.

Gnoli, Raniero. *The Aesthetic Experience According to Abhinavagupta.* Serie Orientale Roma, no. 9. Rome: Instituto Italiano per i Medio ed Estremo Oriente, 1956.

Gode, P. K. "The Date of Rāghavabhaṭṭa, the Commentator of Kālidāsa's *Abhijñānaśākuntalam* and Other Works." *Calcutta Oriental Journal* (1936), 3(6):177–84.

Goyal, S. R. *A History of the Imperial Guptas.* Allahabad: Central Book Depot, 1967.

Grierson, George. "Bhakti Marga." *Encyclopedia of Religion and Ethics,* ed. James Hastings, vol. 2. Edinburgh, 1908–1926.

Harle, James. *Gupta Sculpture.* Oxford: Clarendon Press, 1974.

Heesterman, J. C.. *The Ancient Indian Royal Consecration.* The Hague: Mouton, 1957.

Huizinga, Johan. *Homo Ludens: A Study of the Play Element in Culture.* London: Routledge and Kegan Paul, 1950.

Ingalls, Daniel H. H. *An Anthology of Sanskrit Court Poetry.* Harvard Oriental Series, no. 44. Cambridge, Mass.: Harvard University Press, 1965.

—— "Kālidāsa and the Attitudes of the Golden Age." *Journal of the American Oriental Society* (1976), 96(1):15–26.

Iyer, Bharatha. *Kathakali: The Sacred Dance Drama of Malabar.* London: Luzac, 1955.

Janaki, S. S. "The Vikramorvaśīya of Kālidāsa: A Study of the Poet's Sources." *Samskrita Ranga Annual* (1962–64), 4:12–34.

Jeffers, Keith. "Vidūṣaka Versus Fool." *Journal of South Asian Literature* (1981), 16(1):61–74.

Jones, Clifford R. "Temple Theaters and the Sanskrit Tradition." *Samskrita Ranga Annual* (1972), 6:101–12.

Kakar, Sudhir. *The Inner World: A Psycho-analytic Study of Childhood and Society in India.* Delhi: Oxford University Press, 1978.

Kalla, Lacchmidhar. *The Birthplace of Kālidāsa.* Delhi, 1926.

Kane, P. V. *History of Dharmaśāstra,* 2d ed. 5 vols. Poona: Bhandarkar Oriental Research Institute, 1968–75.

Kantawala, S. G. "The Saṁgamanīya Gem Episode in the *Vikramorvaśīya.*" *Journal of the Ganga Nath Jha Kendriya Samskrit Vidyapeetha* (1969), 25:417–23.

Katre, S. M. *Prakrit Languages and Their Contribution to Indian Culture.* Poona: Deccan College, 1964.

Kaw, R. K. *The Doctrine of Recognition (Pratyabhijñā Philosophy).* Hoshiarpur: Vishveshvaranand Institute, 1967.

Keith, A. B. *The Sanskrit Drama.* Oxford: Clarendon Press, 1924.

Konow, Sten. *Das Indische Drama.* Berlin and Leipzig, 1920. Trans. S. N. Ghosal, *The Indian Drama.* Calcutta: General Printers, 1969.

Kosambi, D. D. *Myth and Reality: Studies in the Formation of Indian Culture.* Bombay: Popular Prakashan, 1962.

Kramrisch, Stella. "Figural Sculpture of the Gupta Period." In *Exploring India's Sacred Art: Selected Writings of Stella Kramrisch,* ed. Barbara Stoler Miller. Philadelphia: University of Pennsylvania Press, 1983.

—— *The Hindu Temple.* Calcutta: University of Calcutta, 1946.

—— "The Indian Great Goddess." *History of Religions* (1975), 14:235–65.

—— "Īśānaśivagurudevapaddhati: Kriyāpāda chapter 26–27." *Journal of the Indian Society of Oriental Art* (1941), 9:151–93.

—— *The Presence of Śiva.* Princeton: Princeton University Press, 1981.

Krishnamoorthy, K. *Kālidāsa.* New York: Twayne Publishers, 1972.

Kuiper, F. B. J. *Varuṇa and Vidūṣaka: On the Origin of the Sanskrit Drama.* Amsterdam: North-Holland Publishing Company, 1979.

—— "The Worship of the Jarjara on the Stage." *Indo-Iranian Journal* (1975), 16:241–68.

Langer, Susanne. *Feeling and Form*. New York: Scribner's, 1953.

Lévi, Sylvain. *Le Théâtre Indien*. Paris, 1890. Trans. N. Mukherji, *The Theatre of India*. 2 vols. Calcutta: Writers' Workshop, 1980.

Liu, James J. Y., *Chinese Theories of Literature*. Chicago: University of Chicago Press, 1975.

Macdonell, A. A. *A History of Sanskrit Literature*. New York: D. Appleton, 1900. Reprint, Delhi: Munshiram Manoharlal, 1961.

Mainkar, T. G. "The Prakrit Verses in the Fourth Act of the Vikramorvaśīyam." In *Some Aspects of Indo-Iranian Literary and Cultural Traditions: Commemoration Volume of Dr. V. G. Paranjpe*. Delhi: Ajanta Publications, 1977.

—— *Studies in Sanskrit Dramatic Criticism*. Delhi: Motilal Banarsidass, 1951.

Majumdar, R. C., et al. *History and Culture of the Indian People,* vols. 2 and 3. Bombay: Bharatiya Vidya Bhavan, 1951, 1954.

Mankad, D. R. "Hindu Theatre." *Indian Historical Quarterly* (1932), 8:480–99; responses from M. Ghosh, A. K. Coomaraswamy, and V. Raghavan in *IHQ* (1933), vol. 9.

Masson, J. L. and M. Patwardhan. *Aesthetic Rapture: The Rasādhyāya of the Nāṭyaśāstra*. 2 vols. Poona: Deccan College, 1970.

Meister, Michael. "Forest and Cave: Temples at Candrabhāgā and Kansuāñ." *Archives of Asian Art* (1981), 24:56–73.

Miller, Barbara Stoler. "The Ādikāvya: Impact of the *Rāmāyaṇa* on Indian Literary Norms." *Literature East and West* (1973), 17(2–3):163–73.

—— "The Divine Duality of Rādhā and Krishna." In *The Divine Consort: Rādhā and the Goddesses of India,* ed. J. S. Hawley and D. M. Wulff. Berkeley: Berkeley Series in Comparative Religion, 1982.

—— *The Hermit and the Love-Thief.* New York: Columbia University Press, 1978.

—— "Kālidāsa's Verbal Icon: Aṣṭamūrti Śiva." In *Discourses on Śiva,* ed. Michael Meister. Philadelphia: University of Pennsylvania Press, 1984.

Mirashi, V. V. "The Rāṣṭrakūṭas of Kuntala and the Date of Kālidāsa." In *Pañcāmṛtam*. Delhi: Lal Bahadur Sastri Rastriya Sanskrit Vidyapeeth, 1968.

Narang, S. P. *Kālidāsa Bibliography* (Delhi: Heritage Publishers, 1976).

Nitti-Dolci, L. *Les Grammairiens Prākrits*. Paris, 1938.

O'Flaherty, Wendy D. *Asceticism and Eroticism in the Mythology of Śiva*. London: Oxford University Press, 1973.

Pal, Pratapaditya. *The Ideal Image: Gupta Sculptural Tradition and Its Influence*. New York: Asia Society, 1978.

Pandey, K. C. *Abhinavagupta*. Banaras: Chowkhambha, 1963.

Pischel, Richard. *Vikramorvaśīya nach drāviḍischen Handscriften*. Monatsberichte der Königlichen Akademie der Wissenschaften. Berlin, 1875.

Potter, Karl. *Presuppositions of India's Philosophies*. Englewood Cliffs, N.J.: Prentice Hall, 1963.

—— ed. *Indian Metaphysics and Epistemology: The Tradition of Nyāya-Vaiśeṣika up to Gaṅgeśa. Encyclopedia of Indian Philosophies,* vol. 1. Princeton: Princeton University Press, 1977.

Preminger, A., F. J. Warnke, and O. B. Hardison, Jr., eds. *Princeton Encyclopedia of Poetry and Poetics.* Princeton: Princeton University Press, 1965.

Raghavan, V., *Bhoja's Śṛṅgāra Prakāśa,* 3d ed. Madras: Punarvasu, 1978.

—— "Music in Ancient Indian Drama." *Journal of the Madras Music Academy* (1952), 25:79 ff.

—— "Gleanings from the Matsya Pūraṇa." *Purāṇa* (1959) 1(1):80 ff.

—— "Kudiyattam—Its Form and Significance as Sanskrit Drama." In *Sanskrita Ranga Annual* (1964–65 and 1966–67) Madras, 1967.

Rangacharya, Adya. *Drama in Sanskrit Literature.* Bombay: Popular Prakashan, 1967.

Rapson, E. J., ed. *Cambridge History of India,* vol. 1. Cambridge: University Press, 1922.

Renou, Louis. "Sur la structure du kāvya." *Journal Asiatique* (1959), 247:1–113.

Robinson, Richard. "Humanism Versus Asceticism in Aśvaghoṣa and Kālidāsa." *Journal of South Asian Literature* (1977), 12(3–4):1–10.

Singh, R. A. "Inquiries into the Spoken Languages of India, From Early Times to Census of 1901." *Census of India, 1961,* vol. I, pt. XI–C(i).

Sircar, D. C. *Ancient Malwa and the Vikramāditya Tradition.* Delhi, 1969.

—— *Indian Epigraphy.* Delhi: Motilal Banarsidass, 1964.

Smith, Vincent A. *The Oxford History of India,* 3d ed. by Percival Spear. Oxford: Clarendon Press, 1958.

Sohoni, S. V. "On Viśākhadatta's Devīcandragupta." *Annals of the Bhandarkar Oriental Research Institute* (1981), 62:169–92.

Srinivasan, S. A. *On the Composition of the Nāṭyaśāstra.* Studien zur Indologie und Iranistik, nos. 5–6. Reinbek: Verlag für orientalische Fachpublicationen, 1980.

Subbanna, N. R. *Kālidāsa Citations.* Delhi: Meharchand Lachhmandas, 1973.

Tāranātha. *rGya-gar-chos-'byuṅ.* Trans. as *A History of Buddhism in India* by Lama Chimpa and Alaka Chattopadhyaya. Simla: Indian Institute of Advanced Study, 1970.

Tarlekar, G. H. *Studies in the Nāṭyaśāstra.* Delhi: Motilal Banarsidass, 1975.

Thapar, Romila. "Renunciation. The Making of a Counter-Culture?" In *Ancient Indian Social History,* pp. 63–104. Delhi: Orient Longman, 1978.

Thieme, P. "Das indische Theater." In *Fernostliches Theater,* ed. H. Kindermann. Stuttgart: Alfred Kroner, 1966.

Thoreau, Henry David. *A Week on the Concord and Merrimack Rivers,* ed. Carl Hovde, et al. Princeton: Princeton University Press, 1980.

Tullu, R. V. "Traditional Accounts of Kālidāsa." *Indian Antiquary* (1878), 7:115–17.

Van Buitenen, J. A. B. *Two Plays of Ancient India*. New York: Columbia University Press, 1968.

Varapande, M. L. *Traditions of Indian Theatre*. Delhi: Abhinav Publications, 1979.

Vatsyayan, Kapila. *Classical Indian Dance in Literature and the Arts*. Delhi: Sangeet Natak Akademi, 1977.

—— *Traditional Indian Theatre: Multiple Streams*. Delhi: National Book Trust, 1980.

Viennot, Odette. *Le Culte de l'Arbre dans l'Inde Ancienne*. Paris: Presses Universitaires de France, 1954).

Warder, A. K. *Indian Kāvya Literature*. 3 vols. Delhi: Motilal Banarsidass, 1972–77.

Wells, Henry and H. H. Anniah Gowda. *Shakespeare Turned East*. Mysore: University of Mysore, 1976.

Wertheim, W. F. *East-West Parallels: Sociological Approaches to Modern Asia*. The Hague: W. Van Hoeve, 1964.

Williams, Joanna. *The Art of Gupta India*. Princeton: Princeton University Press, 1982.

Yates, Frances. *The Art of Memory*. Chicago: University of Chicago Press, 1966.

Yazdani, Ghulam. *Ajantā*. 4 vols. London: Oxford University Press, 1930.

TRANSLATIONS FROM THE ORIENTAL CLASSICS

Major Plays of Chikamatsu, tr. Donald Keene 1961

Four Major Plays of Chikamatsu, tr. Donald Keene. Paperback text edition 1961

Records of the Grand Historian of China, translated from the Shih chi of Ssu-ma Ch'ien, tr. Burton Watson, 2 vols. 1961

Instructions for Practical Living and Other Neo-Confucian Writings by Wang Yang-ming, tr. Wing-tsit Chan 1963

Chuang Tzu: Basic Writings, tr. Burton Watson, paperback ed. only 1964

The Mahābhārata, tr. Chakravarthi V. Narasimhan. Also in paperback ed. 1965

The Manyōshū, Nippon Gakujutsu Shinkokai edition 1965

Su Tung-p'o: Selections from a Sung Dynasty Poet, tr. Burton Watson. Also in paperback ed. 1965

Bhartrihari: Poems, tr. Barbara Stoler Miller. Also in paperback ed. 1967

Basic Writings of Mo Tzu, Hsün Tzu, and Han Fei Tzu, tr. Burton Watson. Also in separate paperback eds. 1967

The Awakening of Faith, Attributed to Aśvaghosha, tr. Yoshito S. Hakeda. Also in paperback ed. 1967

Reflections on Things at Hand: The Neo-Confucian Anthology, comp. Chu-Hsi and Lü Tsu-ch'ien, tr. Wing-tsit Chan 1967

The Platform Sutra of the Sixth Patriarch, tr. Philip B. Yampolsky. Also in paperback ed. 1967

Essays in Idleness: The Tsurezuregusa of Kenkō, tr. Donald Keene. Also in paperback ed. 1967

The Pillow Book of Sei Shōnagon, tr. Ivan Morris, 2 vols. 1967

Two Plays of Ancient India: The Little Clay Cart and the Minister's Seal, tr. J. A. B. van Buitenen 1968

The Complete Works of Chuang Tzu, tr. Burton Watson 1968

The Romance of the Western Chamber (Hsi Hsiang chi), tr. S. I. Hsiung. Also in paperback ed. 1968

The Manyōshū, Nippon Gakujutsu Shinkokai edition. Paperback text edition. 1969

Records of the Historian: Chapters from the Shih chi of Ssu-ma Ch'ien. Paperback text edition, tr. Burton Watson 1969

Cold Mountain: 100 Poems by the T'ang Poet Han-shan, tr. Burton Watson. Also in paperback ed. 1970

Twenty Plays of the Nō Theatre, ed. Donald Keene. Also in paperback ed. 1970
Chūshingura: The Treasury of Loyal Retainers, tr. Donald Keene. Also in paperback ed. 1971
The Zen Master Hakuin: Selected Writings, tr. Philip B. Yampolsky 1971
Chinese Rhyme-Prose: Poems in the Fu Form from the Han and Six Dynasties Periods, tr. Burton Watson. Also in paperback ed. 1971
Kūkai: Major Works, tr. Yoshito S. Hakeda. Also in paperback ed. 1972
The Old Man Who Does as He Pleases: Selections from the Poetry and Prose of Lu Yu, tr. Burton Watson 1973
The Lion's Roar of Queen Śrīmālā, tr. Alex & Hideko Wayman 1974
Courtier and Commoner in Ancient China: Selections from the History of the Former Han by Pan Ku, tr. Burton Watson. Also in paperback ed. 1974
Japanese Literature in Chinese, vol. 1: *Poetry and Prose in Chinese by Japanese Writers of the Early Period*, tr. Burton Watson 1975
Japanese Literature in Chinese, vol. 2: *Poetry and Prose in Chinese by Japanese Writers of the Later Period*, tr. Burton Watson 1976
Scripture of the Lotus Blossom of the Fine Dharma, tr. Leon Hurvitz. Also in paperback ed. 1976
Love Song of the Dark Lord: Jayadeva's Gītagovinda, tr. Barbara Stoler Miller. Also in paperback ed. Cloth ed. includes critical text of the Sanskrit. 1977
Ryōkan: Zen Monk-Poet of Japan, tr. Burton Watson 1977
Calming the Mind and Discerning the Real: From the Lam rim chen mo of Tsoṅ-kha-pa, tr. Alex Wayman 1978
The Hermit and the Love-Thief: Sanskrit Poems of Bhartrihari and Bilhaṇa, tr. Barbara Stoler Miller 1978
The Lute: Kao Ming's P'i-p'a chi, tr. Jean Mulligan. Also in paperback ed. 1980
A Chronicle of Gods and Sovereigns: Jinnō Shōtōki of Kitabatake Chikafusa, tr. H. Paul Varley 1980
Among the Flowers: The Hua-chien chi, tr. Lois Fusek 1982
Grass Hill: Poems and Prose by the Japanese Monk Gensei, tr. Burton Watson 1983

Doctors, Diviners, and Magicians of Ancient China: Biographies of Fang-shih, tr. Kenneth J. DeWoskin. Also in paperback ed. 1983

Theater of Memory: The Plays of Kālidāsa, ed. Barbara Stoler Miller. Also in paperback ed. 1984

MODERN ASIAN LITERATURE SERIES

Modern Japanese Drama: An Anthology, ed. and tr. Ted T. Takaya. Also in paperback ed. 1979

Mask and Sword: Two Plays for the Contemporary Japanese Theater, Yamazaki Masakazu, tr. J. Thomas Rimer 1980

Yokomitsu Riichi, Modernist, by Dennis Keene 1980

Nepali Visions, Nepali Dreams: The Poetry of Laxmiprasad Devkota, tr. David Rubin 1980

Literature of the Hundred Flowers, vol. 1: *Criticism and Polemics*, ed. Hualing Nieh 1981

Literature of the Hundred Flowers, vol. 2: *Poetry and Fiction*, ed. Hualing Nieh 1981

Modern Chinese Stories and Novellas, 1919–1949, ed. Joseph S. M. Lau, C. T. Hsia, and Leo Ou-fan Lee. Also in paperback ed. 1981

A View by the Sea, by Yasuoka Shōtarō, tr. Kären Wigen Lewis 1984

NEO-CONFUCIAN STUDIES

Instructions for Practical Living and Other Neo-Confucian Writings by Wang Yang-ming, tr. Wing-tsit Chan 1963

Reflections on Things at Hand: The Neo-Confucian Anthology, comp. Chu Hsi and Lü Tsu-ch'ien, tr. Wing-tsit Chan 1967

Self and Society in Ming Thought, by Wm. Theodore de Bary and the Conference on Ming Thought. Also in paperback ed. 1970

The Unfolding of Neo-Confucianism, by Wm. Theodore de Bary and the Conference on Seventeenth-Century Chinese Thought. Also in paperback ed. 1975

Principle and Practicality: Essays in Neo-Confucianism and Practical Learning, ed. Wm. Theodore de Bary and Irene Bloom. Also in paperback ed. 1979

The Syncretic Religion of Lin Chao-en, by Judith A. Berling 1980

The Renewal of Buddhism in China: Chu-hung and the Late Ming Synthesis, by Chün-fang Yü 1981

Neo-Confucian Orthodoxy and the Learning of the Mind-and-Heart, by Wm. Theodore de Bary 1981

Yüan Thought: Chinese Thought and Religion Under the Mongols, ed. Hok-lam Chan and Wm. Theodore de Bary 1982

The Liberal Tradition in China, by Wm. Theodore de Bary 1983

The Development and Decline of Chinese Cosmology, by John B. Henderson 1984

STUDIES IN ORIENTAL CULTURE

1. *The Ōnin War: History of Its Origins and Background, with a Selective Translation of the Chronicle of Ōnin,* by H. Paul Varley 1967
2. *Chinese Government in Ming Times: Seven Studies,* ed. Charles O. Hucker 1969
3. *The Actors' Analects (Yakusha Rongo),* ed. and tr. by Charles J. Dunn and Bungo Torigoe 1969
4. *Self and Society in Ming Thought,* by Wm. Theodore de Bary and the Conference on Ming Thought. Also in paperback ed. 1970
5. *A History of Islamic Philosophy,* by Majid Fakhry, 2d ed. 1983
6. *Phantasies of a Love Thief: The Caurapañcāśikā Attributed to Bilhaṇa,* by Barbara Stoler Miller 1971
7. *Iqbal: Poet-Philosopher of Pakistan,* ed. Hafeez Malik 1971
8. *The Golden Tradition: An Anthology of Urdu Poetry,* by Ahmed Ali. Also in paperback edition. 1973
9. *Conquerors and Confucians: Aspects of Political Change in Late Yüan China,* by John W. Dardess 1973
10. *The Unfolding of Neo-Confucianism,* by Wm. Theodore de Bary and the Conference on Seventeenth-Century Chinese Thought. Also in paperback ed. 1975
11. *To Acquire Wisdom: The Way of Wang Yang-ming,* by Julia Ching 1976

12. *Gods, Priests, and Warriors: The Bhṛgus of the Mahābhārata,* by Robert P. Goldman 1977
13. *Mei Yao-ch'en and the Development of Early Sung Poetry,* by Jonathan Chaves 1976
14. *The Legend of Semimaru, Blind Musician of Japan,* by Susan Matisoff 1977
15. *Sir Sayyid Ahmad Khan and Muslim Modernization in India and Pakistan,* by Hafeez Malik 1980
16. *The Khilafat Movement: Religious Symbolism and Political Mobilization in India,* by Gail Minault 1982
17. *The World of K'ung Shang-jen: A Man of Letters in Early Ch'ing China,* by Richard Strassberg 1983
18. *The Lotus Boat: The Origins of Chinese Tz'u Poetry in T'ang Popular Culture,* by Marsha L. Wagner 1984

COMPANIONS TO ASIAN STUDIES

Approaches to the Oriental Classics, ed. Wm. Theodore de Bary 1959

Early Chinese Literature, by Burton Watson. Also in paperback ed. 1962

Approaches to Asian Civilizations, ed. Wm. Theodore de Bary and Ainslie T. Embree 1964

The Classic Chinese Novel: A Critical Introduction, by C. T. Hsia. Also in paperback ed. 1968

Chinese Lyricism: Shih Poetry from the Second to the Twelfth Century, tr. Burton Watson. Also in paperback ed. 1971

A Syllabus of Indian Civilization, by Leonard A. Gordon and Barbara Stoler Miller 1971

Twentieth-Century Chinese Stories, ed. C. T. Hsia and Joseph S. M. Lau. Also in paperback ed. 1971

A Syllabus of Chinese Civilization, by J. Mason Gentzler, 2d ed. 1972

A Syllabus of Japanese Civilization, by H. Paul Varley, 2d ed. 1972

An Introduction to Chinese Civilization, ed. John Meskill, with the assistance of J. Mason Gentzler 1973

An Introduction to Japanese Civilization, ed. Arthur E. Tiedemann 1974

A Guide to Oriental Classics, ed. Wm. Theodore de Bary and Ainslie T. Embree, 2d ed. Also in paperback ed. 1975

Ukifune: Love in The Tale of Genji, ed. Andrew Pekarik 1982

INTRODUCTION TO ORIENTAL CIVILIZATIONS
WM. THEODORE DE BARY, EDITOR

Sources of Japanese Tradition	1958	Paperback ed., 2 vols.,	1964
Sources of Indian Tradition	1958	Paperback ed., 2 vols.,	1964
Sources of Chinese Tradition	1960	Paperback ed., 2 vols.,	1964